Late Neoliberalism and its Discontents in the Economic Crisis

Donatella Della Porta • Massimiliano Andretta • Tiago Fernandes
• Francis O'Connor • Eduardo Romanos • Markos Vogiatzoglou

Late Neoliberalism and its Discontents in the Economic Crisis

Comparing Social Movements in the European Periphery

Donatella Della Porta
Scuola Normale Superiore Florence
Pisa, Italy

Massimiliano Andretta
University of Pisa
Pisa, Italy

Tiago Fernandes
Nova University
Lisbon, Portugal

Francis O'Connor
University of Aarhus
Aarhus, Denmark

Eduardo Romanos
Universidad Complutense de Madrid
Madrid, Spain

Markos Vogiatzoglou
Greek Ministry of State
Athens, Greece

ISBN 978-3-319-35079-0   ISBN 978-3-319-35080-6   (eBook)
DOI 10.1007/978-3-319-35080-6

Library of Congress Control Number: 2016953882

Cover illustration: © SpainCrisis / Alamy Stock Photo

Printed on acid-free paper

This Palgrave Macmillan imprint is published by Springer Nature
The registered company is Springer International Publishing AG
The registered company address is: Gewerbestrasse 11, 6330 Cham, Switzerland

ACKNOWLEDGEMENTS

This volume emerges from a theoretical and an empirical interest. From the theoretical point of view, it aims at bridging social movement studies with political economy, thus developing upon Donatella della Porta's *Social Movements in Times of Austerity* (Polity, 2015). While, however, that work stressed the similarities among the social movements that emerged in late neoliberalism, in this volume the authors look at the ways in which the specificities of the financial and political crises affected the countries at the European periphery. The empirical interest is in reflecting on how social movement traditions interact with contextual characteristics in the development of anti-austerity protests in those countries in Europe that have been hardest hit by the financial crisis and the austerity policies that followed it.

In this endeavour, we have received much needed help of different types and from different sources. First of all, we wish to express our gratitude to our colleagues at the Centre on Social Movement Studies, first at the European University Institute and then at the Scuola Normale Superiore. For long discussions (and some relaxing moments), we thank those who shared with us the Villa Pagliaiuola and then Palazzo Strozzi: among them, Kivanc Atak, Lorenzo Bosi, Lorenzo Cini, Pietro Castelli, Priska Daphi, Konstantinos Eleftheriadis, Andrea Felicetti, Joseba Fernandes, Hara Kouki, Linda Lund Pedersen, Alice Mattoni, Stefan Malthaner, Georgia Mavrodi, Chiara Milan, Emin Poljarevich, Herbert Reiter, Daniel Ritter, Salvatore Sberna, Alberto Vannucci and Lorenzo Zamponi. We have also presented various versions of various chapters at seminars and conferences in various countries: we are grateful for all the comments we have received there. The empirical research would have not been possible without the trust of the activists who spoke with us, as well as the material support of an Advanced Scholars' Grant from the European Research Council on 'Mobilizing for democracy', some of whose results we publish here.

Finally, we are most grateful to Sarah Tarrow, who, with her usual skills and commitment (and also good humour), has helped us to make our ideas not only more communicable but also more clear.

CONTENTS

ABOUT THE AUTHORS

Massimiliano Andretta is Associate Professor at the Department of Political Sciences of the University of Pisa, where he teaches Political Science and Political Communication. His research interests are mainly on social movement and political participation studies. Recent publications include 'Power and arguments in global justice movement settings', in *Meeting Democracy* (2013, edited by D. della Porta and D. Rucht) and 'Il Movimento 5 Stelle in Toscana: un movimento post-subculturale?', in *Gli attivisti del Movimento a 5 Stelle: dal web al territorio* (2015, edited by Roberto Biorcio).

Tiago Fernandes is Assistant Professor of Political Science at Nova University, Lisbon. He holds a PhD from the European University Institute, Florence, and his research interests include political and social revolution, civil society and democratization. Relevant publications include *The Liberal Wing and the End of the Portuguese Dictatorship, 1968–1974* (2006); *Civil Society* (2014); and 'Rethinking Pathways to Democracy: Civil Society in Spain and Portugal, 1960s—2014' (*Democratization*, 2014). *Civil Society, Democracy, and Inequality: Cross-Regional Comparisons (1970s-2015)*, co-edited with Michael Bernhard and Rui Branco, will be published in *Comparative Politics* in 2017. He has been a visiting researcher at Princeton University, the Juan March Foundation, and the Kellogg Institute for International Studies, University of Notre Dame. Currently he is writing a book manuscript on the origins of democracy and dictatorship in France, Italy and Spain from the late nineteenth to the mid twentieth century.

Francis O'Connor is a post-doctoral researcher engaged in the Preventing, Interdicting and Mitigating Extremism (PRIME) project at the University of Aarhus. His research has mostly focused on Kurdish politics and the conflict in Turkey. He has also published on trade union militancy in South Africa and is co-authoring a forthcoming book on social movement participation in the campaign for independence in Scotland and Catalonia. His theoretical interests are on civil wars and political violence, protest and contentious politics, and social movements.

Donatella della Porta is Professor of Political Science and Dean of the Institute for Humanities and the Social Sciences at the Scuola Normale Superiore in Florence, where she is Director of the Centre on Social Movement Studies (Cosmos). She directs a major European Research Council (ERC) project, 'Mobilizing for Democracy', on civil society participation in democratization processes in Europe, the Middle East, Asia and Latin America. Recent publications include *Social Movements in Times of Austerity* (2015); *Methodological Practices in Social Movement Research* (2014); *Spreading Protest* (2014, with Alice Mattoni); *Participatory Democracy in Southern Europe* (2014, with Joan Font and Yves Sintomer); *Mobilizing for Democracy* (2014); *Can Democracy be Saved?* (2013); *Clandestine Political Violence* (2013, edited with D. Snow, B. Klandermans, and D. McAdam); *Blackwell Encyclopedia on Social and Political Movements* (2013); *Mobilizing on the Extreme Right* (2012, with M. Caiani and C. Wagemann); *Meeting Democracy* (2012, edited with D. Rucht); *The Hidden Order of Corruption* (2012, with A. Vannucci). In 2011, she was the recipient of the Mattei Dogan Prize for distinguished achievements in the field of political sociology.

Eduardo Romanos is a Ramón y Cajal Fellow in the Department of Sociology I at the Universidad Complutense de Madrid. Publications include articles in *Social Movement Studies, Contemporary European History, Journal of Historical Sociology, Revista Española de Investigaciones Sociológicas*, and *Revista Internacional de Sociología*. His main research interests are in the areas of political sociology and historical sociology, with a particular focus on social movements and protest.

Markos Vogiatzoglou is a Special Adviser to the Greek Government's Minister of State. He holds a PhD in Political and Social Sciences from the European University Institute. His main research interests are in the areas of political sociology and social movements, with a particular focus on labour organizing and anti-austerity mobilization. Recent publications include the articles 'Lost in the ocean of deregulation? The Greek Labour movement in a time of crisis' (with Lefteris Kretsos), *Relations Industrielles/Industrial Relations*, 70(2); and 'Workers' transnational networks in austerity times: The case of Italy and Greece', *Transfer— European Review of Labour and Research*, 02/2015.

List of Figures

LIST OF TABLES

CHAPTER 1

Late Neoliberalism and Its Discontents: An Introduction

Donatella della Porta

Social movements have long been considered as children of affluent times—or at least of times of opening opportunities. Past research on the labour movement expected strikes to develop when unemployment was low, or at least when economic crisis was accompanied by an opening of political opportunities (as, for example, in the New Deal in the United States). The protests against the Great Recession in the European periphery defy these expectations, however, developing in moments of diminishing opportunities in both the economic and the political realms. Can social movement studies still be useful to understanding these movements of troubled times? This volume offers a positive answer to this question, although specifying the need to bridge contentious politics with other fields, including political economy.

In this chapter, I will first outline the types of crises to which movements had to react as they unfolded at the European Union (EU) level. Second, I will discuss the types of political responses to the crises, and their social and political consequences, setting the contextual political challenges for social movements in the Great Recession. Throughout, I will stress cross-time evolution and cross-national differences in the development of the crises, with particular attention to the European periphery—that is, the area hardest hit, but also the place where social movements against austerity have been more active, although in varying forms. I will attempt

© The Author(s) 2017
D. della Porta et al., *Late Neoliberalism and its Discontents in the Economic Crisis*, DOI 10.1007/978-3-319-35080-6_1

1

to offer a dynamic view of protest in times of austerity, viewing it as: relational, that is, built upon interactions among different actors; constructed, as it is filtered through the social construction of the external reality; and emergent, as it develops from critical junctures that reduce the power of structural constraints, increasing the power of agency (della Porta 2014).

In previous works I had stressed the similarity of movements across the European periphery (della Porta 2015), as contrasted with the rest of Europe. In this volume, however, I focus mainly upon the internal comparison of the countries hardest hit by the crises. I do so to highlight differences in the social movements' strength and breadth and to understand them in terms of three sets of dimensions: (1) the specific characteristics of the socio-economic crisis and its consequences in terms of mobilization potential; (2) the political reactions to it, in what we can define as political opportunities and threats; and (3) the social movement cultures and structures that characterize each country. In each of these parts, I will develop some hypotheses on protests in times of austerity based mainly, but not only, on social movement studies. In this volume, we will discuss these topics through a contextualized analysis of anti-austerity protest in the European periphery.

1.1   What Is This a Crisis of? Late Neoliberalism in the Great Recession

A first question of obvious relevance for an attempt to understand anti-austerity protests is the socio-structural conditions in which they develop. While social movement studies have paid limited attention to this dimension, the field of political economy has recently acquired more and more relevance in its attempt to single out both broad common trends in capitalist development and internal regional differences within global dynamics. Within this literature, reflections on the tensions within democratic capitalism are, therefore, important to understanding neoliberalism and its crisis. With regard to predictions about social movements, Polanyi's concept of countermovements points at cyclical oscillation between free market and social protection: countermovements spontaneously emerge in response to pushes towards free market, defending a moral economy that recognizes some modicum of social protection (Polanyi 1957). Within the world-systems approach, the concept of anti-systemic movements defines broad reactions to exploitation within world capitalism. While the exploitation of the periphery allowed the hegemonic capitalist country to survive—as at the core of the capitalist world-system, extra profits could be invested in granting some benefits to labour—state protection and mercantilistic policies 'increasingly transferred world capitalist competition from the realm of relations among enterprises to the realm of relations among the states' (Arrighi et al. 1989, 12). World system theorists still expect increasing protests as the exploitation grows, as 'When oppression becomes particularly acute, or expectations particularly deceived, or the power of the ruling stratum falters, people have risen up in an almost spontaneous manner to cry halt' (Arrighi et al. 1989, 29).

Indeed, it was the task of anti-systemic movements to resist greedy capitalism, opposing the logic of the system. As Immanuel Wallerstein noted, 'to be antisystemic is to argue that neither liberty nor equality is possible under the existing system and that both are possible only in a transformed world' (Wallerstein 1990, 36). Much historical research on the labour movement stresses its role in defence of the principle of social integration (della Porta 2013). In addition, faced with economic crises, such as the Great Depression between the two wars, it was mobilization from below that pushed for a move towards a reversal of the economic paradigm, from liberalism to interventionist Keynesianism. In its most recent focus on varieties of capitalism as well as late neoliberalism, political economy helps us not only in explaining similarities in the evolution of the crisis and the movements related to it, but also in singling out potential differences even within the same macro region.

Social movement studies could contribute to this enterprise as well, especially in the attempt to specify under which conditions cycles of protest develop. With its focus on political opportunities, social movement studies would correct predictions of almost automatic mobilization in response to growing exploitation. Additionally, in contrast to structuralist views of structures as directly producing reactions, they would stress the role of material as well as cultural resources mobilizable in contentious politics (della Porta and Diani 2006).

Even within its limited attention to strains and grievances, social movement studies would also help in specifying how domestic characteristics and dynamics of a global crisis affect the potential cleavages from which movements mobilized. While not a central focus of social movement studies, strains have been considered as important, as 'protests generally protest against something and we fail to grasp their meaning if we fail to consider what they protest against' (Crossley 2002, 188). Somehow detached from studies on social movements in the North, works on the Global South have particularly emphasized the importance of economic strains in prompting protest. Strains are indeed at the basis of grievances, as feelings of dissatisfaction, resentment, or indignation, in fact, originate in material conditions but, in order to cause mobilization, require psychological processes of comparison with others and cognitive processes producing assessment of procedural injustice (Snow 2013).

In order for people to react to strains, however, we need awareness of the fact that one's own destiny is in large part linked to material conditions (Snow and Lessor 2013), as the responsibility for the unpleasant situation needs to be attributed to a deliberate producer (Klandermans 2013a). For a grievance to emerge over a specific strain, moreover, the situation has to be considered as unjust: a criticism of the ways in which authorities treat social problems/groups has to be framed on the bases of suddenly imposed grievances or assessments of violation of widespread principles (Klandermans 2013b, 5). In fact, injustice frames are extremely important for mobilization, but they require an attribution of responsibility to concrete targets, successfully bridging the abstract and the concrete. As Gamson observed, it is no simple matter to explain 'how the indignities of daily life are sometimes transformed into shared grievances with a focused target of collective action. Different emotions can be stimulated by perceived inequities—cynicism, bemused irony (for example, "Who says life is fair?"), or resignation. But injustice focuses on the righteous anger that puts fire in the belly and iron in the soul' (2013, 607).

These processes are expected to be especially likely in the presence of double deprivation: at both the individual and the group levels. Additionally, exceptional social dislocations are expected to push disadvantaged groups into action, as the loss averse will accept risks in order to defend their subsistence and everyday routines (see Hosoki 2013; Borland 2013 for a synthesis). In this direction, David Snow and his collaborators (1998) have talked of quotidian disruption, emphasizing the relevance of dislocations that disrupt or threaten routines that had been taken for granted. Different degrees of disruption of everyday life as well as different frames in the political attribution of the responsibility for them are, therefore, expected to lead to different degrees and forms of mobilization.

The Great Recession of the 2000s and 2010s has been fuelled by diverse dynamics, and—especially—interpreted in different ways. For the analysis of social movements, the nature of the crisis can be expected to have relevant effects in terms of grievances and claims. Additionally, the interpretation of the crisis by activists as well by other actors is relevant for the protest framing and its resonance. If we want to understand the effects of the crisis on social movements, we have, therefore, to address, at the European as well as the national level, the question, 'what is it a crisis *of?*'

In this volume we address the protests that developed in the EU—especially in its periphery—as the financial crisis spread from the United States to Europe. In general, we can locate the Great Recession within late neoliberalism, that is, a crisis of the turn towards the free market within a Polanyi-like double movement in capitalist development (della Porta 2015). While in the 1980s states were accused of spending too much and moved away from the Keynesian economic policies of full employment—described as being at the basis of a sort of class compromise of advanced Fordist capitalism—post-Fordism brought about a retrenchment of welfare and increased social inequalities. After Fordism and the golden age of the welfare state, the turn towards neoliberalism happened first in the semi-periphery and in the periphery—where new states had risen during cold war rivalry—with multilateral sponsorship, developmental assistance and economic incorporation. After a wave of debt crisis, in the 1970s, the conditionality of structural adjustment programmes (SAPs) imposed by lenders implied a loss of access to basic services and led to major anti-neoliberal policy protest. This was the case, among other places, in Latin America, Asia and the MENA (Middle East and North Africa) regions, where developmental states were radically dismantled through several waves of shock therapy.

Beginning in the 1980s, the core capitalist states experienced a similar turn. First, the United States and Great Britain, led respectively by Ronald Reagan and Margaret Thatcher, moved towards cuts in the welfare state as justified by an ideology of the free market. As increasing inequalities and reduction of public intervention risked depressing the demand for goods, low interest rates were used, in a sort of private Keynesianism, to support demands—ultimately fuelling the 2008 financial crisis. In the face of US and UK economic decline, coordinated market economies—for example the EU and Japan, where firms rely more on non-market relations to organize their activities—seemed to have equal or even superior levels of competitiveness when compared with liberal market economies that rely for coordination on competitive market arrangements (Hall and Soskice 2001;

Streeck 2010). Notwithstanding its diversity, however, that variety of capitalism also moved towards the free market and was hit by the recent financial crisis, showing, indeed, some inherent contradictions of democratic capitalism, with unequal developments in the EU (Stiglitz 2012).

In general, as countries tend to protect their dynamic economic sectors, the United Kingdom and United States allowed for *lax interpretation of financial regulations* (Iversen and Soskice 2012). Given financial fragility in the banking sector, with some European banks heavily dependent on their US counterparts, their crisis reverberated in the EU financial system as EU national governments also oriented themselves to bail out their banks. In 2008, the failure of Lehman Brothers produced such a shock that governments in the EU decided to come to the rescue, an action that was followed by increasing government debt.

Indeed, the crisis took on specific and diverse characteristics in Europe, mutating in time under the effects of world economy transformations and multilevel (mis)governance. In Europe, *the crisis started as a financial one, linked to bank difficulties resulting from reduced liquidity.* The deregulation of the US financial market had brought about highly speculative and risky investments, and the resulting financial crisis reverberated in Europe. After the entrance in force of the euro, in the EU periphery, interest rates initially fell at the German level, while the sudden availability of cheap capital-fuelled credit financed domestic demand—with large investments in housing and consequent price bubbles, especially in Ireland and Spain (Scharpf 2011). Financial bubbles had developed in the years of expansion as capital moved from countries like Germany, with its positive export-import balance, into areas like the European periphery, where countries had a negative balance. In general, inflow of speculative capital facilitated real estate bubbles as well as inflation in deficit countries. In this situation, 'borrowers in trade-deficit countries, including the governments of those countries, came to rely on the continued availability of incoming financial flows. Banks on the other side of these transactions could thus only be assured of receiving expected repayments as long as general credit conditions remained easy' (Armingeon and Baccaro 2012a). In particular, both Iceland and Ireland entered the crisis through 'deregulated national banks dramatically expanding their balance sheets by borrowing in foreign markets to finance a domestic real-estate boom ... when interbank markets froze after the collapse of Lehman Brothers in September 2008, banks collapsed due to creditors' demands repayment and the unwillingness of other banks to issue new loans' (Armingeon and Baccaro 2012a).

After some attempts to develop countercyclical policies, *the crisis aggravated as it was addressed as a debt crisis, derived from the public debt of peripheral EU countries.* In reality, in 2007, while Greece had a public deficit exceeding 6 per cent and a public debt of 107 per cent, the other GIIPS (Greece, Ireland, Italy, Portugal and Spain) countries met the parameters of the Stability and Growth Pact (SGP) (Armingeon and Baccaro 2012a). For them, public debt was not a cause of the crisis but rather a consequence of it, as it increased because of policy decisions to bail out banks and cut taxes, along with some attempts to address growing unemployment. In particular, in Spain and in part in Portugal, some countercyclical policies had developed immediately after the first signs of the crisis, while in Ireland debt skyrocketed after the government intervened to guarantee the liabilities of Irish banks with an investment of 29 per cent of GDP.

However, the crisis had mainly *a structural component as it was fuelled by differential levels of competitiveness in the EU, as well as the general level of competitiveness of Euroland* (Varoufakis et al. 2015). In fact, while nominal unit labour costs had remained basically stable in Germany, they grew in less competitive countries, with the effect of a deficit in the current account, which contrasted with the surplus in Germany. The peripheral economies, hardest hit by the crisis, in fact, shared some characteristics that made them particularly sensitive to the financial earthquake. Their key problem was a decline in competitiveness concurrent with increases in German competitiveness, with persistent current account deficits as 'these imbalances are the mirror image of increasing competiveness and current account surpluses in Germany' (Varoufakis et al. 2015). The European Monetary Union (EMU) produced particular problems for countries with below-average growth, as interest rates proved too high for their economies, 'with the consequence that initially weak economic activity was depressed even further by restrictive monetary impulses' (Scharpf 2011). In fact, EU member states had to find solutions for their unequal competitiveness without the use of monetary exchange rate strategies. On the eve of the crisis, the GIIPS were made particularly vulnerable by severe current account deficits, dependence on capital inflow and over-valued real exchange rates.

The crisis linked to unequal competitiveness then had effects in terms of an imbalance in trade, with growing deficits in the periphery (with the exception of Ireland, where recovery was considered easier). As such, as Armingeon and Baccaro (2012a) observed, 'the sovereign debt crisis is more complex than a simple story about fiscally irresponsible governments which now are being forced by international financial markets to tighten their belts. Ultimately, it is the result of a political decision to create a currency union among economically non-homogenous countries without making any provision for the use of democratically legitimated fiscal transfers to correct asymmetric shocks.'

Having begun as a bank crisis, the situation thus spiralled into a crisis of public debt, then a crisis of investment; *a related social crisis then affected the European periphery* (Varoufakis et al. 2015). In terms of their effects, as had already been assessed for the failure of the SAPs, imposed by international financial institutions in the global South, 'the likeliest outcome is the one underway: ongoing immiseration in the periphery, slower growth across the Eurozone, slow reduction in bank exposure to the peripheral states, degraded politics within the structurally adjusted states, frustrated lenders, and reduced legitimacy for the institutions and countries most prominently associated with the decisions' (Greer 2013). High degrees of unemployment, homelessness, health and poverty indicated the intensity of the social crisis.

In the critical evolution of the crisis, political institutions indeed played an important—and far from positive—role. The first phase of the crisis, which started around 2008, was addressed through interventions oriented towards countercyclical policies. In the first couple of years, with support from international institutions, expansive fiscal measures were applied in an attempt to counterbalance sharp declines. At the beginning of the crisis, 'To avoid a fall in consumer prices that would reduce incentives to spend and thus put further downward pressure on prices, the ECB [European Central Bank] sought to cut market interest rates and increase the money supply. Against the tendency of recession to breed more recession as spending and investment retrench in reaction to reduced demand, governments deployed expanded spending on unemployment support and other automatic stabilizers and—in 2009, at least—explicit demand stimulus' (Woodruff 2014).

Initial responses to the crisis varied cross-nationally, however, with strongly countercyclical efforts by the socialists in government in Spain, moderately countercyclical ones in Portugal, weakly procyclical ones in Greece, and strongly procyclical ones in Ireland, with Italy in between. The government guarantee of the debt also varied. On the one hand, Iceland's government 'refused to guarantee the debt owned by non-foreign residents (which means that they had to take sizeable "haircuts" on their claims); it introduced capital controls to stop capital flight and let the national currency devalue markedly against other currencies' (Armingeon and Baccaro 2012a). In contrast, Ireland 'guaranteed the debt held by foreign lenders, slashed public expenditures, increased taxes and engaged in structural reforms involving, inter alia, public sector wage cuts and cuts in the minimum wage and unemployment benefits' (Armingeon and Baccaro 2012a).

If countercyclical interventions were a characteristic of EU and domestic responses to the first development of the crisis, a second phase started with the emergence of the large Greek debt towards the end of 2009. The immediate effect, fuelled by speculative trends, was a brisk and consistent increase in the interest rate differentials in the Eurozone between the core and the periphery. Given that the interest payments weighed heavily in government spending, 'the danger of self-fulfilling market predictions of debt unsustainability (pessimism breeding higher interest rates breeding deeper pessimism) became significant' (Woodruff 2014).

Beginning in May 2010, the ECB intervened with expanded lending to banks and action in sovereign debt markets oriented to reduce interest rates. Concentrated in the peripheral countries where banks were facing the greatest difficulties, ECB lending served as an alternative source of financing for trade deficits in these countries, compensating for a sudden halt to private financing. Multilateral arrangements, worked out in a large number of Eurozone or broader EU summit meetings, provided fiscal support, including banking rescues, in Portugal, Ireland and Greece in exchange for the acceptance of austerity policies.

So what had started as a financial crisis in 2007 had turned into a sovereign debt crisis in 2009, and 'the European Commission radically changed its recommendations for the peripheral countries. This was the end of the expansive stage and the beginning of the consolidation stage' (Conde-Ruiz and Marín 2013). While it generated initial expansionary reactions, the G20 failed in sustaining cooperation, given the politicization of regulatory issues (Helleiner 2012). Similarly, while in November 2008 the European Commission proposed a recovery programme based on fiscal stimulus, it failed to sustain that plan given its minimal fiscal capacity at the EU level, the lack of an economic government capable of coordinating fiscal and economic policies, together with the constraints of the Stability and Growth Pact (SGT) that limited especially the capacity of weak states, with no budget surplus (Cameron 2012). Therefore, the European institutions ended up supporting in all these countries the same austerity policies: 'Governments of different political orientations, of different political strength and with different capabilities for concertation with the social partners found themselves implementing essentially the same structural adjustment program centered on public sector cuts, pension reform, easing of employment protection legislation, wakening of unemployment insurance, and flexibilization of collective bargaining' (Armingeon and Baccaro 2012b, 182).

In the second phase, responses to the crisis were in fact homogenized around the so-called Washington consensus, imported in the EU in a moment of domination by the centre-right parties at both the domestic and EU levels, and imposed upon a (mollified) centre-left during the crisis. Comparing government responses to the Great Recession of 2008–2009 with government responses to recessions and other economic challenges in the period 1974–1982 in France, Germany, Sweden, the United Kingdom and the United States, Pontusson and Raess (2012) noted two main shifts: a swing away from heterodox policies and a focus instead on fiscal stimulus. Reflecting first and foremost the weakening of labour, which lost the capacity it had in the 1970s to influence directions of crisis management, the range of policy options considered narrowed towards 'combining tax cuts and some spending increases with monetary easing, while resisting protectionist measures and eschewing targeted interventions as well as devaluations'. Massive bailouts of financial institutions added to this, along with the reduced attention to unemployment.[1] A similar policy was applied to the EU as 'a number of governments, pushed by the ECB and other European institutions, made efforts to fight high levels of unemployment through promoting declines in wages—for instance, by reducing minimum wage rates, by decreasing public sector salaries, by reducing unemployment benefits, by weakening and decentralizing collective bargaining, and by forcing renegotiation of labor contracts in recessionary conditions' (Woodruff 2014).

In this second step of the crisis, domestic policies were homogenized—also, according to some interpretations, through the political blackmail of financial panic used by EU institutions. While literature on the variety of capitalism tended to predict different responses to common shocks—as specific domestic policy processes (e.g. coordinated market in Italy versus liberal market economy in Ireland) were expected to produce different answers—this was hampered by the effects of EU intervention. In fact, convergence was imposed from above, as domestic institutions and politics, either party- or interest group-based, have ostensibly played a minor role in selecting the policy response to the sovereign debt crisis. To be sure, there has been and there continues to be a lot of variation in the policy process through which domestic actors have sought to blunt and diffuse popular opposition to the proposed measures. However, none of the country-level variation has (so far) made any difference for the content of the policy packages, which has been very similar across countries and has been imposed from outside… The common response involves public sector expenditure cuts (including cuts in educational expenditures), pension reform, easing of employment protection legislation, weakening of unemployment insurance and flexibilization of collective bargaining rules. (Armingeon and Baccaro 2012a)

The dynamics of the crisis were then affected by the type of public intervention applied to it. It has been noted that the doctrine for recovery imposed by the EU was unsuccessful as it was based on incorrect assumptions and, additionally, did not adequately consider the impact of tradeoffs (particularly in terms of declining demands and investments, with negative effects on public debt) (Monastiriotis et al. 2013). The economic adjustment programmes (EAPs) relied upon an 'expansionary austerity' approach, assuming that growth would ensue from cuts in expenditure that would increase business confidence and hence investments. As SAPs, they were based upon neoclassical economics assumptions, summarized in the so-called Washington consensus: 'limited deficits, free trade, market set interest and exchange rates, deregulation, openness to foreign direct investment, privatization, government expenditure focused on a few areas, tax reform, and property rights'. The similarities between SAPs and EAPs were stressed: pension policies oriented to raises in the retirement age and the imposition of cuts in public sector wages and pensions; decreases in public sector wage bills, with wage and promotion freezes as well as a gradual reduction in staff; lower and shorter-term unemployment benefits; smaller transfers to local and regional governments and state-owned enterprises, as well as lower social contributions, wage freezing and voluntary retirement in the public sector; reduction of social benefits as well as the closing, privatization, or reform of public enterprises (Greer 2013).

In sum, the management of the crisis at the EU level has fuelled rather than quelled its dynamics, as *the crisis was wrongly addressed by the EU as a crisis of fiscal profligacy in all peripheral countries.* In reality, as mentioned, only Greece had high debt at the beginning of the crisis, while in the other GIIPS countries 'fiscal imbalances were largely the result (as opposed to the cause) of the economic shocks that hit them from 2007 on' (Armingeon and Baccaro 2012a). Various decisions by the Troika, composed of representatives of lending institutions including the EU, seem based on a biased (if not racist) vision of peripheral countries as overspending plus cheating.

The EU choice of policies of internal devaluation selectively reduced the potential for growth. As Armingeon and Baccaro (2012a) noted, 'the internal devaluation policy which is being imposed on Greece, Ireland, Italy, Portugal and Spain is ineffective and counterproductive. Internal devaluation depresses growth, and the absence of growth requires further austerity for government [sic] to regain their fiscal credibility, thus generating a vicious cycle.' Broadly applied policies of internal devaluation—with the goal of reducing prices through cuts in wages and employment—have been counterproductive, as not only have gains in competitiveness remained marginal, but they also depressed nominal growth, with the effect of further pessimism spread by rating agencies. Similarly, labour market flexibility reduced incentives to increase productivity.

Researchers have stated that the EU institutions then magnified the Greek crisis, given their lack of capacity to act swiftly on it, and allowed it to spread over Europe. It was noted that, 'Trapped within its own political constraints—excessive trust in the political economy of incentives (the fear of "moral hazard") and a self-defeating adherence to rules—the eurozone was unable to react quickly and boldly to address the solvency problems of Greece. Its sloppiness and indecision fuelled uncertainty with regard to Greece's continued membership in the EMU and assigned an elevated role to financial markets and institutions to dictate economic developments, leading to a realisation of the much-feared domino effect as the crisis spread to Portugal and Spain' (Monastiriotis et al. 2013).

At the same time, *the effects of the crisis were further aggravated as institutions acted in a shock mode.* In fact, the adoption of the approach to the crisis has also been related to 'the nervousness and impatience of Troika lenders (politicians in contributing countries, notably Germany, were worried about the popularity of bailouts; the IMF [International Monetary Fund] was worried about the scale of its lending to Greece relative to other countries and private banks' exposure; and the ECB's participation was hardly envisioned in the EU Treaties), then the response was policy aimed at cutting deficits rapidly' (Greer 2013).

Given large differences in the competitiveness of the Eurozone countries, the crisis dynamics at the periphery were fuelled by the unbalanced archi-

tecture of the euro with its lack of provisions for fiscal transfer. While resting on unequal national economies, the euro system remained without an instrument to buffer these differences in case of shocks as, although the currency is one and the same, the public debt remains national (Varoufakis et al. 2015). Those very differences in competitiveness have increased inequalities, given the unwillingness of member states to control asymmetric shocks and the economic heterogeneity of the countries involved in the currency union. In this situation, macro-economic imbalances result from the creation of a currency union among 'economically non-homogenous countries without making provisions for the use of institutionalised fiscal transfers to correct asymmetric shocks' (Armingeon and Baccaro 2012a). During the crisis, the differential in competitiveness even increased as wage compression and labour flexibility reduced incentives to invest in productivity.

For the countries in the EU periphery, *the crisis has also been worsened by the absence of the main instruments to address economic difficulties*—the possibility of devaluing national currencies and with it the possibility of relying upon their own lender of last resort (Armingeon and Baccaro 2012a). When the demand diminished in peripheral countries as a consequence of the restriction in liquidity, the trade imbalance should have been pursued through an increase in exports—usually facilitated by exchange rate devaluation—which was not available for the European periphery (as it had been for Iceland) because it went against German interests as an export country. Peripheral countries lacked a national central bank as lender of last resort, able 'to deploy a powerful, indeed almost invincible weapon against panic: the use of money creation to buy up assets and coordinate investor expectations about prices. Most students of central banking consider this "lender of last resort" role to be a fundamental advantage of the institution' (Woodruff 2014).

We could expect these crises to have had different depth and speed in different countries in the EU periphery; this would have affected anti-austerity protests. Research on political economy tells us that, notwithstanding the common basis of the crisis, its effects varied in time and cross-nationally. Particularly relevant dimensions seem to be the competitiveness of the domestic economy, the amount and type of public debt, the openness of the market, and the availability of some economic policy measures. The social dimensions of the crises can also be expected to differ. In particular, a combination of these dimensions can explain a stronger shock in Iceland, Spain, Cyprus and Greece, with instead some buffers in Ireland, Portugal and Italy.

1.2   FROM DEMOCRATIC DEFICIT TO A CRISIS OF RESPONSIBILITY IN THE EUROPEAN UNION

The financial crisis fuelled a *democratic crisis*, which can be defined as a crisis of responsibility as political institutions gave away their competences and, with them, the potential to protect citizens' rights (della Porta 2015). Social movement studies have, in general, looked at political opportunities and threats as affecting the level and characteristics of protest. In particular, stable conditions (such as functional divisions of power and channels of access to institutions) as well as conjunctural ones (such as the colour of the governmental coalition or availability of allies) have traditionally been analysed as opportunities and constraints, although filtered by movements' mechanisms of appropriation of them. Research on anti-austerity protest in Latin American shows indeed that, as Polanyi's countermovements developed on the continent since the mid-1990s, their character and outcomes were strongly influenced by political opportunities and constraints provided by the party system. As Kenneth Roberts (2014) noted, while social and political resistance to market liberalization increased, fuelling a revival on the left, the specific forms this revival took were influenced by the domestic forms of neoliberalism as well as the parties' positions on it. In short, the most destabilizing waves of protest developed where party politics did not offer channels for dissent from neoliberal policies, as all major parties supported them. In particular,

> Where conservative actors led the process of market reform and a major party of the left was consistently present as an opposition force, the Polanyian backlash in the post-adjustment era was largely contained within institutional channels. Indeed, societal resistance to market orthodoxy strengthened established parties of the left and eventually enabled them to win the presidency in countries like Chile, Brazil, Uruguay, and El Salvador. In each case, levels of social protest were relatively moderate in the post-adjustment era, established parties remained electorally dominant, and anti-establishment populist figures made little headway in the electoral arena. The political legacies of market liberalization, and the political opportunity structure for mass social or electoral protest, were strikingly different where

center-left or labor-based populist parties played a major role in the process of structural adjustment... In countries like Argentina, Bolivia, Ecuador, and Venezuela, bait-and-switch market reforms left a sequel of explosive social protest that directly or indirectly toppled presidents, led to partial or complete party system breakdowns, and (in the latter three cases) ushered in the election of an anti-system populist figure or a new movement party of the left.

In Europe, as well, today's movements react, indeed, to a legitimacy crisis, although with very different characteristics from the one hypothesized by Habermas (1976) for advanced capitalism. Using his language, one could define the contemporary economic situation, not as a crisis of scarcity or inflation, but as one of redistribution (or lack thereof) (Crouch 2010; Pianta 2012). Today's legitimacy crisis is driven not by excessive state intervention in the market in order to support labour, but rather by state intervention in support of capital and the related stripping off of civic, political and social rights (Sassen 2006). Since 2008, public debt has increased not because of investments in social services and support for the weaker category, but due to huge expenditures of public money to bail out banks and financial institutions from their financially driven crisis as well as by drastic cuts in the taxation of capital. This takes, first of all, the form of a corruption of representative democracy through the overlapping of economic and political power.

On the output side of the political system, this means an abdication of responsibility by representative institutions in the face of citizens' demands. Against the neoliberal promises of defending the market from the state, scholars of various disciplines point at the growing intermingling of the two. In fact, as Crouch wrote about neoliberalism, 'in its attempt to reduce certain kinds of government interventions in the economy, it encourages or provides space for a number of mutual interferences between government and private firms, many of which raise serious problems for both the free market and the probity of public institutions' (2012, 93). Rather than competition, it brought about a concentration of capital with the development of 'giant firms' that distort the market, as 'a "giant" firm is one that is sufficiently dominant within its markets to be able to influence the terms of those markets by its own action, using its organizational capacity to develop market-dominating strategies' (Crouch 2012, 49).

Even more directly, the space for political decisions has been denied, by politicians of different colours, on the basis of the absolute dominance of the so-called 'logic of the market', especially of international markets. As Streeck observed, having been saved by the states, 'As we now read in the papers almost every day, "the markets" have begun in unprecedented ways to dictate what presumably sovereign and democratic states may still do for their citizens and what they must refuse them. Moreover the very same ratings agencies that were instrumental in bringing about the disaster of the global money industry are now threatening to downgrade the bonds of the very same states that had to accept a previously unimaginable level of new debt to rescue that industry and the capitalist economy as a whole' (Streeck 2011, 20). In countries in the Eurozone, the EU management of the crisis increased the democratic deficit at the domestic as well as the European level. These happened through various mechanisms.

First and foremost, *the crisis in the EU was addressed through the imposition of policy choices from electorally unaccountable institutions.* In fact, while formally still in charge of policymaking, national governments have lost the capacity to choose among alternative options and are instead forced to implement unpopular austerity measures. The imposition of conditionality weakened national democracy and sovereignty, as

> The governments of Greece, Ireland, Cyprus, and Portugal ceded autonomy over large areas of their budgets, policies, and economies to a Troika of organizations with very limited democratic accountability: a European Central Bank shielded from politics, accountable to central banks and bound by strict treaty limitations; an IMF that is formally accountable to its shareholder governments; and a European Commission that is closer to European voters, but still only indirectly accountable to governments and the European Parliament. (Greer 2013)

It has been noted that conditionalities increased especially, but not only, for countries that had to sign the Memorandum of Understanding (MoU) and the Memorandum of Agreement (MoA). In what Fritz Scharpf (2011) defined as a 'pre-emption of democracy', 'In countries like Greece and Ireland in particular, anything resembling democracy will be effectively suspended for many years as national governments of whatever political color, forced to behave responsibly as defined by international markets and organizations, will have to impose strict austerity on their societies, at the price of becoming increasingly unresponsive to their citizens' (Streeck 2011, 184). While national governments formally maintain the competence to impose extremely unpopular measures, de facto their sovereignty is denied by the lending institutions. Significantly, the MoU or MoA established the conditionality that countries accepting economic help have to follow, as

> ...the quarterly disbursements of bilateral financial assistance ... are subject to quarterly reviews of conditionality for the duration of the arrangements. The release of the tranches will be based on observance of quantitative performance criteria and a positive evaluation of progress ... The authorities commit to consult with the European Commission, the ECB and the IMF on the adoption of policies which are not consistent with this memorandum ... Prior to the release of the installments, the authorities shall provide a compliance report on the fulfillment of the conditionality'. (Irish and Greek memoranda, cit. in Scharpf 2011, 185)

Thus, all cruelties have to be inflicted by national governments even if dictated by the commission bureaucracy and the self-interest of other countries. If in Greece, Ireland, Portugal and Cyprus neoliberal economic policies were imposed by the Troika of lending institutions (ECB, EC, and IMF) in exchange for financial assistance, in the case of Spain and Italy, it was adopted under indirect pressures.

Policy choices are limited, as deflationary policies are embedded in the EU architecture. Deflationary policies resonated with a Eurozone system that the SGP had pushed towards fiscal rigour since the Maastricht Treaty. Deflationary policies indeed damaged the potential for growth in the GIIPS countries, which not only could not devalue their currency, but also

> ... are unlikely to pull themselves out of their debt problem through inflation, given the ECB's well-known inflation aversion. Their priority should be to resume nominal growth as quickly as possible. Instead they are being forced into an internal devaluation programme by which they are expected to lower wages and prices relative to other countries and thus make up for lost competitiveness. In addition, they are being asked to implement structural measures to increase the degree of competitiveness of the labour and product markets. This policy approach worsens the liquidity problems being experienced by these countries rather than alleviating it. Markets doubt that the countries in question will be able to generate the growth necessary to repay the debt and therefore ask for higher interest rates, which worsens the fiscal position of these governments. In the absence of a lender of last resort that could guarantee the necessary liquidity, these expectations tend to become self-fulfilling. (Armingeon and Baccaro 2012a)

The push towards internal devaluations, embedded in the EU treaty, appeared to have counterproductive effects. As Fritz Scharpf (2011) noted, with the abandonment of Keynesian types of intervention, which assigned leading functions to fiscal policies (as governments are supposed to cut taxes and finance expenditures during recession), the monetarist orientation of the EU policies—with the abandonment of full employment as a goal and the dominance of price stability—was responsible for the type of crisis that developed in the union. After an apparent initial success, 'the political crash programs, through which unlikely candidate countries had achieved an impressive convergence on the Maastricht criteria, had generally not addressed the underlying structural and institutional differences that had originally caused economic divergences. Once access was achieved, these differences would reassert themselves' (Scharpf 2011, 173).

With a rather explicit scorn for representative institutions, neoliberal policies have been imposed by a closed, self-sustained and unchecked class of decision makers with monetarist assumptions that has been empowered during the crisis. It has been in fact observed that:

> In some high-level decisions, these elite bureaucrats—in the ECB (and its predecessor the EMI [European Monetary Institute]), in DG ECFIN [Directorate-General for Economic and Financial Affairs] and in the Economic and Financial Committee (and its predecessor the Monetary Committee)—defined the competences and accountabilities of institutions that would later become their employers, and which some of them would come to lead. This governance structure resulted in like-minded thinkers developing friendships and informal networks, which reinforced their power and career perspectives. But it also meant that these cadres, as they were promoted, moulded the character of the institutions at the core of the euro area and influenced debate, e.g. in determining hiring and promotion policies. Such a setting limited the possibilities for fresh thinking to emerge. Accordingly, the response to the euro crisis has been based on the same perspective of the designers of the EMU architecture, which led to the crisis in the first place. Perhaps the cadres' biggest design failure is that the EU governing institutions do not include the proper checks and balances and insufficient resources were committed to ensuring transparent and robust processes in policy preparation and in decision making ... It should be no wonder then that these cadres made the ECB the most independent central bank in the world. (Cabral 2013)

The effects of this self-referentiality are aggravated by the fact that the governance of the EMU is increasingly devolved to economically oriented actors such as the DG ECFIN, the Council for Economic and Financial Affairs, and the European Central Bank, all of which are oriented by a monetarist paradigm calling for labour market deregulation and cuts in pensions and health care (de la Porte and Heins 2015). The SGP and the monetarist paradigm that underpins it, have not been without criticism—as McNamara (2005, 156) had noted, 'Although the SGP has the word "growth" in its title, it is not likely to promote growth, but rather to be excessively restrictive at precisely the times that European states may need to stimulate their economies, as states are more likely to run up deficits in economic recessions.'

The EU has constrained the democratic dialectics between government and opposition. Politically, the EU has forced on weak economies unchallenged support for its own austerity policy, often imposing—in some cases formally, through conditioned lending, in some case informally, through various forms of pressure—on parties in government and in the opposition to support those policies. This happened in Spain, where the PSOE (Spanish Socialist Workers' Party) in government had addressed the crisis through investments in 2008, but was pushed towards labour market liberalization and austerity. In Portugal, both government and opposition parties were explicitly asked to sign the MoU imposing three austerity packages, as, in 2011, the EU and IMF asked for the adjustment plan to be signed by parties in government as well as in the opposition (Armingeon and Baccaro 2012a). Similarly, in Ireland, after the electoral defeat of Fianna Fáil (which dropped from 77 to 20 seats), the very same policies were imposed on the new governmental coalition formed by Fine Gael and Labour. In Greece, after the socialist victory of 2009, the PASOK promises to increase social protection remained unfulfilled, as its government was replaced by a so-called technical government that, with the support of a broad coalition, had to implement the austerity policies demanded by both the IMF and the EU. In Italy, with a later start to the sovereign debt crisis, in the summer of 2011, the centre-left first supported the emergency austerity package of the centre-right government and then backed (together with the centre-right) a new government, which implemented the EU indications for labour market liberalization that were listed in a supposedly confidential letter sent by both the incoming and outgoing presidents of the ECB.

So, while political outcomes varied to a certain extent in the first part of the crisis, the common outcome of EU intervention was to elide policy differences between left and right, and thus the democratic dynamics of government and opposition. Even if the crisis caused governmental defeats and early elections in Ireland, Portugal, Spain and Greece, policy imposed from above remained unchanged. In fact, grand coalitions and (self-defined) technocratic governments were often appointed under EU pressure.

The EU has intervened on the domestic power of various groups and classes pushing for anti-labour politics. EU policies have been far from neutral in their effects on interest representations as they significantly weakened the unions, which have been manoeuvred—and allowed themselves to be manoeuvred—in corporatist deals, although from a position of weakness. When the unions could not be persuaded to accept austerity measures, the EU line has been to proceed against them. Social pacts (such as the February 2011 agreement on pension reform in Spain, or the 2010 'Croke Park' agreement with public sector unions in Ireland) were concessionary agreements that further weakened unions, which gained at best very minor policy concessions as well as commitment to collaboration in the future. What Polanyi had defined for the first Great Recession as the capitalist fear of labour radicalism found a parallel in the second Great Recession, in the 'neoliberal "Brussels-Frankfurt consensus", strongly entrenched in the European Central Bank. By threatening to allow a self-sustaining market panic unless their conditions were met, ECB leaders were able to "weaponize" market panic to pursue their neoliberal agenda' (Woodruff 2014). With the weakening of labour, in both liberal market and coordinated market capitalism, labour market deregulation and wage moderation were presented as the only options available to gain in competitiveness, given the fiscal constraints imposed by the SGP. While weakening labour, EU policy choices favoured instead the bankers that Polanyi had located as the basis of the financial market government—as 'When a particular gold-backed currency was under threat, Polanyi notes, finance used the prospect of panic to push for austerity and deflation as solutions.' Provisions to 'rescue and oversee private banks, which are in trouble in each country' have been explained by the fact that 'the SAPs, like the EAPs, are heavily influenced by banks whose capital is necessary if the programs are to work' (Greer 2013).

The EU also reduced electoral accountability by moving power from parliaments to the executive (especially, ministers of finance) and independent authorities (above all the ECB). In this respect, the EU democratic deficit is increased by the unaccountability of those formal and informal EU institutions that de facto challenge democratic governments at the domestic level (Cabral 2013). Unaccountable ECB and/or informal Eurogroups have increasing autonomous power to decide whether to create money and under which conditions to distribute it, with the potential for manipulating 'market panic as a disciplinary mechanism' (Woodruff 2014). In this process, in the Eurozone, the loss of monetary autonomy has been followed by a loss of fiscal autonomy as well, with no improvement in the democratic qualities at the European level as policy decisions have moved increasingly towards institutions with limited democratic accountability (for example, the European Commission) (Armingeon and Baccaro 2012a) or, even worse, total lack of transparency (as, for example, the so-called Eurogroup, whose lack of rules for decision making emerged during the Greek crisis).

Fiscal autonomy, and with it national sovereignty, have been dramatically reduced through new EU instruments to impose fiscal probity with strong spillover (restrictive) effects on social policies. In general, 'EU involvement in member state policymaking has clearly escalated as a consequence of the eurozone crisis, after recognition of interdependencies within the EMU' (Sacchi 2015). Recent changes in the management of the crisis have increased the democratic deficit, not only of the EU, but also of the nation state, imposing procyclical policies in a much more stringent way than with the previous SGP. The EU institutions' capacity for enforcement of unaccountable decisions has increased dramatically during the crisis. As an analysis of social policies clearly indicated, 'the nature of EU intervention into domestic welfare states has changed, with an enhanced focus on fiscal consolidation, increased surveillance and enforcement of EU measures. Overall, this represents a radical alteration of EU integration, whereby the European Union is involved in domestic affairs to an unprecedented degree, particularly with regard to national budgets, of which welfare state spending is an important component' (Heins and de la Porte 2015).

At the EU level, increasing controls have been imposed by the Six-Pack, the Fiscal Compact and the Two-Pack. In 1997, the SGP was already fuelling a process of policy coordination entitling EU institutions to impose corrective mechanisms in case of deviations from the EMU prescription, with particular constraints on public expenditures. As the ineffectiveness of the SGP was attributed to its weak capacity of enforcement, however, new and more stringent instruments were developed during the crisis.

First, in December 2011, the Six-Pack increased the strength and the scope of surveillance as well as the specification of objectives and potential sanctions for all member state economies, even more stringently on the Eurozone especially regarding financial sanctions. In particular, country-specific medium-term objectives are set towards budget balance. Surveillance as well as enforcement capacity increased, as the Commission can issue warnings with Alert Mechanism Reports, thus constraining a large range of political decisions through the threat of sanctions. Passed in 2012, the Fiscal Compact is even more binding for euro countries, as it also introduced rules towards curtailing public debt if the limit of 60 per cent of GDP is exceeded; imposes a limit of 0.5 per cent of GDP on structural deficits; and requires member states to report on their national debt to the Commission and the Council with the commitment to discuss any major policy reforms prior to their enactment (de la Porte and Heins 2015). Finally, the Two-Pack, coming into force in May 2013, 'specifies objectives in budgetary policy, together with high enforcement and surveillance mechanisms. Its novelty is to have introduced a common budgetary timeline and rules for all euro area countries. The Two-Pack has a significant impact on "sovereign" budgets—the basis for policymaking—as it requires Member States to send their budget proposals first for approval to the Commission and the Eurogroup, before they are submitted to national parliaments' (de la Porte and Heins 2015).

All of these instruments put unprecedented constraints on social expenditures, as 'tight budgetary criteria will make expansionary public spending difficult even in healthy economies, let alone in crisis-ridden countries. The new instruments were agreed in unusually rapid succession in the context of an ongoing Eurozone crisis, leading to considerable institutional change in the EMU architecture in a short period of time. The resultant institutional architecture holds Member States accountable to the EU ex-ante and ex-post with regard to their budgets and public expenditure, including social expenditure' (de la Porte and Heins 2015).

Germany's veto power has also been stigmatized as producing EU policies that adjust to the interests of one member state. ECB prescriptions were said to promote a 'Brussels-Frankfurt consensus', based upon the financial orthodoxy of the 1920s and 1930s, with its trust in austerity and the promotion of the price mechanism. As its economy developed through exports in the expanding BRICS (Brazil, Russia, India, China and South Africa) countries as well as in Europe, Germany 'has a strong interest in keeping intact a macroeconomic regime in which monetary and fiscal policies remain credibly conservative and is especially wary of fiscal lassitude, which would lead to real exchange-rate appreciation and would thus impair export competitiveness. However, such a neomercantilist model of growth can work for one country (if it is not too big), perhaps a few, but by definition not all countries' (Armingeon and Baccaro 2012a). According to Woodruff, Germany's capacity to blackmail other countries was made credible by the embeddedness of so-called ordoliberalism—a neoliberal doctrine calling for state intervention within constitutionally settled limits. So,

> First, the institutional structure of the Eurozone was such that Germany held an effective veto over many measures needed to promote the protective reaction. Second, the prospect that this veto would be used was in turn rendered credible by the thorough embedding of Ordoliberalism, the particular German variant of neoliberalism, in Germany's institutions and policy-making culture. The strategic power of Ordoliberalism derived from the central role of rule-bound action in this policy approach. Because Ordoliberalism offered resources to justify even catastrophic consequences in an individual case by citing the broader benefits of rules, actors with a commitment to Ordoliberalism could credibly threaten to veto policies required to ward off market panic. (Woodruff 2014)

According to some interpretations, *reactions to financial panic could at times have been instrumentally delayed by the EU institutions, in order to impose austerity policies.* As mentioned, the EU crisis has been seen as fuelled by financial panic, used by political entrepreneurs (such as politicians and technocrats) for increasing their political leverage. In fact, the ECB has often threatened to refuse to function as a lender of last resort for government bonds if specific requests were not accepted. By delaying information about ECB decisions to purchase sovereign bonds in order to calm the markets, the EC kept the panic's pressure on Europe's national governments as well as the opposition. Thus, at the EC meeting of 7 May 2010, then ECB president Jean-Claude Trichet 'described the bond-market panic in dire terms, advocating a rescue fund financed by European governments and a program of budget austerity. He also communicated that adoption of these measures was a precondition for ECB market intervention.' His rejection of the request for immediate intervention by French president Nicolas Sarkozy was supported by Angela Merkel, who threatened a potential intervention of the Bundesverfassungsgericht (the federal constitutional court) against any action seen as inconsistent with the Maastricht Treaty. In this way, 'the shadow of the Bundesverfassungsgericht's Maastricht decision—meant the threat of ECB inaction might well have been viewed credibly' (Woodruff 2014).

While these were general political conditions affecting the European periphery during the Great Recession, we can expect that opportunities and threats had also some specificity by country. Together with the position of the traditional left-wing parties, the degree of trust in (domestic and EU) institutions, the capacity of traditional parties to keep consensus through different means as well as the type of EU requests are among the main dimensions that can affect the degree and type of protests against austerity. Keeping the specific dynamics of the responsibility crisis in mind, we could expect the opposition to austerity policies to take the most disruptive forms in Greece and Spain.

1.3   Anti-austerity Movements

Social movement studies have seen recent changes in the social structure as not particularly conducive to mobilization. In short, not only have processes such as deindustrialization and migration weakened the structural preconditions for the development of a class cleavage, particularly in the working-class forms of mobilization, but recent developments have also jeopardized citizens' rights through poverty, unemployment and job insecurity. In fact,

> Overall, the size of social groups which lack full access to citizenship and its entitlements has grown, whether because they are migrants (legal or illegal), because they are employed in the hidden economy, or engaged in low-paid work. The sense of general instability has been further reinforced by the growth of individual mobility, principally horizontal: and thus more people tend to change jobs several times in the course of one's life—whether out of choice or out of necessity. The multiplication of roles and of professions and of the related stratifications, and the (re)emergence of ethnicity or gender-based lines of fragmentation within socio-economic groups have made it more difficult to identify specific social categories. (della Porta and Diani 2006, 39)

In addition, research on governments' reaction to the Great Recession has suggested that, lacking new powerful social coalitions oriented to lessen economic inequality, 'by and large, governments did not respond to the Great Recession with either striking policy innovations or dramatic institutional change' (Bermeo and Pontusson 2012, 27). In a recent stimulating reflection on the development of capitalism, Wolfgang Streeck (2014) has indeed suggested that it might die due to the absence of opposition rather than because of strong countermovements.

This notwithstanding, strong waves of protest developed in the 1990s and 2000s, first in the global South and then on a worldwide scale, in what was called the global justice movement. These protests had some characteristics that challenged the new social movement paradigm. First of all, from the social point of view, they mobilized coalitions of white- and blue-collar workers, unemployed and students, young and old generations. The need to keep together a heterogeneous social base—as well as the general failures of big ideologies to provide for successful alternative models of social and political organization—fuelled the development of pluralist and tolerant identities, praising diversity and an enriching value. This was reflected at the organizational level through the elaboration of a participatory and deliberative model of decision making (della Porta 2009a, b).

While some research had indicated that the social bases of (left-wing) protest shifted from the industrial working class for the labour movement to the new middle classes for new social movements, anti-austerity protests brought attention back to the mobilization of the losers of globalization. Sometimes called the 'multitude' or 'precariat', those who protested against austerity represented coalitions of various classes and social groups that perceived themselves as the losers of neoliberal development and its crisis.

Precariousness was certainly a social and cultural condition for many movement activists. Overwhelmingly present in protests has been a generation (which in Portugal defines itself as 'without a future') that is characterized by high levels of unemployment and under-employment—that is, employment in positions that are underpaid and unprotected. The most marginalized groups of young people took the lead in the Arab Spring, and those affected by the financial crises mobilized in various forms in Southern Europe. These young people are not those who have traditionally been described as losers: they are rather the well-educated and the mobile, once described as the 'winners' of globalization—but they are far from perceiving themselves as such.

Along with them, we found other social groups that have lost the most from the neoliberal attacks to social and civil rights: from public employees to retired individuals—those once considered as the best-protected social groups and that have instead seen their rights continuously reduced—became, to a greater or lesser extent, precarious themselves in terms of their life conditions, including the loss of fundamental rights such as healthcare, housing and education. Similarly, blue-collar workers of the small but also large factories, shut down or at least in danger of such, have participated in the wave of protest. With high levels of participation by young people and well-educated citizens, the demonstrations brought into the street a sort of (inverted) '2/3' society of those most hit by austerity policies. Traditional workers participated, but so did retired people, unemployed, and precarious workers (although these were more present in other types of protests). Therefore, the protests brought together coalitions of citizens with different socio-biographic backgrounds, but united by their feeling of having been unjustly treated (della Porta 2015).

If neoliberalism produces a liquid culture, destroying the old bases for personal, collective and political identity through forced mobility and related insecurity, identification processes are, however, neither impossible nor automatic. Rather, as social movement studies would predict, they assume once again a central role, although strongly shaped by the changing culture of neoliberalism. While the labour movement had developed a strong identity—supported by a complex ideology—and new social movements had a focus on specific concerns, the identification processes of anti-austerity protesters seemed to challenge the individualization of liquid society as well as its fear and exclusivism, calling instead for state intervention and inclusive citizenship. Defining themselves broadly—as citizens, persons, or the 99 per cent—activists of the anti-austerity movement developed a moral discourse that called for the reinstatement of welfare protections, but they also (indignantly) challenged the injustice of the system. Referring often to the nation, as the basis of reference of a community of solidarity, they nevertheless developed a cosmopolitan vision combining inclusive nationalism with recognition of the need to look for global solutions to global problems.

If scholars reflecting on a liquid society had stressed the presence of multiple individual identities, changing subjective identification, and soft (or weak) collective identities—while others had hopes in the insubordination of the multitudes—much identity work is oriented to a definition of the self, with the re-emergence of a social criticism of capitalism (della Porta 2015). As precariousness, as lost security about life development itself, spread from young unemployed and under-employed to large, once-protected social groups, identification with the overwhelming majority in society might provide some certainty. A strong morality framing grew to contrast the perceived amorality of neoliberalism and its ideology, with attempts to commodify public services. The cynical, neoliberal view of personal responsibility for survival and the proclamation of selfish motives as beneficial have been stigmatized in the name of previously existing rights, with calls for their re-establishment. A stress on solidarity and the return to the commons have been juxtaposed to an unjust and inefficient neoliberal ideology. Differently from the global justice movement, which had presented itself as an alliance of minorities in search of a broad constituency, the anti-austerity movements have constructed a broad definition of the self, as a large majority (contrasted with the network of minorities of the global justice movement) of the citizens. Backward looking, the anti-austerity protests called for the restoration of lost rights, vehemently denouncing the corruption of democracy. However, they also looked forward, combining concerns for social rights with hopes for cultural inclusivity.

As the economic crisis was linked to a legitimacy crisis at the political level—which took the specific form of a crisis of responsibility—more and more groups in society felt themselves non-represented within institutions that were increasingly considered as captured by big business. Collusion between economic and political power then emerged more and more strongly. The effect has been a dramatic acceleration of trends towards declining party membership, loyalty and identification as well as decreases in conventional forms of participation and (especially) institutional trust. Social movements active against austerity policies are embedded in a crisis of legitimacy that takes the particular form of a crisis of lack of responsibility towards citizens' demands. Protesters stigmatize the power of big corporations and (unaccountable) international organizations, with the related loss of national governments' sovereignty. What is more, they hold responsible those governments and the political class at large for what they consider an abduction of democracy. However, rather than developing anti-democratic attitudes, they claim that representative democracy has been corrupted by the collusion of economic and political power, calling for participatory democracy and a general return to public concern with common goods.

Given the extremely low trust in existing representative institutions, these movements have addressed requests to the state, but also experimented with alternative models of participatory and deliberative democracy. With different degrees of radicality, they have combined old and new repertoires of protest. Mostly avoiding violence against people and direct confrontations with police, protests against austerity took the forms of strikes (including general strikes) and mass demonstrations, but also of symbolic performances. As in Latin America for the peasants' movements and the unemployed, blocks of roads or railways have been carried out as ways of attracting attention but also of expressing strong opposition to those who 'block our life'. *Acampadas* became places to prefigure new forms of democracy. In comparison with the global justice movement, the declining confidence in representative institutions is reflected in the weakening of the search for channels of access to public decision making through lobbying or collaboration. Even if there is still a desperate search for politics, its traditional forms are mistrusted and autonomous ones explored. It is not democracy per se that is challenged, however, but rather its degeneration—as 'they call it democracy, but it is not'.

In this sense, these movements are not anti-political but rather propose a different—deliberative and participatory—vision of democracy that they prefigure in their own organizational forms. Although appealing to the citizens beyond traditional parties and associations, these are far from the widespread definitions of populism as an exclusivist and homogenizing discourse, instead suggesting the importance of developing arenas for encounters among persons with different social backgrounds and political ideas. Participants call for deliberation through high-quality discourse rather than charismatic power as a way to find solutions to common problems. In the presence of an institutional system felt as more and more distant, protesters ask for a direct commitment.

This development reflects the perceived challenge in the crisis of neoliberalism: first, the perception of a large and very critical potential basis of the movement in the heterogeneous social groups that have been hit by the crisis; and second, the deep disappointment, not only with representative institutions and political parties, but also with unions and associations of various types, which are stigmatized as unwilling or unable to address the financial crisis. Neither the hierarchical structure of the labour movement nor the networked model of the new social movements seems to fit with the emerging anti-austerity protests (della Porta and Andretta 2013; della Porta and Reiter 2012; della Porta et al. 2015). As neoliberalism attacked the corporatist actors that had driven the social pacts of Fordist capitalism—the unions first but also many civil society associations once integrated in the provision of social protection—the emerging movements began to cherish the idea of a direct democracy of the citizens. Organizational structures have developed following strategic reflections over past successes and failures, but also based on the political and social balances of opportunities and constraints. Both the social characteristics of the reference base and its normative preferences are relevant in explaining the search for new organizational forms. Developing upon the global justice movement's experiences with participatory and deliberative forms of democracy, the anti-austerity protests moved from a 'democracy of the forums' to a 'democracy of the squares', with growing attention to openness, publicity and equality. Deliberative and participatory conceptions and practices of democracy were combined with an emphasis on the direct participation of citizens rather than through networks of associations.

1.4   The Research and This Volume

While these can be considered as general characteristics of the anti-austerity protests, as they emerged in previous research (della Porta 2015), differences have also been noted in the extent of the protests as well as their framing, repertoire of action and organizational models. We might expect these to be rooted in the cultures and structures of various domestic movements, as well as adapting to the characteristics of the socio-economic and political crises. In particular, we might expect organizational structures to resonate with a more horizontal tradition in Spain and Greece, and to a certain extent Iceland, along with a stronger separation of old and new movements; and instead with a more associational heritage in Italy and Portugal, as well as in Ireland and Cyprus. In terms of framing, the balance between left and libertarian traditions can indeed vary—with class discourses more rooted in Southern Europe than in Iceland and Ireland. Finally, we expect the frequency of strikes and marches to be varied by country, with outsiders' strategies more traditionally rooted in Greece or Spain than in Italy or Portugal.

While political opportunities have been considered relevant as either stable (institutional) conditions or contingent ones—as welfare state and party government were taken for granted in traditional reflections of political opportunities—attention to the politics of neoliberalism in post democracies is all the more important to understanding how social movements can adapt to and challenge a situation characterized by high levels of institutional distrust, decline of traditional organizations of political consensus, and the stripping off of political competencies: what I indeed defined as a crisis of responsibility. The different intensity and characteristics of both socio-economic and political crises can be expected to affect the intensity and characteristics of the opposition to austerity—leading it to assume more anti-systemic or countermovement characteristics.

In general, we expect a cross-national comparison of the crises and its discontent in the European periphery to illuminate these relations, in their dynamic evolution. This is what we shall attempt in the rest of this volume, by looking at all these dimensions in the European periphery. As cross-national is linked to transnational analysis, we shall follow in our presentation of the case studies the timing of the spillover of the crisis, starting in Iceland and continuing with Greece, Ireland, Spain, Portugal, Italy and Cyprus.

Focusing on a specific EU periphery—the one that most bitterly experienced the post-2008 crisis—the research design can be located within a most similar comparative approach, with attention to differences within similar cases. At the same time, however, it is not the typical area study, addressing historically homogeneous and geographically proximate cases. By covering not only Southern Europe—as traditionally understood to contain four main countries—but also Iceland, Ireland and Cyprus, we also aim to identify the similarities among geographically distant cases, which have nevertheless occupied similar positions within the crisis of late neoliberalism.

From the point of view of research methods, in all countries we triangulated as much as possible documentary sources (including various databases) with interviews of a theoretically sampled group of about 12 activists of anti-austerity protests in each country (see list in Appendix). The semi-structured questionnaires included questions on the organizational structures, action strategies and framing of anti-austerity protest, with particular attention to the assessment of the socio-economic conditions in late neoliberalism as well as of the legitimacy crisis. In addition, we made use, within a logic of historical comparative analysis, of secondary sources that mainly comprised research in political economy, political participation and social movements.

While data are presented case by case, with a comparative analysis developed in the conclusion, during the research informal meetings and formal conferences allowed for a cross-national vision. The volume is structured as follows, with case studies presented following as much as possible the evolution of the socio-economic crisis and of its discontent.

Chapter 2, *Iceland's Mobilization in the Financial Crisis*, examines the wave of mobilization related to the Icelandic financial crisis, which exploded during the fall of 2008 with the launching of weekly protests in October. Overall, the Icelandic anti-austerity movement consisted of two distinct yet interconnected phases: The Popular Protest (2008–2009), during which (after decades of relative inactivity) grassroots entities and activists emerged as key players in the socio-political scene; and the Constitutional Reform (2009–2012), in which citizens and a handful of more organized collectives engaged in a direct-democratic process in order to draft the new Constitution. Given the relative scarcity of movement-oriented civil society actors in the country, the anti-austerity protesters had largely to reinvent both the organizational formats they adopted and the action repertoire they utilized. Yet, it would be erroneous to characterize the reinvention process as coming out of nowhere. The Iceland protest drew from international experience—but also exercised influence on the anti-austerity mobilizations that would follow, in Europe and beyond.

Chapter 3 is devoted to *The Presence and Absence of Protest in Austerity Ireland*. It has been widely argued that Ireland has been an exception to the other countries toiling under austerity because of the perceived absence of mass protest or political turmoil in opposition to the economic policies imposed by successive governments at the behest of the Troika since 2008. Ireland has been put forth by the Troika as an example of responsible governance because it accepted its collective guilt for the financial recklessness that characterized the Celtic Tiger period. Indeed, this view is not inherently unfounded; until 2013, protest in Ireland was of a lesser extent than could have been expected. Protest did occur, but it was geographically dispersed, fragmented and ideologically inconsistent. Nonetheless, years of harsh austerity led to an incremental groundswell of popular anger and disillusionment with existing parties which crystallized in a massive movement against the imposition of water charges in late 2014. The campaign has seen massive street demonstrations which, proportionate to Ireland's population, have been among the largest expressions of popular opposition to austerity in Europe.

Chapter 4 focuses upon *Turbulent Flow: Anti-Austerity Mobilization in Greece*. The global financial crisis of 2008 arrived in Greece in early 2010, when the newly elected social-democratic government was forced to request an extraordinary 110 billion euros loan from the so-called 'troika' (the International Monetary Fund, the European Central Bank and the European Commission). The loan agreement was accompanied by harsh austerity terms which, by 2014, proved devastating for both the Greek economy and society. These dramatic occurrences left their mark on the social and political scene. Fostered by a particularly strong movement tradition, the anti-austerity mobilizations in Greece—which began as early as May 2010—expanded wave after wave as the crisis years went by. While in 2010 and early 2011 the organizational formats and action repertoire of the anti-austerity protests were similar to those of the previous decades, the Arab Spring and the Spanish *acampadas* of 2011 proved major sources of inspiration for the Greek 'occupy the squares' movement. Later on, contention diffused to football stadiums, military parades and everyday life instances. After 2012, the majority of the movement's resources were devoted to social solidarity structures, in a coordinated effort to relieve the suffering population from austerity's negative consequences. Alongside its materialistic demands, the anti-austerity movement was characterized by its focus on democracy and its content in crisis times. This chapter summarizes the main characteristics of the anti-austerity protest in Greece, on the political, societal and social movement field. It is argued that the ways in which mobilization evolved not only reflected the tradition established by pre-existing social movement organizations, but also allowed for experimentation and development of new social movement practices and organizational forms. The role of critical junctures—during the transition from one protest phase to the next—was particularly important in fostering the aforementioned developments.

Chapter 5 addresses *Late Neoliberalism and Its Indignados: Contention in Austerity Spain*. In May 2011, the so-called Indignados movement emerged in Spain, the mobilizing capacity, visibility and impact of which had no precedent in the country's recent history. Four years later, some of those Indignados are participating in the emergence and development of new political parties that are today ruling some important cities and aspire to do so at the national level after the next elections in December 2015. In the meantime, a strong contentious cycle took place in the country. This chapter analyses this protest cycle, focusing on the socio-economic context, political opportunities, forms of action and organization, and activists' aims, identities and frames. In Spain, the consequences of the Great Recession have been aggravated by neo-liberal policies adopted by different governments under the pressure of electorally unaccountable institutions or the moves of speculators. The authorities' behaviour has eroded citizens' trust in political institutions by uncovering the democratic deficit of a political system that limits the participation channels of civil society while encouraging the enrichment of the elite to the detriment of the living conditions of the majority. These strains are the basis of the indignation which was mobilized first in the streets, and then inside the Parliaments. The Indignados have demanded that authorities reverse the cuts in public services and civil rights, strengthen mechanisms of control and transparency, and create new channels of citizens' access to decision making. Throughout the protest cycle, activists have organized actions of different sorts, with high mobilizing capacity and attracting massive social support. Mobilization has caused a change in the field of social movements with the rise of new actors and the strengthening of existing ones. In their protests and networks, the Indignados opposed the logic of the system with an alternative one based on the model of empowered deliberative democracy, which they updated with a relatively novel concept of organizational inclusiveness directed at potential participants and the transformation of public spaces into open, empathic arenas. They strove to build a movement of 'anyone' based on an extremely inclusive 'we' that aimed to go beyond ideological or partisan affiliations and the auto-referential dynamics, organizational forms, discourses and identities of traditional social movements.

Chapter 6 is on *Late Neoliberalism and Its Discontents: The Case of Portugal*. Portugal during the great recession represents quite an interesting case, since not only was the volume of protest comparatively quite high in the context of southern Europe, but Portugal was also a country in which protest movements tended to form cohesive organizations, create stable and wide coalitions, develop a national scope and establish alliances with unions and left-wing political parties. Moreover, the political and institutional context was favourable to protest, in terms of providing recognition, allies and support. In this chapter we will describe the main traits of the Portuguese social movement and protest dynamics during the Great Recession (collective action repertoires; organizations and actors; identity and frames; and conceptions of democracy), but also try to understand how they were shaped by the socio-economic context (e.g. intensity of austerity and major consequences for the populations' welfare) and national political opportunity structure (e.g. institutional allies, divisions between elites, patterns of government and opposition).

Chapter 7 looks at *Neoliberalism and Its Discontents in Italy: Protests Without Movement?* While Italian social movements have probably been among the most active in creating a strong anti-neoliberal mobilization in Europe, the mobilization against the current economic crisis and the austerity measures taken by Italian governments in the last years has been relatively weak in terms of political outcomes. The chapter reconstructs the main features of the anti-austerity mobilization by underlining the prevalence of a logic of collective action that is fragmented and driven by old actors. The first part of the chapter summarizes the socio-economic and political conditions under which the anti-austerity protests emerged. The following parts are devoted to the analysis of the protests' main characteristics and of how they mirror external political constraints. The concluding part addresses the reasons why the anti-austerity protests have had little impact so far, by referring to three kinds of factors: the political configuration of the governments dealing with the economic crisis, the broader political opportunity structure and the type of civil society. A relatively strong and traditionally party-dominated civil society gives little space for new collective identities to emerge, making the protest field very sensitive to the position of traditional allies within the national political system. The tensions between the left-wing and centre-left parties involved in pro-austerity measures are mirrored in the fragmentation of the protest field and the tensions between social movements and traditional leftist organizations such as trade unions. In addition, the presence of new political actors—such as the Five Star Movement in electoral politics, with few connections with anti-austerity mobilization—limits the possibility for an electoral reconfiguration of the left based on an anti-austerity position.

Chapter 8 analyses *Cyprus' Explosion: Financial Crisis and Anti-Austerity Mobilization.* The chapter addresses the crisis in Cyprus as well as the limited anti-austerity mobilization. During the years that preceded the 2008 financial crisis, Cyprus had achieved relatively high rates of increase in GDP, thanks to its booming tourist and financial sectors. As was the case with other EU countries, however, Cyprus' development had fragile foundations. Its banking sector—accused by many of money laundering and tax-haven services—was unable to sustain the combined systemic shocks of the post-2008 recession, its exposure to Greek public debt, and the tremendous 2011 explosion at a military base, which wrecked the country's main electricity plan and caused damages amounting to almost 10 per cent of the Cypriot GDP. In the ensuing explosion, the government launched negotiations with the EU in the direction of securing a bailout agreement that would allow the country's banks to remain afloat. The austerity terms that would accompany the prospective deal provoked a first wave of public outrage and protest. In November 2012, citizens' groups, unions, and the then newly-formed 'Alliance Against the Memorandum' staged a series of protests. In the spring of 2013, the negotiations' failure and the imposition of capital controls and levies on bank deposits' caused a second round of protest, equally short-lived. In sum, despite the relevant impact of the financial meltdown on the Cypriot economy—and notwithstanding the local social movement's efforts to construct coalitions with other societal groups to counter the austerity measures—organized resistance to the crisis' consequences was scarce and limited, from a certain point on, to individual or uncoordinated actions. Explanations for the above phenomenon include the relative weakness of civil society, the time frame of the protest development, as well as the strong presence of pre-existing, yet marginal, leftist organizations, which hampered the emergence of new protest actors with which a majoritarian part of the society could identify.

In the final chapter, *Late Neoliberalism and Its Discontents: A Comparative Conclusion*, the results of the country cases will be systematically compared in light of the hypotheses put forward in this introductory chapter. First of all, we will assess in each country the characteristics of the anti-austerity protests—looking at their social bases, framing, organizational forms and repertoire of actions. Second, we will introduce and analyse systematic data on the socio-economic disruptiveness as well as the political consequences of the crisis. Finally, we will discuss further potentials for analytic models that aim at bridging social movement studies and political economy, bringing capitalism back into the analysis of contentious politics.

NOTE

1. There was, therefore, a retreat from 'social Keynesianism' as well as from more interventionist policies, protectionism and industrial policies and a move towards so-called liberal Keynesianism: 'Whereas social Keynesianism emphasizes public spending and redistributive measures to sustain long-term prosperity, liberal Keynesianism focuses on demand stimulation during economic downturns and favors tax cuts over spending increases' (Pontusson and Raess 2012).

REFERENCES

Armingeon, K., and L. Baccaro. 2012a. Political Economy of the Sovereign Debt Crisis: The Limits of Internal Devaluation. *Industrial Law Journal* 41(3): 254–275.

———. 2012b. The Sorrows of Young Euro: The Sovereign Debt Crisis in Ireland and Southern Europe. In *Coping with Crisis. Government Reactions to the Great Recession*, eds. N. Bermeo, and J. Pontusson, 162–198. New York: Russell Sage Foundation.

Arrighi, G., T.K. Hopkins, and I. Wallerstein. 1989. *Antisystemic Movements*. London: Verso.

Bermeo, N., and J. Pontusson. 2012. Coping with Crisis. An Introduction. In *Coping with Crisis. Government Reactions to the Great Recession*, eds. N. Bermeo, and J. Pontusson, 1–33. New York: Russell Sage Foundation.

Borland, E. 2013. Disruption. In *The Wiley-Blackwell Encyclopedia of Social and Political Movements*, eds. D. Snow, D. della Porta, B. Klandermans, and D. McAdam, 1038–10341. Oxford: Blackwell.

Cabral, R. 2013. The Euro Crisis and Portugal's Dilemma. *Intereconomics* 48(1): 4–32.

Cameron, D.R. 2012. European Fiscal Responses to the Great Recession. In *Coping with Crisis. Government Reactions to the Great Recession*, eds. N. Bermeo, and J. Pontusson, 91–129. New York: Russell Sage Foundation.

Conde-Ruiz, J.I., and C. Marín. 2013. The Fiscal Crisis in Spain. *Intereconomics* 48(1): 4–32.

Crossley, N. 2002. *Making Sense of Social Movements*. Buckingham: Open University Press.

Crouch, C. 2010. Democracy and the Economy. In *La Democrazia di Fronte Allo Stato Democratico*, ed. Alessandro Pizzorno, 181–192. Feltrinelli: Milan.

———. 2012. *The Strange Non-Death of Neoliberalism*. Oxford: Polity.

de la Porte, C., and E. Heins. 2015. A New Era of European Integration? Governance of Labour Market and Social Policies in the Sovereign Debt Crisis. *Comparative European Politics* 13(1): 8–28.

della Porta, D. 2009a. *Democracy in Social Movements*. London: Palgrave.

———. 2009b. *Another Europe*. London: Routledge.

———. 2013. *Can Democracy be Saved?* Oxford: Polity.

———. 2014. *Mobilizing for Democracy*. Oxford: Oxford University Press.

———. 2015. *Social Movements in Times of Austerity*. Cambridge: Polity.

della Porta, D., and M. Diani. 2006. *Social Movements: An Introduction*. Oxford: Blackwell.

della Porta, D., and M. Andretta. 2013. Protesting for Justice and Democracy. *Contemporary Italian Politics* 5(1): 23–37.

della Porta, D., and H. Reiter. 2012. Desperately Seeking Politics. *Mobilization: An International Quarterly* 17(3): 349–361.

della Porta, D., L. Mosca, and L. Parks. 2015. Subterranean Politics and Visible Protest in Italy. In *Subterranean Politics in Europe*, eds. M. Kaldor, and S. Selchow, 60–93. London: Palgrave.

Gamson, W. 2013. Injustice Frames. In The Wiley-Blackwell Encyclopedia of Social and Political Movements, eds. David Snow, D. della Porta, B. Klandermans, and D. McAdam, pp. 607–608. Oxford: Blackwell.

Greer, S. L. 2013. Structural Adjustment Comes to Europe: Lessons for the Eurozone from the Conditionality Debates. Available at SSRN: http://ssrn.com/abstract=2214866 or doi:10.2139/ssrn.2214866

Habermas, J. 1976. *Legitimation Crisis*. Oxford: Polity.

Hall, P., and D. Soskice, eds. 2001. *Varieties of Capitalism*. Oxford: Oxford University Press.

Heins, E., and C. de la Porte. 2015. The Sovereignty of Debt Crisis, the EU and Welfare State Reforms. *Comparative European Politics* 13(1): 1–7.

Helleiner, E. 2012. Multilateralism Reborn? International Cooperation and the Global Financial Crisis. In *Coping with Crisis. Government Reactions to the Great Recession*, eds. N. Bermeo, and J. Pontusson, 65–90. New York: Russell Sage Foundation.

Hosoki, R.I. 2013. Demography and Social Movements and Revolutions. In *The Wiley-Blackwell Encyclopedia of Social and Political Movements*, eds. D. Snow, D. della Porta, B. Klandermans, and D. McAdam, 344–347. Oxford: Blackwell.

Iversen, T., and D. Soskice. 2012. Modern Capitalust and the Advanced Nation State: Understanding the Causes of the Crisis. In *Coping with Crisis. Government Reactions to the Great Recession*, eds. N. Bermeo, and J. Pontusson, 35–64. New York: Russell Sage Foundation.

Klandermans, B. 2013a. Frustration-Aggression. In *The Wiley-Blackwell Encyclopedia of Social and Political Movements*, eds. D. Snow, D. della Porta, B. Klandermans, and D. McAdam, 493–494. Oxford: Blackwell.

———. 2013b. The Dynamics of Demand. In *The Future of Social Movement Research. Dynamics, Mechanisms, and Processes*, eds. J. van Stekelenburg, C. Roggeband, and B. Klandermans, 3–16. Minneapolis: The University of Minnesota Press.

McNamara, K.R. 2005. Economic and Monetary Union: Innovation and Challenges for the Euro. In *Policy-Making in the European Union*, 5th edn, eds. H. Wallace, W. Wallace, and M.A. Pollack, 141–160. Oxford: Oxford University Press.

Monastiriotis, V., N. Hardiman, A. Regan, C. Goretti, L. Landi, J. Ignacio Conde-Ruiz, C. Marín, and R. Cabral. 2013. Austerity Measures in Crisis Countries: Results and Impact on Mid-term Development. *Intereconomics* 48(1): 4–32.

Pianta, M. 2012. *Nove su Dieci*. Rome: Laterza.

Polanyi, K. 1957 (orig. 1944). *The Great Transformation: The Political and Economic Origins of Our Time*. London: Beacon Press.

Pontusson, J., and D. Raess. 2012. The Politics of Economic Crisis in Historical-Comparative Perspective. *Swiss Political Science Review* 18: 502–507.

Roberts, K. 2014. Populism and Social Movements. In *Oxford Handbook on Social Movements*, eds. D. della Porta and M. Diani Oxford: Oxford University Press.

Sacchi, S. 2015. Conditionality by Other Means: EU Involvement in Italy's Structural Reforms in the Sovereign Debt Crisis. *Comparative European Politics* 13(1): 77–92.

Sassen, S. 2006. *Territory, Authority, Rights: From Medieval to Global Assemblage.* Princeton, NJ: Princeton University Press.

Scharpf, F. 2011. Monetary Union, Fiscal Crisis and the Preemption of Democracy. Working paper, Max Planck Institute for the Study of Societies, Cologne.

Snow, D. 2013. Grievances, Individual and Mobilizing. In *The Wiley-Blackwell Encyclopedia of Social and Political Movements*, eds. D. Snow, D. della Porta, B. Klandermans, and D. McAdam, 540–542. Oxford: Blackwell.

Snow, D., and R.G. Lessor. 2013. Consciousness, Conscience, and Social Movements. In *The Wiley-Blackwell Encyclopedia of Social and Political Movements*, eds. D. Snow, D. della Porta, B. Klandermans, and D. McAdam, 244–249. Oxford: Blackwell.

Snow, D., D.M. Cress, L. Downey, and A.W. Jones. 1998. Disrupting the "Quotidian": Reconceptualizing the Relationship Between Breakdown and the Emergence of Collective Action. *Mobilization* 3: 1–22.

Stiglitz, J.E. 2012. *The Price of Inequality.* New York: Norton and Co.

Streeck, W. 2010. E Pluribus Unum? Varieties and Commonalities of Capitalism. MPIFGF, Discussion Paper 10/12.

———. 2011. The Crisis in Contest. Democratic Capitalism and Its Contradictions. MPIFGF, Discussion Paper 11/15.

———. 2014. Taking Crisis Seriously: Capitalism on Its Way Out. *Stato e Mercato* 100: 45–68.

Varoufakis, Y., S. Holland, and J.K. Galbraith. 2015. *Bescheidener Vorshlag zur Losung der Eurokrise.* Munich: Kunstmann.

Wallerstein, I. 1990. Antisystemic Movements: History and Dilemma. In *Transforming the Revolution*, eds. S. Amin, G. Arrighi, A.G. Frank, and I. Wallerstein. New York: Monthly Review Press.

Woodruff, D.M. 2014. Governing by Panic: The Politics of the Eurozone Crisis. LSE Europe in Question, Working Papers Series.

CHAPTER 2

Iceland's Mobilization in the Financial Crisis

Markos Vogiatzoglou

2.1 INTRODUCTION

This chapter examines the wave of mobilization related to the Icelandic financial crisis, which started in the autumn of 2008. Iceland was the first European country to be directly affected by the Financial Crisis of 2008. As early as October 2008, all three of the country's major private banks had collapsed; their bailout by the state and indirect nationalization provoked a tremendous increase in public debt, whilst the local currency (*króna*) was collapsing, causing further problems to the import-dependent economy.

In response, weekly protests were launched in October 2008. Popular outrage culminated during the Christmas break of 2008–2009, resulting in five days of massive mobilization between 20 and 25 January. Although the participants' main demand was satisfied on the latter date—the government was forced to resign—sporadic protests continued until 15 March 2009. General elections brought a centre-left coalition to government in April 2009. During the autumn of 2009, grassroots organizations and other initiatives launched a National Forum to discuss the possibility of drafting a 'crowd-sourced', new Constitution. The 2010 Constitutional Act provided institutional legitimacy to the process. The draft was completed and approved by a non-binding referendum in 2012. Yet, the government did not proceed with the necessary legislative moves to officially

© The Author(s) 2017
D. della Porta et al., *Late Neoliberalism and its Discontents in the Economic Crisis*, DOI 10.1007/978-3-319-35080-6_2

adopt it, much to the disappointment of the grassroots actors. The general elections of 2013 brought a right-wing government coalition back into power, which immediately put the constitutional reform procedures on hold.

Overall, the Icelandic anti-austerity movement consisted of two distinct, yet interconnected phases: the Popular Protest (2008–2009), during which (after decades of relative inactivity) grassroots entities and activists emerged as key players in the socio-political scene; and the Constitutional Reform (2009–2012), when citizens and a handful of more organized collectives engaged in a direct-democratic process, in order to draft the new Constitution. Given the relative scarcity of movement-oriented civil society actors in the country (and the fact that the previous major mobilization wave in the country dates back to the 1950s anti-NATO protests), the anti-austerity protesters had largely to reinvent both the organizational formats they adopted and the action repertoire they utilized. Yet, it would be erroneous to characterize the reinvention process as coming out of nowhere. The Iceland protest drew from international experience—but also exercised influence on the anti-austerity mobilizations that were to follow, in Europe and beyond.

Movement participants described their experience of participation as 'empowering', 'an imaginative frenzy', 'deeply engaging', fuelling 'the belief that everything could change' (Interviewees IC1, IC2, IC4). It is noteworthy that when asked to comment on the mobilization's outcomes, the interviewees expressed their disappointment and disillusionment, even though some of their demands were actually met. Sentiments aside, the aftermath of the anti-austerity mobilization includes the reintroduction of political and social issues in the public debate, the emergence of radical political formations representing the protesters' viewpoint, and the formation of new coalitions and initiatives in the field of grassroots activism.

2.2   THE SOCIO-ECONOMIC AND POLITICAL CONDITIONS

When the financial meltdown occurred in Iceland, the country was governed by a 'wide coalition' of the right-wing Independence Party and the centre-left Social Democratic Alliance. The coalition held a secure parliamentary majority of 43 out of 63 seats after the 2007 general elections, and the right-wing leader, Geir Haarde, had been appointed prime minister (Statistics Iceland 2014).

The crisis arrived in Iceland in the autumn of 2008: all three major private sector banks (which controlled 80 per cent of the banking system) collapsed and were nationalized in order to prevent their default (Wade and Sigurgeirsdottir 2011). On 6 October, Haarde delivered the infamous 'God Save Iceland' address to the nation, officially terminating the period of prosperity of the previous years (Jónsson 2009; Prasch 2011). The impact of the banking collapse on the Icelandic economy and the measures undertaken to counter it fall beyond the scope of this chapter; yet, two direct consequences which the population endured are noteworthy:

First, the Icelandic citizens suffered direct income losses, due to the currency collapse (which had a significant impact on the country's import-based economy). As noted by a young protester who was a university student at the time of the mobilization:

> Because of the currency collapse imports became too expensive. We have a small agriculture sector, a fishery sector, but we're not self-sufficient. So, a lot of consuming goods became inaccessible to the population. [...] We didn't have any imports coming into Iceland for two weeks. People started worrying, started panicking. [...] The banks had been offering people very cheap loans, to buy things they could not afford. But many of these loans were in foreign currency; the mortgages became astronomically expensive. (Interviewee IC4)

Furthermore, they considered that their government could no longer be trusted. 'We were greatly deceived' was the telling statement by one of the interviewees (Interviewee IC3). Our interviewee expands on that argument: 'when it became clear that the government had greatly deceived the people, the more and more it became clear that the government had been basically lying to those people, the people started protesting' (Interviewee IC4).

What followed was the resignation of the government—which satisfied the main demand of the 2008–2009 protests. The government stepped down on 26 January 2009; financial regulators and the Central Bank of Iceland chief followed immediately afterwards. The results of the April 2009 parliamentary elections shook the country's traditionally stable party system. The Independence Party lost almost 13 per cent of its voters and nine parliamentary seats. All centre-left and left-wing formations recorded gains (Kriesi 2012). A centre-left coalition government was formed, with the participation of the Social Democratic Alliance (SDA) and the Left-Green Movement. Jóhanna Sigurðardóttir (head of SDA) was appointed prime minister, whilst the Citizen's Movement opted to remain in the opposition.

The new government soon fell short of the high expectations its voters had raised. Criticism emerged both from the left—due to the austerity measures implemented, as well as the inability or unwillingness to adopt the new Constitution—and from the right—because of rises in taxation that accompanied pension cuts and high unemployment. Despite the fact that the economy (at least in terms of GDP) moved towards recovery, internal disputes in the coalition parties further undermined their electoral support (Ensor 2013).

In the 2013 general elections, the right-wing formations made an impressive comeback. The Independence Party and the Progressive Party significantly increased their percentages when compared to 2009, whilst the two former government partners, SDA and the Left-Green Movement, suffered record losses. The fragmented left underperformed as well. Of the three parties that participated in the elections, only the Pirate Party managed to enter Parliament. A coalition government was formed, and the 37-year-old leader of the Progressive Party, Sigmundur Davíð Gunnlaugsson, assumed the role of prime minister (The Australian 2013). The newly appointed government changed, to some extent, the external affairs priorities of the country. Iceland is a member of the European Economic Area and has signed the Schengen Treaty. In July 2009, it had applied to join the European Union (EU). But the process has been frozen since 2013, as the two right-wing parties currently governing the country are Eurosceptic.

Moving the focus back to the anti-austerity mobilization, it is important to identify the political and systemic opportunities that facilitated their emergence. As noted by Icelandic scholar Jón Gunnar Bernburg, who conducted qualitative and quantitative research on the 2008–2009 demonstrations, 'a perception of political opportunity among left-wing critics and social activists' can be identified, the careful handling of which, according to him, led to the amplification of the protest activity (Bernburg 2014). The political opportunity, Bernburg explains, emerged from the sharp contrast between the prevailing consumerist and prosperity-for-all narratives of the period directly preceding the financial collapse, and the 'reality check' (as one of our interviewees put it) the Icelandic society was put through directly after the meltdown. The 'fear' and 'panic' the population experienced during the turbulent days of 2008 were complemented by a general sentiment of deception and disillusionment, mostly directed towards government and financial sector officials. It seems reasonable, therefore, that the emergent discourse of the protesters was mostly based on moral grounds. 'Protest participants', notes Bernburg, 'were many more times more likely than non-participants to believe in the reality of political corruption in Iceland and to be in alignment with left-wing political ideas and parties, while socio-economic status and personal economic difficulties had very little effect on participation' (Bernburg 2014, 3).

Political opportunity management by activists also had more practical aspects. As the following long excerpt from Interviewee IC3 confirms, the protesters had clearly identified the party that constituted the weak link of the pre-2009 government coalition, and strategically exercised pressure in the direction of further weakening it.

> On the evening of 21 December 2008, Samfylkingin [the Social Democratic Alliance] had a meeting in Þjóðleikhússkjallarinn [the basement of the National Theatre]. Everybody knew that they did not agree on if they should break off relations with Sjálfstæðisflokkurinn [the Independence Party]. We wanted to encourage them to do so, but all the people were in Austuvöllur [the square in front of the Parliament]. Me and several of my friends just talked to people in Austuvöllur and expressed the idea that the crowd should move to Þjóðleikhúsið. Then six of us went to Þjóðleikhúsið and some other people continued to spread the word in Austurvöllur. We had been sitting in front of Þjóðleikhúsið, the six of us for about 90 minutes and nothing happened, not even our friends came, so we were very disappointed. Then suddenly we hear drums and we see hundreds and hundreds of people flowing from Austurvöllur, singing and shouting, some of them carrying torches, some banners or signs. The first 20–30 came, and together we walked into the building, there was no rush, nobody was violent, nothing was broken or stolen, we just walked down to the basement, urged them to split with Sjálfstæðisflokkurinn and then we left the building very peacefully and joined the crowd outside. (Interviewee IC3)

The state response to the protests was admittedly relatively mild. Mainstream media consistently undermined the demonstrations, and 'Voices of the People' leader Hörður Torfason reported that several anonymous blogs had personally attacked him, the accusations focusing on his personal life and sexual orientation. Yet, none of the above actions could be directly attributed to state apparatuses. The Icelandic police had no (recent) experience of coping with mass protests and political violence of any sort. When confronted with the sporadic contentious incidents of the protest peak (20–25 January 2009), the officers present initially showed signs of disorganization and ambivalence on how they should respond. The disorganization was further aggravated by the fact that all senior police commanders were absent—our interviewees pinpointed that the whole police high command had treated itself to a belated Christmas holiday in a sauna resort outside Reykjavik. Furthermore, internal disputes between the two main police bodies were noted:

> On that date [20 January], the police behaved really badly, they were pepper spraying people and pushing them aside. Then they learnt from their mistakes, they realized that what they did made people angry, also, many of them wanted to be on the other side of the protest obviously, it was a very difficult situation for them I must say. […] They were not organized well enough, they were lacking their supervisors, also the problem is that you have two arms of police in Iceland, the Reykjavik Police and the Iceland Police which controls the Special Forces. The chief of the Reykjavik Police wanted to take a pacifist stance, whilst the chief of the SWAT team wanted to use more violence. They were battling it out, but the Reykjavik Police chief won, in the sense that they were quite pacifist in the end when compared to what they could have done. (Interviewee IC4)

In sum, despite the few injuries suffered by protesters (it is noteworthy that the frozen ground and harsh weather of the time/place made physical confrontation even more challenging for the two sides), it is doubtful whether the state response to the protests was ever perceived as a threat by the participants.

Summing up, the simultaneous presence of the tangible crisis impact on the population's everyday social and economic life and the representation crisis, as well as the lack of any visible direct threats hampering protest activity, did facilitate the emergence and development of the anti-austerity mobilization in the country.

2.3   Protest Events and Protest Campaigns

2.3.1   *Collective Action Repertoires, Organizational Forms and Resources*

Phase 1: Popular Protest (2008–2009)
Given the relative lack of protest culture in the Icelandic society, at least over the last few decades, no protest toolkit was directly available to the

population—nor did any previously organized political actor jump in to direct the dissent. As an anarchist activist recalls, 'People were having informal meetings in coffee-shops and houses, discussing what they can do to change the situation' (Interviewee IC3).

The first recorded public action took place on 11 October 2008, when folksinger Hördur Torfason staged a one-man protest outside the Icelandic Parliament. Torfason repeated the same protest on 18 October, this time joined by dozens of citizens. This was the beginning of the so-called 'Saturday Protests'—which culminated later on in what has been termed the 'Pots and Pans Revolution' (Júlíusson and Helgason 2013). The protests at this stage were totally peaceful and mostly consisted of singing performances and speeches delivered from an impromptu stage, placed on the square in front of the Parliament.

Other citizens were also organizing informative and discussion meetings simultaneously. It is important to trace the trajectory of these 'invisible' gatherings, as not only did they prove to be important mobilization hubs, they also constituted the embryonic forms of what later became the constitutional reform movement. A local journalist, recalls one of these instances:

> There was this guy called Gunmar, an art director who held these 'citizen's meetings', under the slogan 'let's talk, let's stop shouting at each other and educate each other'. There were a lot of these meetings, and lot of people that came and this developed into small groups that were working on thematic issues. (Interviewee IC1)

The weeks went by—and the government refused to resign, despite the demonstrators' appeals. The Saturday Protests grew in numbers. The protesters began building up on the symbolic content of the mobilization. An interviewee recalls that:

> There was a man holding a banner which said 'helvítis fokking fokk' and this became to some extent the main slogan of the protest. It means 'Fuck off from hell' (laughs) as you understand it's a very, sort of, rude, a sort of in-your-face slogan, but became quickly famous. Every Icelandic person who sees this will think back immediately at these times, it's one of the two most famous slogans, along with the other one 'vanhæf ríkisstjórn' which means 'the government is incompetent'. These are the two slogans connected with the revolutionary movement of the time. (Interviewee IC4)

What proved to be a key turning point was the closure of the Icelandic Parliament for 20 days, during the Christmas break of 2008–2009. Our interviewees recall that this incident caused a public outrage, further exacerbated by the luxurious holidays that the MPs enjoyed. The above were considered a provocation, given the economic collapse and the fact that the majority of the people were facing significant economic difficulties. A 25-year-old student at that time remembers that the only issue on the agenda for discussion upon the reopening of the Parliament was whether further limitations in alcohol consumption should be implemented. This was deemed 'irrelevant' to the critical situation of the economy, further adding justification to those calling for the government's resignation. A protest was called to coincide with the reopening of the Parliament, on 20 January 2009. Our student continues:

> The anger was brewing. [...] A lot of people knew as it seems that [the protest] was going to be big, that it was going to be something else. They called it a 'revolution' amongst themselves. A lot of people felt that way. [...] I received a message from a friend, he said come down to the square, it's going to be big, and bring a pot or another piece of metal to make noise with. (Interviewee IC4)

The protest was, indeed, big. Reports vary as to how many people actually participated (secondary data are equally ambivalent). Numbers range from 12,000 to 50,000, an extraordinary level of participation in any case, considering that Reykjavik is home to some 117,000 people, and the whole of Iceland has a population of 315,000 (Statistics Iceland 2015).

The demonstration on 20 January 2009 was the first one where lightly violent tactics were employed on behalf of the protesters. Stones, eggs, shoes, yoghurts and vegetables were thrown at the police and the Parliament's windows. The police responded by pepper spraying and pushing back the participants who had broken the police barriers and climbed up on the building's windows. Several people suffered minor injuries. It is important to note that, when compared with other European countries, the degree of violence was minor, perhaps irrelevant (Note: the police response will be examined in the relevant section, see below). Yet, from the standards of the Icelandic society, and given that most of its members had never witnessed any sort of physical, political confrontation, the scenes caused a tremendous shock. Our interviewees were eager to explain in detail their involvement (or non-involvement) in the ruckus—those with international experience of demonstrations, though, acknowledged the limited degree of violence the protesters exercised, as well as its mostly symbolic nature:

> The protest was not really violent, most of these happened in the evening, and it was made by people who were not really there to protest, but to pick a fight. And they saw prime conditions for it. The people were not aiming to be violent towards police, they wanted to be insulting. They wanted to be aggressive, but not violent. They were throwing yoghurt and eggs [...] it's not really dangerous, it's not something that can hurt you—it can humiliate you but not hurt you. (Interviewee IC4)

The role of informal radical groups in the repertoire escalation is undisputed. The small anarchist circles of Reykjavik acted as a de facto avant-garde protest, providing the necessary expertise to the participants and undertaking several initiatives. This should not be interpreted, though, as a process of verticalization—all instances of the Icelandic financial crisis protest were characterized by a totally horizontal and decentralized coordination of small, mostly informal groups and individuals. Comments from one interviewee are indicative:

> I must emphasize that even if the anarchists became the force that drove the protests, there were no leaders in the ordinary sense of that word. Nobody was in charge, nobody gave any orders. It just happened like that; a few people cut the yellow police ribbons and then the crowd rushed into the area. A few people brought two to three pallets to Austurvöllur [the square in front of the Icelandic Parliament] and lit a fire and an hour later you would see all kinds of people collecting pallets, setting pallets, park benches and everything burnable on fire, singing and dancing around the bonfires. (Interviewee IC1)

Protests continued, on a daily basis now, from 20 to 25 January 2009. More violent incidents were noted: on 21 January, eggs and paint bombs were thrown at the prime minister's car (Waterfield 2009), whilst on the 22nd, police utilized tear gas to disperse protesters, 'for the first time since the 1949 anti-NATO protests' (Gunnarsson and Lawless 2009). On 23 January, the prime minister announced that he would not run for re-election, due to health issues. On 26 January, the government resigned, and the minority coalition that took office announced general elections for the April of the same year, promising to organize a Constitutional

Assembly in order to revise the country's constitution. Sporadic protests continued until 15 March.

Apart from the mobilization's flagship—the 'Saturday Protests'—several other protest events were recorded. They also reflected the decentralized and horizontal character noted above:

> I should also have told you about how very small groups suddenly expanded. There was for example this guy, an ordinary man, not a part of any group or movement, who had been standing alone with his sign in front of Landsbankinn, every day for many weeks. Then one day, forty to fifty people came to the bank and joined him. They went into the bank, shouting—not hurting anyone, not vandalizing as much as one pen, but making a lot of noise. That man—who nobody had ever heard of, was suddenly leading a meaningful demonstration. But nobody told anyone what to do, people just came when they wanted and left when they felt like it. (Interviewee IC3)

In sum, the protest cycle of the October 2008–March 2009 period presented many of the characteristics that became typical for the anti-austerity mobilizations in Europe that followed. Largely populated by people lacking any previous movement experience, more experienced activists provided expertise, but this process took place in an informal manner. Strictly non-partisan and refusing to protest under the banners of established social movement organizations, the Church or other entities, the demonstrators explicitly targeted government and financial institutions. The symbolic choice of the Parliament square as the main field of action bore resemblances to mobilizations in Greece, Tunisia, Egypt and elsewhere (Sergi and Vogiatzoglou 2013). The action repertoire could be considered as innovative and radical only when placed in Iceland's specific *national* context. As one interviewee notes, 'When a lot of these actions are taking place, perhaps not very radical, in the end the mobilization becomes radical, it's like the nation has woken up—we had not seen that before' (Interviewee IC3). This self-perception of radicalization and innovation had important consequences for the aftermath and outcomes of the mobilization, as shall be examined in the concluding section.

Phase 2: Constitutional Reform (2009–2012)

The elections of April 2009 brought to power a coalition of left-wing parties. One of their main electoral promises was the launch of a process of constitutional reform. The particulars on why constitutional reform became the prime issue in the movement's agenda will be examined in the relevant section; it is however worth mentioning at this point that some sort of continuity is to be noted between the popular protests of the previous period and the grassroots initiatives aiming to draft the new Constitution. All of the key actors of the protests were involved in the drafting process; the same was true of new entities that emerged during—or right after—the protest period. Furthermore, the constitutional reform process presents indeed an almost ideal-type example of further democratization of a well-established democratic regime. Finally, the way in which the process developed provides a—perhaps unique—example of grassroots mobilizing and direct-democratic decision making. For these reasons, we consider that it is worth including the constitutional reform of 2009–2012 in our chapter, despite the fact that—technically speaking—it cannot be labelled as a 'protest'.

The constitutional reform process took place in four stages: The National Assemblies of 2009 and 2010; the Constitutional Assembly (later renamed to Constitutional Council) of 2011; and the referendum of 2012.

The first National Assembly, which took place on 14 November 2009, was organized by an umbrella organization of various grassroots initiatives and individuals, called 'The Anthill' (Dessi 2012). Among the organizers, one could find splinter groups from the informal meetings and gatherings that had taken place in the previous period. As an interviewee mentions, 'Among them [i.e. the citizen's meetings] there was a thematic group on the Constitution. And this specific group worked very closely with the National Assembly' (Interviewee IC2). Other key players included:

> [...]Gudjón Mar Gudjonsson, a young entrepreneur with extensive ICT skills, and creator of the Ministry of Ideas, a civic movement promoting participatory democracy. Of the participants of the National Assembly, 1200 were randomly selected from the Icelandic census, and 300 were deliberately selected from among political institutions and relevant associations. (Bergsson and Blokker 2013, 4)

It is important to note how well the initiative was received by the population. Of the 1500 people invited, some 1200 accepted the invitation and came to Reykjavik from all over Iceland. Our interviewees described the event as a 'collective brain-storming' (Interviewee IC3). The participants were distributed in small working groups, discussing specific issues and setting the priorities for the constitutional revision. The Assembly identified nine major thematic fields (education, family, welfare, economy, environment, sustainability, opportunities, equality and public administration), pinpointing directions the reform should follow (Thjodfundur 2009). Parallel to the main discussions, other groups were undertaking projects such as coding and categorizing the parliamentary debates (optional.is 2012).

The experiment was repeated in 2010, this time having secured institutional coverage and governmental support. The 950 (again, randomly chosen) delegates examined in depth the strands that the 2009 Assembly had produced. The governmental mandate was not only to clarify the lines along which the new Constitution would be produced, but also to identify the procedure under which a Constitutional Assembly would be formed, in order to draft the document. The National Assembly decided to call for a direct vote of the whole population, which would elect the 25 Constitutional Assembly members and assign them the task of finalizing the draft over a two-month period. The members were elected in early 2011 and, after a long series of deliberations, judicial obstacles and revisions, the new Constitution was brought for approval in a non-binding (advisory) referendum that took place in October 2012. Despite the relatively low turnout due to high abstention of the rural voters (overall participation reached 49 per cent of the registered voters), the Constitution was approved by a decisive majority (Fontaine 2012).

Only one step remained, but—to the great disappointment of the grassroots activists who had worked hard on the issue during these years—it was never taken. The left-wing government failed (or proved unwilling, depending on the interpretation) to pass the bill approving the Constitution before its mandate was concluded.

Margrét Tryggvadóttir, one of the most passionate supporters of the new Constitution, attributes the failure to get the Constitution passed to a variety of reasons. Some of the MPs raised concerns that elected representatives would lose too much power, whilst the fishing industry and other key economic players lobbied against the increased protection of the country's natural resources, which they interpreted as a threat against their economic activity. Furthermore, personal strategies and factions inside the SDA had an impact on the outcome. More specifically, the parliamentarians elected in the rural areas rejected the abolition of the weighted vote system—rural voters are purposely overrepresented in the Icelandic Parliament. As Tryggvadóttir puts it, 'Parliamentarians who are elected in the country side, they wouldn't be in the next Parliament, and they know that. So it was difficult to get them to say "yes", since they would lose their job' (Interviewee IC5). The 2013 elections brought back to power the right-wing Independent Party and the Progressive Party, which had fiercely opposed the reform procedure, and naturally blocked the new Constitution's adoption.

An important aspect of both mobilization stages is the way through which resources required to sustain the protest were produced or identified, what their source was and how they were allocated. One of the important features of the mobilization in Iceland was its self-organized nature, which helped maintain a particularly cost-effective balance in terms of material resources. The small size of the host city, Reykjavik, also played a role. Additionally, as Iceland is one of the top OECD (Organization for Economic Cooperation and Development) countries in terms of internet deployment, access and use, activists 'spread the word' mostly via digital means (Facebook, Twitter and SMS).

With regard to protest material, the majority of banners were hand-made. Participants brought whatever was available at home—saucepans and other metallic, noise-producing items—as well as objects that were meant to be thrown at the police and the Parliament building. Harsh weather conditions were countered using heavy clothing ('Dress well!' concluded an SMS calling to the protest that one of our interviewees received) and improvised bonfires, where wooden items found in the vicinity were burnt. The stage, truck, and sound system of the 'Saturday Protests' were initially sponsored by the singer Hörður Torfason, but participants almost immediately began collecting donations in order to cover the costs.

An interesting question is how the expertise about the action repertoire was circulated. One interviewee attributes it to small groups of radical activists who had previous movement experience, either at home, or whilst studying/working abroad:

> This is very interesting. You had the *Raddir fólksins* people, who were gathering thousands and thousands, but did not really know what to do. They were just standing there. Then you had these small groups, among which the anarchists, which had quite a different idea on what a protest should look like. [...] The anarchists were much more radical than the rest, they would cut the ribbons of the police and everyone else would follow. (Interviewee IC3)

She admits, though, that there was a mutual learning process between the moderate and the more radical factions of the movement: 'You had this large group of people who had no clue what it is to be an activist. But they became activists, overnight! It was a collective learning process. We need these two forces [...] we need the radicals, and we need these moderate, ordinary people who get all these thousands to join along' (Interviewee IC3).

An interesting characteristic of the protests—which would be encountered later in all the anti-austerity mobilizations in Europe and beyond— was their 'repetitive' nature. Although this was not the first time that a similar type of protest took place at the international level, Hörður Torfason, when asked how he came up with the idea of calling for a protest every Saturday, traced the origins of the idea in his own experiences back in the 1970s. Torfason was then a famous singer and actor. Upon deciding to publicly reveal his sexual orientation, though, he was confronted with hostile reactions from society. His concerts in villages and small towns were suddenly attended only by a handful of people. What he noted, though, was that when returning to the same village for a second concert, the few initial attendants would bring along their friends or family. 'Persistence' and 'patience', he assumed, were more useful than strong statements (Interviewee IC2). Some 40 years later, he tested the impact of persistence and patience in exercising political pressure. In August 2008, he had launched a daily one-man protest in front of a ministry, demanding the recall of an asylum seeker's deportation. Less than a month later, the government satisfied the demand. Naturally, as the objectives of the financial crisis protests were much more ambitious, one had to handle carefully the timing of what was expected to become a long series of protest events.

Turning back to material resources, the political formation 'Citizen's Movement', which emerged during the protests and participated in the 2009 elections, electing four MPs, ran a low-cost electoral campaign. As one of its founding members, recalls:

> We did not have any money. We had Facebook, we had bloggers, we had people like me who knew people in the media, and arranged some interviews. [...] We asked people to support us with money; we got a little money to have a small office on the main street. And from there, volunteers would go in the streets and give people stickers to put on their jackets. That was all. (Interviewee IC1)

2.3.2   Protest Actors, Aims and Framing

The main actor of the first protest stage was the 'Voices of the People' (*Raddir fólksins*)—an impromptu collective founded and led by Torfason.

It was protests every Saturday, and they were led by a man called Hörður Torfason, he's the one that organized the whole thing, made the thing happen. It wouldn't have happened without him. He's a folk singer and a human rights advocate, so to say. [...] He was the first person in Iceland to state openly he's gay, I mean not the first one, but the first one that was [publicly] known and decided to come out of the closet. (Interviewee IC4)

Raddir fólksins introduced the three main demands of the early stages of the protest (see below for details). During their weekly demonstrations, open-air assemblies and public debates were taking place. Despite the cessation of their protest activities in March 2009, they continued to publish editorials and opinion articles on their website until early 2013.[1]

The vast majority of the participants in the Saturday Protests, though, were people with little or no movement experience, having no social movement organization affiliation. As is usually the case, small informal communities, identity and other interest groups joined en masse:

People who had never expressed interest in politics, people who were interested in video games or motorcycles, suddenly were discussing on [sic] politics. They would go together in [sic] the protest, dressed in similar way, in order to establish some identity. I know about a group of motorcyclists, not a member's club, like 'Hell's Angels' or anything, they would show up on their motorcycles, doing a parade during the protests. (Interviewee IC3)

An informal group that, according to participants, played a key role in the development and character of the protests was the radical activists who defined themselves as 'anarchists'. Small anarchist circles were to be found, even before the protests were launched in Iceland. Júlíusson and Helgason (2013) attribute their origins to the punk movement of the 1980s and, even before that, to the resonance of the May 1968 mobilizations in Europe and the United States. Several anarchists had participated in the Saving Iceland environmental organization, which, during the mid-2000s, had staged a series of small-scale actions against the construction of a hydroelectric plant. But our interviewees clarified that the anarchist activists did not have an organized collective of their own, nor were they influential in broader societal circles. While initially their number did not exceed 20 people, there was a significant increase upon the arrival of the crisis: '[When the protests started] the anarchists were around 70 people. It might not sound too much, but in Iceland, you know, we're only 300,000 people, so 70 activists make a difference' (Interviewee IC3).

The activists held informal meetings in private homes, in order to organize themselves in advance of the protests.

> These meetings were started as soon as September 2008 [...] the most radical among the anarchists held meetings in houses. There were a lot of smaller groups working together and coordinating all types of actions. We saw all kinds of performances by performance groups and artists. [...] A feminist group dressed a statue in pink, that sort of action. (Interviewee IC3)

Finally, an important actor—not only in terms of protest organization, but also with regard to discourse production—was the Reykjavik Academy. Defined as 'a sort of liberal center of discussion in the citadel of post-modernist Icelandic academia' and 'a collective of independent scholars' (Júlíusson and Helgason 2013, 199), it actively pursued the creation of spaces where people could participate in open debates. ST, a student at the time, comments:

> There is of course the Reykjavik Academia. Not sure how to describe this, it's a group of academics, civil society actors. Some of them are quite radical. They organized civilian meetings, civil society meetings, where very heated but useful discussions took place in the wake of the crisis. I think this is where the Citizen's Movement was born. (Interviewee IC4)

The Citizen's Movement, mentioned in the interview excerpt above, was a political formation that participated in the April 2009 elections, with the purpose of representing the demonstrators' points of view in the new Parliament. One interviewee was one of its founding members:

> The Citizen's Movement was founded before the Government fell. It was founded during very long, very difficult, very boring meetings, because the people who participated had very different opinions with regard to many issues, for example the European Union and so on. The people who founded it were not activists, well ... they had become activists by then. The core consisted of 20 people, perhaps even less. (Interviewee IC1)

The Citizen's Movement agenda evolved around three main axes: a new constitution, the housing issue (the population had difficulty repaying mortgages in foreign currency due to the *króna* collapse), and the protection of natural resources. Margrét Tryggvadóttir, an MP elected with the Movement in 2009, explains:

> We were thinking that a new constitution was a necessary step towards a better society, a safeguard that what happened in Iceland would never happen again, and that it would give the people tools to react when something was not right. [...] Another thing was that we had to do something for the [people's] home[s] and the economic situation. And the third thing was that we wanted to do something for the energy [...] and in general we wanted to make sure that the companies which are using the country's natural resources pay a fair price, because they didn't and they still don't. (Interviewee IC5)

The Movement did not have a leader—a 'troika' of appointed officials undertook clearly defined responsibilities, complementing one another. Despite their lack of funds and party political experience, they ran a successful, low-cost electoral campaign. Contrary to poll predictions, the list received more than 7 per cent of the votes, easily overcoming the 5 per cent threshold and electing four MPs. But that was when the real problems started:

> It was in many respects a do-it-yourself political formation. It consisted of members of the Reykjavik Academy but also many simple, angry people, who believed that something should be done. It was started a few months before the elections, it was very impromptu—not well organized. It didn't really have a plan on what to do once in the government. They had a clear idea on how to get elected, but not what to do once elected. It became chaotic and sort of dissolved. So they [the MPs elected with it] became orphans in the Parliament, and this happened because the movement behind them had splintered. But still, they did really well, I was happy with them. (Interviewee IC4)

Our interviewee recalls how puzzling the transition between the activist realm and the party politics sphere proved to be: 'We really didn't know how to behave like politicians. We knew how to behave like activists. It was a great experiment, but it blew up in our faces!' (Interviewee IC1).

The MPs elected with the Citizen's Movement moved in the direction of establishing transparency clauses in parliamentary activities. 'They sort of revealed they were total amateurs, but they tried to do some activism in the Parliament, they managed to change some silly traditions, but most importantly, they worked hard to inform the people on what was going on' (Interviewee IC4).

In the end, due to internal disputes, the party list dissolved. The four MPs retained their seats in Parliament as independent members. In the 2013 parliamentary elections, activists participated in three different lists: the *Pirate Party, Dawn* and the *Iceland Democratic Party*. Of the three, only the Pirate Party managed to enter Parliament, electing one representative.

The most important civil society organization, providing knowledge and experience to activists who later became involved with the anti-austerity protest, was the environmental group Saving Iceland. The group undertook various small-scale activities during the mid-2000s, more specifically against the construction of a dam and a hydroelectric plant in the mountainous eastern part of the country. All of our interviewees, who would later become active in the anti-austerity protest, had noted its presence. Hörður Torfason, had participated in some of the group activities, as did several among the anarchist activists. One interviewee considers their presence as an early 'wakening' for the dormant Icelandic social movements:

> There was this activist group called 'Saving Iceland', they were really active before, against hydroelectric plants, for example in 2005–2006 against a dam in the Eastern Part of the country. [...] An Italian company had undertaken the construction and they had hired Chinese workers, with very low wages, in the freezing cold, up in the mountains. That was a wakening as well. (Interviewee IC1)

The leader of the Pirate Party was also a member of Saving Iceland. She is 'still very active in the environmental movement', as an interviewee confirmed.

The second civil society group to play a role in the protests consisted of the remnants of the anti-NATO movement of the 1950s and 1960s. The movement's founding act was the 1949 anti-NATO riots, when thousands of communist-friendly protesters attempted to invade Parliament in order to block the confirmation of Iceland's membership in the Organization. They were blocked by right-wing counterdemonstrators and local police. The heavy military presence of the US army, due to Iceland's key geostrategic position, kept the tensions high in the following decades—occasionally sparking significant mobilizations. Yet, by the early 2000s, the vast majority of US forces had left the country and only a few aged members of the movement remained active. Despite their declining numbers, though, the anti-NATO activists were present in the protests. An interviewee explains:

> The anti-NATO movement had not been forgotten, but it got stronger during the mobilization. You would see younger people joining in the demonstration, which had not happened before. This was the strongest action you had seen in years. Because they got more people, younger people involved. [...] You would see these grannies, these old ladies, protesting—once I saw a group of them wearing masks on their faces—like the anarchists' masks, suddenly even the older were wearing scarfs and masks. (Interviewee IC3)

The unexpected alliance between the youngest, most radical factions of the movement and the traditional activist circles of past decades strengthened movement activities beyond the financial crisis context. For example, 'On January 28, 2009, the government had invited the leaders of NATO for a conference at the Hilton Hotel. Samtök hernaðarandstæðinga [the anti-NATO movement] organized a protest, and the anarchists showed up in support' (Interviewee IC3).

Finally, Júlíusson and Helgason (2013, 196–199) argue that the May 1968 influences in Iceland, as well as their aftermath (small Trotskyist and Maoist parties, the punk culture of the 1980s) resonated with the Icelandic protest, yet the primary empirical data we collected do not confirm such an influence, at least not in a direct manner.

When it comes to protest aims and framing, the 'official' objectives of the early mobilization (before the 2009 parliamentary elections) were rather clear-cut. As an interviewee notes: 'We had a few demands. We wanted the government to resign, we wanted the Central Bank chief to resign, and we wanted the people who were supposed to supervise the financial sector to resign. So we wanted new elections and we wanted to kick out some civil servants' (Interviewee IC4).

All interviewees agree that the above description is accurate. The government's resignation topped the list, and the protesters also demanded the resignation of financial regulators, as well as the head of the Central

Bank of Iceland—considering the latter as the main institution responsible for the financial collapse. The list of three objectives is attributed to the group 'Voices of the People' (*Raddir fólksins*) and their leader Hörður Torfason. Torfason stated that he had collected the three demands during informal discussions with participants in the 'Saturday Protests'. He then jumped onto the stage to ask: 'Do we agree that these three issues constitute our aims?' The participants approved the agenda with cheers (Interviewee IC2). As time went by, though, the agenda was somewhat enriched as new actors joined in the protest. The anarchists, as expected, were promoting a more generic 'no government' agenda. Disabled and elderly people held banners with specific demands concerning their own population groups.

Beyond the explicit claims, though, a set of implicit grievances was expressed during the turbulent winter of 2008–2009. An interviewee stated that what the protesters wanted, in the very end, was to 'make them [i.e., the elites] listen'. 'People were protesting against *everything* at that time [emphasis ours]', added another activist. 'This is what scared the police officers, it scared the parliamentarians obviously. We were making noise; we were hanging on the windows of the Parliament. We were banging the windows, we wanted to disrupt the Parliament, we wanted to make ourselves heard' (Interviewee IC4).

The government's resignation (soon to be followed by those of the other protest targets) satisfied the initial protesters' demands. As the new government was perceived to be movement-friendly, the activists correctly identified a window of opportunity to introduce new aims and objectives in their agenda. According to an activist, there were two main goals in the post-2009 election period. The first one was rather practical. Given that the collapse of the *króna* had placed tremendous burdens on citizens indebted with loans and mortgages in foreign currencies, the movement 'wanted to turn back the clock so that our loans and mortgages will be turned back to the time of 1 January 2008. They would be a little higher but not that expensive. The other big issue we had was the new Constitution' (Interviewee IC1).

Concerning the constitutional reform, an analytical distinction should be made between the reform as a *process*, and the constitution itself as a *document*, as a set of provisions. With regard to the former, an interviewee notes: 'The Constitution problem mattered a lot to many people. [...] When we were working on the new Constitution we viewed it as a very democratic action. Ordinary people participating ... I thought we were seeing something new. It looked like more democracy, more direct democracy, this is how we felt' (Interviewee IC3). With regard to the latter, another interviewee comments: 'We said that there should be something in our law that forces the government, when the people do not trust it anymore, to leave. But there was nothing. So the first idea is that we need to make the Constitution as a standard operating procedure of the government' (Interviewee IC1).

This 'standard operating procedure' included several interesting innovations. Articles 32 to 36 established Icelandic natural resources as 'common property'. Articles 65 and 66 introduced participatory elements to the regime. Namely, referendums may be called and legislative bills may be introduced to the Parliament, following petitions which would be signed by 2 to 10 per cent (depending on the case) of the electoral body. Finally, article 113 'introduces an obligatory referendum regarding constitutional amendments' (Bergsson and Blokker 2013, 8).

Overall, the constitutional reform process sparked a heated and most interesting debate, which reflected the question of what direct democracy could look like in contemporary societies. Several commentators—even among the supporters of the new Constitution—fiercely criticized the process, dismissing the term 'crowd-sourced' used by the National Assembly organizers (Bjarnason 2013). Others attributed the failure to the unwillingness of a significant part of the political elite to concede parts of their authority to the population (Gylfason 2013). Whatever the case, it is beyond any doubt that the perspective of rewriting the country's founding text inspired Iceland's activists to engage in a long, deliberative and participatory process. The latter, complementing the protest period, confirmed the re-emergence of the grassroots and movement organizations in the country's socio-political scene.

2.4   Concluding Notes: The Aftermath and Impact of the Icelandic Mobilization on the Country's Society and Institutions

The protest wave of 2008–2009 and the ensuing direct-democratic constitutional reform process left their mark on Icelandic society, its institutions and its activists. In this concluding section, we aim to categorize the phenomena that are directly related to the protest, along the above three broad axes.

First, with regard to broad societal shifts, all interviewees noted that political debates are much more prominent in the aftermath of the protests—even today. As an interviewee says, 'There is a lot of discussion going on, especially on the internet, you see more people expressing their political views' (Interviewee IC3). Political debates are present on the Facebook pages of Icelanders, their blogs and their everyday lives. According to an interviewee, contemporary Icelanders are 'more involved', 'more aware' than before. Furthermore, as Bernburg had assumed, the financial crisis brought about a rupture with the materialist and consumerist principles that prevailed during the prosperity years.

> I think there is still a lot of materialism, but I think we had some sort of reality check [...] a lot of the materialism died down, because the people could not afford it anymore. [...] Now it's very fashionable among young girls to knit their own clothes, and in general [it is considered fashionable] to do things on your own, collectively. (Interviewee IC4)

The successful conclusion of the protest period, with the resignation of the government and financial sector officials, offered the participants a sense of 'empowerment'. 'People perceived themselves as an "active force"; the mobilization strengthened the feeling of community among us' (Interviewee IC3).

What is more, and despite the conservative formations' electoral victory in 2013, some indications of change can be noted in Iceland's political system. The electoral success of the Citizen's Movement in 2009, followed by the Pirate Party in 2013, brought to Parliament individuals and parties that are considered to represent, to some extent, the protesters' point of view.

> It is very unusual, for example, to have someone like Jon Gnarr in the post of Mayor of Reykjavik. I think more space has been opened for more radical views, than before. [...] The Pirate Party is fighting for transparency, and this is something that you would never have heard before, that is before the protests. (Interviewee IC3)

All-around artist Jon Gnarr—who served as Reykjavik's Mayor until 2014, when he abruptly abandoned politics—is, indeed, an interesting case. Citing as his 'main influences Bakunin, Kropotkin and the British punk band CRASS' (Ruthven 2013), he led a group of fellow artists and musicians (their party was modestly called 'The Best Party') and was elected with 34 per cent in 2010. His term will mostly be remembered for his impressive publicity stunts, but he was also a dedicated human rights supporter.

The above developments, perceived by activists as positive, could not conceal a strong sentiment of disappointment when assessing the political aftermath of the protest. The reasons brought forward were twofold: On the one hand, the rapid re-ascension to power of the political forces considered responsible for the financial crisis; on the other hand, the failure of the centre-left government in adopting the new Constitution.

> I think that what happened, the fact that the people managed to topple the government, gave them a certain feeling of empowerment, but now, we feel like that it didn't matter so much. The government that followed largely disappointed the population. [...] What the voters will never forgive them is that we made a new Constitution and they failed to get it through Parliament. That was the democratic reform that we needed, the crowd-sourced constitution being approved. (Interviewee IC4)

The interpretation activists gave to the shortcomings of the 2009–2013 government was that of systemic deadlock, corruption, and strong alliance networks among the elites, preventing any possibility of 'real change':

> It is still difficult to understand how and why the left-wing government killed the Constitution themselves. After that many people felt angry and hopeless. People got disappointed—a prevailing opinion was that nothing seemed to have changed despite the mobilizations. And, if you take a step back, you can see that indeed, the system did not change. (Interviewee IC4)
> We feel that it's still very corrupted and it hasn't changed so much, especially with the current [right-wing] government. (Interviewee IC3)

Finally, with regard to the impact on the activists themselves and the perspective of further movement activity, all contributors assess in a positive way the 2008–2009 protest cycle. As an interviewee noted, 'Since then, you see many movements working together, you see more cooperation.' The cross-fertilization between various factions of the movement was evident as early as 2009. As an interviewee recalls:

> Activism spread almost overnight and we saw a lot of artistic demonstrations. One example is 12th January 2009 when a group of people, some of whom had never been involved in a solidarity movement, marched to Arnarhóll at

8 o'clock in the morning, carrying dolls and swaddled figures with blood-red streaks, in support of the victims of Gaza. This kind of demonstration was not common before the kitchen tool revolution, but suddenly it became a norm to express your opinions in this way. (Interviewee IC3)

Protests, even large ones (by Iceland's standards) are still taking place. Although significantly weakened with regard to its glory days, the anti-austerity movement remains active:

We had this protest last November [2014]; it was a sort of picnic outside the Parliament. There were 4000 people [...] the protest was against the way they [the Government] were spending the money on the health system, how they are prioritizing the money. [...] So, they were cutting the taxes to big companies, and at the same time cutting down expenses for hospitals, schools. Iceland is a really rich country, there's a lot of money out there, but it's not distributed in a fair way. (Interviewee IC1)

Summing up: the financial crisis mobilization in Iceland was not only, to some extent, successful in achieving its goals; it also had three mid- and long-term consequences: the re-introduction of political and social issues in the country's public debate, the emergence of radical political formations representing the protesters' viewpoints, and the formation of new coalitions and initiatives in the field of grassroots activism. What is more, its early arrival in what would later become a cross-national anti-austerity wave in Europe and beyond, as well as the specific issues it brought forward—the most prominent being the importance of fiscal and currency sovereignty in implementing alternative policies to address the crisis—confirm its significance among the episodes of discontent that late neoliberalism has provoked.

2.5   LIST OF INTERVIEWEES

IC1, member of 'Citizen's Movement', 25 February 2015, Reykjavik
    IC2, founder of the initial mobilization, 26 March 2015, Reykjavik
    IC3, anarchist activist, participated in all major protests, 5 March 2015, Reykjavik
    IC4, student, participated in the main phase of protests, 21 January 2015, Reykjavik
    IC5, member of Parliament (Citizen's movement, Pirate Party), 9 March 2015, Reykjavik

NOTE

1. See http://raddirfolksins.info/

REFERENCES

Bergsson, B. T. and P. Blokker. 2013. The Constitutional Experiment in Iceland. In *Verfassunggebung in Konsolidierten Demokratien: Neubeginn Oder Verfall Eines Systems*, ed. K. Pocza. Baden-Baden: Nomos Verlag. Accessed 5 March 2015. http://papers.ssrn.com/sol3/papers.cfm?abstract_id=2320748

Bernburg, J. G. 2014. Financial Crisis and Protest in Iceland, October 2008–January 2009. *CritCom*. Accessed 5 March 2015. http://councilforeurope-anstudies.org/critcom/financial-crisis-and-protest-in-iceland-october-2008-january-2009/

Bjarnason, B. 2013. Iceland's "Crowd-Sourced" Constitution Is Dead. *Studio Tendra*. Accessed 5 March 2015. http://studiotendra.com/2013/03/29/icelands-crowd-sourced-constitution-is-dead/

Dessi, G. 2012. The Icelandic Constitutional Experiment. *Open Democracy*. Accessed 5 March 2015. https://www.opendemocracy.net/giulia-dessi/icelandic-constitutional-experiment

Ensor, S. 2013. Iceland's Tories are Back. Socialist Review, (381). Accessed 5 March 2015. http://socialistreview.org.uk/381/icelands-tories-are-back

Fontaine, P. 2012. Iceland Says Yes to New Constitution. *The Reykjavik Grapevine*. Accessed 5 March 2015. http://grapevine.is/news/2012/10/22/iceland-says-yes-to-new-constitution/

Gunnarsson, V. and J. Lawless 2009. Icelandic Police Teargas Protesters. *Associated press*. http://web.archive.org/web/20090205093655/http://www.google.com/hostednews/ap/article/ALeqM5gHkIlEVsda4i3Wimog Stwsmm2wrgD95S6Q3O0

Gylfason, T. 2013. Democracy on Ice: A Post-Mortem of the Icelandic Constitution. *Open Democracy*. Accessed 5 March 2015. https://www.opendemocracy.net/can-europe-make-it/thorvaldur-gylfason/democracy-on-ice-post-mortem-of-icelandic-constitution

Jónsson, Á. 2009. *Why Iceland?: How One of the World's Smallest Countries Became the Meltdown's Biggest Casualty*. New York: McGraw-Hill.

Júlíusson, Á.D., and M.S. Helgason. 2013. The Roots of the Saucepan Revolution in Iceland. In *Understanding European Movements: New Social Movements, Global Justice Struggles, Anti-Austerity Protest*, eds. L. Cox, and C. Flesher Fominaya. London and New York: Routledge.

Kriesi, H.-P. 2012. The Political Consequences of the Financial and Economic Crisis in Europe: Electoral Punishment and Popular Protest. *Swiss Political Science Review* 18(4): 518–522.

optional.is. 2012. Þjóðfundur 02009: Data Mining a Government. *optional.is*. Accessed 5 March 2015. http://optional.is/required/2009/11/22/%C3%B Ejo%C3%B0fundur-02009-data-mining-a-government/

Prasch, R.E. 2011. Meltdown Iceland: Lessons on the World Financial Crisis from a Small Bankrupt Island. *Review of Political Economy* 23(2): 327–330. Accessed 5 March 2015. doi:10.1080/09538259.2011.561570?journalCode=crpe20#. VPgf9eFPFMQ.

Ruthven, H. 2013. Anarchism in Iceland: Is True Friendship Possible Under Capitalism? *Ethnographic Encounters* 3(2): 26–32.

Sergi, V., and M. Vogiatzoglou. 2013. Think Globally, Act Locally ? Symbolic Memory and Global Repertoires in the Tunisian Uprising and the Greek Anti-Austerity Mobilizations. In *Understanding European Movements: New Social Movements, Global Justice Struggles, Anti-Austerity Protest*, eds. C.F. Fominaya, and L. Cox. London: Routledge.

Statistics Iceland. 2014. Election to the Althingi and the Presidential Elections 1874–2013. *Statistics Iceland*. Accessed 6 March 2015. http://www.statice.is/ Statistics/Elections/Elections-overview

———. 2015. Key Figures. *Statistics Iceland*. Accessed 6 March 2015. http:// www.statice.is/Pages/1390

The Australian. 2013. Iceland's Austerity Protest Ousts Left. *The Australian*. Accessed 5 March 2015. http://www.theaustralian.com.au/news/world/ icelands-austerity-protest-ousts-left/story-e6frg6so-1226631139255

Thjodfundur. 2009. National Assembly 2009 -. *Thjodfundur.info*. Accessed 5 March 2015. http://www.thjodfundur2009.is/english/

Wade, R. H., and S. Sigurgeirsdottir 2011. Iceland's Meltdown: The Rise and Fall of International Banking in the North Atlantic. Revista de Economia Política, 31(5): 684–697. Accessed 5 March 2015. http://www.scielo.br/scielo. php?script=sci_arttextandpid=S0101-31572011000500001andlng=enandnrm =isoandtlng=en

Waterfield, B. 2009. Protesters Pelt Car of Icelandic Prime Minister. *The Telegraph*. Accessed 5 March 2015. http://www.telegraph.co.uk/news/worldnews/ europe/iceland/4308669/Protesters-pelt-car-of-Icelandic-prime-minister. html

CHAPTER 3

The Presence and Absence of Protest in Austerity Ireland

Francis O'Connor

Ireland was the first European Union (EU) country to succumb to the global financial crisis in 2008. Notwithstanding Irish government narratives of the country's exceptionalism, Ireland should be considered a paradigmatic case of the recent crisis. As della Porta outlined in the introduction to this volume, Ireland's sovereign debt crisis was not a cause of the broader economic turmoil but a consequence of it. When the vast flows of speculative capital that had powered the illusory Celtic Tiger dried up in early 2008, the Irish government was confronted with a liquidity crisis. The Irish government decided to nationalize private banking debt by offering an unlimited guarantee on all banking liabilities in September 2008. This fateful decision has resulted in a country with 1 per cent of the EU's population and 2 per cent of the Eurozone's GDP paying around 41 per cent of the total losses accrued in the European banking crisis (Regan 2014, 30). The Irish economy, the erstwhile 'poster child of free market globalization' was eviscerated (O'Toole 2009, 10). The spiralling crisis rendered it impossible for Ireland to borrow on the financial markets, leading the government to accept a 'rescue package' from the Troika. The Troika obliged successive Irish governments to continue to apply austerity measures, which wreaked havoc on the provision of state services, slashed social welfare and associated payments, and ensured that recession slowly evolved into depression. The fundamental cause of the crisis in the EU states was rooted in the flawed structure of the European

The author is grateful to all those who shared drafts of unpublished work with him and to Frank McNamara and Brian Kitt for feedback on earlier drafts of the chapter.

D. della Porta et al., *Late Neoliberalism and its Discontents in the Economic Crisis*, DOI 10.1007/978-3-319-35080-6_3

Monetary Union (EMU), with the crisis then diverging to take separate trajectories in the respective countries according to the specific varieties of capitalism that prevailed in them. Despite these significant differences, the policy packages imposed by the Troika, either directly (Ireland, Portugal and Greece) or indirectly (Italy and Spain), have not countenanced these variations and have bludgeoned countries into accepting these at times counterproductive policies (Armingeon and Baccaro 2012).

As the crisis took shape according to national and subnational dynamics, naturally, societies' responses to the crisis were similarly varied, reflecting the prevailing cultural and political norms, the relative strength of movements and civil society organizations, and the dynamics between the state and protest actors. The widespread perception took hold that Irish society was quiescent and offered little resistance to the imposition of austerity (see Pappas and O'Malley 2014), unlike the mass unrest witnessed in Greece and Spain. This is a massive oversimplification and, in light of the Right2Water campaign, since 2014, fundamentally incorrect.

This international misconception has arisen for a number of reasons. Successive Irish governments have actively projected an image of a stoic Irish people assuming collective responsibility for the financial recklessness of the Celtic Tiger period. This presumed guilt is rooted in the recognition that the political architects of the crisis were repeatedly validated by resounding electoral victories, even as late as 2007. This view is best exemplified by the November 2010 assertion of the then Minister of Finance, Brian Lenihan, that 'we decided as a people, collectively to have this property boom. That was a collective decision we took as a people. We all partied' (in Kerrigan 2012, 104). A second reason is that until 2014, protest had been overwhelmingly peaceful and relatively small, thus less newsworthy for international audiences. It is also true that many instances of protest were ignored, misrepresented, or underreported by the mainstream Irish media (Mercille 2014a). Thirdly, there was an issue of timing; the extensive mobilization in the early stages of the crisis—a number of national strikes in late 2009—did not attract attention, as it preceded much of the mass protest that subsequently occurred across the GIIPS (Greece, Ireland, Italy, Portugal and Spain) countries. And finally, the mass mobilization of 2014 in the Right2Water campaign came at a time when street protest, as was present at the peak of the European anti-austerity cycle of contention from 2011 to 2012, had largely been channelled into anti-austerity parliamentary politics as in the cases of SYRIZA and Podemos.

This chapter will trace the patterns of protest from 2008 until Ireland's tentative recovery began in 2015. It will begin by briefly describing the context in which the crisis emerged and the measures taken by government to counter it. It will then take a step back and address some of the structural features of the Irish political environment and the historic weakness of the Irish left. It will proceed to analyse how Irish social movements and civil society organizations had been structured and their autonomy undermined by Social Partnership in the immediate run-up to the crisis. It will continue to address initial protest mobilization in the 2008–2010 period, before detailing an intermediate period of fragmented and dispersed protest in the years that followed and describing the intense wave of protest in late 2014 and 2015. It will finally conclude by analysing Ireland's limited economic recovery and summarizing how the years of economic depression have altered the country's political balance of power. This chapter is based on an as yet unpublished, *Scuola Normale Superiore* working paper. It draws on a series of six qualitative interviews with activists in 2014, a vast array of secondary sources and media accounts of the period, and the secondary literature on protest in Ireland. It is also based on the first-hand experiences of the author in the period leading up to 2010.

3.1   THE BANK CRISIS

The banking crisis in Ireland has been the subject of extensive analysis in both journalistic and academic literature (Carswell 2011; Lyons and Carey 2012) as well as three official enquiries commissioned on the topic (Regling and Watson 2010; Honohan 2010; Nyberg 2011). These reports have all reached similar conclusions: the crisis came about because of lax banking regulation and mistaken fiscal policy at the macro level. Most damningly, their findings confirm that 'Ireland's political elite was inappropriately enmeshed with property developers, whose interests were served before those of the national interest' (Kinsella 2012, 225). The matter has also been the subject of a parliamentary enquiry, which has heretofore failed to present its collective findings. It is, therefore, unnecessary for this chapter to delve too deeply into the minute and highly complex details of the banking crisis.

On the night of 30 September 2008, the government decided to guarantee the assets and liabilities of Ireland's six major banks. It was an extremely foolhardy decision, as the government had no idea of the extent of the banks' exposure on the devastated property market (Carswell 2011). It subsequently became public knowledge that Lenihan had been subject to explicit pressure from the ECB (European Central Bank) President Jean-Claude Trichet, who, fearing the risk of contagion, demanded that he [Lenihan] save the banks at all costs (Ó'Riain 2014, 246). It has been surmised that 'in taking over the liabilities of the banks, the government transformed what had been an enormous private debt into a sovereign debt, thereby doubling and potentially tripling the liabilities incurred by the state' (Mair 2011a, 4). The overall financial cost of the guarantee remains contested, but the IMF (International Monetary Fund) declared it the 'costliest banking crisis in advanced economies since at least the Great Depression' (in Mercille 2014a, 48). The increase in national debt due to the crisis, as a proportion of GDP, was 73 per cent (Valencia and Laeven 2012, 19). It was in this context of appalling economic collapse that the Fianna Fáil and Green party government sought to restabilize the Irish economy by launching the first in a series of austerity budgets in 2008.

Ireland was thus confronted with a yawning fiscal deficit primarily resultant from the collapse of its banking sector and exacerbated by the decimation of its tax revenue, which had been overly dependent on regressive forms of indirect taxation in the property sector (Allen 2012, 431). Taxation revenue declined from 47 billion in 2007 to 31 billion in 2010 (Drudy and Collins 2011, 345). The government brought forward the 2009 budget from its usual date in early December to October 2008 in what was the first of eight austerity budgets that cut social spending and raised taxes (*The Economist* 2013). However, the government has been much more assiduous in spending cuts than increasing tax rates, particularly amongst higher earners and on corporations. The cuts to the broader social sector have been substantial. To cite but a few examples: the 2013 budget cut 781 million euros or 5 per cent of the health budget (Leahy et al. 2014), while the 2012 budget projected savings of 812 million euros in Social Protection. These cutbacks 'concentrated on lone parents, the unemployed and short-time workers, the elderly and large families' (Allen 2013, 33).

The drastic measures taken by the government were unable to halt the spiral of decline and arguably further consolidated it. The political and financial chaos culminated in Ireland being unable to borrow on the financial markets because of punitive and unsustainable interest rates of 10 per cent. It was consequently obliged to accept a 'rescue' package from the EU and IMF in November 2010 (Thorhallsson and Kirby 2012, 804). The package came with an interest rate of 5.8 per cent, 'which is generally seen as potentially crippling the Irish economy' (Mair 2011a, 4). The deal transferred all culpability for the banking morass onto the Irish government, disregarding the role of the ECB in enabling perilous lending practices. It also generated resentment because it was clearly forced upon the Irish government (Thorhallsson and Kirby 2012, 809).

The Fianna Fáil–Green coalition collapsed in early 2011, but the timing of the Memorandum prior to the general election would prove to have lasting consequences. Fine Gael and Labour, who formed the new government, had boldly campaigned on a platform of renegotiating the agreement (Mair 2011b, 292), yet they quietly adopted its terms and conditions, thus ensuring continuity in the implementation of austerity (Hardiman and Dellepiane 2012, 17). The undermining of democracy has also taken on institutional force at the national level. The Economic Management Council was established to liaise with the Troika. It consists of the Taoiseach, the Tánaiste, the Minister for Finance, the Minister for Public Expenditure, and a coterie of unelected and unaccountable advisers. Brigid Laffan has described it as an institution of 'unparalleled political authority and power' (in O'Toole 2014). In conjunction with the Troika, it formulates economic policy, which is then presented as a fait accompli to be rubber stamped by the remains of the cabinet and the parliament. The inability of national governments across Europe, irrespective of their ideological position or electoral platforms, to diverge from the economic protocols set down by the Troika has been a recurrent feature in all of the affected countries.

The outcome of these economic measures has been massive unemployment and a return to the mass emigration of decades past. Irish unemployment peaked in 2011 and 2012 at 14.7 per cent (Eurostat 2015a). Although 14.7 per cent is already an astonishing figure, it is thought that it would have been around 20 per cent were it not for emigration (Leahy et al. 2014). A further notable tendency is that of youth unemployment: Eurostat figures show that for the first quarter of 2014, unemployment amongst under-25-year-olds was 26.1 per cent (Eurostat 2015a). In line with EU-wide tendencies, youth unemployment had decreased to 19.6 per cent in November 2015 (Eurostat 2015b). Lower youth unemployment figures are also the result of creative statistical management by the Irish government. The controversial JobBridge Scheme—in which recipients are permitted to take up to a six-month work placement as a means to upskill, while maintaining welfare payments in lieu of a salary—conceals even more extensive youth unemployment (see IMPACT 2015). The brief window between 2004 and 2008 when Ireland attracted huge numbers of Eastern European immigrants has been firmly closed, and the country has become once more a land of emigration. Between 2006 and 2013, a total of 213,000 Irish people emigrated (Glynn et al. 2013, 29). Statistics belie 2012 claims by Minister for Finance, Michael Noonan, that emigration was a lifestyle choice for the country's young (Sheehan et al. 2012): there has been a 400 per cent increase in emigration since the crisis started in 2008 (Glynn et al. 2013, 29). Interestingly, Ireland has a dramatically higher rate of emigration than other affected countries. Eurostat figures show that in 2012 Ireland had a net migration rate per 1000 people of –7.6, followed by the Baltic states and then Greece at –4.0, Portugal at –3.6 and Spain at –3.5 (in Kenny 2013). An ulterior damaging element of emigration is that the contemporary wave of emigrants has higher education qualifications than the general population; accordingly, debate about a 'brain drain' is far from misplaced (Glynn et al. 2013, 29). Finally, although a clear causal relationship is difficult to establish, there is likely a connection between Ireland's relative social peace and youth emigration. As masses of Greek youths besieged parliament in Syntagma Square and the Indignados rose up in Spain, Irish youths were packing their bags, as their forebears had done before them, for Sydney and Holyhead.

3.2   Left-Wing Politics in Ireland

A distinguishing feature of Irish politics has been the weakness of the political left. In a 1992 analysis, Mair explained that Ireland had the low-est parliamentary support for parties of the left in Western Europe (Mair 2014, 117–118), a situation that has not dramatically changed in the interim. Traditionally, Ireland's political culture has been characterized by a consensus-oriented centralism that has not facilitated mobilization at either end of the ideological spectrum. The reasons why a leftist party never obtained mass support are multiple. The salience of nationalism in the early decades of the Free State[1] made it difficult for a party oriented towards working-class issues to gain any traction (Mair 2005, 118). The partition of Ireland had deprived it of its only significant industrial base in Belfast, so the working-class constituency was also rather limited to begin with. These historical and spatial obstacles to left-wing mobilization, coupled with the virulent anti-leftist position of the Catholic church, 'fostered a [political] culture based on loyalty to peasant kinship ties rather than on class solidarity, with values of authoritarianism, conformism and anti-intellectualism predominating' (Kirby and Murphy 2011, 27). Post-independence Ireland was never structurally a propitious environment for a nascent left-wing party, but even in light of these challenges Labour's timid efforts to carve out a left-wing niche have been underwhelming. Historically, the only possible government excluding Fianna Fáil has been a Labour coalition with Fine Gael. This has led Labour to sacrifice its leftism for the dubious honour of junior partnership in government with Ireland's more conservative centre-right party. The failings of the Labour party were cruelly summed up by Fianna Fáil Taoiseach Sean Lemass (1959–1966) in a Dáil speech: 'Far from the Labour Party going "Red"' they are not going anywhere [...] the Labour Party are a nice, respectable, docile, harmless body of men—as harmless a body as ever graced any parliament' (in Finn 2011, 19).

A number of small left-wing parties such as the Socialist Party, Anti-Austerity Alliance (AAA), the People Before Profit Alliance (PBP), the Workers' Party, and an array of left-wing independents have recently found themselves in the spotlight due to their role in the campaign against water charges. They, however, remain fragmented and fractious and their influence is limited to certain urban constituencies. The main left-wing party, especially in light of Labour's servile performance in the contemporary coalition government, is Sinn Féin. The party has been identified by European leftist parties such as SYRIZA and Podemos as their Irish equivalent, much to the chagrin of the AAA and the PBP. In the Republic, Sinn Féin currently boasts 14 TDs,[2] three Member of European Parliament (MEPs), and 157 councillors (out of a total of 949). It has become the leading and most coherent parliamentary opponent to austerity since 2011 and provided a series of alternative budgets (Allen 2013, 145–146). Notwithstanding a series of scandals involving prominent republican figures, it is still currently polling around 20 per cent of votes in opinion polls and is contending with Fianna Fáil for the position of the Republic of Ireland's second largest party. Its left-wing credentials have been brought into question by its role in imposing austerity budgets in the Northern Ireland Assembly and its openness to coalition with other parties. Sinn Féin has played a notably visible role in the Right2Water protests since late 2014, and it remains the only one of the bigger political parties to have signed up to the Right2Change principles, which outline ten policy positions for a 'progressive government'. As will be subsequently outlined, the traditional dearth of strong leftist parties in Ireland is also reflected in the weakness of the left-wing movements.

3.3   'Riot at the Ballot Box'

As Roberts (2015) has argued, social protest and institutional political opportunities are closely intertwined. His analysis of neoliberal reforms in Latin America confirmed that the most destabilizing protest occurred where the party systems did not offer institutionalized channels for opposition to market orthodoxy. One can convincingly argue that the Irish electorate perceived that the election of Labour and to a lesser extent Fine Gael, who had both campaigned for the renegotiation of the Memorandum of Understanding, would have served as such an 'institutional outlet'. These hopes culminated in the dramatic election of 2011. The election was described as a 'revolution at the ballot box' by the incoming Taoiseach Enda Kenny (in Little 2011, 1309), and it was similarly fêted by much of Irish society. It saw the electoral annihilation of Fianna Fáil, reducing it to an enfeebled shadow of its former self. Fianna Fáil, which had been in power for 61 of the previous 79 years, was reduced to the third party in parliament with only 20 TDs, a drop of 57 since the 2007 election. As Mair observed, the loss of Fianna Fáil votes was 'almost unprecedented in a long-established democracy' (2011b, 284). The new Dáil boasted the highest ever proportion of left-leaning TDs in its history, as 'sixty-three TDs were elected on a variety of social democratic, left republican, revolutionary socialist and independent left platforms' (O'Broin 2011). It proved to be Ireland's most volatile election ever, the third most volatile in post-war Europe (Mair 2011b, 285–288).

Notwithstanding the electoral turbulence, the outcome of the election was anything but radical. Labour rejected the opportunity to head a broad left-wing opposition, which would have been in a position to put intense pressure on a Fine Gael minority government. It instead opted to join a coalition with a resurgent Fine Gael party. Accordingly, much of the animation regarding the strong showing of the left proved illusory, as Labour preferred to prop up a right-wing government than attempt to forge a broad critical leftist alternative to austerity. The previous government had accepted the Memorandum of Understanding with the Troika, thereby conceding the country's macro-economic sovereignty. And because, contrary to their pre-election bluster, neither Fine Gael nor Labour were willing to seek a renegotiation of the agreement, the election merely shuffled the players of the game of austerity rather than challenging its rules. As Mair rather bleakly put it: 'democracy in Ireland is […] becoming a democracy without choices, one in which elections might continue to be full of drama, sound and fury, but in which the outcomes might signify little' (Mair 2011b, 29). Subsequent local and European elections and by-elections have, however, suggested that there is a popular demand for a party that genuinely questions the fundamentals upon which recent governments' austerity policies have been based. As aforementioned, Sinn Féin has grown to become a significant political force, with three MEPs and 157 councillors to supplement its Dáil presence. The PBP and the Socialist Party also continued to expand in the local elections, even though they remain strong in almost exclusively urban areas and there is a plethora of leftist independents. The short-sightedness of Labour's participation in government was made apparent, as its share of the vote fell from 14.9 per cent in the 2009 local elections to 5.4 per cent in the local elections of 2014 (Quinlivan 2015, 136), thus rendering Sinn Féin the largest left-wing party in the country.

3.4   SOCIAL MOVEMENTS IN PRE-AUSTERITY IRELAND

The Celtic Tiger period, propelled by the easy availability of credit, brought about deep societal change in Ireland. Years of unprecedented wealth fostered deep political complacency. Any critiques of the unsustainable nature of the economy were dismissed. In 2007, in a speech addressed to the Irish Congress of Trade Unions (ICTU), Taoiseach Bertie Ahern advised those who were downplaying Ireland's economic prospects to commit suicide. The period was characterized by unfettered consumerism and individualism, and it resulted in much depoliticization. However, social movements had not gone entirely dormant. As elsewhere across the world, massive demonstrations were successfully organized against the invasion of Iraq; and more importantly, a long campaign was orchestrated by locals in a remote area of county Mayo against the Corrib Gas Project operated by Shell. The Shell to Sea campaign demanded that the gas refinery be situated offshore, citing safety concerns and planning breaches. The campaign broke into national consciousness when five local men were jailed indefinitely for breaching a court order in June 2005 (Ó Donnabháin 2010; Siggins 2010). The narrative of small farmers and fishermen confronting a multinational oil giant resonated with historic nationalist narratives of oppression and an 'idea of rural populism which associates urban areas with wealth and rural ones with poverty' (Ó Donnabháin 2014, 12). The campaign enjoyed widespread popular sympathy across the country in 2005 before it gradually disintegrated because of its own internal contradictions and a concerted campaign of police violence.

Shell to Sea did highlight certain limitations in the repertoire of contention available to Irish social movements. Firstly, there was the inherent political conservativism of many rural areas. One of the famously imprisoned men, Willie Corduff, declared that 'we are not troublemakers. We do not want to be protesting. We are not activists which we are being called' (in Grant and Domokos 2009). In the teeth of one of the most contentious campaigns in recent decades, Corduff, a leading figure of the movement was unwilling to embrace any form of politicized identity. A second weakness was the unwillingness, particularly of locals in the Rossport area, to embrace more confrontational tactics such as peaceful 'direct action' measures, much to the frustration of the international environmentalists who had set up a solidarity camp to strengthen the local campaign. The third weak point of the campaign was its inability to resist the smear campaign and violence deployed against it by the state. In past decades the state has attempted to discredit nearly every protest campaign as being a front for Republican groups. A concerted media campaign focused on the presence of a number of individual Republicans who took part in various actions related to Shell to Sea, arguably succeeding in twisting public perception of the movement as a group of dangerous and violent radicals (Siggins 2010, 208). In late 2006, as popular consensus began to shift towards the Rossport protesters, a number of days of action were organized, which were characterized by spiralling confrontation between demonstrators and police, numerous instances of police brutality (see Hanahoe et al. 2014), and intimidation by a private security firm called Integrated Risk Management Service (IRMS) hired by Shell (see Barrington 2010, 34–59).[3] As a consequence, members of the local community unilaterally cancelled a planned 'day of action' in November 2006 without consulting the rest of the movement because of safety concerns (Ó Donnabháin 2014, 10), thus leading to a split in the movement between those who prioritized safety and others willing to endure police attacks.

These features of protest have proven to be central to the waves of contention through the years of austerity. Protest remained largely depoliticized until the anti-water charges campaign, theretofore protest demands were deliberately couched in non-ideological language. The depiction of all protesters as republican infiltrators remains a tactic of first resort of the authorities and has been used in efforts to besmirch the anti-water charges campaign (see Brady et al. 2014). And although police violence has been in lesser evidence in anti-austerity protests, with the notable exception of a student protest in 2010, an awareness of the state's lack of compunction in its deployment has informed the constrained repertoire of Irish movements.

3.5   Social Partnership

In the late 1980s, Ireland was characterized by financial instability, inflation, and industrial turmoil (see Culpepper and Regan 2014). In order to bring about a degree of industrial peace and to stave off a potential intervention by the IMF, in 1987 a centralized bargaining structure known as Social Partnership comprising government, business representatives and trade unions was established. In the short term, it brought about the social stability craved by the Irish government and did indeed attract the Foreign Direct Investment that created the conditions for the Celtic Tiger (Baccaro and Simoni 2007). The remarkable feature of Ireland's social partnership, unlike its European counterparts, was that it quickly spread beyond the labour sector to encompass much of civil society including farmers' associations and a broad swath of social justice, religious and community movements in what was known as the Community and Voluntary Pillar. As the Irish economy began to take off, it allowed these community associations and social projects to access central government funds and arguably facilitated a limited degree of influence in the formulation of government policy. However, it became apparent that it was a partnership in name only: the disparity in power between the composite participant organizations and the state confirmed that it was very much a unilateral relationship that operated on the state's terms. It was argued that the community sector's participation in social partnership served to bolster 'the neo-liberal consensus, compensate[d] for public sector withdrawal and studiously avoid[ed] critical assaults on state power' (Meade 2005, 361). Participation in social partnership was contingent upon acceptance of the allegedly non-ideological parameters of the debate. The so-called consensus between the social partners is consensual only because any question of greater redistribution [was] informally prohibited (Murphy 2002, 84; Meade 2005, 359). On occasions where there was an open clash between the social partners and government, 'government easily "trumped" social partnership, especially on tax priorities and incurred relatively little penalty in the way of protest or non-compliance by the social partners' (Hardiman 2006, 366). Social Partnership fundamentally transformed both the role of the state and Irish civil society. It transferred the competences of the public service to external providers in the community sector, thereby rendering the state a coordinator of services rather than their provider (Meade 2005, 351).

In addition to its role in undermining the state's responsibilities in terms of welfare provision, Social Partnership also profoundly impacted the movement habitus of the participating groups. It has been argued that co-option leads to movement bureaucratization (Piven 1977) and professionalization (Cox 2012). Professionalism or the capacity to acquire professional skills tends to exclude the most marginalized segments of society (Meade 2012, 906) which tends to result in middle-class movements *on behalf of* excluded groups rather than organic movements *of* those groups themselves. It thus leads to a less democratic and participatory civil society. Engagement in Social Partnership demands 'an organisational style that is more executive than participative and tactics that are more integrationist than oppositional in type' (Varley and Curtin 2006, 429). As social partners become more akin to a wing of a government department, activist trajectories begin to resemble civil servant careers. As a consequence, one's behaviour as an activist is also subconsciously conditioned by concerns over job security and future prospects. It was these circumstances which ensured that 'communities and movements had lost the habit of mass mobilisation around structural issues in favour of the press release, the research report and the funding application—and had neither the will nor the capacity to return to opposition' (Cox 2012). Finally, civil society organizations were linked vertically to the relevant government departments, in practice in a form of implicit competition with one another for state patronage. This arrangement limited horizontal solidarity across specific social arenas and further enforced the 'depoliticization' of interactions with government for fear of falling into its disfavour. Therefore, the social and political milieu that would have ordinarily fostered counterhegemonic ideas and offered opposition to particular government policies had become de facto agencies of government.

The intrinsic folly of dependence on the state was revealed in 2009, when the government unilaterally withdrew from Social Partnership. As the economy crumbled, the government's social *partners* were no longer of any political utility and were discarded. One can conclude that the state devoured civil society in a time of plenty, to spit out its brittle skeleton when lean times returned. Recent years have served as an intense learning curve in which Irish civil society movements have struggled to re-emerge as actors capable of influencing government policy by the traditional methods of mass mobilization. This was of particular relevance to the Trade Union movement, which emerged particularly discredited from its experience in social partnership.

3.6   First Wave (2008–2010)

By European standards, Ireland has a relatively high, albeit declining trade union density, at 31.7 per cent in 2007 (D'Art and Turner 2011, 162). It is disproportionately located in the public service (Culpepper and Regan 2014, 13). Social Partnership protected Irish unions from the destruction visited on its counterparts in Britain in the 1980s, and also brought about almost two decades of relative industrial peace. It did, however, result in a drastic dulling of union militancy, and over time unions stopped trading 'wage restraint for progressive redistribution policies, but instead for a reduced taxation burden on workers and institutional influence' (Doherty 2011, 376). The Celtic Tiger period also witnessed a concentration of power within trade unions, which has lessened the influence of grassroots members. It has been further asserted that 'two decades of accommodation to cooperative union–management relations have created a union bureaucracy institutionalised in a top-down partnership milieu rather than alternative, bottom-up mobilisation strategies' (McDonough and Dundon 2010, 544–545). Nonetheless, the broader Irish Trade Union movement remains Ireland's largest civil society movement. As the government subjected the country to successive austerity budgets, the trade unions attempted to flex their enfeebled street muscle; ICTU (Irish Congress of Trade Unions) organized two well-attended national demonstrations numbering up to 100,000 protesters, on 9 February and a subsequent one on 6 November 2009. November also saw a one-day strike of 250,000 public sector workers, but a follow-up strike was cancelled in order to facilitate a return to Social Partnership negotiations (Doherty 2011, 382), which of course culminated in the state unilaterally abandoning the system.

ICTU managed to mobilize massive numbers of demonstrators in 2009, but the overwhelming majority of them were public sector employees. A perception gained credence that the trade unions were simply a public sector lobby group indifferent to the needs of those employed in often worse conditions in the private sector. This belief was reinforced by a concerted media campaign, which rather perversely, given the fundamental failures of government and the financial sector, held the unions responsible for Ireland's falling competitiveness and ultimately its dire economic situation. This was a view expounded in particular by a number of newspapers, predominantly those from *Independent News Media*, controlled by Dennis O'Brien (Mercille 2014a; Browne 2013).[4] After the collapse of Social Partnership, the union movement was disoriented and its public sector members' salaries were slashed by 15 per cent (McDonough and Dundon 2010, 553). Rather than adopting a belligerent approach, ICTU took a conciliatory stance and stabilized an agreement between the public sector unions only, and the government. The *Public Service Agreement 2010–2014*, commonly known as the Croke Park Agreement, 'copper-fastens previous unilateral pay reductions while containing a tentative commitment to avoid additional pay cutting measures, unless faced with a further economic crisis' (McDonough and Dundon 2010, 558). It was not, however, universally endorsed; many unions such as UNITE[5] voted against it, only to be outvoted by the larger, more moderate unions such as SIPTU, IMPACT, and INTO[6] (Doherty 2011, 383).

The signing of the Croke Park Agreement had a number of consequences. Firstly, it cemented the division between private and public sectors. Unions can only enjoy popular legitimacy if they are understood as representing all 'those who sell their labour in the service of economic production' (Culpepper and Regan 2014, 20), and the agreement was a definitive betrayal of the wider community of workers in Ireland. Secondly, it guaranteed industrial peace and limited street protest because at that stage unions were the only force capable of mobilizing mass demonstrations. In 2011, at the high point of austerity, only eight strikes were called and a mere 3700 days lost to industrial action (Culpepper and Regan 2014, 13). Thirdly, it resulted in a generational fracture within the unions themselves; older established workers were protected by the Croke Park Agreement while younger recruits were employed on vastly inferior working conditions. This further confirmed the perception that the union movement in Ireland was a part of the state apparatus, protecting relatively well-protected civil servants and banishing its younger members to precarity. Finally, mainstream unions' abdication of their responsibility as a protector of workers in favour of the narrow goal of maintaining their members' rights led to a radicalization of smaller unions that represented more vulnerable private sector workers and lower-paid public sector ones. Unions such as Mandate and UNITE have been at the forefront of the anti-water charges campaign (Holland 2014), which contrasts with the tepid approach of SIPTU.[7]

Aside from the labour movement, there were a number of protests in the 2008–2010 period. The first substantial protest was in response to a government effort to limit the eligibility criteria for free medical care for the over-seventies. The Irish Senior Citizens Parliament (ISCP) and Age Action Ireland (AAI), both formal Social Partners, organized an unprecedented street demonstration drawing a crowd of 15,000 mostly older people to the front of the Dáil. Until the anti-water charges campaign, it was probably the most successful anti-austerity protest in the realization of its objectives. The government was subsequently obliged to maintain extensive criteria for access to free healthcare. Unlike the Trade Union movement, which had essentially lost its ability to forcibly extract concessions from the government, the older people used their significant electoral leverage to force the government's hand. However, the older people's protest operated according to the clientelistic parameters of Irish politics. As Meade argues, 'protesters did not claim or hold out for new political horizons; instead they projected the clientelist bargain on to the national stage' (2015). Claims were levied on a sectional basis, and no questioning of austerity as an approach per se was forwarded; rather, that austerity should not be applied to one subgroup of society. This brief episode of elderly militancy simply reflected the weakness of the vertically fragmented civil society of the moribund Celtic Tiger period.

While the elderly mobilized to defend their interests, Ireland was notable for the passivity of its younger generations. Of course, the ardour of Ireland's youth was tempered by the reality that tens of thousands of them had emigrated or were planning to do so; nonetheless, in the face of disproportionate welfare cuts, massive unemployment and more expensive education, their docility was unexpected. The Irish students' association, USI, coincidentally organized a well-attended demonstration the morning of the day of the elderly people's protest. In general, Irish student politics is markedly different from its European counterparts: it is centrist in orientation and generally viewed as a stepping stone for aspiring career politicians. Current USI President Kevin Donoghue explained the modus operandi of the USI as functioning more like a lobby group than a movement. USI's preference for consensus over confrontation was clear in his declaration that 'if you get anywhere between 500 and 2000 people to turn up at a government party's office, constituency headquarters or in Dublin and tell them they are crap, they are not going to want to work with you' (Interview, October 2014, Dublin).

It did, however, organize one large student protest on 3 November 2010, in the context of national budget negotiations. It was attended by more than 25,000 students, which is huge by the standards of Irish student protests (Flynn 2010). A small breakaway group composed of members and sympathizers of a more militant student organization, FEE (Free Education for Everyone), branched off from the main demonstration and occupied the lobby of the Department of Finance. Outside the department office, other FEE supporters engaged in a peaceful sit-down protest. The protesters outside were baton charged by the police and a number were trampled by horses, which resulted in injuries. The absolutely disproportionate violence of the police seemed to 'represent a government statement of intent, addressed to the general public' (Kerrigan 2010): mass protest would be met with violence. Subsequent to this police brutality, USI president Gary Redmond condemned the actions of the protesters (RTE 2010), again highlighting the limited acceptable means of contention in the eyes of the official student movement. It also highlighted, as occurred in Rossport, that the Gardaí Síochána have no compunction about using violence against peaceful protesters. For the following three years, just as protest was exploding across Europe, the USI did not organize any national demonstrations because, as Donoghue detailed, 'some more senior people in the Students Union at the time, [...] were less inclined to get involved in a national march for fear that something similar would happen again' (Interview, October 2014, Dublin). The student movement essentially succumbed to police intimidation, pointing out the limited repertoire of protest in Ireland.

3.7   SECOND WAVE (2010–2014)

The perception that Ireland meekly accepted austerity is related to this period. Indeed, in comparison to the other countries featured in this volume, there was a much lower incidence of protest than could have been expected. This was primarily because the labour movement was curtailed by the Croke Park Agreement, the student movement had been intimidated into silence, and two decades of social partnership had undermined the capacity of Irish civil society to engage in contentious protest. A dataset covering the period from 2010 to 2013 identified 415 protest events (Naughton 2013). A key feature of these protests was their small size. Only seven involved more than 10,000 demonstrators. They were also almost completely peaceful in nature, with violence present in only two cases which were in relation to small protests organized by Republicans in response to the visit of the Queen of the United Kingdom in May 2011 (Naughton 2013). The protests were almost universally directed against the government across a wide range of topics. Admittedly, many of these protests were not focused on austerity, many centred on the death of Savita Halappanavar,[8] while others were in relation to the Marriage Equality campaign that resulted in the successful 2015 referendum enshrining the right to same-sex marriage in the constitution.

Protest movements in Ireland are often subsumed into dynamics of clientelism which characterize Irish political culture. This is particularly noted in relation to single issue or locally oriented campaigns. Irish TDs are very much engaged with constituency issues and local problems. Traditionally, protest groups have focused their attentions on winning the support of local-elected representatives on a cross-party basis, in order for them to lobby on their behalf. As this occurs across Ireland, and systematic demands are largely absent, it essentially renders various campaign groups as competitors for political patronage and a greater allocation of resources (Naughton 2013). It is also worth noting that such mobilizations have often been successful across a range of issues (Meade 2015). The most notable of these campaigns was the Save Waterford Campaign launched in November 2012 in order to maintain services in the local hospital. A street demonstration attracted 15,000 people in a city of only 50,000 inhabitants. A similar campaign in Roscommon also gained massive local support. Notwithstanding that these groups were mobilizing at the same time on similar issues, there was no coordination between them, thus reinforcing Naughton's (2013) observation that many of these local campaigns are essentially rivals for patronage.

Outside of these locally oriented protests, there were two notable protest initiatives in this period that addressed issues of universal import: the Occupy movement and the Ballyhea Says No campaign. Ballyhea is a small village on the Cork–Limerick border with a rural population of no more than a thousand residents. Established by local sports journalist Diarmuid O'Flynn, the group organizes a weekly protest after mass has finished along the main Cork–Limerick road which passes through the village. The campaign has a singular focus: it argues that the government bailout of the bondholders should be repudiated as it bails out noxious banking debts, accrued in the private sector. The first demonstration was held on 6 March 2011 and has taken place every Sunday since. It is usually attended by small numbers, but its most notable characteristic is its persistence and longevity. As it was for a number of years one of the only movements expressly resisting austerity, it attracted significant media attention. It has inherited one important characteristic from Irish political culture: a refusal to take a specific ideological stance. O'Flynn explained in the run up to the EU election: 'I'm more concerned about right and wrong than right and left' (2014). Its heterogeneous political outlook led it to invite noted right-wing figures such as the economist Constantin Gurdgiev and the controversial politician Declan Ganley for its 300th anniversary march. Ganley has well known links with the US military establishment (Cronin 2009) and founded the right-wing trans-European political party Libertas to compete in the 2009 European Election (Gagatek 2010). Yet, it also invited noted Greek resistance hero Manolis Glezos to join its protest. The campaign has failed to spread beyond the north Cork area, thus suggesting that its longevity is fuelled by pre-existing interpersonal networks and local reciprocal bonds (see McAdam and Paulsen 1993).

The Occupy movement in Ireland took off a little later than elsewhere. A camp was erected outside the Irish Central Bank in October 2011. As one of the participants in Occupy Cork explained:

> There was a direct lineage to the Arab Spring in Tunisia on towards Occupy in the US and then the Occupys were very much the inspiration for the Occupy here which started in September October 2011. [...] It was very much something inspired from outside, from the US. (Interview, October 2014 Dublin)

It enjoyed some support in its early stages and drew crowds of a few thousand to demonstrations in Cork and Dublin. It was remarkable for its innovation in terms of its original repertoires for the Irish context rather than the number of its participants; it held daily open assemblies and meetings, refused to appoint a spokesperson to avoid the personalization of a horizontal movement, and of course occupied a public space. However, it never consolidated its presence as a focus of popular dissent as in Spain. Unlike other European countries, Ireland does not have a significant autonomous- or anarchist-oriented left milieu that would have organically coincided with the horizontal principles of the Occupy movement. Its 'imported' character, the inexperience of its activists, inclement weather, and hostility to the organized movements of the left led to its disintegration without making any significant impact on the Irish political scene.

3.8   THIRD WAVE (2014–2016)

The most unexpected characteristic of anti-austerity protest in Ireland has been the delayed timing of the massive anti-water charges movement, which has served as a vehicle for all of the accumulated grievances throughout the period of austerity. In 2014, at the macro level an incipient recovery had begun to appear, with an anticipated GNP growth rate of 5.2 per cent predicted in 2015, following a figure of 4.9 per cent in 2014 (ESRI 2014) and a slow but steady decline in unemployment to 10.7 per cent in November 2014 (Eurostat 2015a). However, it is not unusual for protest to emerge as conditions improve. De Tocqueville noted in the nineteenth century that:

> Revolutions are not always brought about by a gradual decline from bad to worse. Nations that have endured patiently and almost unconsciously the most overwhelming oppression often burst into rebellion against the yoke the moment it begins to grow lighter. (1856, 214)

A delay in the emergence of protest was also identified in analogous Latin American cases, where it took a number of years of progressive privatization, austerity and economic deterioration before mass resistance emerged (Cox 2011, 16).

Although there have been some other protest events in this period, notably a large ICTU demonstration in February 2013, the anti-water charges campaign is by far the most important. The Right2Water campaign is the largest popular mobilization witnessed in modern Irish history. Since late 2014 it has seen almost 400,000 protesters take to the streets across the country and organized a concerted campaign of pickets of government politicians far beyond the traditional loci of Irish protest (Hearne 2015, 7). The Right2Water campaign has radically altered popular understanding of protest in Ireland. No longer seen just in terms of occasional demonstrations in politically symbolic locations, it has been decentralized and territorialized to towns and neighbourhoods throughout the country. Protest has gone from a periodic to quotidian practice and has taken on a spontaneous and bottom-up character in which the presence of any government official in one's neighbourhood or town is met with improvised pickets. It is an organic movement that has transformed large portions of heretofore passive citizens into activists, engaging in consistent political confrontation. It has succeeded in obtaining dramatic reversals in government policy without so far realizing its principal objective of the abandonment of water charges altogether.

Ireland was unique in Europe because it did not charge for the provision of public water for household consumption. In the context of the negotiation of the Memorandum with the Troika in 2010, the Fianna Fáil–Green government's National Recovery Plan included a proposal to implement water charges, stating that 'we [Irish government] are also planning to move towards full cost-recovery in the provision of water services' (see Hearne 2015). Concrete steps were taken by the Fine Gael–Labour coalition to realize this by the setting up of a semi-state body, Irish Water. The government has attempted to portray it as an environmental imperative to conserve water, asserting that the use of meters will encourage more measured water usage. However, the origins of Irish Water confirm that irrespective of government bluster, it can 'not be dressed up as anything other than a tax' (McGee 2015). It is an additional, socially regressive, indirect tax to add to those previously imposed in recent years. It has been described as 'deeply inegalitarian and unjust' because it does not differentiate based on one's capacity to pay. Furthermore, it cannot be avoided given the fundamental importance of water to daily life (Lynch 2014). Accordingly, the water protests are not simply about this specific charge but rather, as Paul Murphy TD of the AAA put it: 'This has become the lightning rod conducting the accumulated anger and discontent over six years of cuts and taxes to pay for bankers and bondholders' (P. Murphy 2014). An extensive survey of protesters has detailed that for 59.6 per cent of participants, the principal reason for protesting is that 'austerity has gone too far'. The survey also established that the majority of protesters were between 30 and 50 years old, a notable exception to the younger demographic of protesters elsewhere in Europe. Additionally, 54.4 per cent had never previously participated in a protest and there were a disproportionate number from working-class areas (Hearne 2015, 9–17).

The anti-water charges protest is led by the Right2Water campaign. It explicitly states that it is not a movement in itself but rather a platform that facilitates coordination between the large numbers of participating groups. It has three main composite pillars. There are a number of political parties—AAA, PBP, Sinn Féin and the Workers' Party[9]—as well as several independent representatives, some trade unions and community groups. The participating unions—UNITE, Mandate, CPSU, and OPATSI[10]—have provided the funding for the campaign. It has not been endorsed by ICTU or by Ireland's biggest individual union, SIPTU. The three pillars bring different skill sets to the campaign: politicians have political knowledge and access to various public platforms at the national and municipal levels. The unions have organizational skills and economic expertise, while the community groups are present on the ground (Right2Water 2015, 2). The Right2Water campaign has operated on the basis of:

> [...] inclusivity, with the age-old notion that there is strength in numbers and that the greatest way to defeat water charges is by standing together in the largest collective of citizens possible. For Right2Water to enter into the tactical sphere and dictate specific tactics would be to exclude certain groups and individuals from participating in the campaign. (Right2Water 2015)

This inclusivity contrasts with the more exclusionary emphasis of the 'non-political' Ballyhea Says No campaign and the explicit rejection of political parties and trade unions by the Occupy movement. The fact that there is no unified tactical approach facilitates the participation of people willing to commit to various degrees of resistance, ranging from direct action against the installation of water meters, refusal to register or to pay the charges, payment of the charges due to fear but with a determination to punish politicians in favour of them at the next available electoral opportunity and of course participation in street demonstrations. The campaign's decentralization has allowed it to embrace broad swathes of the population of differing political inclinations by encouraging locally appropriate tactics. Accordingly, urban groups in working-class areas of Dublin have engaged in more confrontational activities, whereas initiatives in some rural towns are much less heated and have a more prosaic orientation.

Direct action initiatives began in early 2014, when the installation of water meters began. Local residents in multiple housing estates autonomously organized to prevent the works taking place (Finn 2015, 57). It was particularly prevalent in working-class areas such as Togher in Cork city and areas like Edenmore and Kilbarrack in Dublin (Hearne 2015, 6). These efforts took the form of sit-down protests in front of worksites, blocking the access points to worksites, and simply being present in sufficient numbers to render the continuation of work unsafe. These efforts, usually numbering only tens of people, have proven to be successful in certain areas, leading to postponement of meter installations. These direct action tactics have led to the arrest of a number of protesters.

A more controversial tactic employed by the protesters has been the picketing of government politicians at public appearances, party summits and constituency offices. Although as discussed previously, dispersed pickets were briefly used by the Shell to Sea campaign, they have become a key element in the anti-water charges campaign. The tactic is locally organized and appealing in its simplicity. Once the upcoming appearance of a government figure becomes public knowledge, activists in the area organize a range of disruptive actions ranging from sit ins and chanting to blockading access points. The tactic has come under intense criticism because of its reputed violence and the indiscriminate selection of locations where protests have occurred, such as at the openings of schools and hospitals.

The most notorious incident occurred at an adult education centre in Jobstown in Dublin. A number of protesters performed a sit-in in front of the car belonging to Tánaiste Joan Burton—who had earlier been hit with a water balloon—preventing her from leaving for a number of hours. It triggered a hysterical reaction: Burton herself suggested that the protest had 'parallels with fascism' (Kelly 2014), while the Fine Gael TD Noel Coonan asserted that the country was facing a 'potential ISIS situation' (Carroll and O'Halloran 2014). A massive Garda operation was launched to identify the culprits, which led to the arrest of around 20 suspects including Paul Murphy TD, two city councillors of the AAA, and a number of juveniles in a series of dramatic dawn raids. The accused are currently awaiting trial on charges of false imprisonment and violent disorder. The government has also made recourse to a range of less than virtuous tactics in the struggle against the Right2Water campaign. It has once again played the 'republican card'. Minister for Health Leo Varadkar ominously hinted at republican involvement by mentioning a 'sinister fringe' to the protests. He claimed that 'they abuse the Gardaí, they break the law, they engage in violence, they spread all sorts of misinformation and what I'm worried about is that it is only a matter of time before someone gets hurt' (Independent Newsdesk 2014). Unnamed senior Garda sources also linked North Dublin protests to a faction of the Real Irish Republican Army (RIRA) and its slain leader Alan Ryan (Brady et al. 2014). This is a familiar police tactic and is redolent of similar delegitimizing tactics used against the Shell to Sea campaign. Unsurprisingly, media coverage has also been extremely critical (Mercille 2014b).

There are a number of overlapping reasons why the anti-water charges campaign has been so successful. Firstly, there is the symbolic aspect of water, an element on which we depend for our very survival, rendering it the 'most essential public service of all' (McCann 2014). There have also been the successful campaigns of resistance against water charges to emulate in Dublin in the 1990s and on the international stage against water privatization in Italy in 2011 (Cernison 2014). The second factor is timing: the campaign has come after six years of unremitting austerity. The government has been vaunting improvements in macro-economic indicators, but those effects are far from evident on the ground, exacerbating the general sense of frustration. The charges have simply been the straw that broke the camel's back.

A third key explanation has been the specific spatial dynamics of the campaign. It is important to note that the first mass demonstrations in Dublin occurred only in October 2014, while the pickets and local direct action initiatives began months earlier. Ireland has a peculiarly territorial aspect to its collective psyche, which has led to our fixation with land and property. The fact that Irish Water employees would interfere without permission with one's property triggered a form of defensive territorialism. It is much easier to become motivated when, instead of amorphous austerity, one is confronted by somebody literally digging up one's front garden. Protest then demanded no organizational skills in particular, one simply needed to prevent work being done on or close to their property. There was also a much higher social sanction for neighbours who chose not to participate in protests leading to the critical mass necessary to halt installations. This in turn led to the emergence of local protest identities: demonstrations are populated by groups exhibiting their local identities with banners—in hock to the Ballyhea Says No—such as Jobstown Says No, Limerick Says No and so on. Dynamics of small-group solidarity take hold, and pre-existing bonds become politicized. This local cohesion is further cemented by police repression, whereby the arrest of a fellow activist is also the arrest of a neighbour or friend. The final successful aspect of the campaign has been its geographical diffusion. Irish politics has long been riven with a rural-urban divide. Issues like the septic tank registration fee exclusively affected rural dwellers (McGee 2012), whereas the anti-bin charges campaign was Dublin based (Reilly 2003). The anti-water charges campaign has been successfully diffused across the country. In the Right2Water campaign, diffusion has come about indirectly (Soule 2004), with geographically dispersed groups 'embracing contagion, mimicry, social learning, organized dissemination' (Strang and Soule 1998, 266). Organic local mobilizations have gained strength from the small-group solidarity endogenously gathered through protest actions and have then consolidated their links to the national campaign by attendance at the national demonstrations—all of which has culminated in a campaign that is both national and strongly embedded at the local level.

It is difficult at the current time to assess the long-term outcome of the Right2Water campaign, as it is ongoing. The mass demonstrations have witnessed a steady decline in numbers. A series of demonstrations held in January 2016 attracted at most a few thousand demonstrators. A boycott has been called for the payment of bills and as of July 2015, Irish Water admitted that over 50 per cent of those to whom it provided water had not paid (Finn 2015, 63). It is likely that the campaign will regain some of its momentum surrounding the trials related to the Jobstown protest and the inevitable juridical efforts to punish those who refuse to pay bills.

The Right2Water campaign has also, especially in urban areas, consolidated the electoral presence of the smaller far-left parties and Sinn Féin. Their engagement in the campaign will almost certainly result in electoral dividends at the expense of the Labour party at the next general election. Of the respondents in the Maynooth University Survey, 80 per cent declared that they would be voting for Sinn Féin, the smaller leftist parties, or leftist independents (Finn 2015, 58). Right2Water contemplated running candidates in this year's election but decided to maintain its movement character and stay outside direct engagement in electoral politics. It has instead put forth a ten-point policy document called the Right2Change, which can be described as an openly anti-austerity left-wing document, and called on all of the left-wing parties to endorse its principles. In so doing, it is hoped that the electorate can easily identify candidates that are opposed to austerity and vote accordingly. This is unprecedented in Irish politics: for the first time in modern Irish history, there is an identifiable left-right spectrum. However, the fractious nature of left-wing politics in the country has once again come to the fore with the AAA bickering with Sinn Féin. The AAA has accused Sinn Féin of instrumentalizing the principles to consolidate its own vote at the expense of other leftist parties and has asked its own voters not to share their subsequent vote preferences with Sinn Féin.

In short, the anti-water charges movement has had a profound impact on Irish politics. It has disavowed the simplistic narrative that there was no opposition to austerity in Ireland, introduced an extended repertoire of contention, politicized opposition to austerity on a left-right basis, and empowered huge swathes of Irish society, particularly working-class urban areas. It is also likely to ensure a much larger return of left-wing anti-austerity candidates in the next election but without any possibility of forming an alternative government.

3.9   Conclusion

In less than a decade, Ireland has gone from being the golden child of neoliberalism, to a bankrupt economic basket case, before regaining its status as a stable pro-business open national economy. Undoubtedly, Ireland has moved from a depression to economic growth. The first three-quarters of 2015 returned GDP growth figures of 7 per cent, the highest in the Eurozone (Noonan 2016). And similarly, as Ireland was presented as an example of the unlimited possibilities of a small open economy in the pre-crash period, it is now being exulted as an example of how the rigid imposition of orthodox economic practices can pave the way to recovery.

Yet, the Irish recovery is not all that it seems. Deprivation rates have risen to 31 per cent, a staggering leap from 7 per cent in 2007 and are only marginally behind the levels in Greece (Hearne 2015, 4). The health service is in a status of perpetual crisis, homelessness has reached historic levels, and the embargo enforced on the public service since 2008 has left huge gaps across all government departments. Unemployment has continued to fall, to 8.8 percent in November 2015 (Eurostat 2015b), but 'for each person taking up a job in the last three years, two people of working age emigrated. One in seven young people has left the country' (Taft 2015).

As was outlined in the introduction, the countries beleaguered by austerity have very different political and economic structures and the apparent resolution of the Irish crisis is primarily due to external factors beyond the measures imposed by the Troika or the actions of the Irish government. Importantly, this highlights that the Irish case cannot be emulated in countries such as Greece and Portugal. Regan has explained that 'the *ultimate* cause of Ireland's fragile recovery can be traced to a path dependent effect of an export-led growth regime based on US investment that has nothing to do with the fiscal adjustment' (Regan 2014, 26). The recovery was only possible because of Ireland's particular variety of capitalism: it has had an open economy, with around 85 per cent of all production exported, the majority to the non-euro economies of the United States and the United Kingdom (Regan 2014, 27). Ireland's links to the United States are rooted in historical and cultural relationships that are unavailable to other mainland European economies. Additionally, the Irish government's amenability to large multinationals, its willingness to be utilized as a de facto tax haven, and its offering of the lowest corporation tax rates in the Eurozone have rendered Ireland a unique and not replicable example, in terms of economic recovery. Accordingly, to the extent that the dynamics of Ireland's fiscal crisis and consequent political fallout—and how its social movements mobilized in opposition to austerity—are peculiar to the prevailing political culture and institutions in the country, so too is its recovery.

In terms of electoral politics, the crisis has led to the constitution of a left-right division which had been absent since before the Irish War of Independence. Although no significant new, leftist party has emerged, Sinn Féin's anti-austerity message has won significant popular consensus, and smaller parties of the left will most likely dramatically increase their representation in the Dáil, albeit from a particularly weak starting point. Admittedly, a lot of this growth will come at the expense of the Labour party, which has been utterly discredited by its backing of Fine Gael since 2011.

The most striking political transformation has occurred in the area of social movements. This chapter has briefly outlined how Irish civil society had been rendered toothless and dependent by decades of social partnership. Therefore, when the government began to slash public services and removed social supports to the more vulnerable in society, it was ill-prepared to offer any form of resistance. The chapter then divided the period of austerity into three rough time periods. In the first, initial opposition was led by ICTU and was mostly concerned with protecting further cuts to the public sector. This period ended after the public sector unions signed up to the Croke Park Agreement, thus removing Ireland's largest civil society actor from any significant contestation of austerity. The second phase was marked by disjointed and politically incoherent protest across the country, which paled in comparison with the vastly larger and more militant protests across the continent. Finally, in the third phase, as disquiet settled elsewhere in Europe, protest exploded in Ireland. The anti-water charges movement served as a tangible means to resist what was widely viewed as the 'last straw' in terms of unjust government impositions. The movement was unlike anything previously witnessed in Ireland. It was unashamedly politicized, autonomously organized, employed direct action tactics and diffused across the country. It has politicized heretofore politically inactive sectors of society, particularly in working-class Ireland. Although not successful in reversing broader austerity measures, it has almost completely derailed the government's efforts to impose water charges.

Contrary to ill-informed accounts, the austerity years in Ireland have witnessed enormous social and political tumult. Protest in Ireland has evolved at its own pace, at somewhat of a remove from developments in other GIIPS states. It has remained overwhelmingly peaceful and has often been framed in politically inconsistent or locally oriented discourse. Yet, one hundred years after the execution of the Irish socialist James Connolly, and a century of political marginalization in a land of social conservatism and small-holder capitalism, the left has returned to take a prominent position in Irish politics.

NOTES

1. After the War of Independence in 1921, Ireland did not obtain full independence and existed as a British dominion until 1937. A new constitution in that year rendered it a Republic in all but name, and Ireland formally became a republic in 1949.
2. A *Teachta Dála* is a deputy of the Irish Parliament, *Dáil Éireann*. It is the equivalent of the English term *Member of Parliament (MP)*.
3. An Irish IRMS employee who worked at Rossport was subsequently killed in Bolivia while he was reputedly working in cohort with a group of mercenaries who were attempting to kill President Evo Morales. Another IRMS employee was also involved in the plot, but he managed to avoid capture and went on to found a far-right organization called the *Szeckler Legion* to fight for the

rights of the Hungarian minority in Romania (Barrington 2010, 38–42).

4. The Irish media played a notable role in exacerbating the excesses of the Celtic Tiger period and championing the austerity policies implemented by successive governments. As Julien Mercille observed, 'the media do not present a broad range of opinions, but rather a relatively narrow spectrum of ideas. They present elites' economic prescriptions favourably to the public and thus contribute to shape dominant political and economic ideologies' (2014a, 1).

5. UNITE represents a very diverse array of both public and private sector workers ranging from health and construction to municipal employees and factory workers.

6. SIPTU represents 40 per cent of all workers in ICTU; it is also a mixed union representing private and public sectors. INTO represents primary school teachers, and IMPACT largely represents lower-level civil servants.

7. SIPTU has a formal institutional relationship with the Labour party and was a strong supporter of the Croke Park Agreement.

8. Halappanavar was denied an abortion that would likely have saved her life because of Ireland's restrictive abortion laws; a midwife explained to the victim, an Indian national, that the laws were as such because Ireland was a 'Catholic country' (Cullen and Holland 2013). The following weeks saw a number of protests and vigils across the country demanding reform of abortion legislation. A demonstration on 17 November 2012 attracted in excess of 10,000 people (McDonald 2012)

9. The Workers' Party does not have representatives in the Dáil, although a number of Independents have links with them.

10. The Civil Public and Services Union is a public sector union. The Operative Plasterers and Allied Trades Society of Ireland represents workers in the construction sector.

References

Allen, K. 2012. The Model Pupil Who Faked the Test: Social Policy in the Irish Crisis. *Critical Social Policy* 32(3):422–439. doi:10.1177/0261018312444418.

———. 2013. *Austerity Ireland: The Failure of Irish Capitalism*. London: Pluto Press.

Armingeon, K., and L. Baccaro. 2012. Political Economy of the Sovereign Debt Crisis: The Limits of Internal Devaluation. *Industrial Law Journal* 41(3): 254–275. doi:10.1093/indlaw/dws029.

Baccaro, L., and M. Simoni. 2007. Centralized Wage Bargaining and the "Celtic Tiger" Phenomenon. *Industrial Relations: A Journal of Economy and Society* 46(3): 426–455. doi:10.1111/j.1468-232X.2007.00476.x.

Barrington, B. 2010. Breakdown of Trust: A Report on the Corrib Gas Dispute. Frontline Defenders.

Brady, T., N. O'Connor, and F. Sheahan. 2014. Water Protests Infiltrated by Dissidents as Meters on Hold. *Irish Independent.* http://www.independent.ie/irish-news/water/water-protests-infiltrated-by-dissidents-as-meters-on-hold-30725389.html

Browne, V. 2013. O'Brien's Record Should Disbar Him from Having a Disproportionate Hold on Media. *Irish Times.* http://www.irishtimes.com/business/o-brien-s-record-should-disbar-him-from-having-a-disproportionate-hold-on-media-1.1493100

Carroll, S., and M. O'Halloran. 2014. State Faces "Potential Isis Situation" Over Water Protests. *Irish Times.* http://www.irishtimes.com/news/politics/state-faces-potential-isis-situation-over-water-protests-1.2009289

Carswell, S. 2011. *Anglo Republic: Inside the Bank That Broke Ireland/Simon Carswell.* Dublin: Penguin Ireland.

Cernison, M. 2014. Online Communication Spheres in Social Movements Campaigns: The Italian Referendum on Water. PhD Thesis. Florence: European University Institute.

Cox, L. 2011. Gramsci in Mayo: A Marxist Perspective on Social Movements in Ireland. In *Proceedings of New Agendas in Social Movement Studies Conference.* National University of Ireland Maynooth. http://eprints.maynoothuniversity.ie/2889/

———. 2012. Challenging Austerity in Ireland. *Concept* 3 (2).

Cronin, D. 2009. Learning from Libertas. *Guardian.*

Cullen, P., and K. Holland. 2013. Midwife Manager "Regrets" using "Catholic Country" Remark to Savita Halappanavar. *Irish Times.* http://www.irishtimes.com/news/health/midwife-manager-regrets-using-catholic-country-remark-to-savita-halappanavar-1.1355895

Culpepper, P. D., and A. Regan. 2014. Why Don't Governments Need Trade Unions Anymore? The Death of Social Pacts in Ireland and Italy. *Socio-Economic Review*, February, mwt028. doi:10.1093/ser/mwt028.

D'Art, D., and T. Turner. 2011. Irish Trade Unions Under Social Partnership: A Faustian Bargain? *Industrial Relations Journal* 42(2): 157–173. doi:10.1111/j.1468-2338.2011.00617.x.

Doherty, M. 2011. It Must Have Been Love … but It's Over Now: The Crisis and Collapse of Social Partnership in Ireland. *Transfer: European Review of Labour and Research* 17(3): 371–385. doi:10.1177/1024258911410803.

Drudy, P.J., and M.L. Collins. 2011. Ireland: From Boom to Austerity. *Cambridge Journal of Regions, Economy and Society* 4(3): 339–354. doi:10.1093/cjres/rsr021.

ESRI. 2014. Latest Quarterly Economic Commentary. *Quarterly Economic Commentary.*

Eurostat. 2015a. Euro Area Unemployment Rate at 11.5%. Eurostat News Release Euro Indicators 1/2015.

———. 2015b. Euro Area Unemployment Rate at 10.5%. Eurostat News Release Euro Indicators.

Finn, D. 2011. Ireland on the Turn? *New Left Review*, no. 67, 5.

———. 2015. Daniel Finn: Ireland's Water Wars. New Left Review 95, September–October 2015. *New Left Review* 95(Oct.): 49–63.

Flynn, S. 2010. 25,000 Protest Against Fees Increase. *Irish Times.* http://www.irishtimes.com/news/25-000-protest-against-fees-increase-1.672194

Gagatek, W. 2010. *The 2009 Elections to the European Parliament Country Reports.* European University Institute: RSCAS Books. Florence.

Glynn, I., T. Kelly, and P. Mac Éinrí. 2013. Irish Emigration in an Age of Austerity. University College Cork.

Grant, H., and J. Domokos. 2009. Rossport's Gas Pipeline: Harriet Grant and John Domokos on How Emotions are Running High. *Guardian.* https://www.theguardian.com/environment/2009/jun/10/rossport-gas-pipeline-shell

Hanahoe, T., T. Conway, and J. Monaghon 2014. We Need to Talk About the Gardaí Village. *Village*, 11 March.

Hardiman, N. 2006. Politics and Social Partnership: Flexible Network Governance. *Economic and Social Review.* Economic and Social Research Institute.

Hardiman, N., and S. Dellepiane. 2012. The New Politics of Austerity: Fiscal Responses to Crisis in Ireland and Spain. SSRN Scholarly Paper ID 2013238. Rochester, NY: Social Science Research Network. http://papers.ssrn.com/abstract=2013238

Hearne, R. 2015. The Irish Water War, Austerity and the "Risen People" an Analysis of Participant Opinions, Social and Political Impacts and Transformative Potential of the Irish Anti Water-Charges Movement. Department of Geography, Maynooth University.

Holland, K. 2014. Water Charges March a "Tipping Point" After "Years of Hurt". *Irish Times.* http://www.irishtimes.com/news/social-affairs/water-charges-march-a-tipping-point-after-years-of-hurt-1.1961040

Honohan, P. 2010. The Irish Banking Crisis Regulatory and Financial Stability Policy 2003–2008. Dublin.

IMPACT. 2015. Jobbridge—Time to Start Again. A Proposal to Reframe, Restrict and Resize Irish Internship Policy. IMPACT Education Division. http://www.impact.ie/wp-content/uploads/2015/04/JobBridgeReport2015.pdf

Independent Newsdesk. 2014. Leo Varadkar Slams "Sinister Fringe" to Water Protests. *Irish Independent*. http://www.independent.ie/irish-news/water/leo-varadkar-slams-sinister-fringe-to-water-protests-30723122.html

Kelly, F. 2014. Fascism Thoughts as Burton Held in Car at Water Protest. *Irish Times*. http://www.irishtimes.com/news/politics/fascism-thoughts-as-burton-held-in-car-at-water-protest-1.2045757

Kenny, C. 2013. Ireland Has Highest Net Emigration Level in Europe. *Irish Times*. http://www.irishtimes.com/blogs/generationemigration/2013/11/21/graphic-ireland-has-highest-net-emigration-level-in-europe/

Kerrigan, G. 2010. The Charge of the Not-so-Light Brigade. *Independent.ie* http://www.independent.ie/opinion/columnists/gene-kerrigan/gene-kerrigan-the-charge-of-the-notsolight-brigade-26697472.html

———. 2012. *The Big Lie: Who Profits from Ireland's Austerity?* Dublin: Transworld Ireland.

Kinsella, S. 2012. Is Ireland Really the Role Model for Austerity? *Cambridge Journal of Economics* 36(1): 223–235. doi:10.1093/cje/ber032.

Kirby, P., and M. Murphy. 2011. *Towards a Second Republic: Irish Politics after the Celtic Tiger*. London: Pluto Press.

Leahy, A., S. Healy, and M. Murphy. 2014. The European Crisis and Its Human Cost. A Call for Fair Alternatives and Solutions. A Caritas Report by Social Justice Ireland.

Little, C. 2011. The General Election of 2011 in the Republic of Ireland: All Changed Utterly? *West European Politics* 34(6): 1304–1313. doi:10.1080/01402382.2011.616669.

Lynch, K. 2014. Water Taxes Are Indirect Taxes—Deeply Unjust. *Right2 Water*.

Lyons, T., and B. Carey. 2012. *The FitzPatrick Tapes: The Rise and Fall of One Man, One Bank, and One Country*. Dublin: Penguin.

Mair, P. 2005. Party Competition and the Changing Party System. In *Politics in the Republic of Ireland*, Fourth edition. London: Routledge.

———. 2011a. Bini Smaghi vs. the Parties: Representative Government and Institutional Constraints. Working Paper. http://cadmus.eui.eu/handle/1814/16354

———. 2011b. The Election in Context. In *How Ireland Voted 2011: The Full Story of Ireland's Earthquake Election*. Basingstoke: Palgrave Macmillan.

———. 2014. Explaining the Absence of Class Politics in Ireland. In *On Parties, Party Systems and Democracy: Selected Writings of Peter Mair. ECPR Essays*, Ingrid van Biezen. Colchester, UK: ECPR Press.

McAdam, D., and R. Paulsen. 1993. Specifying the Relationship Between Social Ties and Activism. *American Journal of Sociology* 99(3): 640–667. doi:10.1086/230319.

McCann, E. 2014. Why Water, Why Now? Ireland Takes to the Streets. *Irish Times*.

McDonald, H. 2012. Thousands March in Dublin Over Abortion Rights. *Guardian.* https://www.theguardian.com/world/2012/nov/17/march-dublin-abortion-death

McDonough, T., and T. Dundon. 2010. Thatcherism Delayed? The Irish Crisis and the Paradox of Social Partnership. SSRN Scholarly Paper ID 1702602. Rochester, NY: Social Science Research Network. http://papers.ssrn.com/abstract=1702602

McGee, H. 2012. Dáil Protest at Septic Tank Fee. *Irish Times.* http://www.irish-times.com/news/d%C3%A1il-protest-at-septic-tank-fee-1.451372

———. 2015. Jury Out on Success of Irish Water Strategy as Deadline Passes. *Irish Times.* http://www.irishtimes.com/news/politics/jury-out-on-success-of-irish-water-strategy-as-deadline-passes-1.2088581

Meade, R. 2005. We Hate It Here, Please Let Us Stay! Irish Social Partnership and the Community/Voluntary Sector's Conflicted Experiences of Recognition. *Critical Social Policy* 25(3): 349–373.

———. 2012. Government and Community Development in Ireland: The Contested Subjects of Professionalism and Expertise. *Antipode* 44(3): 889–910. doi:10.1111/j.1467-8330.2011.00924.x.

———. 2015. The Older People's Uprising 2008. In *Defining Events: Power, Resistance and Identity in 21st Century Ireland.* Manchester: Manchester University Press.

Mercille, J. 2014a. *The Political Economy and Media Coverage of the European Economic Crisis: The Case of Ireland.* Routledge Frontiers of Political Economy. New York: Routledge.

———. 2014b. What Is a Sinister Fringe and Are Water Protesters ISIS Affiliates?— The Media on the Water Charges Protests. *Right2 Water.* http://www.right-2water.ie/blog/what-sinister-fringe-and-are-water-protesters-isis-affiliates-media-water-charges-protests

Murphy, M. 2002. Social Partnership—Is It "The Only Game in Town"? *Community Development Journal* 37(1): 80–90. doi:10.1093/cdj/37.1.80.

Murphy, P. 2014. Head to Head on Water Charges: Is It Time for the Public to Pay Up? No. *Irish Times.*

Naughton, M. 2013. An Interrogation of the Character of Irish Protest Since the Bailout, Unpublished Dissertation, School of Politics and International Relations, University College Dublin. School of Politics and International Relations: University College Dublin.

Noonan, Ml. 2016. Ireland's Economy: A Solid Recovery. *OECD Data.* http://data.oecd.org/chart/4qCg

Nyberg, P. 2011. Misjudging Risk: Causes of the Systemic Banking Crisis in Ireland: Report of the Commission of Investigation into the Banking Sector in Ireland.

O'Broin, E. 2011. 2011—An Interesting Year for the Left. *Irish Left Review.*

Ó Donnabháin, St J. 2010. The Struggle Against the Corrib Gas Pipeline: A Story of State and Corporate Corruption. *Left Curve*.

———. 2014. Ideological Diversity and Alliance Building Across Difference in Social Movements: The Campaign Against Shell in Ireland. National University Ireland Maynooth.

O'Flynn, D. 2014. My Political Philosophy. Accessed 3 March 2015. http://diarmuidoflynn.com/2014/03/DiarmuidOFlynn-MEP-political-philosophy.html

Ó'Riain, S. 2014. *The Rise and Fall of Ireland's Celtic Tiger: Liberalism, Boom and Bust*. Cambridge: Cambridge University Press.

O'Toole, F. 2009. *Ship of Fools: How Stupidity and Corruption Sank the Celtic Tiger*. London: Faber and Faber.

———. 2014. How Gang of Four Runs the Country. *Irish Times*. http://www.irishtimes.com/opinion/fintan-o-toole-how-gang-of-four-runs-the-country-1.2038643

Pappas, T.S., and E. O'Malley. 2014. Civil Compliance and "Political Luddism": Explaining Variance in Social Unrest During Crisis in Ireland and Greece. *American Behavioral Scientist* 58(12): 1592–1613.

Piven, F.F. 1977. *Poor People's Movements: Why They Succeed, How They Fail*. New York: Pantheon Books.

Quinlivan, A. 2015. The 2014 Local Elections in the Republic of Ireland. *Irish Political Studies* 30(1): 132–142. doi:10.1080/07907184.2014.990959.

Regan, A. 2014. What Explains Ireland's Fragile Recovery from the Crisis? The Politics of Comparative Institutional Advantage. *CESifo Forum* 15(2): 26–31.

Regling, K., and M. Watson. 2010. A Preliminary Report on the Sources of Ireland's Banking Crisis. Commissioned by the Minister of Finance Brian Lenihan.

Reilly, J. 2003. Far Left Pulling the Strings on Bin Charge Campaign. *Irish Independent*. http://www.independent.ie/opinion/analysis/far-left-pulling-the-strings-on-bin-charge-campaign-26236172.html

Right2Water. 2015. Right2Water—Strategy, Tactics, Unity. *Right2 Water*. Accessed 4 March 2015.

Roberts, K. M. 2015. Populism, Social Movements, and Popular Subjectivity. In The Oxford Handbook of Social Movements, 681–696. Oxford University Press.

RTE. 2010. Gardaí, Students Clash in Dublin. RTE News, 3 November.

Sheehan, F., B. Keenan, and L. Hogan. 2012. Family Fury as Noonan Says Young Emigrate for Lifestyle. *Irish Independent*. http://www.independent.ie/irish-news/family-fury-as-noonan-says-young-emigrate-for-lifestyle-26813027.html

Siggins, L. 2010. *Once Upon a Time in the West: The Corrib Gas Controversy*. Dublin: Transworld Ireland.

Soule, S. A. 2004. Diffusion Processes Within and Across Social Movements. In *The Blackwell Companion to Social Movements*, D.A. Snow, S. A. Soule, and H. Kriesi. Malden: Blackwell Publishing.

Strang, D., and S.A. Soule. 1998. Diffusion in Organizations and Social Movements: From Hybrid Corn to Poison Pills. *Annual Review of Sociology* 24: 265–290.

Taft, M. 2015. Ireland Is No Model for Greece. *The Guardian*, 10 July, Sec. World News. http://www.theguardian.com/world/economics-blog/2015/jul/10/ireland-no-model-greece-troika-austerity

The Economist. 2013. The Eighth Austerity Budget. *The Economist*, 19 October. http://www.economist.com/news/europe/21588110-government-end-economic-emergency-sight-eighth-austerity-budget

Thorhallsson, B., and P. Kirby. 2012. Financial Crises in Iceland and Ireland: Does European Union and Euro Membership Matter? *JCMS: Journal of Common Market Studies* 50(5): 801–818. doi:10.1111/j.1468-5965.2012.02258.x.

de Tocqueville, A. 1856. *The Old Regime and the Revolution*. Harper and Brothers.

Valencia, F. and L. Laeven. 2012. Systemic Banking Crises Database: An Update. IMF Working Paper 12/163. International Monetary Fund. http://econpapers.repec.org/paper/imfimfwpa/12_2f163.htm

Varley, T. and C. Curtin. 2006. The Politics of Empowerment: Power, Populism and Partnership in Rural Ireland. In *Economic and Social Review*. Economic and Social Research Institute.

CHAPTER 4

Turbulent Flow: Anti-Austerity Mobilization in Greece

Markos Vogiatzoglou

4.1 Introduction

This chapter examines the ways in which the anti-austerity mobilization developed in Greece in the years 2010–2014. The first protests were launched just days after the Greek government's plea for financial assistance to the institutions that would later be called the 'Troika'— the International Monetary Fund, the European Central Bank and the European Commission (EC). We distinguish four mobilization phases. The first one, which we define as 'traditional mobilization', lasted for a year—May 2010 to May 2011. The second stage, the main characteristics of which reflected the inefficiency of the previous period's collective action repertoire as well as the strong resonance of international developments, is the brief but intense 'occupy the squares' movement (May 2011–September 2011). The third stage (September 2011–June 2012) is mostly characterized by diffused contention across the societal sphere; during this period, the 40-year-old Greek political party system was significantly shaken and the seeds of a new socio-political balance were planted. Finally, in the fourth stage, since the elections of 2012 and until January 2015, when snap elections brought to power the left-wing SYRIZA party, the country witnessed a notable weakening of street protest activity, as the anti-austerity movement focused its action on two different fronts: shoring up the social solidarity structures, and countering the threat of the neo-Nazi party Golden Dawn.

© The Author(s) 2017
D. della Porta et al., *Late Neoliberalism and its Discontents in the Economic Crisis*, DOI 10.1007/978-3-319-35080-6_4

During these turbulent years, practically all pre-existing social movement organizations, left-wing political parties, trade and student unions became involved in one way or another in the anti-austerity mobilizations. New actors emerged as well, and thousands of citizens without any prior movement experience took to the streets. The organizational structures employed reflected the well-established horizontal tradition of the Greek movement. Material claims and grievances were raised, alongside calls to reinvent the country's democratic framework. The collective action repertoire included: a large (even by the Greek trade unions' standards) number of politically charged general strikes; hundreds of protests, among them 25 large protest events that brought together as many as 500,000 participants (Diani and Kousis 2014; Kousis 2013); occupations of public spaces and buildings; several incidents of mass political violence; and the provision of services and basic goods to the suffering population.

In sum, the anti-austerity mobilization in Greece—the EU country that suffered, perhaps, the gravest consequences from the application of late neoliberalism's policies—became also a laboratory of experimentation and development for social movement practices and organizational forms. In what follows, we shall first examine the socio-economic and political context of the crisis. Then, the organizational formats and collective action repertoires undertaken by the anti-austerity protest's main actors are brought forward. The protest aims and discursive practices follow, with a special focus on the ways protesters approached the democracy and democratization issues. The chapter concludes with a discussion and analysis of the main findings.

4.2   Socio-Economic and Political Context of the Protests

4.2.1   The Origins of the Crisis and Its Consequences

The global economic crisis that began in 2008 in the United States of America, influencing first the real estate market and then the banks and the financial sector, by no means presaged the explosion of the EU countries' debt crisis, especially in the nations of the European South.

In Greece, during the initial stages of the crisis, economic and political elites seemed confident and reassured that the Greek society and economy were sufficiently shielded from the negative influence of the major international banks and credit institutions' crisis. This confidence derived from the exceptionally positive course of the Greek economy during the previous decade. Indeed, from 2000 onward, the Greek GDP was rising at an impressive rate, higher than the EU's median (Blavoukos and Pagoulatos 2013), whilst the Greek banks and major corporations were expanding their operations in the Balkan and south-eastern Mediterranean regions (Petrakis 2012). This positive economic environment helped the centre-right party New Democracy (ND) to secure a second contiguous electoral victory, in October 2007. Two years later, the government resigned and early elections were proclaimed. The government's resignation was justified by the need for crucial decisions to be taken, due to an undefined threat the Greek economy would face in the near future. These developments stunned the Greek society and the political elites, yet during the electoral campaign, no serious discussion ensued on the forthcoming unfavourable occurrences. The social-democratic party PASOK assured the public that the economy faced no problems, that the former government had resigned simply due to its fatigue (incapacity) towards managing the country's political affairs.

In this climate of relative political euphoria, George Papandreou's Panhellenic Socialist Movement was elected, securing a wide parliamentary majority. The electoral public warmly approved PASOK's pre-electoral promise for a redistributive set of policies that would define the terms and means of yet another developmental leap.

Just three months later, due to the public debt crisis and the difficulties in refinancing its loans through the international financial market, Greece was forced to accept an extraordinary 110 billion euros loan from the so-called 'Troika'. The loan agreement was accompanied by a Memorandum of Cooperation between the country and its creditors. The terms of the Memorandum obliged Greece to proceed to an immediate and extensive privatization of many public enterprises and public real estate; to drastically reduce the number of employees in the public sector; to adopt flexibilization policies in labour relations; to increase retirement age limits; and to reduce—by 30 to 40 per cent—salaries and pensions in both the public and the private sectors. Following an urgent request from Papandreou's government in April 2010, the Troika negotiated an economic adjustment programme with the Greek authorities. The set of measures, which covered the period 2010–2013, was agreed upon by the European Council on

2 May 2010. In late 2011 and early 2012, a second economic adjustment programme was negotiated with the Greek authorities. The programme, approved by the European Council on March 2012, initially covered the period 2012–2014, but was subsequently extended by two years until 2016. The combined financial assistance amounts to 240 billion euros, consisting of 110 billion euros from the first programme and 130 billion euros from the second.

The overarching objective of the programme is to restore Greece's credibility to private investors by ensuring fiscal sustainability, as well as by safeguarding the stability of the financial system and boosting growth and competitiveness. To this end, the programme consists of a comprehensive set of ambitious policies that reinforce each other. Namely, those policies refer mainly to fiscal adjustment (with the objective of reaching a primary surplus of 1.5 per cent in 2014 and 4.5 per cent of GDP in 2016). There is also a restructuring plan for the banking sector. The plan involves bank liquidity support, as well as measures to recapitalize banks without infringing on competition rules, with an emphasis on the establishment of the Hellenic Financial Stability Fund (HFSF). Finally, the economic adjustment programme entails numerous structural reforms to foster economic growth and boost competitiveness. Typical examples include the modernization of the public sector, as well as regulations intended to make product and labour markets more efficient and flexible, with the goal of creating a more open and accessible business environment for domestic and foreign investors. Privatization of public assets is also considered a necessary step to guarantee the above objectives.

Nevertheless, Greece's economic performance remains devastating according to data from the national statistical authorities (ELSTAT). Public debt stood at 175.7 per cent at the end of 2013, despite the fact that the majority of memorandum commitments were met on time. Real incomes have declined, and the proportion of the population facing poverty risk has dramatically risen. Along these lines, non-performing loans (NPLs) continue to expand. Unemployment, in turn, rose to 28.1 per cent, while youth unemployment was as high as 62.1 per cent (data for December 2013) and those at risk of poverty was 34.6 per cent in 2012. Depressed growth of more than 25 per cent of the GDP since 2008 has seriously dented the productive capacity of the Greek economy.

Further, the social impact of fiscal consolidation has been aggravated by the lack of a general safety net, as well as low social spending and a traditionally weak welfare state. The Greek social protection system is characterized by fragmentation of benefits, with limited targeting and no general minimum income support mechanism (Guillén and Matsaganis 2000). Another worrying development is the increase in the number of suicides. Previously a very unusual phenomenon in Greek society, suicides have risen enormously since 2010 (Karanikolos et al. 2013). In general, almost all headline macro-economic and social well-being indicators signal dramatic changes and unfortunate developments for the vast majority of working people in Greece.

Further, reversal trends of recovery are not in sight, even if recent Organization for Economic Cooperation and Development (OECD) and Troika reports forecast economic growth by 2015 if austerity and internal devaluation policies continue to be the main policy dogma. Nevertheless, it remains a mystery how such optimism can come to fruition in an economy that has to reabsorb more than 30 per cent of its workforce (almost 1.5 million unemployed people) as well as dealing with huge losses in salaries (35 per cent on average) and other dramatic cuts in social spending and care. For example, a recent article in the medical journal *Lancet* provides mounting evidence of a Greek public health tragedy due to austerity cuts in health services budgets (Kentikelenis et al. 2014). In a similar vein, a report on Greece sketches the social and humanitarian crisis provoked by the triumph of policies that mainly aim to increase the volume and frequency of transactions on the back of the far-reaching labour market reforms in 2010–2013 (Kretsos 2014). The therapy has proven more dangerous than the disease, and most working people in Greece have seen their lives turned upside down in the matter of a few months.

4.2.2   *Political Context*

As mentioned above, the crisis landed in Greece shortly after the election of a particularly strong government, led by PASOK's George Papandreou (2009 general elections, 44 per cent of the votes, 160 seats out of 300). Although the outcome had secured a safe parliamentary majority for PASOK, the consecutive votes on austerity packages narrowed it down as time went by. Several MPs split from the party, refusing to approve the Memoranda and their accompanying legislative initiatives. It is important to note, though, that the fall of the Papandreou government cannot be attributed to an actual loss of parliamentary majority, but rather to a general climate of fear, insecurity and loss of orientation among the government officials and MPs, which had rendered governance unsustainable (Lentzou 2011; Pikoulas 2011).

In November 2011, in an attempt to find a way out of the political deadlock, Papandreou suggested a referendum to decide the country's future in the Eurozone. The proposal was dismissed by the creditors, and although reports vary on what followed (there is some speculation on whether EU officials were in coordination with centre-right ND leader Antonis Samaras and Papandreou's successor in the PASOK leadership, Evangelos Venizelos), Papandreou stepped down on 6 November 2011 and a technocrat cabinet was formed, enjoying the parliamentary support of a three party-coalition (PASOK, ND and the extreme-right party LAOS). Banker Loukas Papademos was appointed Prime Minister, in a move that unavoidably brings to mind similar events in Italy (Monti government) just a few days later.

The Papademos government was unpopular from the very beginning. Whilst ND wanted elections to take place as soon as possible (given that polls were giving them a clear lead), PASOK officials aimed to delay them, in order to have time to regroup and reduce the expected electoral losses. Although the initial plan was to schedule elections for 19 February 2012, they were delayed until May 2012, to allow the Papademos government to negotiate the second bailout package and its accompanying austerity measures (second Memorandum).

The elections on 6 May 2012 proved to be an earthquake for the previously relatively stable, post-dictatorship Greek political system. ND ranked first, losing some 14 per cent of the vote when compared to 2009. PASOK suffered record losses (more than 30 per cent of their 2009 vote), ranking third. LAOS was wiped off the political map. The leftist coalition SYRIZA became the major opposition party, increasing its support from 4 to almost 17 per cent. Furthermore, a formerly marginal neo-Nazi party, Golden Dawn, managed to enter the Parliament, securing almost 7 per cent of the vote.

The fragmentation of the new Parliament prohibited the formation of a coalition government. A second round of general elections was called for 17 June 2012. There, the foundations for a new type of bipolar political system were laid. Both ND and SYRIZA increased their proportion of the vote (when compared to May 2012) by approximately 10 per cent, establishing themselves as the key political players in the field. Thanks to a 50-seat bonus offered to the first party, ND managed to form a coalition government with PASOK and the centre-left DIMAR (Democratic Left). ND's Samaras was sworn in as Prime Minister.

The new government held a most secure parliamentary majority (173 seats out of 300). Yet, in June 2013, DIMAR left the government, reducing the majority (which had already been weakened due to split-offs by MPs who rejected austerity legislative packages) to a mere 153 seats out of 300. The 2014 euro-elections confirmed SYRIZA's lead, whilst opinion polls depicted the unpopularity of the ND-PASOK coalition.

In late 2014, the Samaras government called for an early election for President of the Republic.[1] Unable to gather the necessary consensus to elect a president, the Parliament was dissolved and elections were held on 25 January 2015. An anti-austerity coalition government emerged, and SYRIZA's Tsipras was sworn in as Prime Minister the day after.

Table 4.1 shows the three main political parties' performance in the 2009–2014 period.

Finally, with respect to public opinion, as was posited earlier in this chapter (see Introduction), the financial crisis was indeed accompanied by a crisis of representation. Similar to other austerity-ridden countries, Greek citizens show low trust for political and social institutions, such as political parties, trade unions, and the Parliament (European Commission 2013; Laoutaris 2011). In 2013, more than 60 per cent of Greeks reported low or no trust in the EU (European Commission 2013). In contrast, a more or less stable two-thirds of the society expressed, during the crisis years, their wish for Greece to remain in the Eurozone (European Commission 2011, 2013, 2014).Throughout the crisis years, the Greek population was particularly pessimistic with respect to their country's and personal perspectives, especially regarding the economic and labour market situation (European Commission 2011, 2014).

Table 4.1   PASOK, New Democracy (ND) and SYRIZA's electoral results

Party	2009	May 2012	June 2012	2015
PASOK	43.9%	13.2%	12.3%	4.68%
New Democracy (ND)	33.5%	18.9%	29.7%	27.8%
SYRIZA	4.6%	16.8%	26.9%	36.3%

4.3   Contemporary Anti-Austerity Protest

4.3.1   Organizational Formats and Collective Action Repertoires

Given the explicit austerity focus of the Memorandum of Understanding (MoU) that was signed between the Greek government and its creditors, the country's social movement organizations, trade unions and opposition parties (especially of the left) commenced preparing themselves for a campaign, the main goal of which would be to block the austerity measures. Broadly speaking, the official kick-off of the anti-austerity campaign could be traced to the general strike of 5 May 2010, which was proclaimed by both confederations of the Greek trade union system. In the days and weeks that preceded the strike, various organizations engaged in preparations, publicizing and organizing their members, for what they considered would be a long-term campaign (Kanellopoulos and Kostopoulos 2014).

One may distinguish four different stages of the anti-austerity mobilization, based on their main organizational characteristics and collective action repertoires employed.

Stage 1 (May 2010–May 2011): Traditional Mobilization
During this period, the Greek movement behaved in a similar manner to the mobilizations of the recent past. The repertoire included the usual general strikes[2] (and their respective protests), demonstrations, clashes with the police and typical protests in many Greek cities. As one interviewee notes, 'The first protests of that period are similar to the ones of the Metapolitefsi period: the ones during the day of a national strike, the ones of 1st May, we see trade unions, parties, many common features' (Interviewee GR3).

The starting point of the mobilization (which proved to be a most significant point, as shall be examined in what follows) was the general strike and protest of 5 May 2015. Demonstrators arrived at the entrance of the Parliament, where they were confronted by riot police. Participation in both the strike and the protest was exceptionally high (some 250,000 people were reported to participate in the Athens protest [Kousis 2012]); but the incident that overshadowed everything else that occurred that day was the arson of Marfin Bank and the consequent death of three of its employees.

The Marfin incident turned the 5 May protest into an eventful one for two reasons. First, the pro-government media utilized the killings in order to promote a 'law and order' versus anarchy discourse, which facilitated the government's argument in favour of the agreement. Second, and more importantly, the death of the three bank employees was a tremendous shock to the protesters,[3] especially those who utilized a more contentious repertoire. As one interviewee notes, '[...] the Marfin incident shocked the people that participated in the movements. They suddenly begun to stay back [from concrete actions] and wonder what happened' (Interviewee GR4).

The assessment and self-criticism process that followed radically altered one of the most visible actors of the protests, that is, the anarchist and anti-authoritarian (A/A) organizations (See Main Protest Actors section for more details). What is more, perhaps for the first time in years, the social legitimization for mass political violence decreased, and the more pacifist elements of the mobilization had a strong argument in their arsenal, which at a later stage contributed to creating the 'non-violent' discourse of the Syntagma Square occupiers.

After a six-month period with few and weak demonstrations, protest activity resumed towards the end of 2010 and intensified during the winter of 2010–2011. It is important to note that the protests were peaceful—for the standards of the Greek movement scene—and similar to the traditional pattern, as depicted above.

Stage 2 (May 2011–September 2011): Occupied Squares
After a year of unsuccessful mobilizations against the austerity measures, it became obvious to organizers that the traditional repertoire was insufficient. Following a wide debate (and self-reflection) on the strategic failures of the previous period, inspired by the Arab Spring, and adopting the organizational patterns of the Spanish Indignados, the 'occupy the squares' movement participants launched their mobilization in Thessaloniki and Athens, to spread a few weeks later to the main squares of several Greek cities. The mobilization enjoyed huge popularity. According to a poll, an impressive 20 per cent of the Greek population participated in at least one protest event during May and June 2011 (alerthess.gr 2011).

The Greek version of the so-called 'Indignados' movement was launched on 25 May 2011 when, following a widespread call to mobilization through social networking websites, thousands of people showed up to protest in front of the Greek Parliament, in Syntagma Square, Athens and the White Tower, Thessaloniki. Several hundred remained in the two squares after the end of the protest, formed an improvised 'popular assembly', and decided to remain there until 'the troika, the government, everyone leaves' (Interviewee GR8).

The initial calls to mobilization were circulated through Facebook pages. Subsequently, the news of the forthcoming protest began spreading in other ways: emails were sent in large numbers, articles in blogs and news sites appeared, hashtags were introduced on Twitter. The political affiliation and socio-political background of those who formulated the initial calls remain unknown.

This was not the first time that calls to squat the Syntagma Square were issued. Yet, it was the first time that a truly bottom-up mobilization was attempted. According to an activist who participated in the Syntagma Square Assembly, 'It was clear to everyone that all parties should stay out. If they [the party members] wanted to come, they should come as citizens, as individuals, not to gather their votes or sell their newspapers' (quoted in Sergi and Vogiatzoglou 2013).

On the designated day, some 50,000 people showed up in Athens, and some 5000 in Thessaloniki, according to media reports (Kousis 2012). In Athens, whilst on the upper side of the square thousands were protesting against the government and the international creditors, on the lower side hundreds participated in the popular assembly, in an attempt to 'trace a common path for their struggle'. The decision taken was to form an 'acampada'-style camp on the square, squat the square and call for daily demonstrations to be followed by popular assemblies.

The daily assembly was the main organizational and decision-making apparatus of the mobilization, during the months that it lasted. The assembly operated as follows: 'In the beginning [...] we would decide on which issues to discuss. Those who wanted to speak would take a paper with a number, then we had a "lottery", and the numbers drawn would speak' (Interviewee GR7, quoted in Sergi and Vogiatzoglou 2013).

Apart from the assembly, another characteristic inherited from the Spanish Indignados was the formation of working groups, which would undertake specific tasks and provide constant feedback to the assembly in terms of refining its political positions, proposing texts to be circulated, and 'producing actions, producing initiatives for people towards getting involved and participating in various activities' (Interviewee GR11).

Another important feature of the Syntagma Square mobilization was the distinction between the so-called 'upper square' and 'lower square'.

During the daily demonstrations, the protesters who gathered in front of the Parliament were waving Greek flags and shouting slogans against the politicians and the Troika of creditors, whilst the lower side of the square, where the assemblies were taking place, was the regular meeting point for the more politicized and leftist protesters.

The peak of the Greek version of the Indignados movement was the 'Battle for Syntagma Square' of 28–29 June 2011, when tens of thousands of people protested against yet another set of austerity measures. During these two days, the measures were discussed and voted in a besieged Parliament, whilst all around it protesters were fiercely clashing with riot police. Practically all the Greek Social Movement Organizations, political parties of the left, trade unions, and various professional and other groups joined forces in and around Syntagma Square, in order to implement the Parliament blockade plan the Indignados Assembly had formulated. What followed were two days of street blockades, barricades, attempts to invade the Parliament, counteroffensives by the police forces, fierce clashes and property destruction. The 'Battle for Syntagma Square' left behind almost 800 people injured and millions of euros in damages. Yet, the austerity package was ultimately approved by the Parliament, as the police managed to secure a safe corridor for the MPs to enter and vote.

Despite the fact that, during the feverish days of the Syntagma Square Battle, an unprecedented 'unity in action' spirit was evident in the majority of the Greek social movement organizations—and despite the recapturing of the square by the protesters after an evacuation operation by the riot police—the movement, lacking a clear and achievable goal, did not manage to reach the mobilization peaks of the previous period, and slowly faded. When, in mid-August (a period when the majority of the Greek population is on holiday), the riot police returned to dismantle the *acampada*, only a few dozen campers were present, and only a few hundred protested, the same day, against the eviction imposed.

One may distinguish four important characteristics of the protests that took place in May and June 2011, in the context of the 'Indignados'-style protest.

1. Their frequency and duration: the protests occurred on a daily basis (every evening at 18:00) and lasted until late at night (occasionally after midnight). The most populated protests were those that coincided with general strikes (15, 28 and 29 June 2011), followed by the Sunday protests.

2. Their explicitly non-violent character: for the first time in recent years, there was a consensus among the protesters in the direction of avoiding direct confrontation with the police forces. This element is by no means unrelated to the Marfin incident, noted above.

3. The use of innovative means, at least with regard to the traditional repertoire of Greek movements: laser pointers, choreographies, improvised banners and so on. The most significant innovation, at least for this generation of activists, was the multi-day occupation of Syntagma Square. Whilst the idea of multi-day public space occupations was largely inherited from the December Riots of 2008, camping outside the Parliament 'until the government resigns' was a unique means that had never been invoked.

4. Finally, with regard to the participants' socio-political characteristics, the crowd that attended both the demonstrations and the assemblies was significantly diverse, compared to all mobilizations of the post-dictatorship era. Greece has relatively strong social movement organizations, and it had been quite common in the past to organize protests in which the attendance was monopolized by the 'usual suspects'. Yet, this time, those 'usual suspects' were not particularly welcome (since they were considered as belonging to parties and organizations that were part of the problem, not of the potential solution). Therefore, when present, the party and organizations' members were obliged to refrain from openly referring to their political identity. This characteristic gradually changed in time, as the movement became more and more politicized. During the demonstration peaks, however (for example during the general strikes proclaimed by the Greek Trade Union Confederation on 28–29 June 2011), when maximum mobilization was an explicit goal, all potential participants were welcomed. Furthermore, some complaints were raised against political entities that refused to assist in a 'unity in action' joint protest. According to a 34-year-old anarchist who did not actively participate in the movement, considering it apolitical and reformist,

> ...the craziest contradiction of Syntagma was towards the parties and organizations. They were removing the leftists' banners and posters, but when, for example, the Greek Communist Party [which also did not support the Indignados movement] would hold a demonstration outside the Parliament, they were booing them for not participating enough! (Interviewee GR9)

Stage 3 (September 2011–June 2012): Diffused Contention

The third phase of the anti-austerity movement is characterized by the massive participation of workers' organizations, and by widespread discontent expressed by various social groups, mostly through acts of civil disobedience: refusal to pay newly imposed taxes, verbal and physical attacks against politicians in public spaces, protesting in previously non-politicized settings (such as football stadiums, military and school parades) (Insider 2012; Karatziou 2012; to vima 2011).

In terms of labour mobilization, apart from the usual general strikes (the most important of which took place on 19–20 October 2011 and 12 February 2012), several productive sector unions engaged in multi-day strikes (hospital doctors, lawyers, port workers), whilst the emblematic Chalyvourgia Ellados strike and factory occupation was launched. The steelworkers of Chalyvourgia went on strike and occupied their factory over a nine-month period in order to resist their employer's plan to sack numerous colleagues and impose wage cuts on the remaining workers. The strike (and occupation) ended after the workers were forcefully evicted during a riot police operation.

With respect to the football stadiums, an interesting development was the abandonment of the 'No Politica' dogma (Dunning 2000) by several football teams' organized fans. Anti-government and anti-Troika banners were raised, slogans were shouted and clashes with riot police occasionally erupted. The football fans took active part in the public debate over the rise of the neo-Nazi party Golden Dawn; whilst some teams' fan clubs were infiltrated by extreme-right militants (as is often the case in other European countries), others' responded by adopting an anti-fascist stance and occasionally collaborating with political entities in the anti-fascist self-defence groups that emerged in the aftermath of June 2012 elections.

The two main protest events of this period were the general strikes of 21 October 2011 and 12 February 2012. According to Kousis, some 500,000 people participated in each (Kousis 2013). Both ended in violence, albeit of a different nature: whilst the 2011 one was characterized by physical confrontation between different protesters' groups,[4] the 12 February protest was a full-scale conflict between protesters and the police. For several hours, rioting took place all over the city centre of Athens, ending in severe property destruction, dozens of injuries and arrests.

It is widely perceived that the 12 February demonstration was the last major protest event of the period. A few weeks after the events, the

Papademos technocrat government resigned, opening the path for the June 2012 elections, after which new forms, tactics and strategic goals of the anti-austerity protesters were brought forward. As one interviewee comments:

> The 12th of February was a turning point. We fought with the cops for hours, I hadn't seen such a thing since December 2008. And for what? Another Memorandum had been voted, another time we had been tear-gassed; we had failed. And afterwards the elections came and everyone, instead of pro-testing, put their hopes to SYRIZA. But it was not just SYRIZA, we had also failed. (Interviewee GR10)

Another interviewee agrees that the February 2012 demonstration was an important turning point for the anti-austerity movement: 'the demonstration was crucial to the movement; one may assume that we had witnessed a radicalization of the movement from 2008 to that date; henceforward what we'd witness would only be de-radicalization' (Interviewee GR4).

Stage 4 (June 2012–December 2014): Social Solidarity

In the aftermath of the June 2012 elections, which brought to power the PASOK–ND–DIMAR coalition government, a radical shift in both the collective action repertoires and the organizational frames of the anti-austerity mobilization was noted. The reasons for this transition will be examined inthe the next section Protest Aims, Identity, Collective Frames and Actors.

The few anti-austerity protest events were focused around labour issues (in a sort of continuation of the struggles of the previous period). In 2013, two major productive sector strikes took place: the metro workers' and the high-school teachers'. Both were met with extreme repression on behalf of the State: apart from the 'political recruitment' of strikers,[5] riot police intervened to clear the respective workplaces from strikers and workers standing in solidarity with them. In June 2013, the announcement of the closure of the public TV/Radio broadcaster (ERT) and the sacking of its employees was met with a spontaneous demonstration of some 50,000 people outside the company's headquarters. ERT studios were occupied all over Greece, and the television and radio stations continued broadcasting clandestinely—until, once again, the riot police intervened to re-occupy them.

All of the other anti-austerity activities were undertaken by the so-called 'social solidarity structures' which sprang up all over the country from 2012 and onwards. Their initial purpose was to provide the societal response to the humanitarian impact of the austerity measures. These structures include social hospitals, pharmacies, grocery stores, soup kitchens and electricians' crews (which illegally reconnect the electricity to those who could not afford to pay their bills). All the above operate on a volunteer basis and provide their services and goods to the poorest among the population, migrants and locals included. They present a flexible and direct-democratic, assembly-based structure, which aims to cover the gap left by the receding Greek welfare state.

As Kantzara puts it:

> [...] one could argue that the way solidarity is expressed in Greece goes two directions: it sustains social ties and at the same time it helps changing social relations from bottom up. Solidarity helps citizens survive, while interdependence between and among them becomes more visible in a positive sense and societal cohesion is retained. Solidarity as it is expressed in the last couple of years, not only in Greece, gradually contributes to changing society from bottom up, due to the great variety of activities and organizations involved. (Kantzara 2014, 276)

It is important to note that the volunteers themselves (with the exception of a small radical minority) do not wish to extend their activity beyond what is absolutely necessary; they perceive their actions as an emergency response to an extraordinary situation, that is, the dismantling of the Greek welfare state. The political project on which they all agree (some disagreement being noted, of course, in the procedure to follow and the expected outcome) is the re-establishment of some sort of societal care for the weak, without the latter being offered on a volunteer, charity-like basis. As noted in a March 2015 statement by the Metropolitan Community Clinic at Hellinikon (MKIE), perhaps the biggest organization operating in the field:

> The role of social clinics/pharmacies is unfortunately still important, we hope though that in the next few months it will be diminished and, why not, become extinct. Our permanent demand, which is the establishment of a National Health System which offers decent, free services to all citizens, is still valid and will be valid until realized. (MKIE Press Release, 13 March 2015)

4.3.2   Protest Aims, Identity, Collective Frames and Actors

As expected, the common frame of all the protests and activities that took place in the period under scrutiny was the anti-austerity focus. Indeed, from the very beginning of the mobilization, the explicit goal was to block or abolish (at a later stage) the austerity measures that were (to be) introduced. One interviewee, a young leftist activist, was quite straightforward when asked what kind of grievances launched the protests: 'The decrease in wages and income, the increase in taxes, the loss of jobs, the beginning of house auctions' (Interviewee GR5).

Soon enough, though, the agenda was diversified in order to include broader demands and claims. This diversification perplexed our interviewees. As one interviewee responded, when asked what the protesters were demanding:

> This is difficult to answer, because for example in the 'Indignados' demonstration the main demand was 'direct democracy', but trying to translate that ... to understand what it actually means ... it's inconclusive. For example in Athens, the Syntagma Square was divided in the upper part and the lower part, with different discourses, and different demands. (Interviewee GR4)

Another interviewee confirms the above distinction, adding that: '[...] the demands were sometimes contradictory. In the "upper square" the demands were more nationalistic, whereas in the "lower square" were more anti-authoritarian and in terms of direct democracy' (Interviewee GR3).

In order to disentangle the variety of discourses and claims that were raised, one needs to carefully observe the various periods the mobilization went through and the discursive dynamics that characterized each one. First of all, even during the first period of the protest, the general strikes turned political in the literal sense, as a large number of participants expressed their demand for the government to resign. This can also serve as a potential explanation for the choice of Syntagma Square as the main site of protest during the whole 2010–2012 period (see Sect. 4.3.1.2 for more details). The protesters attempted to overthrow the government by exercising pressure on MPs to vote against the austerity packages.[6] It is important to note, though, that contrary to mobilizations of the previous decades, no efforts were made to secure channels of access to public decisions through collaboration or lobbying. The protests had a very confrontational character and clearly reflected the declining confidence in representative institutions.

Diani and Kousis have conducted an in-depth examination of the anti-austerity movement's claims for the period 2010–2012. They distinguished two types of claims: first, the materialistic ones, closely related with the impoverishment of large parts of the population and the dissolution of a—formerly prosperous—middle class; and second, the political claims directly related with democratization and sovereignty, 'voicing deep worries about the current state of Greek democracy and about threats to national sovereignty (a theme that, incidentally, resonates well across traditional left-right divides)' (Diani and Kousis 2014, 401). The prevalence of democratization claims was such that, according to the authors, 'The only set of claims that one finds consistently linked by strong ties across the three phases of the protest consisted of claims focusing on "democracy", which acted as bridges between claims on "sovereignty" and claims on "austerity measures"' (Diani and Kousis 2014).

An interesting addition to the above is the assumption, made by many, that the squares' movement was self-fulfilling, in the sense that it provided the field for participants to intervene in the political decision-making procedures, get informed and freely debate on the crisis' causes and the consequences it bore on their lives. As one interviewee notes: 'Furthermore, I believe that the Indignados movement was a self-worth event, people went to the protest areas to have some fun or to try to find some meaning in all this, something that was not present in the traditional demonstrations' (Interviewee GR3).

In the post-June 2012 stage of the protest, the aims and goals of the movement became more 'productive', in the sense that instead of raising demands towards authorities, the anti-austerity activists mobilized to provide services and goods to the population. One cannot speak of a clearly prefigurative way of doing politics, in the sense that, as mentioned above, most solidarity structures perceive themselves as temporary, emergency respondents to a harsh socio-economic situation. Yet, it is beyond any doubt that the horizontal, direct-democratic, anti-bureaucratic character of the social solidarity structures is one that the activists would wish to bequeath to the welfare state services of the future.

The extent to which the anti-austerity mobilization managed to achieve its aforementioned goals is a debated issue among movement activists (and scholars). One interviewee sums up the arguments raised by both sides:

For most people the movement failed. For example, the protests of 2011 against the vote on the 'medium-term agreement' failed, as the agreement was voted for. For others, another non-achievement of the 2011 mobilization was that it could not stop the 'delegation' rationale which was the biggest problem and the biggest enemy when we asked for direct democracy. On the plus side, people were radicalized, and with the 'aid' of the prolonged crisis we ended up in the establishment of a Left Government. The fact that we have structures of solidarity which arose from this movement, is an achievement, as well as the fact that people from the traditional left and from the anarchist movement can now sit on the same table and debate. There were small achievements every time, which in the long term built up into something concrete. (Interviewee GR4)

Another interviewee agrees that the rise to government of the left-wing party SYRIZA was related to the anti-austerity mobilization, as well as a positive development: 'The fact that SYRIZA rose from the squares' movement to become the government is a kind of an achievement' (Interviewee GR5). It is noteworthy that the commenter is an ANTARSYA (which stands for Anti-capitalist, Left-wing Collaboration for the Subversion) militant and has never voted or supported SYRIZA, which he considers a rival political force.

A SYRIZA-friendly interviewee confirms the above assumptions, with an important addition: the SYRIZA government by no means compensates for the defeat the movement suffered in terms of its direct claims. One should expect the turbulence to continue, until the deep wounds the crisis left to the Greek society are healed:

On one hand the main demands were not met, for example the non-abolishment of collective bargaining or the wage cuts. On the other hand the fall of the Papandreou administration should be considered as an outcome of the mobilizations, due to its clear de-legitimization. Also the rise in power of SYRIZA would be impossible without the mobilization background. [Yet] I think it will be hard to achieve social harmony, in the sense of post WWII consensus, socially or politically, no matter what happens with the SYRIZA administration and the ongoing negotiations. [with the creditors] (Interviewee GR3)

Main Protest Actors
Perhaps for the first time in the post-dictatorship period, the vast majority of the people who protested against austerity in the years 2010–2014

were not organized in any political or other entity, and were quite reluctant to demonstrate under any collective/party/union's banner. Yet, it would be a fatal mistake to attribute the mobilization to some sort of 'spontaneous impulse' that made the people take to the streets and protest for years in a row. Rather on the contrary, I argue that there was not a single trace of spontaneity in the way the movement developed. The way the mobilization was organized drew from the country's pre-existing social movement 'toolkit' and the international stimuli. The same goes for the action repertoire. This occurred as the organizers of each activity were trained, experienced activists able to invoke the expertise they had amassed from previous mobilizations. As one interviewee notes, practically all Greek social movement organizations' activists and left-wing party militants got involved in the anti-austerity protests of the period under scrutiny:

> I can't identify anyone who wasn't involved. It is a big period and if one didn't participate in a protest, they participated in a latter one. The left, the extra parliamentary left, even the anarchists and this was impressive, to some extent took part in the 'Indignados' protests. The middle class participated in the movement, which was something we weren't used at. In terms of age, we see a huge range, from very young to very old, pensioners. In Syntagma Square we saw together the left and the right, but in terms of inexperienced in protesting, there were in individual level, no unusual political organizations. (Interviewee GR4)

Especially with regard to the activities that required a high degree of commitment (occupy the squares, social solidarity structures), the main organizers included trained activists, as well as newcomers who were eager to learn and commit themselves to the collective project. 'We didn't know how these things work, but, you know, we had to become activists overnight', commented one of our interviewees, who had participated in the collective kitchen of Syntagma Square (Interviewee GR7).

In what follows, we shall examine the contribution of the social movement organizations and other organized entities that participated in the anti-austerity protest.

Among the organizations that contributed to the protest was SYRIZA. Back in 2009, SYRIZA was particularly weak in terms of membership and influence, both with regard to the party itself, as well as its representatives in unions, student organizations and so on. It participated, though, in all the mobilizations. Its youth branch was particularly active, as well as some of its leftist fractions (SYRIZA was a coalition of smaller parties and other political collectives until 2012). Especially with respect to the Syntagma Square occupation, our fieldwork has documented the covert presence of a large number of movement-friendly members and low- and mid-ranking officials. They participated in working groups and held a prominent role in organizing the assemblies. They respected the horizontal nature of the protest, yet it is beyond doubt that some sort of coordination behind the scenes took place.

In the aftermath of 2012 elections, SYRIZA invested heavily in assisting the solidarity structures. Apart from the local initiatives, which the party members and voters were invited to populate, SYRIZA founded an umbrella organization entitled 'Solidarity for all', which undertook the task of coordinating the distribution of goods and services across the country. Although not everyone agrees, there is a general feeling that they managed to handle in a delicate manner the balance between assisting initiatives and occupying them. SYRIZA profited, in electoral terms, from the above, as the party built a wide network of alliances at the grassroots level, something that was missing in the past, as noted. Also present in the protest was ANTARSYA, a marginal extra-parliamentary party, which has a significant presence in grassroots unions and student organizations.

Among the political parties, on the other hand, the KKE (Communist Party of Greece) remained more marginal. Prior to the crisis, KKE's main strength was in trade unions and student organizations. The party managed to mobilize its base on many occasions, yet their main shortcoming was the 'isolationist' policy they applied to their actions, their effort to avoid coordinating with other factions of the movement (the KKE-affiliated organizations traditionally organize separate demonstrations in order to preserve the 'class-based focus' of their mobilizations). The party's organizations paid a heavy toll for the above, being accused of complacency and inactivity. In electoral terms, KKE lost its dominant position in the Greek left by SYRIZA.

Important actors were anarchist and anti-authoritarian organizations (A/A) and activists, a constellation of small groups, squats, social centres, political organizations and unorganized individuals, adopting the most diverse tactical repertoires and ideologies. The A/A can mobilize up to 10,000 people nationwide. Their broader contribution to the Greek social movement is twofold: in organizational terms, they advocate for horizontal, direct-democratic, assembly-based decision-making. In the aftermath of December 2008, this mode of organizing has become prevalent in most mobilizations, whilst the more structured party-like schemes are being rejected. In terms of action repertoire, the A/A generally consider as legitimate the physical confrontation with riot police, as well as property destruction during demonstrations. It is important to note that in Greece, mass political violence (usually in the form of rioting) enjoys much higher social legitimacy than in most other European countries. The Marfin incident in 2010 temporarily reversed this climate of tolerance, but the police interventions during the 'occupy the squares' stage of the mobilization raised the levels of contention to an unprecedented peak. In this setting, the A/A acted as a de facto avant-garde of the more militant part of the movement, given their expertise and refined organization when rioting. After 2012, the A/A invested their resources in two different fields: first, by constructing their own solidarity structures; second, by populating the self-defence squads that confronted the neo-Nazis in the streets of the main Greek cities.

Unions also mobilized in the anti-austerity protest period. In Greece, two complementary trade union confederations are to be found: the GSEE, representing the workers of the private sector; and ADEDY, representing public officials. GSEE, being the only officially recognized private sector workers' confederation in the Greek trade union system, is by default *pluralist* in political terms—that is, its structures are populated by representatives whose political beliefs range from the extra-parliamentary left to the extreme right. The current composition of its Administrative Board[7] is shown in Table 4.2.

The contribution of the Greek trade unions to the anti-austerity movement was mostly through the proclamation of general strikes. The first

Table 4.2   Composition of the GSEE's administrative board

Union factions	Political affiliation	Votes	Seats
PASKE	PASOK (social-democrat)	146	16
DAKE	ND (right-wing)	103	11
DAS-PAME	KKE (communist)	94	10
AP	SYRIZA (radical left)	44	5
EMEIS	None (moderate left)	32	3
Other	Extra-parliamentary radical left	4	0
Total		423	45

Source: GSEE press release (unnumbered), 24 March 2013

such strike was called for 5 May 2010; 11 more would follow in the course of that year. The number exploded in 2011–2012, when more than 30 days of general strikes were called. Overall, 52 days of 24-hour general strikes were called during the period under scrutiny.

The symbolic weight of these strikes was most important in the development of the movement. Research has confirmed that all the major protest events occurred during the strike days (Diani and Kousis 2014; Kousis and Kanellopoulos 2013; Kousis 2012). During these days, tens of thousands (occasionally, hundreds of thousands) of protesters would march in the streets of Athens and the other major Greek cities, clashes with the police and other violent action being a frequent phenomena. The concrete achievements of these impressive mobilizations were minimal; facing an opponent who had mobilized all available resources, based its actions on a very clear political strategy, and was assisted by a strong propaganda mechanism launched by the mainstream media, the unions failed to block any of the proposed measures. As if the above were not enough, trade union officials had to cope with the widespread public accusation that their response was insufficient and/or irrelevant to the occasion. In a 2013 opinion poll, an impressive 95.2 per cent of respondents considered that the unions did 'very few things or nothing' to block the austerity tempest (Lykavitos 2013).

The grassroots unions operating in Greece were more successful in establishing themselves as important players. On the one hand, a horizontal coordination of grassroots unions launched a large union assembly in 2010 in order to issue a separate call from that of the GSEE (and a separate meeting point) for the general strike demonstrations (aformi 2010). The message conveyed to the potential protesters was that one could participate in the anti-austerity protest without identifying with the Confederation—considered as 'government-friendly' and ineffective. The call was soon embraced by many other organizations, including the small left-wing parties, student unions and even NGOs (non-governmental organizations). The outcome was astonishing: whilst the precarious workers' unions gathered tens, occasionally hundreds of thousands of protesters at their meeting point—thus spearheading all the anti-austerity marches—the GSEE never managed to gather more than ten thousand participants in the square they had set as their starting point.

On the other hand, the radical grassroots unions' members soon populated the non-labour-related movement actions, offering their expertise and technical skills to the movement's services. Examples include the audio-visual workers' collective 'Diakoptes', which played a key role in setting up the Syntagma Square media team. Freelance programmers and network technicians from the telecommunications unions provided the internet infrastructure of the occupied square. The Athens 'Waiters and Chefs' Union' was the first to set up a 'strike soup kitchen' in 2010—soon to be followed by dozens of other collectives which provide, today, free meals to the impoverished population.

Democracy: Frames and Concepts

Based on a large corpus of inter-disciplinary research, scholars addressing the issue of social memory construction have produced a significant theoretical work, both in a general sociological perspective (for a brief overview, see Kansteiner 2002; Olick and Robbins 1998; Olick 1999) and from a standpoint more focused on social movements (Armstrong and Crage 2006; Edy 2006; Harris 2006). As Gongaware eloquently put it, the movement's memory construction is a complex process, which 'allows participants to consider new ideas as though they are extensions of what the movement is already doing or has already done' (2011, 41). Yet, as Harris warns, during this process the members 'may actually consciously or unconsciously block out some events of the past while privileging others that are more favorable to their experience' (2006, 20).

The ways in which democratization was conceptualized during the anti-austerity protest movement drew heavily from the mnemonic constructions that were articulated among participants and organizers. In 2013, in a joint project with colleague Vittorio Sergi, we had documented the symbolic weight the Syntagma Square bore for the Greek activists:

> In Greece, the most prominent banner decorating Syntagma Square was quoting the final article of the Greek constitution: 'Observance of the constitution is entrusted to the patriotism of the Greeks who shall have the right and the duty to resist by all possible means against anyone who attempts the violent abolition of the Constitution' (Hellenic Parliament 2008). The reference—or threat—was obviously directed to the government and the MPs overlooking the squat from the Parliament's windows. Yet it had an additional connotation: 'Syntagma' in English means 'Constitution'. The name was given to the square after the 1843 popular revolt against the King, the epicentre of which was the square, and which ended up in the approval of the first Greek Constitution. Thus, even the name of the site chosen for the mobilization was a reminder to participants, by-standers and claimees that

the struggle for democracy (as perceived by protesters) was drawing from the past but also involved the contemporary provisions of the nation-state's founding texts. (Sergi and Vogiatzoglou 2013)

What is more, towards the end of World War II, Syntagma Square had become the theatre of the Greek civil war's prelude. In December 1944, a demonstration organized by the partisans' organization EAM–ELAS was met with live ammunition by the police force, resulting in several deaths and numerous injuries. The partisans' response was the '*Dekemvriana*' revolt—widely acknowledged as the first episode of the 1946–1949 Civil War that followed. The banner held by partisans in this demonstration read: 'When the people are confronted with the danger of tyranny, they have to choose between chains and arms.'

Interestingly, the same slogan was invoked during the anti-austerity protest, by the most diverse actors: anarchists, anti-fascists, but also nationalist left-wingers (such as EPAM) utilized it, occasionally replacing the 'arms' conclusion with the more generic 'resistance'.

The legacies of the anti-dictatorship struggle were present in another recurrent slogan of the anti-austerity protest: 'The Junta did not end in 1973, [what we're asking for is] Bread-Education-Freedom'. 'Bread-Education-Freedom' was the iconic slogan of the Polytechnic Rebellion of 17 November 1973. Having occupied their university for several days, thousands of students—as well as the workers who came to their support—were confronted by the Special Forces and tanks of the Greek army, sent by the dictatorship to disperse them. The military invasion in the Polytechnic School bore a heavy toll: at least 40 dead and 1000 injured. It is impossible to exhaustively describe the tremendous impact the Polytechnic Rebellion has had on the Greek movement ever since. Indicatively, one could highlight the following:

1. The commemoration demonstration, which takes place each year, attracts thousands of people, its content being enriched in accordance with the political context of the period.
2. In spatial terms, the Rebellion confirmed the role of the Exarchia neighbourhood (where the Polytechnic is situated) as the epicentre of movement and radical political activity.
3. The Polytechnic incidents became the main axis of reference for a whole generation of anti-dictatorship activists, who are broadly defined as 'the Polytechnic Generation'.

As one interviewee says:

> The experience of the Polytechnic Rebellion is so strong that we carry it throughout the Metapolitefsi period, the left as well as the anarchists. It's not coincidental that we have the commemoration protest every year, and that the buildings of the Polytechnic School are to be found in the area where the clash with the police takes place most commonly. During the anti-austerity mobilizations we heard the slogan 'Bread-Education-Freedom'— the junta did not end in 1973. (Interviewee GR3)

The slogan 'Bread-Education-Freedom' was always present, at the margins of the Greek movements (especially those related to education), in the years that followed the Metapolitefsi. It became prominent again during the crisis times, as it combined the materialistic element ('bread') with the activists' efforts to respond to what democracy should look like in contemporary times. The way in which the Polytechnic Rebellion memory was reconceptualized, utilized, and further developed by the anti-austerity protesters emerges from the words of one interviewee:

> The way that the memory of Polytechnic Rebellion was used in 2008 and onwards was quite different than the way it was used before. Up until 2008, the annual ceremony was used as a means to learn, remember and simulate what had happened but also to radicalize the 'new entrants' of the movement. Since 2008 there has been a re-appropriation of this memory, we no longer recreate what had happened, but we now live our own 'Polytechnio', the murder of Grigoropoulos. (Interviewee GR4)

In general terms, conceptualizing and framing democracy was one of the main goals of the anti-austerity mobilization, especially during its second stage and afterwards ('occupy the squares', May–September 2011). Whilst the mainstream conceptualization of democracy (dominated by the interpretation given by the main political actors of the Metapolitefsi period) was fiercely rejected, the mobilization participants explored the potentials of direct democratic provisions. They did so in two ways. The first way was through concrete actions, in a sort of prefigurative politics' implementation of direct-democratic decision-making. As one interviewee confirms: 'Direct democracy was the main feature [of the period]. It worked, partially, thanks to the popular assemblies' (Interviewee GR5).

The second way was through a theoretical and conceptual exploration of what could replace the current, considered as failed and/or inadequate system of democratic representation. An interviewee sums up the developments as follows: 'During the Indignados movement the main concept of democracy is identified either with the depreciation of representative democracy (slogans such as "they are all the same", "they are all thieves"), or with more radical ways such as the "lower square" assembly, the demand of direct democracy' (Interviewee GR3).

Despite the fact that the Greeks adopted the 15M organizational frame, they soon rejected both the term '*indignados*' ('*aganaktismenoi*' in Greek) and the slogan 'Real Democracy Now!' as 'too vague, too generic' (Interviewee GR11). They replaced it with 'Direct Democracy Now!' The assembly of Syntagma Square organized many debates and events with constitutionalists, political scientists, philosophers and economists, in an attempt to produce a design for how to introduce direct-democratic provisions in the Greek constitution. The idea that prevailed was that a Constitutional Assembly (in a similar manner to the Icelandic one of 2010–2012) would be required, and the demand was introduced in the assembly's claims agenda.

4.4   Concluding Remarks

The anti-austerity mobilization that took place in Greece between the years 2010–2014 reflected all the characteristics of the post-2008 socio-economic environment. What began as a financial crisis, aggravated by the country's immense public debt and relatively low competitiveness when compared to its neighbours, became a social crisis when Greece's creditors demanded internal devaluation policies—in other words, harsh austerity—to be applied in exchange for a new round of loans. The social crisis then provoked a political one, as it became evident to the population that the citizens were offered no substantial path to express their opinions on the country's future. It is interesting to note that the anti-austerity protesters did not only address their criticism to the Troika's democratically unaccountable decision makers; they considered the crisis of representation as encompassing, first and foremost, their nation-level political system. Despite the fact that the anti-austerity mobilization contributed to the toppling of three different governments from November 2011 to December 2014, the protest did not recede until the country's political party system lay in ruins and new political forces had consolidated their presence in the field.

The way in which the mobilization developed followed in broad terms the Southern European anti-austerity protest pattern: a broad repertoire of action with high mobilizing capacity and attracting massive social support; a strong commitment to empowered deliberative democracy in the movement's street politics; and the combined focus on material and democracy-deepening claims. It also featured, however, some of the long-standing, distinct characteristics of the country's social movement tradition: the general strike as a symbolic resource and a driving force for the protest; relatively high levels of mass political violence; and the intensive use of references to the country's movement memory to construct the mobilization frame.

When the history of the crisis era is written, the anti-austerity mobilization will not pass unnoticed. The rise of the left-wing party SYRIZA in power, the establishment of the social solidarity structures, and the shifts in the country's movement itself, following an extensive self-reflection of movement participants on the successes and inefficiencies of their strategies, leave no doubts with respect to the protest's long-term impact. Yet, to what extent the five-year-long multifaceted mobilization managed (or will manage) to achieve its explicit goals still remains an open question. As these lines are being written, SYRIZA's capitulation to the Troika's demands is producing the first sparks of what might become, in the near future, a new round of anti-austerity action—the major difference being that, this time, there seems to be no left-wing alternative on which the demonstrators can place their hopes and aspirations. Whether this will signify a major push towards the right for Greece's socio-political balance, or whether new, unexpected societal forces will once again emerge to lead the struggle forward, is perhaps the biggest challenge to which the country's activists will have to respond.

4.5   List of Interviewees

GR1, pilot Interview, 1 April 2015, Athens

GR2, active against the dictatorship as a student, a SYRIZA voter ever since, had abandoned movement activity until the crisis arrived, 5 April 2015, Athens

GR3, committed activist since the democratic transition period, journalist for SYRIZA's newspaper AVGI, 2 June 2015, Athens

GR4, anarchist activist, 9 June 2015, Athens

GR5, member of the extreme-left party ANTARSYA, 20 June 2015, Athens

GR6, Syntagma Square Assembly participant (interviewed twice, see GR10), 2012, Athens

GR7, Syntagma Square Assembly participant, 25 June 2015, Athens

GR8, activist/academic (interviewed twice, see GR11), 2012, Athens

GR9, anarchist activist, 2012, Athens

GR10, Syntagma Square Assembly participant (interviewed twice, see GR6), 21 June 2015, Athens

GR11, Activist/Academic (interviewed twice, see GR8), 28 June 2015, Athens

NOTES

1. The President of the Hellenic Republic—a mostly symbolic figure in the Greek political system—is elected indirectly; the electoral system is complicated, but in this specific case, the candidate of the governing coalition would need 180 MP votes out of 300 to get elected.
2. As Kelly and Hamann (2010) affirm, Greece led the scoreboard for general strikes in Western Europe from 1980–2008, with 38 general strikes out of a total of 85 strikes overall.
3. One needs to keep in mind that it was the first time in the post-dictatorship era that a death occurring during a protest was attributed to the protesters themselves.
4. Members of the Communist Party of Greece (KKE) blockaded the streets around the Parliament. Other protestors requested a corridor be made available for non-KKE affiliated groups to participate in the encirclement. The refusal by KKE officials led to scuffles. Hundreds of anarchist activists (who have a long history of physical confrontations with KKE members) attacked the KKE with Molotov cocktails, stones and wooden sticks. The latter counterattacked, together with the riot police, and the demonstration was dissolved amidst a general ruckus. Some 50 people were injured, whilst a KKE member died of a heart attack.
5. The 'political recruitment' is a legislative provision allowing the government to break a strike on grounds of public safety. The provision was cancelled in April 2015 by the SYRIZA government.

6. All of the austerity packages that were voted held a de facto confidence vote status for the government, as party discipline was invoked in order to avoid differentiations.
7. In accordance with the results of the GSEE latest General Congress (March 2013).

REFERENCES

aformi. 2010. Grassroots Unions Coordination: An Interview with Panagiotis Sotiris. Accessed 26 July 2010 http://aformi.wordpress.com/2010/06/17/

alerthess.gr. 2011. MRB Issues New Poll on the "Indignados". Accessed 31 December 2011 http://www.alterthess.gr/node/8839

Armstrong, E.A., and S.M. Crage. 2006. Movements and Memory: The Making of the Stonewall Myth. *American Sociological Review* 71(5): 724–751. doi:10.1177/000312240607100502.

Blavoukos, S., and G. Pagoulatos 2013. On the Greek Trajectory to the Crisis: Not Much of a Riddle, Wrapped in a Mystery, Inside an Enigma! In *Conference of European Studies*, Amsterdam.

Diani, M., and M. Kousis. 2014. The Duality of Claims and Events: The Greek Campaign Against Troika's Memoranda and Austerity, 2010–2012. *Mobilization: An International Quarterly* 19(4): 387–404.

Dunning, E. 2000. Towards a Sociological Understanding of Football Hooliganism as a World Phenomenon. *European Journal on Criminal Policy and Research* 8: 141–162.

Edy, J.A. 2006. *Troubled Pasts: News and the Collective Memory of Social Unrest.* Philadelphia: Temple University Press.

European Commission. 2011. *Eurobarometer 76. Eurobarometer—Public Opinion in the European Union.* Brussels. http://ec.europa.eu/public_opinion/archives/eb/eb76/eb76_first_en.pdf

———. 2013. Eurobarometer 79. Accessed 21 May 2015 http://ec.europa.eu/public_opinion/archives/eb/eb79/eb79_first_en.pdf

———. 2014. *Eurobarometer 81. Eurobarometer—Public Opinion in the European Union2.* Brussels. http://ec.europa.eu/citizenship/pdf/spring_eurobarometer_july_2014.pdf

Gongaware, T. 2011. Keying the Past to the Present: Collective Memories and Continuity in Collective Identity Change. *Social Movement Studies* 10(1): 39–54. doi:10.1080/14742837.2011.545226.

Guillén, A.M., and M. Matsaganis. 2000. Testing the "Social Dumping" Hypothesis in Southern Europe: Welfare Policies in Greece and Spain During the Last 20 Years. *Journal of European Social Policy* 10(2): 120–145.

Harris, F.C. 2006. It Takes a Tragedy to Arouse Them: Collective Memory and Collective Action During the Civil Rights Movement. *Social Movement Studies* 5(1): 19–43. doi:10.1080/14742830600621159.

Hellenic Parliament. 2008. The Greek Constitution. Athens: Hellenic Parliament. http://www.hellenicparliament.gr/UserFiles/f3c70a23-7696-49db-9148-f24dce6a27c8/001-156 aggliko.pdf

Insider. 2012. The Fans of PAO and the Controversial Banner. Accessed 4 June 2012 http://www.theinsider.gr/index.php?option=com_contentandview=articleandid=16157:the-angry-supporters-of-pao-and-the-controversial-banneran dcatid=34:footballandItemid=88

Kanellopoulos, K., and K. Kostopoulos. 2014. The Major Organizations/Groups Behind the Greek Anti-Austerity Campaign. Repertoires of Action and Political Claims. In *ECPR General Conference*, Glasgow.

Kansteiner, W. 2002. Finding Meaning in Memory: A Methodological Critique of Collective Memory Studies. *History and Theory* 41(2): 179–197. doi:10.1111/0018-2656.00198.

Kantzara, V. 2014. Solidarity in Times of Crisis: Emergent Practices and Potential for Paradigmatic Change. Notes from Greece. *Studi Di Sociologia* 3: 261–280.

Karanikolos, M., P. Mladovsky, J. Cylus, S. Thomson, S. Basu, D. Stuckler, J.P. Mackenbach, and M. McKee. 2013. Financial Crisis, Austerity, and Health in Europe. *Lancet* 381(9874): 1323–1331. doi:10.1016/S0140-6736(13)60102-6.

Karatziou, N. 2012. Am I Not Paying or I Cannot Afford to Pay? Accessed 4 June 2012 http://monopressgr.wordpress.com/2012/03/25/%CE%B4%CE%B5 %CE%BD-%CF%80%CE%BB%CE%B7%CF%81%CF%8E%CE%BD%CF%89- %CE%AE-%CE%B4%CE%B5%CE%BD-%CE%AD%CF%87%CF%89- %CF%84%CE%B7%CF%82-%CE%BD%CF%84%CE%AF% CE%BD%CE%B1%CF%82-%CE%BA%CE%B1%CF%81%CE%AC%CF%84/

Kelly, J., and K. Hamann. 2010. General Strikes in Western Europe, 1980–2008. In *European Regional Congress of the International Industrial Relations Association*, Copenhagen. http://faos.ku.dk/pdf/iirakongres2010/track4/28.pdf

Kentikelenis, A., M. Karanikolos, A. Reeves, M. McKee, and D. Stuckler. 2014. Greece's Health Crisis: From Austerity to Denialism. *Lancet* 383(9918): 748–753. doi:10.1016/S0140-6736(13)62291-6.

Kousis, M. 2012. Greek Mega Protests Against Austerity Measures: A Relational Approach. In *XXII World Congress of Political Science*, Madrid.

———. 2013. The Spatial Dimension of the Greek Anti-Austerity Campaign, 2010–2013. In *CES Conference*, Amsterdam.

Kousis, M., and K. Kanellopoulos. 2013. Impacts of the Greek Crisis on Contentious and Conventional Politics, 2010–2012. Proceedings of the 1st Midterm International Conference of the 'Disaster, Conflict and Social Crisis Research Network' of the European Sociological Association.

Kretsos, L. 2014. Youth Policy in Austerity Europe: The Case of Greece. *International Journal of Adolescence and Youth* 19: 35–47. doi:10.1080/0267 3843.2013.862730.

Laoutaris, G. 2011. The Blurry Image of Local Administration. Accessed 14 December 2013 http://laoutaris.wordpress.com/tag/δημοσκόπηση/

Lentzou, I. 2011. MPs are Being Assaulted and Threatened in Every Public Appearance—Public Outrage Gets Worse. Accessed 21 May 2015 http://www.newsit.gr/default.php?pname=Articleandart_id=85235andcatid=9

Lykavitos. 2013. Opinion Poll: What the Greeks are Afraid of. Accessed 14 December 2013 http://lykavitos.gr/archives/77016

Olick, J.K. 1999. Collective Memory: The Two Cultures. *Sociological Theory* 17(3): 333–348. doi:10.1111/0735-2751.00083/abstract.

Olick, J.K., and J. Robbins. 1998. Social Memory Studies: From "Collective Memory" to the Historical Sociology of Mnemonic Practices. *Annual Review of Sociology* 24: 105–140. doi:10.2307/223476.

Petrakis, P. 2012. The Pre-Crisis Growth of the Greek Economy. In *The Greek Economy and the Crisis*. Berlin: Springer.

Pikoulas, Y. 2011. Siege of the Parliament and Extremist Actions. *Ethnos*. Athens. http://www.ethnos.gr/article.asp?catid=22768andsubid=2andpu bid=63108973

Sergi, V., and M. Vogiatzoglou. 2013. Think Globally, Act Locally? Symbolic Memory and Global Repertoires in the Tunisian Uprising and the Greek Anti-Austerity Mobilizations. In *Understanding European Movements: New Social Movements, Global Justice Struggles, Anti-Austerity Protest*, eds. C.F. Fominaya, and L. Cox. London: Routledge.

to vima. 2011. Riots and Cancellation of the Parades All Over the Country. Accessed 4 June 2012 http://www.tovima.gr/society/article/?aid=427388

CHAPTER 5

Late Neoliberalism and Its Indignados: Contention in Austerity Spain

Eduardo Romanos

On 15 May 2011, a call for protest marches in Spain ignited a social movement, the mobilizing capacity, visibility and impact of which had no precedent in the country's recent history. Four years later, some of the Indignados who mobilized against the authorities' response to the financial crisis and the deficits of Spanish democracy have participated in the emergence and development of new political parties that are now ruling some important cities and became an important actor at the national level after elections in December 2015. In the meantime, a strong contentious cycle has taken place in the country. Social movement activists have resorted to a broad repertoire of action, from confrontational tactics to more conventional ones, adopting a horizontal, inclusive, assembly-based organizational model in their groups and networks. Mobilization has caused a change in the domestic field of social movements with the rise of new actors and the strengthening of existing ones. Throughout the cycle, activists have demanded a number of basic citizenship rights that political elites had neglected while prioritizing the interests of powerful economic actors. Activists have also clarified that the crisis was not only of the economy but also of an institutional system that facilitates corruption and impedes the emergence and development of alternatives to neoliberal policies.

In this chapter, I present an overview of this protest cycle, focusing on the socio-economic context, the political opportunities, the forms of action

© The Author(s) 2017
D. della Porta et al., *Late Neoliberalism and its Discontents in the Economic Crisis*, DOI 10.1007/978-3-319-35080-6_5

and organization, and the activists' aims, identities and frames. The data analysed include documents, websites and six semi-structured, face-to-face individual interviews with key informants among contemporary social movement activists. Interviews were conducted in Madrid and Barcelona in the autumn of 2014 and the winter of 2015. Half of the interviewees were men and half were women. The interviews solicited organizational information and the interviewee's interpretation of movement processes and protests. Some basic information on the interviewees and the dates and places of the interviews are listed at the end of the chapter.

5.1   FINANCIAL CRISIS AND CRISIS OF RESPONSIVENESS

The impact of the 'great recession', along with the austerity measures taken by successive governments during the crisis period, has led to a dramatic increase in unemployment, poverty and inequality in Spain. At the height of the crisis (end of 2012 and beginning of 2013), the number of unemployed broke the six million threshold, with an unemployment rate of 27 per cent (57 per cent among the young). Even among those at work, wage devaluation, rising prices, loss of purchasing power, worsening public services and precarious labour conditions have contributed to social exclusion and poverty (Requena and Picazo 2013). The poverty rate reached 22 per cent in 2013, while soup kitchens and food banks supported 1.5 million people in 2012—twice as many as three years earlier (Sahuquillo et al. 2013).[1] Every 15 minutes a family is evicted from their home because they are unable to meet their mortgage payments (Romanos 2014). However, the crisis has not had the same effect on everyone. Its impact has been much more severe for those in the middle and lower tiers of the wage scale. In 2014, Eurostat declared Spain the second most unequal country in the EU, behind Latvia.

In this context, the Spanish population regards political responses as inadequate. Support for both the government and the opposition parties has dropped, especially for the former. Public support for the Spanish Socialist Workers' Party (PSOE), which was in office until November 2011, has suffered dramatically, following the perception that they were unprepared for the situation. The socialist government of José Luis Rodríguez Zapatero first denied the very existence of the crisis, and then implemented moderate countercyclical fiscal stimulus measures against it. In May 2010, the government changed strategy in order to adopt a number of severe and unpopular neoliberal policies, including cuts in the pension system, civil servants' salary, assistance to handicapped people and the state's public investment. Prime Minister Rodríguez Zapatero defined these policies as 'indispensable and fair', while the number of people who thought that the PSOE depends on the support of large economic groups doubled between 2009 and 2011 (Barreiro and Sánchez-Cuenca 2012; see also Lobera and Ferrándiz 2013). The Spanish government adopted these and other austerity measures under pressure from electorally unaccountable institutions. The first significant constitutional reform, expediently passed in August 2011 with the support of the two main parties (PSOE and People's Party—PP), introduced the principle of budget stability in order to combat public debt. This step was taken after the European Central Bank (ECB) insistently demanded that urgent measures be taken towards the recovery of the credibility of Spanish bonds, as recently admitted by Rodríguez Zapatero in his memoirs. In the summer of 2012, the moves of speculators raised the Spanish risk premium to over 600 points.

Distrust of the political parties, which is perceived as one of the country's major problems, has extended to other political institutions at the local, national and supranational levels. In general, the population was dissatisfied with the democratic system in its current form. However, the lack of confidence in the political system has not resulted in a widespread attitude of apathy and political alienation (Orriols and Rico 2014, 77–78). In fact, interest in politics and trust in politicians followed opposite trends: institutional disaffection increased, but the detachment of citizens from politics did not (Adell 2011).

The shock caused by the austerity measures adopted by the centre-left intensified with the cuts and reforms of the new centre-right government from November 2011. In the first three months in office, the new government froze the salaries of civil servants and the minimum wage, limited the spending of all state institutions, announced a 40 per cent cut in public investment and presented a 'very aggressive' labour reform (in the words of Luis de Guindos, the new Minister of Economy) that eased employment protection and limited the scope of collective bargaining (Gómez 2012). Shortly thereafter, the government announced an additional cut of 10,000 million euros in the education and health budgets, which had already been cut by 21 and 14 per cent, respectively.

Since the economic crisis began, a large proportion of the Spanish population has perceived the democratic system as deficient, and these people are demanding a (new) political system in which citizens can become more involved in decision-making processes. According to public opinion, politicians may be better qualified, but they are also less honest than other social groups (Font et al. 2012; Font and Alarcón 2012). Indeed, even more than the economic crisis, the many cases of corruption and the deficits of the democratic system seem to be the main motives for participation in the protest movement that emerged in May 2011, the so-called 'Indignados' or 15M movement (Redes, Movimientos y Tecnopolítica 2014; cf. Likki 2012).[2]

5.2   Indignados at the Gates of the Polity

As with anti-austerity contention in Latin America (Roberts 2014), consensus among the major parties with respect to the neoliberal reforms implemented during the crisis found strong criticism in the streets in the Spanish case.[3] The Indignados sustained a strong critique of these parties and the (bipartisan) party system 'who supported austerity measures and have not taken care of citizen needs in the wake of the crisis, instead using public money to socialize private banking debt' (Flesher Fominaya 2014). The 1978 Constitution embodied a representative government model based on a two-party system, political alternation, a decentralized territorial structure, and an electoral system that favoured the formation of parliamentary majorities and strong and stable governments (Gunther et al. 2004; Laiz 2002). The new institutional design gave precedence to the executive power over the legislative, and imposed severe limitations on direct democracy mechanisms (Jiménez 2007). In fact, 'Policy priorities were mainly defined by the prime minister's inner core [while] weak parliamentarianism inhibited the development of regular and institutionalized links between parties and [organized] civil society, weakening, in the long term, both parties and voluntary associations' (Fernandes 2014, 15). The political elites designed an institutional framework that isolated representatives from the direct social pressure of protest movements in a political context of social effervescence, the atomization of parties, and strong resistance from the right and the army to the moves that were being made to leave Franco's dictatorship behind. The blockages are also related to the sensitivity of the political authorities to the voices of the street. The authorities pay little or no attention to street protests, ignoring the numbers and concerns of protesters. This applies to both conservative and progressive political parties, and the same attitude is projected through mass media (Fishman 2011; Sampedro 1997; Asens 2004).

Two legal initiatives illustrate the sustained distance between institutions and social movements during the recent contentious cycle, each with a different party in office. First is the so-called 'transparency law', the approval of which the socialist government of Rodríguez Zapatero promised to accelerate soon after the beginning of the protests. MPs from other political parties used the occasion to propose that a commission be created to study the demands of the Indignados for the purpose of 'deepening democracy and political participation, in addition to transparency and accountability in democratic institutions'.[4] The majority groups rejected the initiative. Instead, they passed a non-binding motion with a series of recommendations, for example, publishing the assets of politicians, removing compensations for retiring politicians and tightening the system of public incompatibility. Ultimately, the government did not follow through on their promises due, according to them, to the calling of a snap election (Sánchez 2013), which the socialists eventually lost. In December 2013, the new conservative majority in parliament adopted a law of 'transparency, public access to information and good governance', the contents of which still leave Spain below international standards, as the Indignados and other civil society organizations have noted. The second legislative initiative was concerned with Spain's acute housing problems. Since 2011, the activists from the movement against evictions had promoted a Popular Legislation Initiative (PLI) which, among other measures, included the regulation of a system of retrospective payments in kind for distressed mortgage holders, the blocking of evictions and the promotion of social housing initiatives. They collected almost 1.5 million signatures in support of their initiative (the required number is half a million in order to be processed), but the new conservative majority in parliament blocked the PLI and passed a bill that did not include the bulk of the activists' demands (Romanos 2014).

Roberts (2014, 687) shows that in Latin American countries 'where center-left or labor-based populist parties played a major role in the process of structural adjustment ... a sequel of explosive social protest that directly or indirectly toppled presidents, led to partial or complete party system breakdowns, and [in some cases] ushered in the election of an anti-system populist figure or a new movement party of the left'. In Spain, where a centre-left party 'voluntarily' initiated the implementation of neoliberal policies (i.e. under the pressure of supranational European institutions) in the context of financial crisis, the contentious cycle has so far been partially similar. The decline in the protest cycle has coincided with the emergence of new political parties, which are in one way or another related to the 15M (Romanos and Sádaba 2015). The best known of these is Podemos (We Can), which in May 2014, only three months after its foundation, had an unprecedented electoral success: it attracted 1.2 million votes and gained five MPs in the elections for the European Parliament. Essentially, the party leaders seized the opportunity presented by the structural changes resulting from the economic and political crisis and created their own political party. The party reacted to the emotions of the public to transform the wave of indignation connected with the 15M movement into excitement for political change via the electoral process. The success of Podemos in the European elections and the decline of the two main parties (which, in aggregate, attracted for the first time less than 50 per cent of the votes, in what some have framed as the 'crisis of the two-party system') appears to have caused a major upheaval in the political landscape.

Elections affect social movements in many different ways, also by altering the opportunity structure (Heaney 2013). As elections draw nearer, activists show an increasing tendency to resort to the electoral mechanism to channel their demands (Blee and Currier 2006). In this regard, the 15M movement has followed the pattern. The 15M emerged a week before the 2011 local and regional elections. Four years later, many activists have regarded the new electoral cycle (local and regional elections in May 2015, and general elections in December of the same year) as the opening of a window of opportunity that may counterbalance the lack of political response prompted by the previous protest cycle. This comes on top of the effects of the 2014 European elections and their surprising outcome for Podemos, which seems to have affected the activists' perception of the possibilities of accessing political power through institutional channels that are already in place:

> This anti-austerity cycle has demonstrated that massive mobilization is not equivalent to success ... I think that this is now a common idea among those amongst us who have always believed that mobilization is essential. We are in a transitional stage, first, because there is a window of opportunity open, and second because people are beginning to believe: to believe that if we reach certain institutions we shall be able to do something.

Before Ganemos and Podemos appeared, the people working for social movements held thousands of meetings in order to figure out what we could do, along with mobilization, with the institutional tools at our disposal. It is hatching now, but this has always been the idea. Clearly, those are not the candidates of the 15M, or the candidates of the cycle of mobilization, but candidates that can only be understood after four years of mobilization and a situation of institutional blockage. If these levels of mobilization had achieved three or four core targets, the institutional channel would not have been quite so successful. People working in social movements have been left no other option. I cannot think what else we could have done that we haven't already done; what else we could do to get out of a situation of social emergency like the one we are currently going through in this country. (Interviewee SP1)

Despite the fact that law and order are not among the main public concerns (as reflected in public opinion polls) and that the increase in the number of protests has not resulted in violence (the police resorted to force in only 0.08 per cent of the 87,000 protest events staged in the period 2013–2015, according to the data provided by the Ministry of the Interior), in March 2015 the government passed a new internal security law and a new criminal code which human rights organizations have described as 'the most restrictive since Francoism' (No Somos Delito, Dossier de Prensa, March 2015). These norms enact measures that 'have the effect of extending the range of punishable behaviour in the context of demonstrations, increasing the severity of the punishments which can be imposed and reducing the procedural guarantees available to those accused of them' (Amnesty International 2014). Even police trade unions have joined in the criticism, denouncing the vulnerability of both the citizens and the police officers, who lack judicial support and the training to apply the new norms adequately.

5.3 ANTI-AUSTERITY PROTEST IN SPAIN: THE INDIGNADOS AND BEYOND

On 15 May 2011, over 50 protest marches drew together tens of thousands of people from all over Spain.[5] These marches had been convened by the Democracia Real Ya (DRY [meaning Real Democracy Now]) digital platform under the slogan 'We are not goods in the hands of politicians and bankers'. They took place a week before the municipal and regional elections. In Madrid, some of the protesters decided to continue with the march, blocking traffic in the centre of the city with a sit-down protest. After confrontations with police, a situation that led to some arrests, a group of about 40 people remained at the Puerta del Sol in order to, among other reasons, 'support the detainees and continue with the demonstrations'. This meeting soon turned into an assembly 'with the main idea of creating and maintaining a permanent encampment'. Thus *acampadasol* was born, the general form of which replicated the encampment organized in early January by Egyptian protesters in Tahrir Square, Cairo, within the so-called Arab Spring (Patel 2013).

The encampment in Madrid grew around various committees that worked on the maintenance of the camp and the logistics of the assembly process, as well as several working groups concerned with generating discourse for the articulation of the emerging protest movement. In the afternoons, committees and working groups participated in a general assembly that was open to everyone. The support received by the movement grew on the internet and at the square. The #spanishrevolution became a worldwide trending topic on Twitter, while more and more people appeared at the Puerta del Sol. The website tomalaplaza.net gathered information on what was happening in the square and at other locations where protesters had gathered, including those organized by Spanish emigrants abroad. The Provincial Electoral Committee of Madrid banned protests one day before election day, during the so called *jornada de reflexión* [day of reflection], but some 25,000 people challenged this decision at Puerta del Sol in a massive act of civil disobedience (Romanos 2013).

The encampment broke up on 12 June after long internal discussions and strong pressure from the authorities. Up to that day, it was the epicentre of a protest movement, the so-called Indignados (also known as the 15M movement), whose mobilization, which was also related to a wider transnational cycle, was the trigger for an important protest cycle that swept the whole country. The 15M attracted a large number of participants, many of whom had not previously been active in protest. At the same time, the movement was widely regarded with sympathy by broad sectors of the population (Romanos 2013; Sampedro and Lobera 2014). The Indignados have resorted to a broad repertoire of action, from confrontational tactics (e.g. city encampments, building occupations, sit-ins and irruptions) to more conventional ones (marches, petitions and a citizens' referendum), and they have even exercised a certain degree of low-intensity violence (the so-called 'escraches' and some clashes with the police). Mobilization has caused a change in the field of social movements with the rise of new actors (e.g. local assemblies, collective self-management initiatives such as consumer cooperatives and food banks, the so-called 'tides' on labour sectors such as health and education) and the strengthening of existing ones (among others, the Platform of those Affected by Mortgages and the wider movement against evictions). These more specific actors managed to keep high standards of mobilization until mid-2013 (Portos 2016), when a decline in the protest cycle began, coinciding with the emergence of new political parties which are, in one way or another, related to the 15M—such as Partido X, Ganemos, and Podemos (Romanos and Sádaba 2015). At the international level, the 15M has also influenced the emergence of other social movements in other countries such as Occupy Wall Street in the United States (Romanos 2016).

5.3.1   Collective Action Repertoires

Massive assemblies and relatively long encampments in city centres are at the core of actions organized by the Spanish Indignados. The two forms of action are closely related. The first encampment was born in Madrid in an assembly. In turn, the encampments have hosted 'general' assemblies (of the movement at the local level) as well as other more specific ones (of working groups and commissions created in the encampments). Protest encampments are, however, not an innovation but a well-known tactic in Spanish contention. Adell (2011, 9) points to at least 42 encampments in the past 25 years in Madrid in relation to various issues (labour, neighbourhood, global justice and solidarity). The innovation lies in placing these encampments in the centre of the cities, as well as in their (massive) magnitude. Indignados encampments became sort of mini-republics (Elola 2011) organized around different tasks and facilities that largely replicated the 'Tahrir Square model' (Patel 2013; Patel and Bunce 2012).

The assemblies organized by the Indignados in the encampments and elsewhere follow the model of 'empowered deliberative democracy' practised by the anti-globalization movement (see below). Over time, the assemblies moved from the central square of the city to the neighbourhoods, 'expanding a movement that put democracy in a central position' (Interviewee SP4). The so-called Neighbourhood Assemblies reproduced the model of *acampadasol*, forming working groups and committees

(Corsín and Estalella 2011). These assemblies 'varied widely from one neighbourhood to the next, in terms of size, intensity and issues under discussion' (Estalella and Corsín 2013), and little coordination existed between them (García Espín 2012). With decentralization, the number of participants progressively dwindled (Perugorría and Tejerina 2013).

The Indignados also organized massive marches that have been characterized by the deliberate absence of flags and symbols related to political parties, unions or other organizations, thus reproducing a common practice of local autonomous social movements (Flesher Fominaya 2005). In these marches, many activists carry self-made banners, written at home or during the course of the march itself, often with humorous messages (Romanos 2012). The marches have usually been oriented from the periphery to the political centre, local, national and even European. In summer 2011, the so-called Outraged People's March organized in six columns from different points of Spain to Madrid in order to 'strengthen the contacts between assemblies created or expanded as a result of 15M (in neighbourhoods and villages)' and share citizens' problems and demands across the country. Once finished, some participants called for another march to Brussels, in which proposals were collected 'in order to improve the coordination of movement internationally and reach a common frame for action' (Público 2011). Other important protest marches within this same mobilization cycle were the so-called Dignity Marches (Marchas de la Dignidad), which culminated in a massive march on 22 March 2012 in Madrid.[6] On this occasion, the protest ended with 24 people arrested and around 100 wounded during clashes with police.

Over time, workers of particular public services have organized massive sector marches against privatization policies. These marches have been titled as 'tides', with different colours according to different services. 15M activists have been involved in the 'tides', and movement networks have given coverage and support to them. The most significant among these have been the 'green tide' (education) and the 'white tide' (healthcare).[7] The 'green tide' was created in summer 2011, fuelled by various Facebook pages, Twitter accounts and mailing lists, through which teachers began to demand a coordinated response to the budget cuts in education (Sánchez 2013). The most intense conflict took place in Madrid, where the activists, organized in school assemblies, called for a ten-day strike in autumn 2011, with the support of the trade unions. The conflict was rekindled by the new Education Act (LOMCE), which was passed by the government in late 2013. This event caused two more strikes nationwide. The 'white tide' was created in Madrid in 2013 in response to the planned budget cuts in healthcare announced by the regional government (Pastor 2013). It was supported by both professionals from different categories and users of the public healthcare system. Activists organized mass demonstrations and petitions, in five days reaching almost a million signatures against privatization.[8] They have also taken legal action in the courts, whose judgements have blocked the government's plans and caused the resignation of its political responsible (Adell and Olayo 2014).

The 15M movement has also called for frequent mass gatherings, often in seats of government and political parties. These have sometimes turned into impromptu marches ending in the main square of the city. Usually these actions have been reactive to news broadcasts by the media (e.g. in connection with corruption scandals) or events related to the institutional agenda (e.g. the appointment of mayors in the summer of 2011). Mass gatherings have also been organized on the anniversaries of major events for the movement, and to show solidarity with other protests. In these cases, the gatherings have taken place in the iconic centre of the movement, for example, the Puerta del Sol in Madrid and Plaza Catalunya in Barcelona. On occasion, marches and rallies have ended with blocking traffic in the inner city, sometimes in the form of sit-ins leading to impromptu assemblies. Sit-ins have also been used to block home evictions.

Although less frequently, the 15M movement has used other forms of action, both conventional and confrontational. Conventional actions include: petitions on issues ranging from the refusal of government decrees to limiting privileges for political elites or support to activists under arrest; legal actions in defence of detainees and against corrupt politicians and bankers; and the creation of cooperatives and consumer groups. Confrontational actions include: the occupation of buildings to create housing and social centres; sit-ins in banks and government offices; and irruptions in bank branches, which activists accessed by posing as customers and, once inside, organized creative and humorous performances. On 25 September 2012, a coalition of various groups and assemblies organized a gathering under the title 'Surround Parliament', which aimed to dissolve the parliament and begin a constituent process, rescuing the institutions and popular sovereignty from the mandates of the Troika and the financial markets. The activists blamed most political parties for having accepted and cooperated with this enslavement (Aguado i Hernández 2013). This action, however, was not supported by the majority of the

Indignados' assemblies, which regarded it as an attempt to radicalize protests (Pastor 2013). As Spanish legislation prohibits protests in the vicinity of the parliament building (Fishman 2011), the authorities could criminalize the protesters, present the action as illegal in the media and deploy massive police force (Fernández de Mosteyrín 2013). This allowed the police to launch 'a sequence of arbitrary, and in many cases also clearly illegal, actions' (Pisarello and Asens 2012). The use of violence, by protesters as well, marked a turning point in the general support for the movement (Sampedro and Lobera 2014).[9]

While non-violence is one of the pillars of the Indignados (Mir et al. 2013), activists have occasionally participated in violent clashes with the police (after some marches, mass gatherings and blockades) and low-intensity disruptive action against people, such as the so-called 'escraches'. Recalling the old charivari, still used in some regions, these actions consist of the public condemnation of those responsible for an injustice, with the objective of exposing and upsetting them. The word was created in Buenos Aires, where human rights activists used this form of protest against those responsible for crimes during the dictatorship so that their neighbours and workmates would come to know who they really were and what they had done. In Spain, *escraches* targeted politicians who objected to a Popular Legislation Initiative (PLI) supported by the Plataforma de Afectados por la Hipoteca (PAH; Platform of Those Affected by Mortgages). The PAH emerged in 2009 as part of a broader social movement that had been campaigning for access to decent housing since 2003. The period of intense mobilization initiated in May 2011 has facilitated the recruitment of a large number of people into the PAH activities and organizational structure, while the 15M movement has adopted the protests against evictions as its own and used its networks to give visibility to the calls for action over the housing problem (Romanos 2014; Adell 2013; Martínez and García 2011). Citizens wholeheartedly supported these initiatives, especially at the beginning (between 78 and 89 per cent of popular support, according to some opinion polls [Garea 2013]). Over time, *escraches* have become a widespread form of protest held outside the headquarters of banks in order to damage their corporate image. They have also been carried out by other groups negatively affected by austerity policies such as cutbacks in health and education. These people have held *escraches* outside the offices of firms that have benefitted from the privatization plans enacted by various regional governments. In addition to the *escraches* and the aforementioned PLI, the PAH led the campaign 'Stop Desahucios', which, according to the association, has managed to stop 2045 evictions (August 2016). At the same time, the activists have rehoused 2500 people in occupied buildings, in a policy that they brand 'the PAH's social programme'.

The Indignados' repertoire also includes dramatized actions with a strong expressive component. Specific groups have organized these amidst irruptions, marches, rallies and assemblies. Usually such actions are clearly humorous, the activists being aware of the benefits associated with the strategic use of humour in order to, among other things, cool tempers at moments of great stress, cause onlookers to identify with the demands of the movement, lower the costs of activism related to fatigue, communicate possible internal anger and criticism in a less dramatic and conflictual way, strengthen internal cohesion and ridicule opponents (Romanos 2012).

5.3.2   Protest Aims, Identity and Collective Frames

The slogan of the Democracia Real Ya (DRY) protest on 15 May 2011 ('We are not goods in the hands of politicians and bankers') identified a social problem (the commodification of citizens) and those responsible for this problem (political and economic elites, in coalition to defend their own interests), while pointing out a possible solution (more democracy and more participatory). The call for the protest included a number of basic citizenship rights that political elites had neglected while prioritizing the interests of powerful economic actors. These rights are the access to housing, employment, culture, health, education, political participation, free personal development and consumption of goods necessary for a healthy and happy life. The messages of the placards carried by the Indignados in this and subsequent protests largely reproduced this frame while underlining the context of crisis. This was not only an economic crisis but also a political one, of an institutional system that facilitates corruption and impedes the emergence and development of alternatives to neoliberal policies (Adell 2011; Fishman 2011).

Regarding specific demands, the protest campaign organized by DRY asked for 'eliminating the privileges of the political class, the control of banks, the right to housing, unemployment measures, quality public services, a new fiscal system, participatory democracy and reducing military spending' (Toret 2012, 55). The working groups in the encampments expanded these demands. In Barcelona, activists included issues related to the protection of labour rights and the environment (Delclós and Viejo 2012), while in Madrid the discussions revolved around four major topics: the reform of the electoral law, the fight against corruption, effective separation of powers and citizens' control over politicians.

Claims have remained stable over time (Martínez and Domingo 2014; Delclós and Viejo 2012), although certain issues reached greater visibility—for example, the housing problem and the privatization of public services, thanks to the mobilization of PAH and of the 'tides', respectively. 'The PAH's discourse has revolved around the situation of a social group that lives precariously (the "evicted families"), direct appeals to the State (demanding a legal reform that ensures that mortgage loans are regarded as nonrecourse debt and that affordable social houses are made available), the direct intermediation with banks for the solution of specific cases, and a premeditated high media profile' (Martínez and García 2011). This discourse has tried to raise the housing issue from the individual (those who 'lived beyond their means') to the collective sphere (defining the economic crisis as a massive fraud affecting all citizens) (Mangot Sala 2013). For their part, the 'tides' have stood up in defence of the consideration of public services (especially education and healthcare) as universal and free rights, and have also tried to improve the working conditions therein (Cortese and Masa 2013). Protesters wore appropriately coloured t-shirts, caps, pins and banners, thus facilitating identity building while making their actions more visible and their numbers more apparent (Adell 2013).

The construction of easily identifiable actors responsible for particular grievances combined in the activists' mobilizing message with an inclusive 'we', made up of '*personas*' instead of 'activists' or '*militantes*'—terms usually associated with the '*old way of doing politics*', based on ideological or partisan affiliations (Perugorría and Tejerina 2013) and the auto-referential dynamics, organization forms, discourses and identities of traditional social movements (Arribas 2015). Inclusiveness is a fundamental value in the Indignados movement, but it is hardly new in the field of social movements (Mansbridge 1986; della Porta 2005). In Spain, inclusiveness, openness, and loosely structured participation have been relevant in some historical developments of the working-class movement (Romanos 2007; Fishman 1990; Sartorius 1977). However, there are two aspects of inclusiveness which are somewhat new in the Indignados. First, the inclusiveness that they promote is not targeted at those who are already part of the movement—in order to establish mechanisms that will ensure their inclusion in the decision-making process—but rather at potential participants. Here, the square plays an important role. One of the novel aspects of the 15M movement was how it experimented with new models of democracy at the centre of a public space. In this way, the movement brought practices of deliberative democracy—which had previously been confined to more or less limited spaces such as social forums, social movement headquarters, peace encampments and social centres—out into public squares, where passers-by were invited to join in. This seems to be an important difference from the practices of previous movements (Romanos 2013). The change of focus implies a change in movement orientation towards the ordinary people outside the assembly rather than on the activities of those internal to these gatherings (Lawrence 2013). Second, the Indignados movement developed a less rational, more affective sense of inclusiveness—one that is not so much oriented to the decision-making process but rather to the transformation of public spaces into an arena that is also open to empathy. In August 2011, the Indignados reflected upon the basic features of their movement in Spain, one of which was 'INCLUSIVENESS. The power of this movement relies on the fact that we are many and that we are different [...] The spaces that make us strong, that give us joy and make us powerful, are those which allow each one of us to *feel* it as their own.'[10]

Beyond the encampments, inclusiveness has been a feature of all actions and campaigns of the current protest cycle, and it has been assimilated by post-15M political parties such as Podemos, led by political science scholar Pablo Iglesias. As pointed out by Flesher Fominaya (2014), participants in the 15M 'took as a central challenge the need to develop a political language that transcended Spain's deep long lasting political cleavages, and whose activists strategically and ideologically cast themselves as *ordinary people just like you*. This is exactly the line taken by [Pablo] Iglesias and Podemos, populist in the purest sense of the term, and an extremely effective one it is. His campaign letter combines 15-M's *ordinary citizen* discourse with its anti-corruption and democratic regeneration stance.'

In addition, the widespread use of humour has contributed to the creation of a distinctive style that sets it apart from other movements and forms of collective action, also within the left. As already mentioned, participants in the massive marches organized in the recent cycle of protest often carry self-made banners, written at home or during the course of the march itself, often with humorous messages (Romanos 2012). In her research on the anti-globalization movement in the early 2000s in Madrid,

Flesher Fominaya (2007) showed how humour was a key tool by means of which activists integrated new and marginal group members, and at the same time conceptualized direct actions whose intended audience was the general public. Humour also facilitated the creation of a new political identity, distinct from that of the institutional left. However, the same research by Flesher Fominaya also stated that the recognition of humour's potential for subversion in political activism was a relatively new concept in Spanish movement circles in 2007.

The visibility and relevance of humour in the Indignados (Romanos 2012) suggest that this is no longer the case. Innovations in social movements, as in many other areas, are usually the work of new generations. The change in style among Spanish activists, which can be seen at a broader level as part of a transnational change (Shepard 2011), seems to be no exception to this rule, as it was driven by the arrival of a new generation of activists. This new generation has diverse skills, among them knowing how to make strategic use of information and communication tools, which have proved to be useful in the drawing up and dissemination of humorous content.

5.3.3   Protest Actors and Organizational Formats

As previously noted, the protests and marches that took place on 15 May 2011 were organized by Democracia Real Ya (DRY). This protest campaign, which over time has become a social movement organization, has its origin in a small group of young people who at the end of 2010 decided to form a Facebook group, Juventud en Acción (Young People in Action) (Elola 2011). Influenced by the saucepan revolution in Iceland and the Arab Spring, the group's members soon identified a series of problems which they wished to protest about: the distance between formal politics and the people, the stranglehold of the two main parties on the system of representative democracy, and the subjugation of politics to the markets. The group set up a website to organize the protest, to which more established civil society organizations gradually came to offer their support. Other groups, either newer or with a lesser degree of internal structure, also joined the campaign. These more loosely structured actors organized a series of protest campaigns that helped prepare the way for what was to occur on 15 May (Romanos 2013). Thus DRY can be seen as a 'mesomobilization actor' whose protest campaign managed to integrate and, to some degree, coordinate other 'micromobilization actors' who, in turn, managed to motivate and mobilize individuals both inside and outside the micromobilization groups themselves (see Gerhards and Rucht 1992). After the marches, while the encampments were being set up, the activists of DRY were very active on social networks, which had the effect of multiplying their followers: the official Facebook profile of the campaign swelled from 25,000 to 200,000 followers between 10 and 19 May (Piñeiro-Otero and Costa Sánchez 2012). This political use of social media continued for as long as the encampments remained and beyond, during the neighbourhood assemblies, when 'alternative' social networks (Gil 2012), created by the activists themselves, were also experimented with.

Surveys carried out in the early marches, encampments and assemblies (Anduiza et al. 2013; Arellano et al. 2012; Calvo et al. 2011; Likki 2012) show that the activists' average age was about 30, they were well educated and there were roughly equal numbers of men and women. With regard to labour market participation, Anduiza et al. (2013) indicate that 64 per cent of the participants in the demonstration in Madrid on 15 May were in paid employment, while 14 per cent were unemployed and 7 per cent were pensioners. On the basis of these data they hold that the Indignados 'were more likely to be women and unemployed; they were younger and more educated than participants in other [previous] demonstrations [between January 2010 and May 2011] ... It seems that the unemployed felt closer to the 15M demands than to the unions, which may be seen as representing the rights of those that already have a job' (Anduiza et al. 2013, 11).

In Madrid, 66 per cent were graduates or in higher education (Likki 2012).[11] The economic level of the Indignados was also relatively higher than average: 70 per cent of the people interviewed in Madrid considered their financial situation to be good (32 per cent) or so-so (38 per cent); 10 per cent thought they were poor or worse; and 20 per cent felt they were wealthy or financially better off than most people in Spain (Likki 2012). With regard to occupations, Anduiza et al. (2013)[12] indicate that very few manual workers were among the participants in the protest on 15 May 2011 in Madrid. Only 3 per cent of respondents came from the categories of industry, agriculture and construction. Civil servants, health, social services and education workers, as well as other professionals, made up more than two-thirds of the activists (66.3 per cent). When compared to the data for the general population of the Comunidad de Madrid (UGT-Madrid 2011), manual workers are clearly underrepresented in the movement (3 per cent of the activists as compared to 15.8 per cent of the

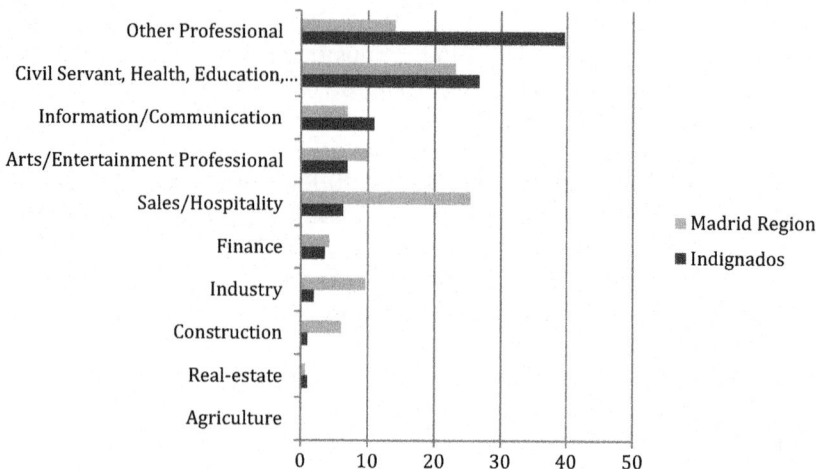

Fig. 5.1 Types of occupations of the Indignados compared with the general population of the Madrid region (percentage)

general population), and the same can be said of those working in retail and hospitality (6.3 per cent of the activists versus 25.4 per cent of the general population), while the liberal professions are clearly overrepresented in the movement (88.7 per cent of activists compared to 58.8 per cent) (Fig. 5.1).

After the encampments had been set up, the protests adopted a horizontal, assembly-based organizational model, which is time-consuming and dependent on the availability of ample human resources. The strong involvement of the activists, therefore, has been crucial for the continuation of campaigns over time. The protests launched against the privatization of healthcare and education have promoted horizontal deliberation processes through debates on social networks, where 'opinions are proffered, and politics are discussed, but where there are no hierarchical differences and nobody has to do what a works council has dictated' (Interviewee SP2). One of the most novel features of these protest actions is the marginal role played by trade unions, with which activists have often maintained a strained relationship (Adell 2013; Sánchez 2013). In the words of a 'white tide' activist, the trade unions had nothing to do with the organization of the protests: 'the movement amply demonstrated the ability and the will to self-organize ... the occupation [of hospitals] was the most visible form of protest ... and that also helped us to set up a radically democratic system ... to organize a series of novel actions that had little to do with the typical corporatism [of healthcare professionals]'. During mobilization, 'trade unions were regarded with scorn ... we preferred to start anew rather than using old systems, and that created some friction between the trade unions and the movement' (Interviewee SP2). The 'tides' also took part in the organization of a protest campaign 'against the financial coup', which grouped together around 350 associations and drew support from social movements in other countries, for example Portugal. Similarly, 'tide' activists have participated in international actions, especially the European march celebrated on 1 June 2013, which was initially organized by the Portuguese group 'Que se lixe a Troika' (Pastor 2013).

The PAH, one of the most prominent organizations during the anti-austerity cycle, forms a network of territorial nodes (223 are currently active) and organizations that operate at the neighbourhood, metropolitan, and national levels (Abellán and Janoschka 2013). Decisions are taken in assemblies, and the direct involvement and tutelage of the victims of mortgage malpractice are actively sought (Colau and Alemany 2012). Their actions enjoy ample popular support, as shown by the 1.5 million signatures collected in endorsement of the PLI. As an activist in 15M and Ganemos observed:

> [The PAH] has brought together very different things, which is something that the other movements or organizations have not achieved: it is a movement of citizens without a well-defined ideological bias; it concerns the 99 per cent, that is, anyone; it tackles a specific and widespread problem; it has managed to advise the victims and turn them into activists; it has brought solutions and improved people's lives by solving their problem; it spelled out the names of the perpetrators behind the housing problem, and it has named the causes, offering solutions and alternatives; it has, in addition, created a real movement, with rules, organization and structure. (Interviewee SP3)

The PAH has united activists with very different profiles, including 'women and immigrants, groups that have been less visible in other movements' (Interviewee SP1). At the same time, the PAH has attained a good capacity to network with other movements, especially neighbourhood associations and 15M assemblies (Colau and Alemany 2012).

The initiative Rodea el Congreso came from an ad hoc federation ('coordinadora') of political, social, and workers' organizations (Fernández de Mosteyrín 2013). These were later joined by some neighbourhood assemblies related to the 15M, which were to play an essential role in terms of organizational resources (Pastor 2012). The campaign operated through the organization of assemblies: 'we met regularly in order to debate, give and receive information and take decisions on actions and proposals; this we did horizontally, without hierarchies. We also interacted with other groups, in the belief that change is possible if we can coordinate action, even if our discourses vary. Our assemblies are open and are publicly announced on our website; anyone can participate; the only caveat is that violence, sexism and racism are not tolerated'.

Finally, the Marchas de la Dignidad were organized by a wide constellation of groups, including organizations and platforms against neoliberalism (e.g. ATTAC), civil rights movements (e.g. 'tides' and PAH), and other agents which are more in line with a classic understanding of the left—for example the Sindicato Andaluz de Trabajadores (SAT), which played an important role in the organization and dissemination of the protest. For some, the SAT is a 'paradigmatic example of trade union renovation' (Roca and Díaz 2013). It often resorts to 'direct action, it interacts with social movements and associations, and it links the specific labour problems of its members with broader issues of social justice' (Hyman 2007). In this way, the SAT presents itself as an 'alternative class trade union; an advocate of direct democracy and open participation, independent and autonomous from political parties and public institutions alike'; it promotes coordination with 'social movements and collective associations, such as squatters ("okupas"), antimilitarist groups, the 15M and immigrants' associations' (Roca and Díaz 2013). In any case, the SAT has a classic organizational structure, with executive cadres and well-defined leadership. They have actively denounced social problems (especially in Andalusia) by staging disruptive actions of civil disobedience, for example 'assaulting' supermarkets and taking food, which was later distributed among families in need. These actions received much media attention. These and other actions are framed within a discourse that decries economic precariousness and unemployment and demands a democracy based on social justice.

5.3.4 Democracy: Frames and Concepts

There was a negative period followed by a positive one, carried forward from the bottom up. The former was characterized by 'we are lacking in democracy', 'there is no democracy' and 'they call it a democracy, but it is not'; we tried to prove, to pass the message that even if they said that Spain was a formal democracy, this was not real. A democracy that only happens once every four years is not a democracy. We wanted more democracy ... we wanted to be heard. This was the initial part of the cycle, and it was very important. Later, for the second part, we said 'if they don't want to be democratic, we shall be more so, and better'. We began trying to find small spaces for democracy and participation. In Madrid, that involved taking the encampment to the neighbourhoods, the neighbourhood assemblies, the working groups, etc. It was a time for experimentation, for basic democracy, horizontality ... Once we realized the limitations of this system, a third stage began. All this that we are building is necessary and good, but if we are unable to democratize the government institutions, there will always be a glass ceiling, a block that will not let us go forward. The decisions that are made from above affect our lives so much, they put us at risk every day, and we cannot change them with micro-politics. Then we have to tackle these institutions, democratize them, change them. Now is the time for the 'yes, we can'. (Interviewee SP3)

This testimony by an activist in 15M and Ganemos divides the recent protest cycle into three phases with regard to the idea of democracy. The first phase corresponds to the preparation stage for the 15 May protest, the setting up of the encampments and the organization of open assemblies in the squares. During this phase, protesters criticized the quality of the democratic system, demanding more and more efficient, political participation and deliberation channels. These demands were also related to the degree of control that the economic structures exercise over political decision making ('there is no democracy if the markets rule over us'). The activists have identified austerity policies with the absence of democracy (and sovereignty). In addition, corruption (the main concern among Spanish citizens, according to the CIS's opinion polls) is regarded as the product of a democratic system whose control mechanisms are weak and of a political system that has encouraged the enrichment of some politicians to the detriment of the living conditions of the majority. Slogans such as 'they don't represent us' or 'they call it a democracy, but it isn't' were used to criticize the democratic model established during the Transition, which is now perceived as a 'low-intensity democracy' (Arribas 2015): a system whereby elites fight to safeguard the privileged position of the main political parties and trade unions while limiting the participation channels of civil society.

Along with the construction of a 'well-founded critique of traditional leadership and representative forms of political action' (Espinoza Pino 2013, 230), 15M groups, committees and assemblies demonstrated, as previously noted, a strong commitment to the empowered deliberative democracy model, 'whose principles are equality, inclusiveness, transparency, a quality communicative process and the transformation of individual preferences for the common good' (della Porta 2005). The implementation of this model corresponded to the second phase of the mentioned process. Those taking part in the 15M open-deliberation spaces felt that they were among equals, that they were members of a shared project: 'An assembly is a space for equality, for people who have the same aims.'[13] During these assemblies, inclusive language was used: one prominent example is the default use of a feminine term to refer to those present ('personas'). Inclusivity ('absolute, of everybody') was essential if the movement was to retain a subjective and diverse character. Transparency was not only demanded of the adversary (the political and economic establishment), but was presented as one of the movement's key features. Actions undertaken and agreements reached by committees and work groups were made available online. The attitude of the Indignados towards the role of 'collective thinking' and 'active listening' during assemblies is, in a way, reflective of the transformation of individual preferences:

> Collective thought directly opposes the current system, which is ruled by individual thought ... Generally, two people with opposing ideas tend to confront each other, defending their point of view ferociously, trying to convince, win or, at the very least, reach a middle ground. The target of collective thinking is to build. That is, two people with different ideas who come together to create something. So, it is neither your idea nor mine. Both ideas are part of a new thing that neither of us knew before. That is why active listening is so important, because we are listening, not preparing our response. Collective thinking is achieved once we understand that all opinions, ours and those of others, are necessary if agreement is to be reached. It is an idea that, once constructed, transforms us indirectly ... [Collective thinking is] something like the result of the synthesis of the individual intellects and ideas; not an eclectic jumble, but a synthesis; individual intelligence at the service of the common good; creation that starts from an understanding of difference as a way to enrich the common idea.[14]

For preferences to change, the deliberation process must be based on good-quality communication (della Porta and Diani 2006). The Indignados used the idea of representative democracy to explain the contrasting nature of consensus-oriented deliberative processes:

> The best arguments are sought in order to adopt those decisions which respond best to different opinions; not between opposing doctrines, like we do when we cast our vote. The process must be peaceful, all opinions must be respected, and prejudices and ideologies must be left at home ... It is important not to gesticulate excessively, not to transmit to the assembly our personal feelings or grudges. When stalemates occur or the temperature rises, a smile is priceless.[15]

The 'assembly stimulation' (*dinamización de asambleas*) committee was responsible for the quality of communication and the principle of deliberative democracy within the movement. The members of the committee were usually part of rotating teams of moderators, and they disseminated several documents (in written and audio-visual formats) that tried 'to help with this new way of doing politics'. These documents specified the roles that needed to be fulfilled for the assemblies to function adequately, for example, moderators and facilitators, but also other things such as the way to arrange the physical setting (from the formation of aisles so participants could move within the assembly, to sound systems and facilities for people with impaired mobility), the way turns should be allocated, and how sign language translation and record keeping would be undertaken. These documents, in short, present the spatial structure, the relationships and the mechanisms involved in the 'assembly decision-making model'.

The incipient institutionalization of the movement in a number of new political parties (Podemos, Ganemos, Partido X) began a third phase in the development of the notion of democracy within the protest cycle. This institutionalization is somewhat surprising, given the activists' poor opinion of traditional political parties and, in general, the current system of political representation. In this regard, one of the results of the 2011 protests appears to have been the emergence of new ways of articulating the relationship between social movements and political parties. In some ways, we are now presented with a movement-party within which the evolution of one form of collective action into another may be observed. The new technologies seem to have played a significant role in this evolution (Romanos and Sádaba 2015). The extensive use of digital tools, which encourage participation and deliberation in the creation and development of these new parties, in some ways reproduces essential values and practices of the movement, thus facilitating the identification between the 15M activists and the parties. The use of these digital tools has been accompanied by the development of a certain technophilic frame that stresses the potential of new technologies for democratic deepening. The frame developed by post-15M parties illustrates a new concept of representation. The classic, delegated political representation is abandoned in favour of a distributed representation model (decentralized networks are used as a vehicle for the representation of the citizens). Deliberative and distributed representation models, which the internet has made possible, are like horizontal, assembly-based schemes in which the process of consultation is permanent—a sort of constant referendum (Gimmler 2001). A technological imaginary, according to which digital networks are regarded as invisible hands working to put together different opinions in a coherent and efficient manner, is therefore essential. We could even say that decentralized digital networks 'simulate' a real democracy; this is, in any case, the opinion of activists, who regard this simulacrum as a political experiment with real value:

> I think that social networks, because they are networks and, therefore, horizontal and accessible, were the space where we could simulate and experiment with this massive participation forum. I think that this lab has been at the basis of many of the proposals that we have drawn up explaining what we want. I think it has been essential (Interviewee SP3).
>
> I think that social networks have made us aware of the fact that politics is something that happens every day. Politics must not be reduced to isolated events. Everyday life is politics, and this political content must be understood, interpreted and denounced (Interviewee SP1).
>
> The idea has spread that trade unions are no longer useful for our struggle. Something different must be done. This is combined with the use of social networks, whose role has been, I think, enormous; Facebook profiles, WhatsApp groups, etc. ... where politics are talked about, where opinions are heard and where nobody holds the floor ... Technological developments have created a favourable environment for opinion, for the idea that nobody's opinion is better than anybody else's. I think that technological developments have been a breakthrough for this longing for democracy and representation. (Interviewee SP2)

It is also true that some of these party-movements have made use, simultaneously, of the figure of charismatic leadership, but always in combination with decentralized assemblies and communication networks such as circles (Podemos), assemblies (Ganemos) and citizen networks (Partido X). That is, all these parties have appealed to ideas of decentralized democratic participation, deliberative networks, public assemblies, connected political forums, participation mechanisms, horizontality and debate devices among peers. This notion has gone so far that the interviewed activists associated social networks with 'new democratic uses' and saw the internet as a fully functional political space (in the same way that a neighbourhood, a city or a territory can be):

> Interaction in a social network, such as Twitter and Facebook, is generating new ways to make democracy, and there is even more to it. The way Reddit is being used may turn it into one of the key agoras for this new democracy. I think that this was a common opinion during the protests: internet is not a tool; it is a neighbourhood, like all other neighbourhoods, but one which can be everybody's, big enough for all and open to the opinions of everyone. (Interviewee SP3)
>
> Then, new technologies are beginning to be used differently; not only are the mainstream resources being used, for example Twitter, but new tools are also being created in order to share, debate and so on ... This is essential in the creation of frameworks of debate. Concerning what I said earlier, that politics happen every day, what we are most interested in talking about is our everyday problems, and understanding that our everyday problems are the result of a series of political decisions that need not have been applied. Policies can change. Social networks are essential for showing what is going on and for presenting alternatives. (Interviewee SP1)
>
> The idea is that these are not democratic devices, but can generate much democracy. It is a multilayered idea: the outcome of the use of opaque devices in which participation does not feature is more participation. Was the Acampadasol Twitter account managed democratically? Not at all. Did it generate democracy? Endlessly. I think this has to do with the generation of a belief in possibilities, in activation, and with the possibility of expanding networks. (Interviewee SP4)

These party-movements, after all, emerged at the moment when the internet came to be perceived as a ubiquitous and efficacious communication system (Kelty 2008). In this regard, social movements have regarded digital networks as spaces that can be appropriated, where action is possible, and where no restrictions or caveats apply (Treré and Barranquero 2013). Indeed, the appropriation and occupation of the digital spaces is a recurrent idea among movement activists, as observed by an activist in 15M and social centres: '[The digital space] has been particularly valuable for our movements, to begin with because we have made it our own natural habitat … the 15M, after all, started there, even if only symbolically the 15M began as a Facebook call … we have managed the social networks so that they are, at least in Spain, a space for movements' (Interviewee SP3).

Some activists have entered the institutions as a result of the 2015 local and regional elections, especially at the local level, where 'popular unity' electoral platforms created on the initiative of social movements (while integrating representatives of political parties, including in several cities Podemos) have won and now govern cities as important as Madrid, Barcelona and Zaragoza. While in the case of Podemos (as SYRIZA in Greece), the party imitates or incorporates organizational aspects of the movements, the local platforms mean the transformation of the very social movements in the form of movement institutionalization (Martín 2015, 113). The links are also visible in terms of leadership: some new mayors have played a leading role in the movement, as in the case of Barcelona, where Ada Colau had been the PAH's spokeswoman for years. Among other measures, the new councils are implementing open government systems based on participatory and deliberative concepts of democracy in which citizens can raise and discuss proposals. These new systems have been designed by or in collaboration with 'tech activists' involved in the anti-austerity protests and previous social movements.

5.4   OTHER MOVEMENTS IN THE CONTENTIOUS CYCLE: WORKERS, WOMEN AND STUDENTS

Since the beginning of the crisis, trade unions have suffered a severe loss of prestige. The Eurobarometer indicates a reduction in trust from 38 to 30 per cent in 2007–2010. Moreover, periodical CIS opinion polls suggest that this drop continued in the following years, down to a score of 4.11 in 2010 (on a scale of 0 to 10, where 0 indicates no trust at all) and 2.45 in 2014. Despite these disappointing figures, trade unions have played an important role in the anti-austerity protest cycle, at least from a quantitative point of view. According to data provided by the Ministry of the Interior, trade unions have organized the most protests during the current protest cycle, relating to firm-specific labour conflicts (redundancies, wage cuts, loss of workers' rights) or to broader issues (including three recent general strikes). The first general strike took place on 29 September 2010, triggered by a new labour policy and the announced reform of the public pension system. The trade unions claimed that Spain had relinquished its sovereignty, as these measures were adopted at the instigation of the Troika (European Commission, ECB, and International Monetary Fund), and criticized the fact that the consequences of the economic crisis were being suffered mainly by workers and pensioners. A total of 70 per cent of workers went on strike, and the associated protest march in Madrid was attended by half a million people, according to the trade unions. On 29 March 2012, the trade unions organized another general strike, using the same arguments. On 14 November 2012, Spanish trade unions tried to raise the stakes by organizing a general strike at the European level; Portuguese (CGTP-IN) and Italian (CGIL) trade unions, and also French and Greek workers, followed suit.

The 15M's criticism of the political system includes, albeit indirectly, the major trade unions (Calle and Candón 2013; Espinoza Pino 2013; see also Ripa et al. 2013). While the main trade unions have progressively come to support the initiatives put forward by the Indignados, 15M groups, committees and assemblies have tended to cooperate more closely with alternative trade unions, especially those associated with the anarchism movement, which has increased the strength and visibility of these trade unions (Ripa et al. 2013). The Indignados have also taken part in the general strikes, some of them 'taking' (that is, conquering) it in order to drive a process of inner democratization 'from below'. This can be seen as an extension of the tactic of 'taking the square'. The Indignados published a manifesto calling for 'taking the strike to invent new ways to strike'. They created a 'repository of virtual and physical forms to be joining the [29 March strike] and overflowing this with imagination, our organizational skills and our networks'. They say 'Let's make a strike which anyone could live as her/his own; an inclusive and open strike'.[16] Occasionally, the disagreements between the Indignados and the main trade unions (CCOO and UGT) have been obvious, for example, when the former declined to join the Cumbre Social (Social Summit), a CCOO- and UGT-promoted platform against austerity. The Indignados criticized the initiative because of 'the clear lack of real contents, and the apparent attempt to mollify the social discontent ... the "social model of the last 35 years" cannot be defended, like the trade unions have done in the Social Summit's initial public statement, because those four decades have allowed for the progressive emergence of the neo-liberal model'.

Feminists have criticized some expressions of structural violence within the 15M in the form of 'lack of representation in committees and assemblies, patronising behaviour (when setting out their arguments) and sexist stereotyping, mainly having to do with women's demands being considered not universal' (Gámez 2015, 2). They have even denounced cases of sexist violence in the encampments. Despite these problems, feminist activists have seen the 15M as an opportunity to stress the relationship between patriarchy and capitalism. 'Indeed, women have transformed the 15M spaces by connecting the political struggle to the materiality of their bodies and to the everyday strategies of care they have deployed. Thus, they argue that through their unpaid everyday work they counter the effects of capitalist cuts in health, education and social services. But they have also provided, along with other fellow encampment activists, care and support to families in precarious situations, such as prior to evictions' (Gámez 2015, 4–5). The feminist movement has also participated in the organization of the 'violet tide', which denounces the impact of budget cuts on women, with the endorsement of the 15M assemblies, trade unions and equality secretariats from left-wing parties. In opposition to the government's plans to impose a more restrictive regulation on abortion and the general restriction of women's rights, the feminists organized a protest campaign which included the so-called 'Liberty train', a massive protest march held in Madrid on 1 February 2014 gathering women from all parts of Spain alongside trade unions and left-wing parties. The government finally withdrew the proposed legislation, bringing about the resignation of the project's main advocate, the Minister of Justice. A restricted version of the bill, which focuses on making it harder for minors to have an abortion without their parents' permission, was passed in April 2015.

Within the student movement, Juventud Sin Futuro (JSF) was a key organization in the mobilizations that preceded the emergence of the 15M (Romanos 2013). JSF is a platform that unites several student associations in Madrid. The platform emerged in the aftermath of the mobilization cycle against the so-called Bologna Process (Fernández 2014). JSF's discourse sought to represent young people as subjects with a full set of rights confronted with a series of material problems, such as access to housing and labour precariousness. These problems have resulted in the mass emigration of young Spaniards in search of jobs, as stressed by a public campaign whose main slogan was 'we're not leaving, they are kicking us out'. The slogan of JSF's protest march, one month before the emergence of 15M was 'without a home, without a job, without pension, without fear'. JSF has carried out disruptive protests and acts of civil disobedience, such as 'reclaiming the streets' (for instance after the 15 May protest march) or the symbolic use of actions borrowed from other countries, such as the 'book block', imported from Italy (Fernández 2014).[17] Within this protest cycle, the student movement has organized other campaigns—for example, 'Toma la Facultad' (Take the Faculty), which criticized budget cuts in education and the use of the public debt as a financial instrument to attack public services (in this case, the university), as well as 'La Universidad en la calle' (University on the streets), which used public spaces, especially in Madrid and Barcelona, to increase the visibility of their demands. The activists created the Platform of Victims of University Tuition Fees (Plataforma de Afectados por las Tasas) as a space of solidarity and support for those students who cannot pay these fees. This platform performs actions of civil disobedience in order to force academic institutions to negotiate the cases of students at risk of having to discontinue their university education (Fernández 2013).

5.5   Conclusions

In Spain, the consequences of the Great Recession have been aggravated by neoliberal policies adopted by both centre-left and centre-right governments under pressure from electorally unaccountable institutions such as the ECB or the moves of speculators. The authorities' behaviour has eroded citizens' trust in political institutions (at the local, national and supranational levels) by making visible the democratic deficit of a political system that limits the participation channels of the civil society while encouraging the enrichment of the elite, to the detriment of the living conditions of the majority. These strains are the basis of the indignation that was mobilized first in the streets, and then inside the parliaments. Thousands of people have participated in a protest movement that has sought to shift responsibility for the crisis from the individual to the collective sphere; from the unemployed, the pensioner, the evicted, the 'youth with no future' and other precarious persons to the political and economic elites. This movement has demanded that authorities reverse the cuts in public services and civil rights, strengthen mechanisms of control and transparency, and create new channels of citizens' access to decision making. However, authorities have shown little receptiveness to them. This unresponsiveness has been facilitated by the institutional framework designed during the transition to democracy in the late 1970s, which tends to isolate representatives from the direct pressure of social protest movements. In fact, the most direct response has been negative in the form of new, more repressive laws that extend the range of punishable behaviour in the context of protests. In this environment, some activists have created new political parties that are trying to enter the institutions in order to reverse neoliberal policies and change the political system from within.

Throughout the anti-austerity cycle, activists have organized a broad range of actions—more conventional, more confrontational—with high mobilizing capacity and attracting massive social support. Mobilization has caused a change in the field of social movements with the rise of new actors (e.g. local assemblies, collective self-management initiatives, the so-called 'tides' on labour sectors such as health and education) and the strengthening of existing ones (among others, the Platform of those Affected by Mortgages and the wider movement against evictions). In their protests and networks, the Indignados opposed the logic of the system with an alternative one based on the model of empowered deliberative democracy, which they updated with a relatively novel concept of organizational inclusiveness directed at potential participants and the transformation of public spaces into open, empathic arenas. They brought practices of deliberative democracy out into public squares, where passers-by were invited to join in. This implies a change in movement orientation towards the ordinary people outside the gatherings rather than on the activities of those internal to these. The Indignados strove to build a movement of 'anyone' based on an extremely inclusive 'we' that aimed to go beyond ideological or partisan affiliations and the auto-referential dynamics, organizational forms, discourses and identities of traditional social movements.

5.6   LIST OF INTERVIEWEES

Contemporary anti-austerity activists:

SP1, activist in student and 15M movements, and member of Podemos, Madrid, 19 October 2014

SP2, activist in "white tide", Madrid, 3 November 2014

SP3, activist in global justice and 15M movements, Madrid, 5 November 2014

SP4, activist in global justice and 15M movements, and member of Ganemos, Madrid, 26 November 2014

SP5, activist in global justice, free culture and 15M movements, Madrid, 9 December 2014

SP6, activist in PAH, Barcelona, 16 March 2015

NOTES

1. Unemployment and poverty rates provided by the Spanish Statistical Office in the Economically Active Population Survey (2013, Q1) and Living Conditions Survey (2014, with data from 2013), respectively (www.ine.es).
2. Two years after the emergence of this movement, the problems that caused it were still in place: 63 per cent believed that political corruption had increased, 54 per cent claimed that corruption was a worse problem than in other countries, and up to 95 per cent distrusted the motivations of political parties and the efficiency of the court system to tackle the problem (Metroscopia 2013).
3. Indeed, 'PPSOE' and 'PSOE, PP, la misma mierda es' [PSOE, PP, they are the same shit] were among the most popular slogans in the anti-austerity protests (Basteiro 2013).
4. Press note, 21 June 2011 (available at www.congreso.es).
5. The number of participants varied according to the source: 20,000 (according to the police), 80,000 (according to *El País*), or 130,000 (according to the organizers).
6. The organizers claim that 1.5 million people attended the march; authorities claim only 50,000.
7. Other 'tides' include mobilization of social workers ('orange tide'), feminists ('violet tide'), and Spanish migrants abroad ('deep red tide').
8. An open poll was celebrated between 5 and 10 May 2013, with the participation of 950,000 people—94 per cent of whom voted in favour of a public and universal healthcare system (Pastor 2013).
9. Until then, the *indignados* received broad, cross-sectorial support among the general population in Spain, affecting people of differ-

ent ages, genders, employment situations and levels of urbanization. Three-quarters of the people supported the *indignados'* main demands, while one-half supported their strategy (Sampedro and Lobera 2014).

10. http://madrid.tomalaplaza.net/2011/08/12/. Capitals in the original; my italics.
11. Similar data shows that Occupy Wall Street activists were better educated than average (Milkman et al. 2013).
12. I am grateful to Camilo Cristancho for sending me the data in advance and to the team members of the 'Caught in the Act of Protest: Contextualising Contestation' project (http://www.protestsurvey.eu) for their permission to use it here. Data is now available in DANS (http://dans.knaw.nl/). The data refers to activists with paid work, the unemployed, and pensioners. In the case of the last two categories, the last job held is referred to.
13. http://madrid.tomalaplaza.net/2011/05/31/
14. *Guía rápida para la dinamización de asambleas populares* (31 May 2011, available at http://madrid.tomalaplaza.net).
15. Ibid.
16. http://www.madrilonia.org/2012/03/comunicado-de-toma-la-huelga/
17. The 'book block' is a tactic used by university protesters 'who fabricate shields made in the form of books, symbolizing the idea of books (critical thinking) as weapons' (Flesher Fominaya 2014, 168).

REFERENCES

Abellán, J., and M. Janoschka. 2013. Dos años de movimiento por la vivienda en Madrid (2011–2013): Desobediencia, rupturas y luchas en el contexto de la crisis urbana. *Paper presented at XI Congreso FES*, July, Madrid.

Adell, R. 2013. Re-movilización social en contexto de crisis. *Paper presented at XI Congreso FES*, July, Madrid.

———. 2011. La movilización de los indignados del 15-M. Aportaciones desde la sociología de la protesta. *Sociedad y Utopía* 38: 141–170.

Adell, R., and A. Olayo. 2014. De la indignación a la dignidad. Balance de la protesta 2013. In *Anuario del Conflicto Social 2013*, (de) S. Aguilar, 190–223. Barcelona: UAB.

Aguado i Hernández, J. A. 2013. Los repertorios de herramientas de los movimientos sociales como *jiu-jitsu* político: El caso del 15-M y otras movilizaciones. *Paper presented at XI Congreso FES*, July, Madrid.

Amnesty International. 2014. Spain: The Right to Protest Under Threat. Accessed 9 June 2014 http://www.amnesty.org/en/library/info/EUR41/001/2014/en

Anduiza, E., C. Cristancho, and J.M. Sabucedo. 2013. Mobilization Through Online Social Networks: The Political Protest of the Indignados in Spain. *Information, Communication and Society* (online).

Arellano, J., I. Basterretxea, and C. de la Cruz. 2012. *Estudio de dinámicas sociales en torno a las movilizaciones del 15-M en Bilbao.* Vitoria: Gobierno Vasco.

Arribas, A. 2015. Recordar el 15 M para reimaginar el presente: Los movimientos sociales más allá del ciclo electoral de 2015. *Interface* 7(1): 150–164.

Asens, J. 2004. La Presión al Movimiento de las Okupaciones: Del Apartato Policial a los Mass Media. In *Dónde Están las Llamas: El Movimiento Okupa: Prácticas y Contextos Sociales,* eds. R. Adell and M. Martínez, 293–338. Madrid: Los Libros de la Catarata.

Barreiro, B., and I. Sánchez-Cuenca. 2012. In the Whirlwind of the Economic Crisis: Local and Regional Elections in Spain, May 2011. *South European Society and Politics* 17(2): 281–294.

Basteiro, D. 2013. García-Page: "Tenemos que acabar con el lema del 15-; 'PSOE y PP, la misma mierda es". *El Huffington Post,* 7 November.

Blee, K., and A. Currier. 2006. How Local Social Movement Groups Handle a Presidential Election. *Qualitative Sociology* 29(3): 261–280.

Calle, Á., and J. Candón. 2013. Sindicalismo y 15 M. In *La democracia del futuro: Del 15-M a la emergencia de una sociedad civil viva,* eds. M. Cruells and P. Ibarra, 151–186. Barcelona: Icaria.

Calvo, K., T. Gómez-Pastrana, and L. Mena. 2011. Movimiento 15 M: Quiénes son y qué reivindican? *ZoomPolítico* 4: 4–17.

Colau, A., and A. Alemany. 2012. *Vidas hipotecadas. De la burbuja inmobiliaria al derecho a la vivienda.* Barcelona: Cuadrilátero de Libros.

Corsín Jiménez, A., and A. Estalella. 2011. #spanishrevolution. *Anthropology Today* 27(4): 19–23.

Cortese, F., and O. Masa. 2013. La Marea Verde o la salida democrática a la doble crisis de la educación. *El Viejo Topo,* 306-7, 61–65.

Delclós, C., and R. Viejo. 2012. Beyond the Indignation: Spain's Indignados and the Political Agenda. *Policy and Practice* 15. Accessed 23 May 2014 http://www.developmenteducationreview.com/issue15-perspectives4?page=show

della Porta, D. 2005. Making the Polis: Social Forums and Democracy in the Global Justice Movement. *Mobilization* 10(1): 73–94.

della Porta, D., and M. Diani. 2006. *Social Movements: An Introduction.* Malden: Blackwell.

Elola, J. 2011. El 15-M sacude el sistema. *El País,* 22 May.

Espinoza Pino, M. 2013. Politics of Indignation: Radical Democracy and Class Struggle Beyond Postmodernity. *Rethinking Marxism* 25(2): 228–241.

Estalella, A., and A. Corsín Jiménez. 2013. Asambleas populares: El ritmo urbano de una política de la experimentación. In *La democracia del futuro: Del 15-M a la emergencia de una sociedad civil viva*, eds. P. Ibarra and M. Cruells, 61–80. Barcelona: Icaria.

Fernandes, T. 2014. Rethinking Pathways to Democracy: Civil Society in Portugal and Spain, 1960s–2000s. *Democratization* 37: 1–31.

Fernández de Mosteyrín, L. 2013. Rodea el Congreso: Un caso para explorar las bases del Estado securitario. In *Anuario del Conflicto Social 2012*, ed. S. Aguilar, 1129–1152. UAB: Barcelona.

Fernández, J. 2013. The Student Movement in Barcelona: A Renovated Movement Against Austerity Measures? *Paper presented at the ESA 11th Conference*, Turin.

———. 2014. *Los movimientos estudiantiles desde las teorías de acción colectiva: El caso del movimiento anti-Bolonia en el Estado Español*. Tesis doctoral. Bilbao: Servicio de Publicaciones UPV-EHU.

Fishman, R.M. 1990. *Working-Class Organization and the Return to Democracy in Spain*. Ithaca, NY: Cornell University Press.

———. 2011. Democratic Practice After the Revolution: The Case of Portugal and Beyond. *Politics and Society* 39(2): 233–267.

Flesher Fominaya, C. 2005. *The Logic of Autonomy*. Berkeley: University of California.

———. 2007. Autonomous Movements and the Institutional Left: Two Approaches in Tension in Madrid's Anti-globalization Network. *South European Society and Politics* 12(3): 335–358.

———. 2014. *Social Movements and Globalization: How Protests, Occupations and Uprisings are Changing the World*. New York: Palgrave Macmillan.

Font, J., and P. Alarcón. 2012. Cómo queremos que se tomen las decisiones políticas. *Zoom Político* 2.

Font, J., J. Clemente, M. Wojcieszak, and P. Alarcón. 2012. *Democracia sigilosa' en España? Preferencias de la ciudadanía española sobre las formas de decisión política y sus factores explicativos*. Madrid: CIS.

Gámez Fuentes, M.J. 2015. Feminisms and the 15 M Movement in Spain: Between Frames of Recognition and Contexts of Action. *Social Movement Studies: Journal of Social, Cultural and Political Protest*. doi:10.1080/147428 37.2014.994492.

García Espín, P. 2012. De vuelta al barrio como espacio de lo político? *Revista Internacional de Pensamiento Político* 7: 291.

Garea, F. 2013. El 15-M mantiene la simpatía ciudadana dos años después. *El País*, 18 May.

Gerhards, J., and D. Rucht. 1992. Mesomobilization: Organizing and Framing in Two Protest Campaigns in West Germany. *American Journal of Sociology* 98: 555–596.

Gil, J. 2012. Las redes sociales como infraestructura de la acción colectiva: Análisis comparativo entre Facebook y N-1 a través del 15 M. *Sistema* 128(10): 65–80.

Gimmler, A. 2001. Deliberative Democracy, the Public Sphere and the Internet. *Philosophy and Social Criticism* 27(4): 21–39.

Gómez, M.V. 2012. Guindos: La reforma laboral va a ser extremadamente agresiva. *El País*, 10 February.

Gunther, R., J.R. Montero, and J. Botella. 2004. *Democracy in Modern Spain*. New Haven, CT: Yale University Press.

Heaney, M.T. 2013. Elections and Social Movements. In *The Wiley-Blackwell Encyclopedia of Social and Political Movements*, eds. D. A. Snow, D. della Porta, B. Klandermans, and D. McAdam. Chichester; Malden: Wiley-Blackwell.

Hyman, R. 2007. How Can Trade Unions Act Strategically? *Transfer* 13(2): 193–210.

Jiménez, M. 2007. Mobilizations Against the Iraq War in Spain: Background, Participants and Electoral Implications. *South European Society and Politics* 12(3): 399–420.

Kelty, C. 2008. *Two Bits: The Cultural Significance of Free Software and the Internet*. Durham: Duke University Press.

Laiz Castro, C. 2002. Las elecciones y los sistemas electorales. In *Sistema Político Español*, P. Román. Madrid: McGraw-Hill.

Lawrence, J. 2013. The International Roots of the 99 % and the "politics of any-one". *IC—Revista Científica de Información y Comunicación* 10: 1–19.

Likki, T. 2012. 15 M Revisited: A Diverse Movement United for Change. *ZoomPolitico* 11: 1–16.

Lobera, J., and J.P. Ferrándiz. 2013. El peso de la desconfianza política en la dinámica electoral en España. In *Partidos, medios y electores en procesos de cambio. Las Elecciones Generales española de 2011*, eds. I. Crespo et al., 41–65. Tirant lo Blanch: Valencia.

Mangot Sala, Ll. 2013. La Plataforma de Afectados por la Hipoteca. De la Crisis a la Estafa. Del Prozac al Empoderamiento'. *Clivatge* n° 2, 56–88.

Mansbridge, J.J. 1986. *Why We Lost the ERA*. Chicago: University of Chicago Press.

Martín, I. 2015. Podemos y otros modelos de partido-movimiento. *Revista Española de Sociología* 24: 107–114.

Martínez, M., and A. García. 2011. *Ocupar Las Plazas, Liberar Los Espacios*. Unpublished Paper. Accessed 10 January 2012 http://www.miguelangel-martinez.net/?Ocupar-las-plazas-liberar-los

Martínez, M.A., and E. Domingo. 2014. *Social and Political Impacts of the 15 M Movement in Spain*. Unpublished Paper. Accessed 9 June 2014 http://www.miguelangelmartinez.net/IMG/pdf/M15_impacts_v3_0_April_2014.pdf

Metroscopia. 2013. Clima social de España (43ᵃ oleada), 11 January.

Milkman, R., S. Luce, and P. Lewis. 2013. Changing the Subject: A Bottom-up Account of Occupy Wall Street in New York City, CUNY.

Mir, J., J. Franca, C. Macías, and P. Veciana. 2013. Fundamentos de la Plataforma de Afetcados por la Hipoteca: Activismo, asesoramiento colectivo y desobediencia civil no violenta. *Educación Social: Revista de Intervención socioeducativa* 55: 52–61.

Orriols, Ll, and G. Rico. 2014. El clima de opinión. In *Elecciones generales 2011*, eds. E. Anduiza, A. Agustí Bosch, Ll. Orriols, and G. Rico, 63–82. Madrid: CIS.

Pastor, J. 2012. El Movimiento 15-M en Madrid, 2012. In *Anuario del Conflicto Social 2012*, de. S. Aguilar, 205–214. Barcelona: UAB.

———. 2013. El 15-M, las Mareas y su relación con la política sistémica. El caso de Madrid. *Paper Presented at the XI Congreso AECPA*.

Patel, D.S. 2013. *Roundabouts and Revolutions: Public Squares, Coordination, and the Diffusion of the Arab Uprisings*. Unpublished Paper.

Patel, D.S., and V.J. Bunce. 2012. Turning Points and The Cross-National Diffusion of Popular Protest. *APSA Comparative Democratization Newsletter* 10(1): 10–13.

Perugorría, I., and B. Tejerina. 2013. Politics of the Encounter. Cognition, Emotion and Networks in the Spanish 15-M. *Current Sociology* 61(4): 424–442.

Piñeiro-Otero, T., and C. Costa Sánchez. 2012. Ciberactivismo y redes sociales. El uso de facebook por uno de los colectivos impulsores de la "spanish revolution", Democracia Real Ya (DRY). *Observatorio Journal* 6(3): 89–104.

Pisarello, G., and J. Asens. 2012. Golpismo y democracia, Caffè Reggio, 2 October. http://www.caffereggio.net/2012/10/02/golpismo-y-democracia-de-gerardo-pisarello-y-jaume-asens-en-publico/

Portos, M. 2016. Taking to the Streets in the Context of Austerity: A Chronology of the Cycle of Protests in Spain, 2007–2015, *Partecipazione and Conflitto* 9(1): 181–210.

Público. 2011. La marcha a Bruselas del 15-M concluye mañana, 7 November http://www.publico.es/espana/marcha-bruselas-del-15-m.html

Redes, Movimientos y Tecnopolítica. 2014. *#Encuesta15M2014* [Fichero de datos]. Barcelona: IN3, Universitat Oberta de Catalunya. http://civilsc.net/encuesta1m2014_datos

Requena, A., and B. Picazo. 2013. La pobreza laboral aumenta en España. *eldiario. es*, 2 April, http://www.eldiario.es/economia/pobreza-laboral-aumenta-Espana_0_115488999.html

Ripa, D., J. Rodríguez, and A. Fuente. 2013. Sindicalismo, crisis económica y movimientos sociales: Identidades, debilidades y fortalezas del sindicalismo y escenarios futuros. Paper presented at the Congress Políticas sociales entre crisis y post-crisis. Universidad de Alcalá, 6–7 June.

Roberts, K. 2014 Populism and Social Movements. In *Oxford Handbook on Social Movements*, eds. D. della Porta and M. Diani. Oxford: Oxford University Press.

Roca, B., and I. Díaz. 2013. De la tierra a los supermercados: El SAT como ejemplo de particularismo militante y de renovación sindical. In *Anuario del Conflicto Social 2012*, (de) S. Aguilar, 855–876. Barcelona: UAB.

Romanos, E. 2007. *Ideología libertaria y movilización clandestina. El anarquismo español durante el franquismo (1939–1975)*. PhD dissertation, European University Institute.

———. 2012. The Strategic use of Humor in the Spanish 15 M Movement. *Paper Presented at The Politics and Protest Workshop, CUNY*, NYC, 4 October.

———. 2013. Collective Learning Processes Within Social Movements: Some Insights into the Spanish 15-M/Indignados Movement. In *Understanding European Movements: New Social Movements, Global Justice Struggles, Anti-Austerity Protest*, eds. C. Flesher Fominaya, and L. Cox, 203–219. London: Routledge.

———. 2014. Evictions, Petitions and *Escraches*: Contentious Housing in Austerity Spain. *Social Movement Studies* 13(2): 296–302.

———. 2016. Immigrants As Brokers: Dialogical Diffusion from Spanish *Indignados* to Occupy Wall Street. *Social Movement Studies* 15(3): 247–262.

Romanos, E., and I. Sádaba. 2015. La evolución de los marcos (tecno) discursivos del movimiento 15 M y sus consecuencias. *Empiria* 32: 15–36.

Sahuquillo, M.R., J.A. Aunión, and A. Mars. 2013. 2008–2013: Balance de daños, *El País*, 27 December.

Sampedro, V. 1997. The Media Politics of Social Protest. *Mobilization* 2(2): 185–205.

Sampedro, V., and J. Lobera. 2014. The Spanish 15-M Movement: A Consensual Dissent? *Journal of Spanish Cultural Studies* 15(1–2): 61–80.

Sánchez, J.L. 2013. *Las 10 Mareas del Cambio. Claves para comprender los nuevos discursos sociales*. Madrid: Ed.eldiario.es.

Sartorius, N. 1977. *El sindicalismo de nuevo tipo: Ensayos sobre Comisiones Obreras*. Barcelona: Laia.

Shepard, B.H. 2011. *Play, Creativity, and Social Movements: If I Can't Dance, It's Not My Revolution*. New York: Routledge.

Toret, J. 2012. Una Mirada Tecnopolítica Sobre Los Primeros Días Del #15 M. In *Tecnopolítica, Internet y r-evoluciones*, eds. Alcazan, Arnaumonty, Axebra, Quodlibetat, Simona Levi, Sunotissima, Takethesquare, and Toret, 50–69. Barcelona: Icaria.

Treré, E., and A. Barranquero. 2013. De mitos y sublimes digitales: Movimientos sociales y tecnologías de la comunicación desde una perspectiva histórica. *Redes.com* 8, 27–47.

UGT-Madrid. 2011. *Evolución del empleo por sectores de actividad: Comunidad de Madrid, 2008–2011*. Madrid: UGT-Madrid, Secretaría de Empleo y Formación. Accessed 20 December 2013 at http://madrid.ugt.org/Informes/

CHAPTER 6

Late Neoliberalism and Its Discontents: The Case of Portugal

Tiago Fernandes

6.1 Introduction

Although an existing body of research has shown that citizens' protest and the formation of social movements are less likely to emerge in conditions of economic recession, there is also much variation in this regard.[1] Portugal during the Great Recession represents quite an interesting case, since not only was the volume of protest comparatively high in the context of southern Europe, but Portugal was also a country where protest movements tended to form cohesive organizations, create stable and wide coalitions, have a national scope, and establish alliances with unions and left-wing political parties. Moreover, the political and institutional context was favourable to protest, providing recognition, allies and support.

In this chapter we will describe the main traits of the Portuguese social movement and protest dynamics during the Great Recession (collective action repertoires; organizations and actors; identity and frames; and conceptions of democracy), but also try to understand how they were shaped by the socio-economic context (e.g. intensity of austerity and major consequences for the population's welfare) and national political opportunity structure (e.g. institutional allies, divisions between elites, patterns of government and opposition). Specifically, we will argue that two interrelated features explain the singularity of Portuguese social protest dynamics. First, the impact of the crisis on the welfare of the popula-

© The Author(s) 2017
D. della Porta et al., *Late Neoliberalism and its Discontents in the Economic Crisis*, DOI 10.1007/978-3-319-35080-6_6

tion was less severe than in most southern European countries (e.g. risk of poverty). This was the effect of two institutional legacies. The pro-austerity government did not dismantle and even expanded a state-civil society partnership for policy delivery to the poor, unique in Southern Europe, which had been established in the 1980s; and an active constitutional court rolled back many of the more severe austerity measures. Second, the political and institutional context facilitated the availability of allies, voice and resources for social movements. State repression was low, even with vast segments of the military and police forces aligning with anti-austerity protesters; the parliament was open and receptive to some protesters' demands and provided alliances with all political parties of the left (socialists, communists and the left bloc); and at the height of the protest cycle, movements received support from an additional plethora of organizations including the Catholic church, the media and some employers' organizations.

6.2   POLITICAL AND SOCIO-ECONOMIC CONTEXT

Almost immediately after the fall of Lehman Brothers in September 2008, a severe economic and financial crisis hit Portugal. The first reactions of the incumbent government—led by the Socialist Party, and in tune with European Union (EU) directives—were to promote fiscal expansion and implement Keynesian policies. But very few months afterwards, and again in line with a new European policy, the government resorted to fiscal consolidation and procyclical measures (Moury and Freire 2015, 123–124).

The first austerity programme was approved on 13 April 2010, when the Socialist minority government, with the support of the opposition centre-right PSD (Partido Social Democrata, or Social Democratic Party), implemented a series of budgetary cuts to meet the deficit limits imposed by the EU. These included pay freezes, higher limits to unemployment benefits, stricter requirements for the unemployed to accept available jobs, and cancellation of temporary social protection and employment support.

A second package of austerity started in September 2010, again with the support of the PSD, with the aim of reducing the budget deficit even more significantly. It included wage cuts for public employees (between 3.5 and 10 per cent for wages above 1500 euros per month); cancellation of promotions; reduction in spending on pensions and other social benefits like family allowances; an increase in the value-added tax (VAT) from

21 to 23 per cent; cancellation of all public investments; and privatizations of the transport sector.

In December 2010 a third package of austerity was debated at the European Council—though this time without the support of the PSD. Finally, on 12 March 2011, another austerity plan was announced, which included measures like additional decreases in pensions, higher taxes and cuts to health and welfare services. This last plan had not been discussed in parliament or the with social partners (unions and employers' organizations), provoking not only negative reactions from the parliamentary opposition on both the left and the right, but also large popular demonstrations against austerity, including a demonstration by the major union confederation, CGTP, on 19 March. The plan was rejected in parliament, and under great pressure from popular mobilizations, the socialist government resigned. On the 6 April, international financial assistance was requested by the Portuguese government, after the downgrading of the Portuguese debt had led to interest rates above 7 per cent (Lima and Artiles 2011).

Negotiations for a bailout with a Troika composed of three lending institutions (the EC, ECB, and IMF) agreed on a 78 billion euros loan. At the beginning of May 2011, the socialists (PS, or Partido Socialista), the centre-right (labelled social democrats in Portugal, or PSD) and the right (CDS-PP) signed a memorandum with the Troika. The two remaining left parties (the communist party, PCP, and the Left Bloc, BE or Bloco de Esquerda) opposed the agreement and did not even meet with the Troika.

The Memorandum of Understanding (MoU) included seven main points: (i) fiscal policy; (ii) financial sector regulation and supervision; (iii) fiscal-structural measures (which also included public administration and healthcare); (iv) labour market and education; (v) markets for goods and services; (vi) housing; and (vii) framework conditions (including judicial system competition, public procurement and business environment). The labour market measures were directed at revising the unemployment insurance system, but at the same time designed to strengthen social security; employment protection legislation was also to be changed in order to end labour market segmentation and ease the transition of workers across occupations and sectors; working time arrangements would be eased; and labour costs would be reduced in order to advance job creation and competitiveness (González and Figueiredo 2014).

During the electoral campaign that followed the resignation of the PS government, the socialist party—although accepting the terms of the

Troika agreement—also argued that the cuts to the welfare state and to universal education would be much deeper if the right won the elections. In turn, the PSD declared its goal to implement reforms even more liberal than the Troika proposed, while blaming the socialists for the bailout (Magalhães 2014).

In fact, the PSD clearly ran on a neoliberal agenda. Attacking the excessive presence of the State in the economy and stressing the supposed costs the state functioning and social rights imposed on the economy, it proposed a series of constitutional changes that aimed to end the notion of free, universal national health and education services and to eliminate the 'fair cause' limitation for the dismissal of workers. Moreover, it declared its intention to revise the constitution, specifically to abolish all the articles related to a free and universal welfare state and educational system. The left (Communist Party and Left Bloc) declared its opposition to the agreement and its support for the renegotiation of the debt (Magalhães 2014, 20–22).

In the June 2011 elections the socialists lost to the PSD, which formed a coalition government with the right-wing CDS-PP, thus allowing it to govern with an absolute majority. The PSD won with 38.7 per cent of the vote (9.5 per cent more than in the previous general elections of 2009) and the CDS earned 11.7 per cent (1.2 per cent more), whereas the PS achieved 28.1 per cent of the vote (8.5 per cent less than in 2009). On the left, the PCP won 7.4 per cent (0.04 per cent more) and the BE 5.2 (4.6 per cent less). Abstention was 42 per cent (1.6 per cent more than in 2009).

The new right-wing government set out not only to implement but even to radicalize the Troika programme (with the global aim of reducing the budget deficit-to-GDP ratio from 5.9 per cent in 2011 to 3 per cent in 2013). This foresaw privatizations in the electricity, gas markets, railways, telecommunication and postal sectors; deregulation of the labour market; reduction of the number of public sector workers and pay freezes of public employees; the fusion of local municipalities in order to reduce administrative costs; a series of cost-reducing reforms in the pension system (in pensions above 1500 euros); cuts in the amount and duration of unemployment benefits; increases in class sizes at the primary and secondary levels in the field of education; higher fees in the national health service; and an increase in taxes (VAT, corporate and personal income).

Most of the cuts in salaries, pensions, and the welfare state were well beyond the original Troika agreement (Moury and Standring 2013,

16–18; Rodrigues and Silva 2015, 34), as were the 2011 3.5 per cent extra tax on income and the increase in the energy VAT (González and Figueiredo 2014). The MoU gave particular importance to unemployment and employment security and working time arrangements, alongside active labour market policies; it stressed the need for improving human capital; emphasized social dialogue; and considered the need to look at the constitutional implications of the measures to be implemented—none of which the government took into consideration (González and Figueiredo 2014, 309–310).

In 2011, the main measures were public sector wage cuts between 3.5 and 10 per cent to salaries above 1500 euros; reduction of the Christmas bonus by 50 per cent; cuts of up to 10 per cent on pension benefits above 1500 euros per month; an increase in the early retirement age from 55 to 57 years and in the standard retirement age up to 67 or 68 years; stronger means-tested approaches to welfare benefits and a reduction in employers' contributions; 3.5 per cent extra tax on income; and raising the VAT on energy (Estanque et al. 2013, 33–34; González and Figueiredo 2014, 309–310; Natali and Stamati 2014, 320–321).

Even more, harsher austerity measures were implemented in the second half of 2012. The public sector bonuses for Christmas and summer holidays were again reduced by half, although in July 2012 the Constitutional Court reversed this measure by deeming it unconstitutional (Estanque et al. 2013, 33–34). In the pension system, a gradual reduction in benefits for salaries between 600 and 1100 euros was enacted, access to early retirement benefits was suspended, and the retirement age was increased (Natali and Stamati 2014, 320–321). In 2013, the state budget again increased the tax burden (Estanque et al. 2013, 33–34), and the 2014 state budget introduced cuts to gross salaries above 675 euros, starting at 2.5 per cent and rising to 12 per cent for gross wages above 2000 euros per month (Freire 2014, 5–6).

In terms of political attitudes (as shown by opinion polls), the crisis deepened dissatisfaction with the institutions of democracy, although this trend was already clear before the crisis. Since 1985 there has been a decline in satisfaction with the functioning of democracy, particularly pronounced between 2006 and 2008 (41 per cent of the adult population). In 2011 it was 33 per cent and in 2012 it fell to 10.2 per cent (Freire 2014, 199).

Still, some institutions were more trusted than others. At the start of the crisis in 2011, when asked about who better represented their interests, citizens placed the president and the social movements above political parties (Sousa, Magalhães and Amaral 2014). At the end of 2012, confidence in political institutions and banks and financial systems was much lower than for other institutions like the church, the armed forces and the press. Moreover, the unions were the institutions in which the Portuguese had the most trust. Actually, trust in the trade unions was the only indicator to show increased growth between 2008 and 2012 (Freire 2014, 7–8). Inversely, citizens' support of the EU has shown a decline since at least the mid-2000s (Freire 2014, 19).

Another survey showed that trust in several democratic institutions had a negative trend between 2008 and 2012. The presidency was the institution that had the highest level of trust in 2008 (73 per cent), but in 2012 it had declined substantially (35 per cent). The government was trusted by 45 per cent of the population in 2008 and only 14 per cent in 2012. Trust in parliament fell from 49 to 22 per cent. And political parties suffered a decrease of 11 per cent, though the level of trust in 2008 was already low (less than 30 per cent) (Pequito, Tsatsanis and Belchior 2014, 501).

At the same time, diffuse support for the democratic regime did not decline substantially and remained at high levels. In 2008, 95.4 per cent of Portuguese agreed with the statement that the democratic political system is a very good or fairly good way of governing the country. In 2012 this percentage had only decreased to 91.3 per cent (Pequito, Tsatsanis and Belchior 2014, 501).

With the onset of the crisis and the adoption of pro-austerity policies, socio-economic and welfare indicators in Portugal have considerably worsened. At the same time, it should be noted that in this regard Portugal performed better than most of its southern European counterparts—that is, the impact of the crisis was less severe. Unemployment in Portugal rose from 8.6 per cent of the labour force in 2008 to 15.3 in 2013, but in 2014 it declined to 12.2 per cent (Eurostat). According to one study the largest contributors to unemployment are people over 45 (30.4 per cent of total unemployment in 2012), and those with low levels of education (60 per cent of total unemployment). There was also a fall in the share of the unemployed covered by unemployment benefits (61 per cent in 2008; 46 per cent in 2012) (González and Figueiredo 2014).

In the last decade, jobs offering permanent contracts have decreased, while fixed-term contracts increased. Precarious work has increased. In 2010 there were 37.6 per cent of workers between the ages of 15 and

34 working on fixed-term contracts; in the age group 15–24 years it was almost 50 per cent (Estanque, Costa and Soeiro 2013, 33).

Inequality in the late 1990s and early 2000s did not show substantial changes, but after the mid-2000s there was a clear decrease in inequality, which was interrupted in 2011. In addition, the share of wages in GDP fell from 58.4 per cent in 2010 to 55.6 per cent in 2012, and it is forecast to fall to 54.1 per cent in 2014 (Estanque, Costa and Soeiro 2013, 33). In terms of the evolution of income distribution, the top decile declined from 2011 to 2012. The share of the lowest deciles (1 and 2) did not show drastic changes in recent years. Deciles 3 to 8, which correspond to the middle class and constitute 60 per cent of the population, also kept their share of income during austerity. There was also a high risk of poverty or social exclusion among children (aged 17 or below): 28.6 per cent in 2011 compared with 24.4 per cent for the population as a whole (González and Figueiredo 2014).

Although in a cross-temporal comparison Portugal has shown a negative performance in terms of socio-economic indicators, compared with the other southern European democracies, the picture is less negative. According to Gutiérrez, Portugal has been the best performer in terms of employment rates between 1995 and 2013: in 2013 Greece had a rate of employment of 53 per cent, Spain 58 per cent, Italy 60 per cent and Portugal 66 per cent. Unemployment rates at the end of 2013 were 27.2 per cent in Greece and 26.1 per cent in Spain, while in Portugal they were 16.3 per cent and in Italy 11.4 per cent. In terms of youth employment rates (categories 20–43 years old), as well, Portugal looks better than any other southern European country (Gutiérrez 2014, 386).

The risk of poverty for 2011–2013 (60 per cent of median equalized income, starting in 2005) was 17 per cent in Portugal, 18 per cent in Italy, 20.5 per cent in Spain, and 23 per cent in Greece. The severe material deprivation rate for the period 2005–2012 rose in Greece from 12 per cent of the population to 20 per cent, in Portugal from 8 to 9 per cent, in Italy from 6 to 14 per cent, and in Spain from 4 to 6 per cent (Gutiérrez 2014, 377, 386).

Other studies are congruent with the previous findings. In terms of relative poverty during the period 2009–2013, Greece went from 20 per cent to 45 per cent of the population, Spain from 22 to 25 per cent, Italy from 17.5 to 20 per cent, and Portugal from 16 to 23 per cent (Matsaganis and Leventi 2014, 201). During the same period, the Gini index increased very steeply in Greece (from 0.321 to 0.364), rose a bit in Spain (from 0.314 to 0.318), stayed more or less stable in Italy (0.308 to 0.311), but declined steadily in Portugal, from 0.322 to 0.310. This picture is also confirmed if one measures inequality by the distribution in terms of income quintile share ratio S80/S20 (measuring the income share of the richest 20 per cent relative to that of the poorest 20 per cent): in Greece it rose from 5.27 to 7.77, in Spain from 5.79 to 5.94, in Italy 5.07 to 5.20, and in Portugal it declined from 4.95 to 4.75 (Matsaganis and Leventi 2014, 403).

This is confirmed by Eurostat data for 2014. Portugal performs reasonably well in most indicators. Unemployment was the second lowest (12.2 per cent), with Italy only slightly better (11.8 per cent) and well ahead of Greece (25 per cent) and Spain (21.6 per cent). Youth unemployment (under 25) was the lowest (31 per cent), compared with Greece (48.6 per cent), Spain (46.7 per cent), and Italy (40.5 per cent). The same goes for female unemployment (12.6 per cent), almost equal to Italy (12.5 per cent) and much better than Greece (29.4 per cent) and Spain (23 per cent). In Portugal, the number of people at risk of poverty or social exclusion is also the lowest in southern Europe (27.5 per cent), with Greece achieving 36 per cent, Spain 29.2 per cent, and Italy 28.1 per cent.

In terms of inequality, the quintile share ratio (S80/S20) was the second best in southern Europe (6.2), after Italy (5.4) but ahead of Greece (6.5) and Spain (6.8). Only in the Gini coefficient of disposable income was Portugal in the middle of the classification (34.5, the same value as Greece), after Italy (32.5), but ahead of Spain (34.7).

6.3   ANTI-AUSTERITY PROTESTS

6.3.1   Collective Action Repertoires

Most types of collective action rose in Portugal during the crisis. Participation in legal demonstrations grew from 4.2 to 7.4 per cent (Lima and Artiles 2013, 150), or from 3.7 to 6.8 per cent of the population, from 2008 to 2012 (Accornero and Ramos Pinto 2014, 2). Research based on national surveys shows even higher percentages for the period 2008–2012. The percentage of Portuguese signing a petition rose from 21 to 32 per cent; participating in demonstrations, from 12 to 24 per cent; participating in legal strikes, from 11 to 25 per cent; occupying buildings, from 1 to 3 per cent; and blocking roads and railways, from 1 to 2 per cent

(Amador 2013, 34). Moreover, Portugal was probably the site of the biggest demonstrations, some of which comprised between 800,000 and 1.5 million participants—about 8–15 per cent of the population.

In terms of forms of collective action, the number of demonstrations also grew. In the city of Lisbon, it increased from 244 in 2010 to 298 in 2011 and to 579 (one every 15 hours) in 2012. Overall, in Portugal there is a predominance of strikes. Of 163 events, 66 were demonstrations (40.5 per cent), but 76 were strikes (46.6 per cent) of varying duration and scope. Other types of action, including petitions, public assemblies and occupations, characterize only 12.9 per cent of protest events (Accornero and Ramos Pinto 2014, 19).

In the first half of 2010, labour-based protest occurred mainly in the private sector, over pay and layoffs; but gradually during the crisis, public sector workers and trade union federations assumed the leading role. In addition, strikes across multiple companies (a sign of coordination) increased from 18.6 per cent of strike events in 2010, peaking at 39.7 per cent in 2011 to 28.3 per cent in 2012. Finally, there was also a higher use of the general strike as a tactic. During 1974–2009 there were five general strikes, but since 2010 a similar number has occurred as a result of a deeper collaboration between the two main trade union federations (Accornero and Ramos Pinto 2014).

Another study, covering the period between 2010 and 2012, shows that 384 strikes occurred, involving about 224,500 workers just in the private sector (Estanque 2014, 65–66). Sectoral strikes were also widespread and frequent. Besides the general strikes, the available data shows that the number of ordinary strikes increased from 123 to 127 per year, as did the average number of workers affected by strikes (from 71 to 92) and the number of working days lost (from 71 to 113) (Freire 2014, 14–16).

Forms of collective action like open assemblies and occupations created at the centre of demonstrations have failed. Inspired by the Spanish 15M, Rossio Square was occupied during 15–20 May 2011 (Fonseca 2012b, 12–16; Estanque 2014, 65), but it attracted very few people (at most 100) and lasted only 6 days. The occupation of a former school building in Porto in April 2011 was also forcibly ended one year later (Baumgarten 2013a, 2). In June 2011 the Indignados de Lisboa were formed, organizing assemblies, debates and cultural activities; but apart from Rossio Square in Lisbon, only two assemblies were created (in the Lisbon neighbourhoods of Benfica and Graça).

In the aftermath of the protest of 15 October 2011 (the Day of Global Action, an international protest day occurring in 82 countries and 951 cities around the world), Ocupar Lisboa, the Occupy Lisbon Movement, camped in a small area in front of the Portuguese parliament until 12 December 2011 (Baumgarten 2013a, 461). This effort also failed. Finally, in the aftermath of the Global Spring demonstration (a day of protest 'For Global Democracy and Social Justice', which celebrated the anniversary of public Spanish protests of the year before), on 12 May 2012, after a two-day meeting of groups called Activar ('to activate'), it was decided to occupy the large Eduardo VII park in Lisbon. Activists were evicted after six days (Baumgarten 2013a, 2).

In terms of occupations, the level of commitment of activists in Portugal seems to be weak. Most participants did not stay overnight. During the day, the various assemblies, workshops and shared meals organized by the activists tended to have very low participation and failed to generate public interest. In addition, all occupations were small (e.g. only five tents at 'Primavera Global Portuguesa') (Baumgarten 2013a, 461–462). In their meetings, activists also abandoned the principle of consensus, and voting became more widespread. There was a general feeling of frustration with the meetings because of a perception that some of the activist groups simply repeated their positions and no real debate occurred (Baumgarten 2013a, 462–464).

Instead, activists of some of the major demonstrations have used petitions to the parliament. This confirms Robert Fishman's insight that parliament is the central institution by which activists address politicians (Fishman 2011). On 12 March 2011, during the 'Desperate Generation' (*Geração à Rasca*) demonstration—at the time considered the largest street protest in Portugal since the revolutionary period of 1974–1975, with 200,000–500,000 protesters in several Portuguese cities—its promoters delivered 2000 pieces of paper to the parliament containing specific demands by the people who attended the protest (Baumgarten 2013a; Soeiro 2014, 71 ff).

In November 2011, the APRE—Associação de Reformados e Pensionistas (Pensioners' Association)—delivered a petition for the rights of pensioners (Petição pelos Direitos dos Aposentados, Pensionistas e Reformados), with about 13,500 subscribers. Finally, in December 2011 a group for the Citizen Audit on Sovereign Debt was created (Auditoria Cidadã à Dívida Pública). It included left-wing parties like the PCP and the BE, a former secretary general of the CGTP, a former socialist junior minister, trade unionists and activists from various anti-austerity movements, which presented to the parliament on 31 January 2014 a petition advocating the restructuring of the Portuguese debt (Baumgarten 2013a).

Perhaps even more importantly, FERVE and Precários Inflexíveis (PI), both precarious workers' movements, and the M12M (Movimento 12 de Março) launched the Iniciativa Legislativa de Cidadãos (ILC, or Citizen's Legislative Initiative) on 19 April 2011. In Portugal since 2003 there is the legal possibility, which was always contained in the Portuguese constitution (article 167), for citizens to have legislative initiatives as long as they gather a minimum subscription of 35,000 individuals. This was used to present the Lei Contra a Precariedade (Law Against Precariousness) (Fonseca 2011, 11–14). This initiative was welcomed by parliament and although it took one year to be discussed, it can be considered a partial success since it led to the formation of a specific parliamentary commission devoted to this issue, and several of the proposal's claims were approved (Interview with Tiago Gillot).

It has also been common for demonstrators to assemble in front of the parliament, or to end their marches there. The biggest demonstration of the whole period—the *Screw the Troika. We want our lives back!* (*Que se Lixe a Troika* [QSLT]. *Queremos as nossas vidas de volta!*) demonstrations on 15 September 2012—started with a press conference in front of the parliament on 12 September, which was broadcast on radio and television. This was the biggest protest event of the austerity period (2010–2015), taking place in about 30 cities and estimated to include one million participants, with 500,000 in Lisbon alone (*Público*, 16 September 2012). Activists considered this the peak of the protest cycle (Interview with Hugo Evangelista).

Moreover, it has been common for protesters to enter the parliament itself, such as on 3 May 2013, when pensioners interrupted the president of parliament's speech by singing the 1974 revolutionary song *Grândola*. Other major demonstrations in Portugal that have finished in front of the parliament included the police forces' demonstrations of September 2011 (with about 10,000 policemen) and 6 November 2012; the Day of Global Action on 15 October 2011; the general strikes of 24 November 2011 and 14 November 2012; and the January 2014 pensioners' demonstration organized by APRE.

The presidency has also been a place for activists to gather. Demonstrators usually demand that the president dismiss the government (as he can do by constitutional norm) or block the government's budget proposal.

Cases included the demonstration of public employees and the military on 12 November 2011; the demonstration of 21 September 2012 by the QSLT platform; and the July 2013 demonstration called by the CGTP, in collaboration with the PI, P-15O and QSLT.[2]

Forms of civil disobedience and boycotts have very rarely been used by Portuguese protesters, with the interesting exception of the police. As strategies of protest they have collectively engaged in calling in sick to work (a habit which spread to several cities), refused to apply traffic fines, and on one occasion organized a form of action called 'Levantamento de Rancho'. This form of rebellious act was used during the colonial wars and consists in the collective refusal to eat on the premises of police buildings. At the time, it was penalized with prison.

Grandoladas were an innovative repertoire that was, among a series of other protest events, inspired by the QSLT protest of 15 September 2012. *Grândolar* was a term invented after activists interrupted a prime minister's speech in Parliament by singing the 1974 revolutionary song *Grândola*. This action was soon copied by various groups around the country and was practised when government officials or ministers visited. According to Paula Gil, 'the *Grândolas* were great peaks of mobilization' (Interview). As mentioned above, on 3 May 2013, pensioners interrupted the speech of president of the parliament with this song (Estanque 2014, 65–66). On 2 March 2013, a protest march organized nationally by Que. se Lixe a Troika platform created in its aftermath a new wave of *Grandoladas*, boycotting any government officials that happened to participate in public ceremonies around the country (Estanque 2014, 65–66).

The level of violence has been low. On 15 October 2011, the Day of Global Action, activists who wanted to occupy the main stairways of the parliament threw eggs at police. Two of them were arrested briefly (*Público*, 16 October 2011). At the general strike of 24 November 2011 there was one person injured by the police and seven detained, after people again tried to force the stairs of the parliament (DN, 26 November 2011, 5). The general strike of 22 March 2012 saw clashes between activists and police, but also between union members and activists of the Plataforma 15 de Outubro (P-15O). This was the only occasion on which activist groups fought among themselves. The CGTP leadership later declared that the Platform was too radical and had the purpose of creating incidents with the police (DN, 24 March 2012, 17; DN, 05 April 2012, 18).

It was during the general strike of 14 November 2012 that the more serious incidents would occur. Fifteen people were imprisoned by police after pelting the barriers in front of the parliament with stones for two hours. Forty-eight people were slightly injured (21 policemen and 27 activists). The CGTP again condemned the groups that started the confrontations (supposedly Tugaleaks and Anonymous PT). At the same time, this incident led to the dismissal of the president of Portuguese public television (RTP), after he illegally (without a judicial order) ceded the police images of the protesters (DN, 23 November 2012, 1).

Larger demonstrations have occurred throughout the national territory. The 12 March 2011 'Desperate Generation' demonstration, with 200,000–500,000 protesters, although initially called in Lisbon, spread to several cities in the country (Soeiro 2014, 71 ff). Police protests between May and December 2011 occurred in the north, the centre and the south, in the cities of Braga, Espinho, Lisbon and Faro. The protest of 15 October 2011 (Day of Global Action) comprised about 100,000 people in Lisbon alone, but also spread to the cities of Angra do Heroísmo, Braga, Coimbra, Évora, Faro, Ponta Delgada, Santarém and Porto (50,000), which in fact covers the whole national territory. The demonstration against the closing of *freguesias* (counties) on 1 April 2012 occurred in Lisbon but stimulated a series of protests all over the country until September 2012 against the lack of state services at the local level (public works, railroads, doctors, courts, hospitals and schools).

The Screw the Troika demonstrations of 15 September 2012 also occurred in the cities of Faro, Viseu, Pombal, Leiria, Braga, Funchal, Aveiro, Bragança, Évora and Coimbra. Again, this covers the whole national territory. Finally, the cultural demonstrations organized by Que se Lixe a Troika on 2 March 2013 occurred in 23 cities (mainly in Porto, Coimbra, Braga, Aveiro, Viseu, Faro, Viana do Castelo, Beja, Portimão and Lisbon) (Baumgarten 2013a, 1–3).

It was common to see the spread of smaller and local protest events in the aftermath of a major national event. For instance, in the aftermath of the national demonstration against the extinction of *freguesias*, and until September 2012, there were frequent local demonstrations all over the country against the closing of public services and infrastructure (railroads, courts, hospitals and schools) (*Público*, 12 April 2012).

6.3.2 Protest Aims, Identity and Collective Frames

Almost all major anti-austerity protest events were framed within the culture and tradition of the Portuguese revolution of 1974. Right from the start of the protest cycle in 2011, there was the systematic use of the key songs of the revolutionary period of 1974–1975; the slogans raised the memory of the revolution as something that should be repeated or as a standard by which contemporary politics should be evaluated.

For example, in the Geração à Rasca demonstration of 12 March 2011, under the banner 'several generations, one struggle', older revolutionary slogans were also recurrent: the singing of the revolutionary song *Grândola*, phrases like '*Povo unido jamais será vencido*' (the united people shall never be defeated), '*25 de abril sempre*' (25th of April forever), and '*fascismo nunca mais*' ('fascism, never again') (*Público*, 13 March 2011). This pattern continued in 2012. At the Screw the Troika demonstrations, these same slogans and songs were attuned to present day issues: 'another world is possible', 'all we have is past', 'the people in poverty, politicians in big life', 'IMF out of here' (*Público*, 16 September 2012).

Another important frame, although not as widespread as the revolutionary songs and slogans, were the messages and self-presentations of the 1990s student demonstrations. This decade had seen immense student mobilization against the rise in university fees and student struggles for equal and democratic access to the university schools. A famous journalist had used the pejorative '*geração rasca*' (trashy, cheap generation) to describe high school and university students, after some protest events in which acts of violence occurred (destruction of automobiles and the use of slang words). On 15 September, Screw the Troika activists sang some slogans from the 1990s student demonstrations ('*não pagamos*'; we don't pay) in front of parliament. But more importantly, the first big demonstration of the austerity period, the 12 March 2011 'Geração à Rasca', reformulated the word *rasca* for contemporary purposes (*rasca* can also mean desperate).

Finally, another frame is intergenerational solidarity. This frame is expressed, for example, in the main slogan of the 12 March 2011 demonstration: 'several generations, one struggle' (*Público*, 13 February 2011).

6.3.3   *Protest Actors and Organizational Formats*

Unions have been quite important in the mobilization for protest, not only for strikes, but also for marches and demonstrations. Moreover, it has been common for the two main union confederations to collaborate in the organization of protest. The general strikes of 24 November 2010 and 27 June 2013, as well as the 8 November 2013 public sector strike, were all called jointly by CGTP and UGT. Only in 1988 did the two union confederations unite in a general strike. In the general strike of 22 March 2012, although UGT did not adhere, 20 of its main unions disobeyed the confederation and supported the CGTP (Accornero and Ramos Pinto 2014; Lima and Artiles 2011).

The main socio-professional organizations of the police and the military have also been important in calling for protest (ASPP/PSP, Associação Sindical dos Funcionários de Investigação Criminal da PJ, Associação dos Profissionais de Guarda, Sindicato Nacional de Polícia-SINAPOL, Associação Sindical dos Profissionais de Polícia). They have also collaborated with public sector unions (Frente Comum, Fesap, Sindicato dos Quadros Técnicos do Estado), for example in their joint demonstration on 12 November 2011.

It has also been common for unions and anti-austerity social movements to join and support the mobilization for each other's protest events. This was the case for the demonstrations of 12 March 2011 ('Desperate Generation') and 15 October 2011 (Day of Global Action), which saw participation by unions, especially the CGTP. In addition, several demonstrations organized by unions have been supported and joined by other movements. The CGTP demonstration on 29 September 2012 had the support of QSLT Platform (*Público*, 30 September 2012); the general strike of 14 November 2012 was joined by social movements like Precários Inflexíveis (PI), Intermitentes do Espetáculo, Estudantes pela Greve, Platform 15 October (P-15O), and Movement 12 March (M12M) (Soeiro 2014, 67–71); and the July 2013 CGTP demonstration in front of the presidential palace was joined by PI, P-15O and QSLT. According to Soeiro, because of the participation of other social movements in their protest events, unions have chosen long marches and demonstrations as repertoires of protest in addition to strikes (Soeiro 2014, 71–73).

There was also a tendency for the formalization of social movements during the cycle of protest. For instance, in the case of two existing associations of precarious workers—FERVE (Fartos Destes Recibos Verdes/Sick of These Green Receipts) and Precários Inflexíveis (Inflexible Precarious)—the two organizations have reinforced formal and bureaucratic traits as well as fusing into one single association of precarious workers.

FERVE was founded in March 2007. Mainly based in Oporto, it gradually acquired national scope. Initially it was organized to denounce situations of irregular labour relations and exploitation of precarious workers, and to mobilize for protest, but it gradually evolved into an organization for the defence of labour rights (Fonseca 2011, 7–9).

The Precários Inflexíveis (PI) was created after the first May Day demonstrations in Lisbon in 2007. Initially based in the Lisbon area, they soon spread to the entire country. They started by organizing around a network structure, but evolved into a more formal organization. The internet and social media are important tools for their activism, but less so than in FERVE (Fonseca 2011).

In the second half of 2012, FERVE ceased its activity and was absorbed by Precários Inflexíveis (Fonseca 2011). On 7 July 2012, PI acquired a formal structure and was legally registered as an association (with statutes, organs and fiscal identity). This recognition facilitated not only access to all parliamentary parties, but especially capacity to recruit members (200 in 2012, which pay quotas between 1–50 euros/month). It has also developed permanent relationships with the CGTP, women's organizations, and pensioners' associations (APRE), creating offices in Portugal's two major cities, Lisbon and OPorto (Fonseca 2012a, 11).

Pensioners have also created a successful formal organization, APRE (Associação de Reformados e Pensionistas). Corresponding to the model of the traditional civic association, with formal dues paying membership and chapters spread through the country, it aims to be considered among the social concertation bodies and consulted in policy-making. APRE was founded on 14 December 2012 in the aftermath of the measures falling over pensioners contained in the 2013 state budget. Starting out with 300 members, its membership soon rose to 2331 individuals, which have elected their leadership in voting booths in Lisbon, OPorto and Coimbra. Organizationally, it created regional and local delegations. Regional delegations make the connection between local chapters and the national direction. There are 12 local chapters (Portimão, Faro, Braga, Cabaceiras de Basto, Almada, Guimarães, Viseu, Aveiro, Porto, Coimbra, Évora and Lisbon) (Alves 2014). According to João Camargo, one of the leaders of PI, 'APRE is highly important and it is the organization which became more strengthened during the crisis' (Interview).

Another important pre-crisis association was the Associação Nacional de Freguesias (National Association of Counties), which represented all the elected counties of Portugal (more than 4000 political units). Founded in the aftermath of the revolution, it played an important role during austerity by organizing the demonstration of 1 April 2012, which clearly defeated the government's plans for the extinction of 1500 *freguesias*. It brought together local officeholders from all parties.

It also should be noted that in Portugal it was common during the austerity cycle for protest events to lead to the formation of platforms of social movements (with the participation of radical left political parties as well), which then become consolidated and organized further protest events. These are platforms which are run on an equal basis among the organizations that constitute them. At the same time, none of these platforms has survived the period of the crisis or succeeded in generating stronger and unified social and/or political movements for political reform and democratic deepening (in the mould of SYRIZA or Podemos).

The first major protest event, the 'Desperate Generation' demonstration of 12 March 2011 was the most spontaneous (Baumgarten 2013a). After a Facebook group called for protest via social media, autonomous groups started to appear in several cities of the country asking people to join the protest, while at the same time contacting social organizations (Fonseca 2012b). Precarious workers and unemployed youth showed up massively, but the protest was also intergenerational, with the participation of students, parents and grandparents, as well as middle-aged unemployed (Estanque, Costa and Soeiro 2013).

In terms of movements, there was participation from women's organizations, precarious associations (like Precários Inflexíveis), LGBT groups, the main union confederation CGTP, radical left parties like the Left Bloc (BE) and PCP, and even the centre-right party youth JSD (Soeiro 2014, 7; Público, 13 March 2011). In the aftermath of the protest, after a national convention in Lisbon, they created a national organization, the Platform M12M (Plataforma Movimento 12 de Março) (Fonseca 2012b). At the same time, the platform received its main support from a political party, the Left Bloc. The platform also organized a national convention to discuss policy solutions to the economic crisis (the Forum Gerações) and in May 2011, during the national election campaign, it claimed for a citizen audit of the public debt (Soeiro 2014, 7). Still, it gradually faded away in importance after the summer of 2011, resuming activities mainly through the organization of debates in a newly founded forum in Lisbon called Academia Cidadã (Citizen's Academy) (Interview with João Camargo).

The second platform created in 2011 was Platform 15th October (P-15O), brought into being at the Rossio occupations of April and May 2011. It gathered more than 30 groups with the aim of preparing the International Day of Global Action on 15 October 2011 (Baumgarten 2013a, 1). By the summer of 2011, the platform also included anti-austerity and precarious organizations (M12M, Indignados Lisboa, Acampada Lisboa—Democracia Verdadeira Já, Protesto dos Professores Contratados e Desempregados and FERVE); environmental (GAIA), LBGT and women's groups; left-wing journals (*Revista Rubra*), as well as anti-racism organizations (SOS Racismo) and ATTAC Portugal. Its meetings were 'highly participated ... usually with a minimum of 80, 100 people' (Interview with Nuno Rodrigues).

This platform also failed, because of internal conflicts and divergences over political strategy. Activists favouring direct action and confrontation with authorities—as well as conceptions of direct and participatory and assembly democracy (the group Ruptura/Fer, a faction of the BE, which later would leave BE and form a new party, MAS, or Movimento Alternativa Socialismo)—clashed with the remaining groups that preferred alliances with unions and peaceful protest. Especially the unions and Precários Inflexíveis (which are closer to BE) rejected this strategy, as evident in the 15 October 2011 Day of Global Action demonstrations when small groups of activists clashed with police (Soeiro 2014, 75–76; Interview with Nuno Rodrigues). Also according to Nuno Rodrigues, the Plataforma 'never had a direction and statutes' (Interview).

The third, and most successful, platform was Que se Lixe a Troika (QSLT). Created on 27 August 2012 by a group of 29 activists from different movements and political parties in order to prepare the demonstration of 15 September 2012, it was a much wider platform than the previous ones. It included the PI, M12M, and P-15O platforms, and it contained representatives of left-wing parties (the PCP and the BE), the trade union federation CGTP, politicians of the socialist party (historic leader Manuel Alegre and Lisbon city counsellor Helena Roseta), prominent revolutionary military of 1974 (captains Vasco Lourenço and Sousa e Castro), as well as civil society organizations like ATTAC, SOS Racismo, UMAR (women's organization), colectivo habita, panteras rosas (gay rights), the workers' commissions of the public television and the autoeuropa factory, and the military officers' association (Accornero and Ramos Pinto 2014, 15–17; Baumgarten 2013b, 7–9; Camargo 2013, 137; Soeiro 2014, 72–73).

The commitment of the communist party was also quite strong, with the nomination of several activists to its leadership. Internally it had a democratic structure; according to Nuno Rodrigues, 'although there was a direction, someone responsible for the group, they were elected in a democratic way. The model was democratic, everybody in order to speak had to register, there was a list and everybody spoke in their turn' (Interview).

Finally, there were initiatives for the creation of a unified progressive platform of movements, parties and groups fighting austerity. This was the 'Democratic Congress for Alternatives' (Congresso Democrático das Alternativas–CDA), which took place in October 2012 and brought 1500 activists of the M12M, CGTP and BE, as well as independent figures of the left and a few socialists (Accornero and Ramos Pinto 2014, 15–17). An outgrowth of the congress was the creation of a new political party, Livre (Free), which positioned itself between the extreme left (BE and PCP) and the centre-left (PS). It was an anti-austerity and pro-Europe party, espousing a mix of social-democratic and libertarian values. One of its main aims was to sponsor the unity of the left. It had a collegial leadership of 15 people, selected in party primaries. This party was able to achieve an expressive vote in European elections (though it was unable to elect an MP), but it failed totally in the general elections of October 2015.

The use of the internet and social media has been quite important for the start of the protest events. The 12 March 2011 Geração à Rasca demonstration was organized mainly through Facebook and blog groups, although its organizers had a personal history of political engagement. Paula Gil was a member of the political party Left Bloc (BE), and Alexandre Carvalho and João Labrincha were ex-members of the communist and socialist youths, respectively. In Oporto, the group of activists belonged either to BE, the communist youth, or FERVE (*Público*, 12 March 2011).

In terms of the social groups or sociological categories participating in the demonstrations, these have been quite varied. On the Day of Global Action on 15 October 2011, the social composition of demonstrators included teachers, designers, pensioners, doctors and young precarious (*Público*, 16 October 2011). In the demonstration of 21 September 2012, when thousands of people protested in front of the Portuguese presidency asking for the dismissal of the government, there was a presence from a diversity of social movements and political groups: MPs of the BE and the Communist Party, anonymous, anarchists and precarious workers. But the demonstration was also attended by housewives, pensioners, liberal professionals, actors, small entrepreneurs, students, ex-military and dock workers (*Público*, 16 September 2012).

At the 2 March 2013 protest march organized nationally by the Que se Lixe a Troika platform, participating associations included precarious workers' groups like the Movimento sem Emprego and Precários

Inflexíveis; social movement platforms like the M12M; the major union confederation (CGTP); gay rights organizations; and some military associations. The printed media referred to participants from social categories that included students, teachers, pensioners, women and doctors (*Público*, 02 March 2013). Again, the march also had the support of the CGTP and the PCP, BE and some PS deputies.

National surveys conducted in 2008 and 2012 showed that the people who participated in the protest events tended to be of urban origin, literate, with strong traits of attachment with the political system, namely identification with a political party and interest in politics. Moreover, both the young and the old participated (Viegas, Teixeira, Amador 2015, 211–213).

As mentioned above, left-wing parties and local civil society associations have actively participated in most demonstrations. For instance, the 1 April 2012 national demonstration against the extinction of *freguesias*, called by the Associação Nacional de Freguesias (National Association of Parishes), included participation of elected local officers of several parties, although with a preponderance of the BE and PCP. The population participated massively, with more than 150,000 demonstrators. Local associations came from all over the country for the protest event: musical bands, cultural and leisure associations, sports clubs (*Público*, 12 April 2012).

Although Portuguese activists have been inspired by protest events taking place in other countries, the targets of Portuguese protests remained mainly at the national level. This was true even in demonstrations like the 15 October 2011 and 12 May 2012, which were organized as a part of international days of action (Baumgarten 2013a, 468–469).

6.3.4   Democracy: Frames and Concepts

During the Portuguese cycle of protest, protest claims were filtered through the frame of social and labour rights. The notion behind this is that full democracy is only complete when, in combination with political and civic rights, there is a full set of economic rights that equalize socio-economic conditions. In this sense, the centrality of labour and socio-economic issues is unique to the Portuguese case. This is reflected in interviews with activists: 'I always thought that to speak of democracy is to speak of rights; it is only through the real implementation of rights that you avoid having differences between citizens' (Interview with João Camargo).

This framing can also be seen in the banners shown in several of the demonstrations. On 15 October 2011, the major demand was 'work with rights'. At the 29 September 2012 demonstration organized by the CGTP with the support of QSLT, banners held the following phrases: 'We want work. We demand rights against impoverishment and injustices.'

The centrality of work and its dignity is also present in the self-conceptions of the people participating in the demonstrations. In the 25 March 2011 demonstration, organizers asked each person to bring a sheet of paper with a relevant problem written on it, which would then be delivered to parliament. An analysis of the several categories showed that labour issues were the most important (49 per cent). Issues related to the political system and transparency of public decisions and the struggle against corruption accounted for a much smaller percentage of the claims (14 and 9 per cent, respectively) (Soeiro 2014, 71 ff). Moreover, the main slogan of the 2 March 2013 protest march organized nationally by the Que se Lixe a Troika platform was: 'emprego, saúde e educação, troika não' ('Jobs, health and education! Not Troika!') (Público, 03 March 2013).

Protests have also been framed as demands for 'more democracy' and 'real democracy' (as in some banners of the demonstration on 25 March 2011; Fonseca 2012b, 15). At the demonstration on the Day of Global Action of 15 October 2011, João Labrincha, one of the organizers, considered the originality of this protest event to be related to the re-emergence of popular assemblies, as well as to the memory of the revolution. As he said, 'there were moments during the PREC (as is known the revolutionary process of 1974–1975, meaning processo revolucionário em curso, or ongoing revolutionary process) where people could participate in popular assemblies but since then it had not happened again' (Público, 16 October 2011). This was very close to a conception of democracy based solely on the social movements themselves. As a demonstrator defended in the Global Spring protests of 12 May 2012, new policy solutions to austerity 'must come out of the movement itself' (Público, 13 May 2012).

Still, this fell short of a conception of participatory democracy. It reflected more of a disappointment with the functioning of existing democracy, which needed not to be replaced by a totally new system but deepened by people's activism and self-autonomy. 'There is an immense relevance of representative democracy ... the aim is to try a bigger popular participation, around people's sovereignty and the possibility to contribute in specific ways to electoral programmes, that the people's voice be heard. It is a Conception of representative democracy but with a wider focus than today' (Interview with Paula Gil). One of the memorable slogans of the Platform M12M was the expression of the Portuguese Nobel prize-winner in literature, José Saramago, 'to make every citizen a politician'. In addition, at the demonstration on 15 September 2012, banners read: '*sejam as pessoas a decidir as suas vidas*' (the people should decide their lives).

There was also a general appeal to revolt and, although within the confines of representative democracy and existing civic rights, a stress on participatory democracy: 'if they want us to accept unemployment, precariousness and inequality as a way of life, we will answer with the strength of democracy, freedom, mobilization and struggle' (Soeiro 2014, 71–72).

There was also the conception that austerity 'destroys dignity and destroys democracy', as well as a widespread discontentment with political parties and the way representative democracy is working. One of the slogans at the March 2011 demonstration in Lisbon was, 'The people united don't need parties' (Estanque, Costa and Soeiro 2013).

But non-parliamentary conceptions of democracy have been a minority, mainly defended by small groups like MAS. Most activists rejected this conception as a waste of time, prone to be manipulated by small groups, and not representative, since only in very few groups can direct democracy work (Interviews with João Camargo and Tiago Gillott). Still, some activists also think that 'change will never be done through parliament, but in the neighbourhoods, workplaces. ... Moreover, political parties like BE and *Livre* think that it will always be possible class conciliation. But I don't think so. ... The PCP does think it is impossible class conciliation, it defends the working class but it has a much closed structure, based on Stalinism.' Instead, the 'MAS vision is the unity of all small parties: MRPP, PAN, PCP, BE and *Livre*' (Interview with Nuno Rodrigues).

6.4   Interpretations

Two interrelated features help explain the singularity of Portuguese social protest dynamics. First, the indirect impact of institutions and policy legacies had the effect of making the crisis less severe in terms of the welfare of the population. Two dimensions were essential: the legacy of state-civil society partnerships for policy delivery to the poor, with a wide network established since the 1980s and unique in southern Europe, and the role of the constitutional court in cutting back many of the harshest austerity measures. Second, the direct impact of the political context provided allies, voice and resources for social movements.

At the start of the crisis the government adopted a Social Emergency Plan, based on a greater role for social welfare organizations (IPSS, Instituições Privadas de Solidariedade Social), which were partly state funded. Some of the measures enacted placed more workers in the IPSS, increasing the number of meals it served and fostering volunteering (time banks in firms which allow workers to volunteer). State expenses with IPSS devoted to social action also grew 7.9 per cent between 2011 and 2014. By the end of 2014, there were about 16,413 agreements between the state and the IPSS, which covered about 532,035 people (namely in the areas of elderly and child support). Moreover, in Portugal the government never cut the smallest old-age pensions, which kept their nominal value (Joaquim 2015, 16–19, 26).

While it was clear that the existing funds were not enough and that this coincided with a decline in investment in direct services by the state in welfare and social support (Joaquim 2015, 62), this programme also seems to be unique to Portugal when compared to the other southern European democracies. The authors of a recent study note that there was never any state-civil society partnership for welfare services in Greece; in Italy it has existed but had problems of implementation; and in Spain it is very recent, only having started in the late 1990s (Ascoli, Glatzer and Sotiropoulos 2013, 20–22). In Portugal, on the contrary, a programme of this type was created in the early 1980s as a direct consequence of the revolutionary period of 1974–1975 (Fernandes 2014).

The constitutional court's blockade of major government laws and satisfying popular demands made austerity less harsh, as well as fuelling protest within the existing system. The Constitutional Court (CT) has repeatedly rejected some of the government's harsher initiatives on the grounds of violating the equality principle in the constitution, as well as norms emanating from the revolutionary period. It rejected in July 2012 the Holiday and Christmas bonus cuts, on 26 September the Labour Code, and in May 2014 all cuts that had been made to public servants' wages from 2011 onwards (Accornero and Ramos Pinto 2014). This led the first minister of finance to resign in the summer of 2012 (Freire 2014, 12; González and Figueiredo 2014, 312).

Moreover, one of the motives in the constitution that is recognized as valid for collective action is the defence of the constitution itself. This proved to be quite important in the present cycle of anti-austerity protest, since much collective action against austerity was framed on this basis. For instance, the manifesto of the Platform P-15O read as follows: 'According to the constitutional principle achieved on 25 April 1974 ... the economy ... must be subordinated to the general interest of society' (Baumgarten 2013a, 468–469).

In terms of state repression, the police and the armed forces had almost no repressive role, besides keeping minimal order in major demonstrations. At the main demonstration of the austerity period, the QSLT demonstration on September 2012, the police forces had orders from the government not to react violently if attacked (DN, 23 September 2012, 3). At the same time, the National Commission for the Protection of Data published a document making it illegal for the police to use cameras to register demonstrations and possibly single activist actions (DN, 15 October 2012, 7).

But even more crucially, the professional and civic associations representative of the armed forces and the police were vocally critical of austerity policies, expressed strong opposition to the minister of defence, and organized several anti-austerity demonstrations during this period. Major protest events organized by the police and the military were the week of indignation (*semana de indignação*, 21–28 September 2011) of all police forces (PSP, GNR, ASAE), organized by the respective unions— Sindicato Nacional de Polícia (SINAPOL) and Associação Sindical dos Profissionais de Polícia (ASPP)—which culminated in a demonstration of 10,000 policemen in front of the Portuguese parliament. In addition, on 10 November 2012, 10,000 military demonstrated against the state budget before the Lisbon City Hall.

The police have also presented themselves as guardians of citizens' rights. On the banners of the police demonstrations of November 2011 it could be read: '*Polícia democrática ao serviço do cidadão*' (Democratic police at the service of citizens). Moreover, the military frequently declared that they would never be used to repress the rights of the Portuguese to demonstrate (DN, 06 November 2012 and 11 November 2012, 20). In fact, during the QSLT protests of 2 March 2012, the president of the national association of sergeants demanded the resignation of the government (*Público*, 03 March 2012).

In this sense, the police and military served as allies of anti-austerity protest movements, thus contributing to very low levels of violence in Portugal. The number of people sent to prison or physically injured was quite low (*Público*, 03 March 2012).

Another important aspect was the openness of institutions, namely the parliament, to protesters. Petitions presented to parliament have been an important part of the repertoire of protest in Portugal. During the crisis, not only did the number of petitions grow, but the response time from the parliament was much shorter than in the past (Tibúrcio 2015).

Even before the crisis, precarious movements such as FERVE presented petitions to parliament—in this case in July 2008 to end the so-called false green receipts, signed by 5257 people (Fonseca 2011, 7–9). On 20 November 2009, FERVE, Precários Inflexíveis, and Plataforma dos Intermitentes do Espectáculo e do Audiovisual presented the document 'Antes da Dívida Temos Direitos!' (Before the Debt We Have Rights), with 12,125 signatures. They were able to meet the president of the parliament and the head of the commission of work and social security, and the report was debated in parliament (Fonseca 2011, 11–14).

Moreover, parliament included two strong left-wing parties, the PCP and the BE, with historically deep roots in civil society and openness to protesters' demands. Together comprising almost 20 per cent of the seats, these two parties were thus central to the success of protest events. During the whole democratic period they have helped to organize protest and given voice to activists within institutions, while at the same time keeping social movements' repertoires of action within the older models of the strike and the legal demonstration. Just to give an example, the Portuguese social forum was born with the active support of the PCP and the BE, not only in terms of organization building but also in decision making. This was unique to the Portuguese social forum (Baumgarten 2013b, 13–14).

During the crisis, the PCP also had a solid organic linkage with organizations like CGTP (the biggest union confederation in Portugal), the Confederação Nacional de Agricultores (Agriculture National Confederation, CNA), the National Confederation of Pensioners and Elders (MURPI), and several cooperative associations. It also has successful ancillary organizations like youth and women's organizations (Juventude Comunista Portuguesa and Movimento Democrático de Mulheres, respectively). As of 2013, 60 per cent of communist parliament candidates were also members of a trade union (Lisi 2013).

In addition, with the emergence of the 'global justice movements' in the early 2000s, the BE created a position responsible for collaboration and the establishment of permanent linkages with these movements (Lisi 2013). During the first May Day in 2007, it furnished logistical and material support to the mobilization of precarious movements (FERVE, Precários Inflexíveis, and performing artists Intermitentes do Espectáculo) as well as in the drafting of specific legislative proposals. In early February 2011, it launched a campaign with the slogan 'precariousness is not the future' on small advertising billboards. Leaders of some of the precarious groups are also members of the main national BE bodies (Lisi 2013).

But social movements were also able to find allies in the socialist party. In early 2012, MPs from PS and BE developed a successful joint petition to the constitutional court in order to reverse that year's budget, especially regarding public sector cuts in salaries, pensions and summer and Christmas subsidies. In 2013 the strategic orientation of the PS was to work together with the radical left in order to reject the budgets in parliament and to present a parliamentary motion of no confidence in April (De Giorgi, Moury and Ruivo 2015).

In the aftermath of the European elections on 25 May 2014, the PS went through a change in leadership, which also moved it more clearly to the left. The socialist leader José Seguro, after an internal dispute, was replaced by his rival, António Costa, the president of Lisbon's city hall and a more left-wing politician who had ruled Lisbon in coalition with the radical left political party BE along with a plethora of citizen's movements. Interestingly, this was done thorough a new process, primary elections involving non-militants, with high participation (Raimundo and Pinto 2014).

A direct consequence of this strategic change of the PS was the formation of a political alliance with the BE and the PCP in the aftermath of the general elections of 4 October 2015. Although the centre-right PSD–CDS coalition had won the electoral contest (36.8 per cent of the vote) and the PS was the second most voted party (32.3 per cent), on 10 November 2015 the right-wing government was brought down in parliament by a vote of no-confidence of all the left parties (PS, PCP and BE). At the same time, these parties presented to the president a common agreement of support for a socialist minority government. This was guaranteed by the fact that all left parties combined had the majority of the votes and seats in parliament (the BE achieved 10.1 per cent and the PCP 8.2 per cent).

This strong connection with political parties probably also explains the rise in conventional political participation in Portugal during the crisis. Between 2008 and 2012, activities like 'contact a politician' grew from

5 to 9 per cent and 'distribute party propaganda' from 5 to 7 per cent (Viegas, Teixeira, and Amador 2015, 211–213).

Moreover, manifestos and public declarations by prominent politicians and national figures of the left and centre have appeared at crucial moments, supporting and calling for protest. On 11 November 2011 was published a 'Manifesto in defence of democracy, equality and public services'. This resulted in the presentation of a petition to parliament, which had collected 6759 signatures in just one week and which was debated during a parliamentary plenary session (Freire 2014, 14–16). In addition, on the day before the general strike of 24 November 2011, Mário Soares (socialist party founder, ex-prime minister and president of the country, considered the father of Portuguese democracy) and eight other personalities published a manifesto appealing to the Portuguese to struggle against austerity. The manifesto declared that 'this is the moment to mobilize the citizens of the left, who believe in social justice and in the deepening of democracy as ways to fight the crisis'. This position was echoed in the left-wing parties, with the PS and the PCP supporting the strike (DN, 20 November 2011, 12).

Another manifesto was published on 11 March 2014, the 'Manifesto 3D' (Dignity, Democracy and Development), inspired by the famous expression of the three D's of the Portuguese revolution (Decolonize, Democratize, Develop). It was signed by major centre and left-wing figures (from PSD, PS, PCP and BE). It presented a petition (with almost 34,000 signatures) to the Portuguese parliament aimed both at the restructuring of the Portuguese debt and at state investment policies destined to promote growth and employment (*Público*, 11 March 2014; *Público*, 19 March 2014).

Finally, in the summer of 2014, about 30 centre and left personalities published the manifesto 'Por uma Democracia de Qualidade' (For a Democracy with Quality), in which they asked for deep institutional changes like the reform of the electoral system, transparency in the financing of political parties, and attention to the growing divide between citizens and politicians (Alves 2014, 57).

There were also a series of allies in civil society, especially at the height of the protest in September 2012, including some employers' associations, the church, the national confederation of social welfare associations, and the media. Employers' organizations were quite sceptical of austerity programmes during this period (in contrast to selected economic groups like distribution chains or big banks). In June 2013, the four employers'

confederations represented in the corporatist concertation body (CES–
Conselho Económico e Social) publicly presented a document criticizing
government policies. It said that 'it is urgent to reconcile government
targets with reality [...]. The fiscal consolidation policy continues to be
based on a reduction of domestic demand, an unwise tax increase and
scarce financing opportunities for small and medium-sized firms [...].
Austerity has been a short-term answer (implemented as if it was the only
possible answer) but nowadays, given its results, it would be irresponsible
to pursue or, even worse, to further develop this approach [...] we cannot
insist on a policy that is not a solution for Portugal and from which, if we
insist on it, there can be no way back' (González and Figueiredo 2014).

Specific policies have also been actively opposed by employers, which
supported at the same time the demands of unions and social movements.
When in the summer of 2013 the government increased private sector
workers' social security contributions to 18 per cent (while also decreasing contributions in the same proportion), there was widespread discontent both from unions and employers. As the head of the Manufacturing
and Construction Employers' Confederation said at the time, 'the pillar of social stability and coordinated market economy is under attack'
(González and Figueiredo 2014, 311).

Furthermore, employers' organizations were sympathetic to protest. In
the aftermath of the massive QSLT demonstrations in September 2012,
António Saraiva, president of the industry confederation, claimed that 'the
government must learn from the protest and find alternative policies to
the TSU. There must be more public investment' (DN, 18 September
2012, 5); the Catholic Church, through the council of Portuguese bishops
appealed to 'political stability' and 'equity in the solutions and distribution
of benefits' (DN, 19 September 2012, 1); and Eugénio Fonseca, president
of the biggest platform of social welfare organizations in Portugal, also
lent support to the protesters. As he said, not only does the 'government
ha[ve] to be sensible to the protest', but a strong civil society is decisive to
'make sure capital is not so dominant' (*Público*, 03 March 2012).

Finally, media coverage of the large demonstrations, according to
Baumgarten, was complete and positive. This confirms Robert Fishman's
assertion that a 'crucial feature of Portugal's post-revolutionary democratic practice is the openness of the communication media to the voices of
relatively powerless protesters' (Fishman 2011, 5). The QSLT demonstration of 15 September 2012 started being mentioned on 27 August, and
on this day the main newspaper *O Público* gave an overview of the many

austerity measures in Portugal since 2010. The media referred to the high numbers of people who confirmed their participation on the Facebook pages of the protest events, and the demonstration was reported on all four major television stations. The protests of the Geração à Rasca were also widely supported by the media. The main daily newspapers *O Público* and *Diário de Notícias* reported about the high numbers of people who announced their participation on Facebook as well, and asked demonstrators about their reasons for joining the protest. The *Diário de Notícias* also noted that Portugal is one of the countries with the highest rates of fixed-term contracts and connected this information to the protests. Moreover, almost all of the smaller demonstrations were announced by the daily newspapers and by national television and radio (Baumgarten 2013a, 10–11).

6.5   NEWSPAPERS

Diário de Notícias (DN)
Público

6.6   LIST OF INTERVIEWEES

Contemporary anti-austerity activists:
   João Camargo (PI, QSLT, BE)
   Nuno Rodrigues (PI, P-15O, MAS)
   Tiago Gillot (PI, May Day, Auditoria Cidadã)
   Paula Gil (Geração à Rasca, M12M, Iniciativa Legislativa de Cidadãos/ Lei contra a Precariedade)
   Hugo Evangelista (PI, May Day)

NOTES

1. Interviews have been made at the Department of Political Studies, Nova University, between March and June 2014.
2. Plataforma 15 de Outubro (PLatform 15th of October)

REFERENCES

Accornero, Guya, and Pedro Ramos Pinto. 2014. "Mild Mannered"? Protest and Mobilisation in Portugal under Austerity, 2010–2013. *West European Politics* 40: 1–25.

Alves, Carlos. 2014. *Crises económicas e movimentos sociais de protesto: O caso de Portugal, 2011–2014.* PhD Project, Nova University, Lisbon.

Amador, Inês. 2013. *Protesto Político nas Democracias da Europa do Sul (Portugal, Espanha e Grécia): Uma análise comparada e longitudinal (2002–2012).* Master's thesis in Political Science, ISCTE-IUL.

Ascoli, Ugo, Miguel Glatzer, and Dimitri A. Sotiropulos. 2013. Southern European Welfare and Social Services: The Role of the Third Sector. *Conference of Europeanists*, Amsterdam, June 25–27.

Baumgarten, Britta. 2013a. Geração à Rasca and Beyond: Mobilizations in Portugal After 12 March 2011. *Current Sociology* 61(4): 457–473.

———. 2013b. Why Did Suddenly so Many People Appear? The Success of the Portuguese 15 September 2012 Protests. *Paper for the Political Science Seminar at FCSH/UNL.*

Camargo, João. 2013. *Que se lixe a troika!* Deriva: Porto.

De Giorgi, Elisabetta, Catherine Moury, and João Pedro Ruivo. 2015. Incumbents, Opposition and International Lenders: Governing Portugal in Times of Crisis. *The Journal of Legislative Studies* 21(1): 54–74.

Estanque, Elísio. 2014. Rebeliões de classe média? Precariedade e movimentos sociais em Portugal e no Brasil (2011–2013). *Revista Crítica de Ciências Sociais* 103: 53–80.

Estanque, Elisio, Hermes Augusto Costa, and José Soeiro. 2013. The New Global Cycle of Protest and the Portuguese Case. *Journal of Social Science Education* 12(1): 31–40.

Fernandes, Tiago. March 2014. Rethinking Pathways to Democracy: Civil Society in Spain and Portugal, 1960s–2000s. Democratization 22: 1074–1104.

Fishman, Robert M. 2011. Democratic Practice after the Revolution: The Case of Portugal and Beyond. *Politics and Society* 39(2): 233–267.

Fonseca, Dora. 2012a. The Crisis in Europe, the Precariat's Movements and Trade Unionism: Differences and Possibilities of Cooperation in Action. *Council for European Studies Conference*, Amsterdam.

———. 2012b. A mobilização de 12 de Março em Portugal: Movimento social ou 'explosão'? Atores, processos e consequências. *Sociologia, Revista da Faculdade de Letras da Universidade do Porto* 24: 113–131.

———. 2011. Precariedade laboral e a emergência de novos actores sociolaborais: Os movimentos de trabalhadores precários em Portugal. *XI Congresso Luso Afro Brasileiro de Ciências Sociais*, Salvador, 7–10 August 2011.

Freire, André. 2014. The Condition of Portuguese Democracy During the Troika's Intervention. *Paper Delivered at the Conference Crisis politics in Southern Europe: Challenges to Democratic Governance*, University of Nicosia, Cyprus, 24 April 2014.

González, Pilar and António Figueiredo. 2014. The European Social Model in a Context of Crisis and Austerity in Portugal. In The European Social Model in Times of Economic Crisis and Austerity Policies, ed. Daniel Vaughan-Whitehead. International Labor Organization.

Gutiérrez, Rodolfo. 2014. Welfare Performance in Southern Europe: Employment Crisis and Poverty Risk. *South European Society and Politics* 19(3): 371–392.

Joaquim, Claudia. 2015. *O Terceiro Sector e a Protecção Social: Que Modelo para Portugal?* M.Phil. Dissertation, ISCTE, Lisbon.

Lima, Maria da Paz Campos, and Antonio Martín Artiles. 2013. Youth voice(s) in EU Countries and Social Movements in Southern Europe. *Transfer* 19(3): 345–363.

———. 2011. Crisis and Trade Union Challenges in Portugal and Spain: Between General Strikes and Social Pacts. *Transfer* 17(3): 387–402.

Lisi, Marco. 2013. Rediscovering Civil Society? Renewal and Continuity in the Portuguese Radical Left. *South European Society and Politics* 18: 21–39.

Magalhães, Pedro. 2014. After the Bailout: Responsibility, Policy, and Valence in the Portuguese Legislative Election of June 2011. *South European Society and Politics* 17(2): 309–327.

Matsaganis, Manos, and Chrysa Leventi. 2014. The Distributional Impact of Austerity and the Recession in Southern Europe. *South European Society and Politics* 19(3): 393–412.

Moury, Catherine, and Adam Standring. 2013. *"Não há alternativas": Discursive Depoliticization and the Construction of Crisis Meta-Narratives in Portuguese Austerity Policies.* FCSH-UNL: Draft Paper.

Moury, Catherine, and André Freire. 2015. A Política e as políticas de austeridade: O caso português. In *Crise Económica, Políticas de Austeridade e Representação Política*, eds. André Freire, José Manuel Leite Viegas, Marco Lisi. Lisbon, Assembleia da República, Coleção Parlamento.

Natali, David, and Furio Stamati. 2014. Reassessing South European Pensions after the Crisis: Evidence from Two Decades of Reforms. *South European Society and Politics* 19(3): 309–330.

Pequito Teixeira, Conceição, Emmanouil Tsatsanis, and Ana Maria Belchior. 2014. Support for Democracy in Times of Crisis: Diffuse and Specific Regime Support in Portugal and Greece. *South European Society and Politics* 19(4): 501–518.

Raimundo, Filipa, and António Costa Pinto. 2014. When Parties Succeed: Party System (In)Stability and the 2008 Financial Crisis in Portugal. Paper Prepared for the 2014 Annual Meeting of the American Political Science Association, Washington DC, August 28–31.

Rodrigues, Maria de Lurdes, and Pedro Adão e Silva. 2015. A Execução do Memorando de Entendimento. *Governar com a Troika. Políticas Públicas em Tempo de Austeridade*, eds. Maria de Lurdes Rodrigues and Pedro Adão e Silva. Lisboa, Almedina.

Soeiro, José. 2014. Da Geração à Rasca ao Que se Lixe a Troika. Portugal no novo ciclo internacional de protesto. *Sociologia. Revista da Faculdade de Letras da Universidade do Porto*, Vol. XXVIII: 55–79

Sousa, Luís de, Pedro Magalhães, and Luciano Amaral. 2014. Sovereign Debt and Governance Failures Portuguese Democracy and the Financial Crisis. *American Behavioral Scientist* 58(12): 1517–1541.

Tibúrcio, Tiago. 2015. O Parlamento e os cidadãos em Portugal: O direito de petição antes e depois do acordo da Troika, à luz de critérios de eficácia. In *Crise Económica, Políticas de Austeridade e Representação Política*, eds. André Freire, José Manuel Leite Viegas, Marco Lisi, Lisbon, Assembleia da República, Coleção Parlamento.

Viegas, José Manuel Leite, Conceição Pequito Teixeira, and Inês Amador. 2015. Formas e estiloes de participação política na Europa: antes e depois da crise económica de 2008. In *Crise Económica, Políticas de Austeridade e Representação Política*, ed. André Freire, José Manuel Leite Viegas, and Marco Lisi. Lisbon: Assembleia da República, Colecção Parlamento.

CHAPTER 7

Neoliberalism and Its Discontents in Italy: Protests Without Movement?

Massimiliano Andretta

7.1 Introduction

In the early 2000s, Italian social movements have probably been among the most active in creating a strong anti-neoliberal mobilization in Europe (della Porta et al. 2006; Andretta et al. 2002). The Italian branch of the global justice movement has in fact been characterized by a network of different social movement sectors. Along with active involvement of organizations originating in the labour movement and an impressive presence of groups with a Catholic background, the movement includes activists from the social centres of the 1990s as well as the 'new' social movements of the 1970s and 1980s.

Nonetheless, the mobilization against the current economic crisis and the austerity measures undertaken by Italian governments in recent years has been relatively weak in terms of political outcomes. First, the anti-austerity protest field was dominated by old actors, and was not able to produce the strong social and political coalitions that emerged in the anti-neoliberal mobilization phase. Second, the mobilization has not, so far, had an impact on the political and party system that could at least create the conditions for challenging the neoliberal, austerity-oriented responses to the economic crisis.

The still ongoing economic crisis has triggered widespread protest, especially against the Italian governments' austerity measures. In this

The author is grateful to Mario Morroni for his comments on a previous draft of this chapter.

D. della Porta et al., *Late Neoliberalism and its Discontents in the Economic Crisis*, DOI 10.1007/978-3-319-35080-6_7

chapter, I will single out the main characteristics of Italian anti-austerity mobilization from 2009 to 2014, making use of different types of sources and integrating qualitative and quantitative methods of analysis: in-depth interviews with activists involved in the most visible organizations mobilizing against austerity (see Appendixat the end of this chapter); the documents of social movement organizations, available online and selected on the basis of personal knowledge and information gathered through newspapers and the above mentioned interviews; and, finally, a protest event analysis based on newspaper articles from *La Repubblica* (2009–2014). The aims of this chapter are, first, to contextualize the Italian anti-austerity mobilization in its economic, social and political context; second, to describe its main characteristics; and, finally, to provide an explanation for the comparative weakness of such mobilization in terms of political outcomes.

In the next section, we will summarize the socio-economic and political contexts in which the recent anti-austerity protest emerged; in the section Anti-Austerity Mobilization, we will analyse the main characteristics of the anti-austerity protests, by singling out the number of protest events throughout the considered period, the issues around which the protests occurred, the main organizational actors, the forms the protests took, and their main targets. In the section Anti-Austerity Repertoire, we will reconstruct the frame of the crisis developed by the actors of the anti-austerity mobilization by underlining the importance of democracy within it. In the section Framing the Crisis, we will suggest that the relative weakness of the anti-austerity mobilization is related to a specific relationship between progressive social movements and their potential allies. The economic crisis and the related austerity policies represent a real 'threat' for the constituency of many civil society organizations, especially trade unions and social movements. However, due to a peculiar political opportunity structure, which operates upon a specific type of civil society, this threat did not foster broad social and political anti-austerity coalitions. Although protest mobilization against anti-austerity measures was relatively high, an anti-austerity movement failed to emerge (see the section on Explaining Mobilization). In the conclusions, we will address the Italian case in a comparative perspective.

7.2   THE CRISIS IN THE CRISIS: THE SOCIO-ECONOMIC AND POLITICAL CONDITIONS OF ANTI-AUSTERITY PROTEST IN ITALY

Contemporary Italian protests must be contextualized in what we can call a 'multilevel' crisis. On one hand, in Italy, the financial crisis did not have a strong effect on the banking system, as 'the tradition of the Banca d'Italia controls, the prudency of the intermediaries, the recent restructuration of the financial industry, the lower private indebtedness, the less lively economy, all contributed to the result ... of luring Italy away from the international financial instability' (Ciocca 2010, 52–4). The turbulent financial market, however, hit Italy as well as the other South European countries, creating obstacles to the refinancing plans for the growing public deficit (which increased in Italy from –1.59 in 2007 to –5.36 in 2009)[1] and a spectacular increase in the differential between interest rates in Italy and Germany. Moreover, given its chronically low level of productivity, Italy has been strongly affected by the world real economic crisis, induced by the financial crisis, with a drop in the GDP (Fig. 7.1). Even worse, 'Italy had already been experiencing for several years a creeping crisis, characterized by stagnation and inflation ... with a progressive erosion in terms

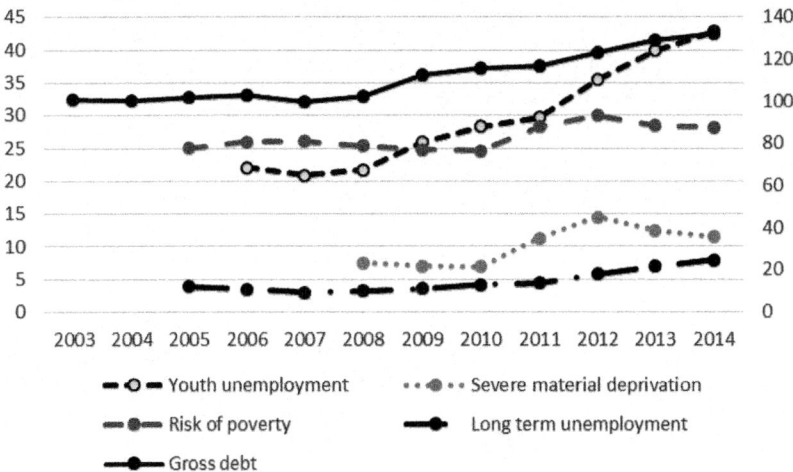

Fig. 7.1   Socio-economic indicators in Italy *Source*: Eurostat, our elaboration

of competitiveness and per capita income in comparison with the other European countries' (D'Ippoliti and Roncaglia 2011, 213). According to some authors, the 'crisis' of recent years only worsened the already existing Italian crisis, which is more structural than conjunctural: the low competitiveness is the result of a productivity based on low investment in technologies, high use of the labour force (Lucidi and Kleinknecht 2010), and specialization on labour intensive sectors (D'Ippoliti and Roncaglia 2010, 214).

When the current economic crisis began, the Italian government was led by Silvio Berlusconi and his centre-right coalition. The Italian government's difficulties in facing the turbulent financial markets and the sovereign debt crisis led the prime minister to resign under domestic and European pressures. In 2011, a new, so-called caretaker government was formed under the leadership of the economist Mario Monti, supported by a large coalition in the Parliament, including both the People of the Liberty (PDL)[2] and the Democratic Party (PD),[3] the Italian President of the Republic, Giorgio Napolitano, and the European Union (EU) institutions. The Monti government was to introduce further austerity policies. Under Monti, the Italian government received the infamous secret letter from the European Central Bank explicitly asking it to proceed with the necessary 'structural reforms', which included liberalization, job flexibility, privatization and cuts in public sectors employed salaries, all considered important measures to increase the Italian growth potential (*Sole 24 Ore*, 29 September 2011; *Corriere della Sera*, 29 September 2011).

In 2013, new national elections were held. Given an electoral law that assigns majority prizes at the national level for the Chamber of Deputies and at the regional level for the Senate, the centre-left coalition, formed by the Democratic Party and Sinistra, Ecologia e Libertà (SEL, Left, Ecology, and Liberty)[4] won the majority of seats in the former but not in the latter. Besides the electoral law, the centre-left was kept to a mere 29.55 per cent of votes not only by the electoral performance of the centre-right coalition (including the PDL, the Lega Nord [North League] and other small right-wing parties), which obtained 29.18 per cent, but also due to the unforeseen success of the Movimento 5 Stelle (M5S, the Five Star Movement), which earned 25 per cent of the votes, a good part of them from former centre-left voters (Bordignon and Ceccarini 2013). The spectacular electoral performance of the M5S has been interpreted as the voters' reaction to the austerity measures undertaken by mainstream left and right political parties, as its electoral manifesto focused on strong criticism towards the European institutions and their diktats (Alonso 2014, 20; Franzosi, Marone, and Salvati 2015).

The electoral results led the President of the Republic to play a key role in creating a large new coalition government, led by Enrico Letta (PD), with the support of the PD, Scelta Civica (Civic Choice, the party created by Mario Monti), and the Nuovo Centro Destra (NCD, New Centre Right, originated from a split in the PDL), as well as Forza Italia, which withdrew after a couple of weeks. The new government lasted until February 2014, when Letta was replaced by the new secretary of the PD, Matteo Renzi, who formed a new government with the same parliamentary support. After the end of the Berlusconi government, the PD was then at the centre of the new governments that had to deal with the austerity measures that had been aggressively promoted by the European Commission, the International Monetary Fund (IMF) and the European Central Bank (ECB).

However, austerity policies had already been introduced before the Monti government. A recent report on 'the impact of the crisis on fundamental rights across member states of the EU' (Nastasi and Palmisano 2015), commissioned by the LIBE committee (Committee on Civil Rights, Justice and Home Affairs) of the European Parliament, summarized the Italian governments' measures linked to the crisis since 2008 in relevant sectors. Here we focus on only four sectors: educational, healthcare, labour market and budget. In the educational sector, looking only at compulsory education, the report mentions the Decreto Brunetta (Decree-Law 112/2008), which ' sought to slash spending on public schools by 8 billion euros, increase the number of students per teacher, and reduce schools' non-teaching staff' (Nastasi and Palmisano 2015, 11). There were cuts in the education system in 2010, the merging of schools with less than 1000 pupils, and reduction of personnel in 2011 (ibid., 18–23). In addition, the university system received cuts in the ordinary financing fund (FFO), accelerated by the economic measures accompanying the so-called Riforma Gelmini (Law 240/2010) and increasing in the following years until 2014. As the report concludes, 'This and other measures in the sector are in line with Italy's long tradition of underinvestment in education: Italy is the only country in the OECD [Organization for Economic Cooperation and Development] not to have increased expenditure per student since 1995; by comparison, spending in other OECD countries increased on average by 62 %' (Nastasi and Palmisano 2015, 10).

Other policies have addressed the healthcare system, through austerity measures introduced by the so-called health pacts between the state and the regions. Budgetary constraints 'have limited the possibility for the Regions to provide healthcare services beyond national basic service standards (*livelli essenziali di assistenza* or LEA)' and, in addition, 'there are also indications that waiting times for medical services may be longer than acceptable and that reduced spending on pharmaceuticals may hinder or delay Italy's access to the most expensive, newer drugs' (Nastasi and Palmisano 2015).

As for the labour market, Italy has traditionally been characterized by activity and employment rates below the EU member states' average (D'Ippoliti and Roncaglia, 2011, 214). Labour market reforms began to be implemented at the end of the 1990s, with the aim of lowering the obstacles to work entrance and exit and decentralizing salary negotiations. Even if these measures initially had some positive impacts in terms of employment for women and youth, 'certainly these measures had a negative impact in terms of work quality and precariousness' (D'Ippoliti and Roncaglia 2011; see also Corsi et al. 2007). The report to the European Parliament states that Law 92/2012:

> ... made it easier to dismiss workers. It also sought to limit the practice of using certain cooperation contracts that offer employees lower protection than the standard permanent employment contract. Evidence suggests, however, that the reform did not succeed in reducing the prevalence of precarious forms of work on the Italian labour market. Some argued that easier dismissals have actually resulted in people losing their jobs, without making access to the job market any easier for others. (Nastasi and Palmisano 2015, 11)

The data shown in Figs. 7.1 and 7.2 confirm this conclusion.

Budget reforms have been introduced through three types of measures: pension reforms, spending reviews and a constitutional amendment. Pension reforms started to be implemented in 1992 (Decree 53/1992)—when the retirement age was raised and the calculation for determining pension amounts gradually extended to the entire work life—and then again in 1995 (Law 335/1995) with the so-called Dini reform, through which the pension calculation system, formerly characterized by a retributive mechanism, moved towards a contributive process. Other reforms raising the retirement age, incentivizing the retirement delay, reinforcing the contributive mechanism, and facilitating access to the supplementary

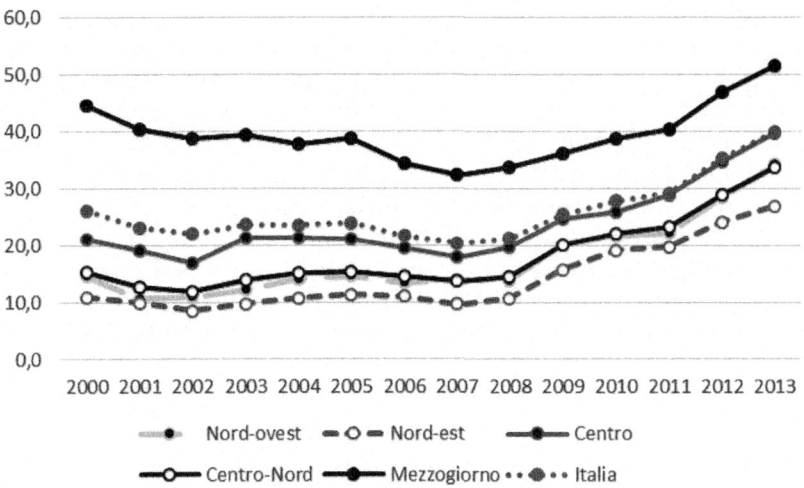

Fig. 7.2 Youth unemployment rate (ages 15–24) *Source*: Istat, our elaboration

pension systems were passed in 2000 (legislative Decree 47/2000), 2004 (Enabling Law 243/2004), and 2007 (Law 247/2007) by both centre-right and centre-left governments (Ferrera 2006; Natali 2007).

As for the legislation passed during the crisis, the report mentions the pension reform of 2010 (DL 78/2010, converted into L 122/2010), introducing 'stricter age and contribution requirements, particularly for public employees, automatic periodic adjustment of benefits and require-ments to life expectancy' (Nastasi and Palmisano, 2015, 22). In addition, the Decree-Law 201/2011 (*Decreto Salva Italia*—Save Italy Decree) changed the age and contribution requirements for retirement, as well as the methodology for calculating the amount of retirement pensions (Nastasi and Palmisano 2015, 59). The report underlines that:

A particularly regrettable side-effect of the new rules on retirement age and contribution requirements was the so-called *esodati* issue—workers who had agreed with their employers to leave their post to their children, accepting to resign earlier than retirement age but with the expectation, under the applicable laws, to acquire the right to pension within a few years. When the retirement age was increased, they found themselves without a job or pension for much longer than they had envisaged. (Nastasi and Palmisano 2015)

Spending reviews have reorganized the welfare and judicial systems by merging bodies, cutting expenditures, reorganizing and limiting local services, and introducing a cost review process in 2011, 2012 and 2014 (when further cuts in expenditures were planned as follows: 4.5 billion euros in 2014, 17 billion euros in 2015, 32 billion euros in 2016) (Nastasi and Palmisano 2015, 18–23). In 2012, the obligation of a structural budget balance was introduced into the Italian Constitution.

As for the effects of these interventions, even if the GDP stopped declining in 2012 (see Fig. 7.1), it is still well below the European average. Moreover, the national GDP 'growth' (very limited in any case) hides visible regional differences. For instance, in the period 2008–2012, while the Italian GDP decreased by 6.9 per cent on average, in the so-called Mezzogiorno (South and the main islands), it declined to –10.1 per cent.[5] In addition, in the period under consideration, there was an acceleration of the already existing (Galbraith and Garcilazo 2004) income redistribution towards the healthier sectors of the population (Sylos Labini 2009); an increase in unemployment, more strongly affecting young Italians (especially, but not only, in the South, Fig. 7.2); and the related impoverishment of the population (Fig. 7.1).

Overall, both the crisis and the austerity policies have worsened the social conditions of the Italian population, and it is not surprising that the austerity measures were highly unpopular. According to the results of an opinion poll survey conducted in 2013 by Gallup,[6] 62 per cent of Italians believe that the 'policy of austerity in Europe' is not working, only 3 per cent that it is working, and 28 per cent that it is working, but it takes time. At the same time, 76 per cent said that those policies are serving the interests of only certain countries (mostly Germany), and 67 per cent believe that 'there are alternatives'. The same survey shows that 66 per cent of Italians are rather pessimistic about the future of young people in Europe: as many as 92 per cent believe that young people will have fewer opportunities than their parents' generation to have a secure job; 87 per cent a satisfying job; 93 per cent a secure pension; 92 per cent a high salary, and 54 per cent a comfortable accommodation. In Italy, as in Greece, Spain, Portugal and Ireland, trust in the principal institutions at both the national and the European levels has drastically fallen starting from January 2010 (Alonso 2014). Even if in Italy the crisis of the political system and of its relations with the voters dates to long before the current economic crisis and related austerity measures, the perception that voters can do little in affecting policies is also signalled by the fall in electoral participation in the most recent years.

7.3   ANTI-AUSTERITY MOBILIZATION: PROTEST WITHOUT MOVEMENT?

It was in this economic, political and cultural context that Italian anti-austerity protests emerged. According to protest events data we gathered between 2009 and 2014, *La Repubblica* reported on 1140 protests in Italy.[7] Anti-austerity related claims of the protest events (economic crisis, budget cuts, privatization, labour issues, cuts in welfare—education, health system, culture)[8] are present in as much as 70 per cent of the protest events and, as it appears in Fig. 7.3, the correlation between anti-austerity protest and all protest events by month is very strong (Pearson = 0.89, significant at 0.001 level). The government and institutions have been the main target throughout the six years selected, addressed by about 83 per cent of the protest events. While this politicization of claim making is quite common, it is worth noting that as much as 21 per cent of the events targeted a firm or a bank. The level of the target in the reported events was national in more than 84 per cent of the protest events, while in about 7 per cent the target was at the EU or international level.

The peak of the protest cycle was reached in 2010, when the crisis started to become evident in Italy under the centre-right government still led by Silvio Berlusconi (Fig. 7.3). Moreover, while in each year the protests concentrate mainly in the autumn, when the stability law is discussed in parliament, during the Berlusconi government two peaks of the protest were also reached in March–May 2010 and March–May 2011. It is also interesting to note that, apart from January 2012, the government led by Mario Monti and the current Renzi government have been relatively less often targeted by the protest: the total mean number of protest events per month is 15.6 (the mean under Berlusconi is 17, under Monti 12.8, under Letta 15.8 and, finally, under Renzi 12).

Almost all of the activists and the key witnesses interviewed agree on three thematic areas that have been at the core of the protest arena in Italy in the last years: labour, environment and housing. In the words of the leader of the grassroots trade union COBAS, there are:

> ... three blocks, the labour question, the precariousness where there is a vast area of squatted social centres, students, part of the grassroots trade unionism; the environmental issue in all its variants—water, big infrastructures, garbage disposals; the housing issue which is a big issue especially because

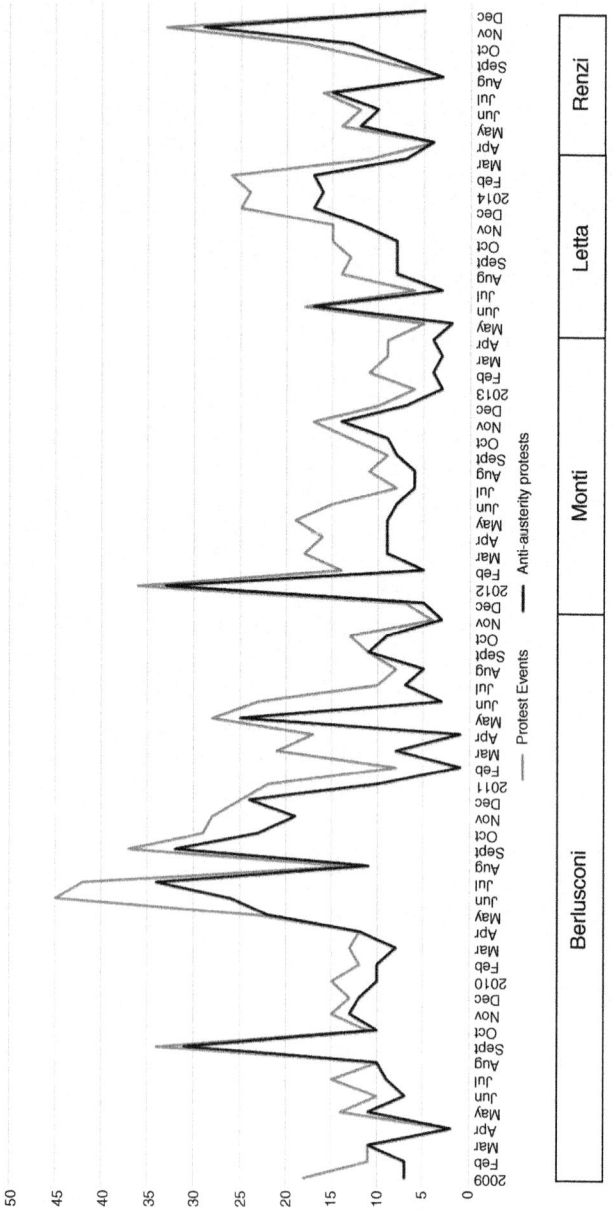

Fig. 7.3 Protests and anti-austerity protests in Italy 2009–2014, by month and government

it includes the migrants, with a very consistent, large migrant participation, and that will become even bigger for the attacks against them by the North League and other fascist areas. (Interviewee IT1, see also Interviewees IT2, IT4 and IT5)

The role of the student movement is also stressed. As a former student movement activist explained, 'the student movement had a key role for two reasons: because it expressed a time continuity since the "Onda" [the Wave, a strong national student mobilization] of 2008 and then occupying the protest field with strong organizations till 2011; and because it had a transversal character which allowed the relations with other actors', such as workers, precarious workers and the social centres.

The social profiles of the protestors, as reported by the newspaper articles, also seem to confirm that workers (present in 62 per cent of protest events), precarious workers (8 per cent), students (15 per cent), and to a lesser extent unemployed (2 per cent) and immigrants (5 per cent), are more present in the protest arena.[9] The dominant social profile is by far that of the 'workers', which means public and private employed. Only under the Berlusconi government and at the beginning of the Monti government did the precarious social profile, which includes students, immigrants, unemployed and precarious workers (Standing 2011), show up in protest arena in the same way as the traditionally employed (Fig. 7.4).

7.3.1   The Organizational Field of Anti-Austerity Protest

Organizationally speaking, our respondents underline the role of established trade unions (such as the CGIL and the FIOM), grassroots unions, student organizations, local committees, squatted social centres and other informal groups; but also of formal associations. They also emphasize the declining presence of political parties (especially of the radical leftists, but also in some cases of the Five Star Movement, which has been particularly present on environmental issues) (Interviewees IT1, IT2, IT3, IT4, IT5, IT6, IT8 and IT10).

According to the Protest Event Analysis (PEA) data, about 45 per cent of the total protest events have included trade unions: 52 per cent under the Berlusconi government, only 23 per cent under Monti, 44 per cent under Letta, and as much as 65 per cent under Renzi. A claim related to anti-austerity was present in 95 per cent of trade union protest events—although 50 per cent of all anti-austerity protests fall under different types

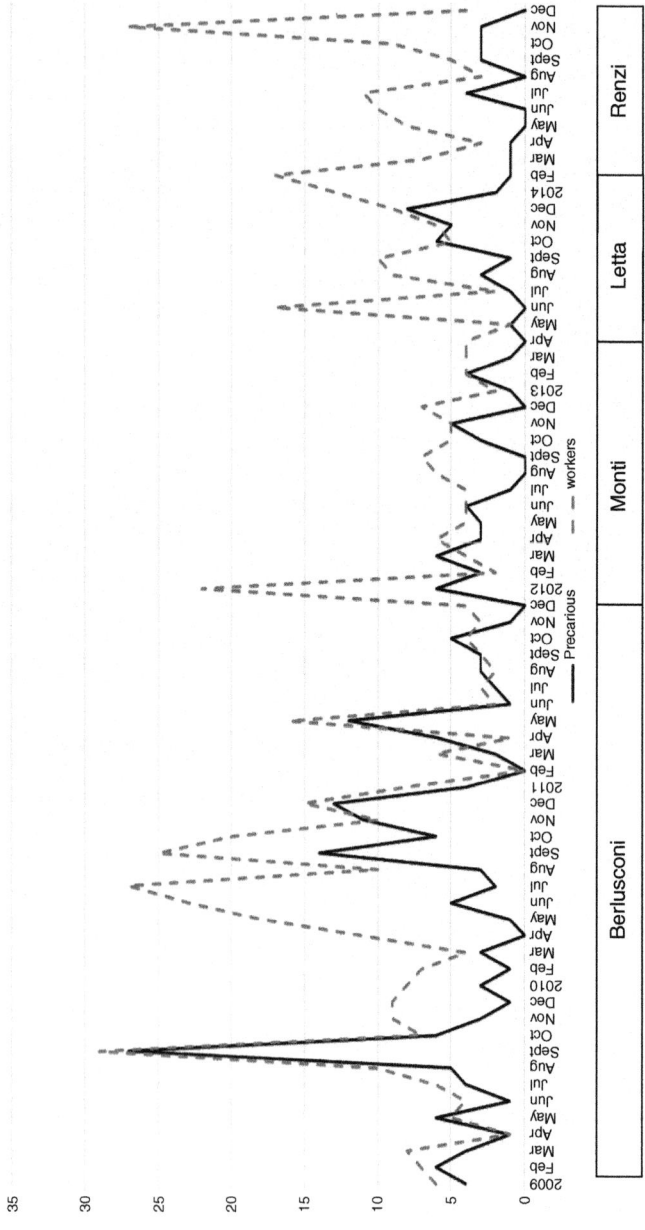

Fig. 7.4 Workers and precarious protests per month and government (absolute numbers) (Italy)

of mobilization. In about 62 per cent of the total trade union protest events, the traditional trade union confederations were present: the CGIL or its affiliate metalworker trade union (FIOM) was present in 52 per cent, while the three confederations protested together in about 22 per cent of the total trade union protest events. Grassroots trade unions, traditionally leftist and critical of the three main Confederations, were present in about 40 per cent of the total trade union protest events. Notwithstanding tensions between the leftist grassroots and the confederations, the former protested with the CGIL in about 15 per cent of the total trade union protest events. Interestingly enough, the percentage of co-staged protest is higher under the Berlusconi government (18 per cent) and lower under Monti (9 per cent) and Renzi (7 per cent).

What is more, the protest event analysis indicates that while established trade unions are central throughout the whole cycle of anti-austerity protest, their protest mobilization declined under the Monti government. And if we look at the type of trade unions in the protest arena, we see that, while the CGIL and the confederations decreased their presence, grassroots trade unions prevailed in the protest events under Monti and Letta (Figs. 7.5 and 7.6).

Although the Italian anti-austerity protest cycle has been channelled by trade unions, other social movement organizations have been (even a bit more) present (43 per cent of the total, if we consider formal and informal social movement organizations together). While, however, non-union social movements were present in only 33 per cent of the anti-austerity related protests, vice-versa, anti-austerity claims were present in only 55 per cent of the total social movements' protests. If the student movement was more inclined to engage in anti-austerity protests, other movements such as environmental and women's movements framed their claims in a different way.

Social movement-led protests were relatively more common under the Monti government, when there was a decline in the protest cycle (they were present in 65 per cent of the total protest events in that period). Moreover, social movements protesting under the Monti government were more likely to be grassroots and informal (53 per cent, Fig. 7.6), as much as the trade unions protesting in that period were grassroots (Fig. 7.7).

Social movement organizations and trade unions seem to have lost their traditional connections in the protest arena. Especially, the leftist CGIL and its metalworker-affiliated FIOM have a tradition of interactions,

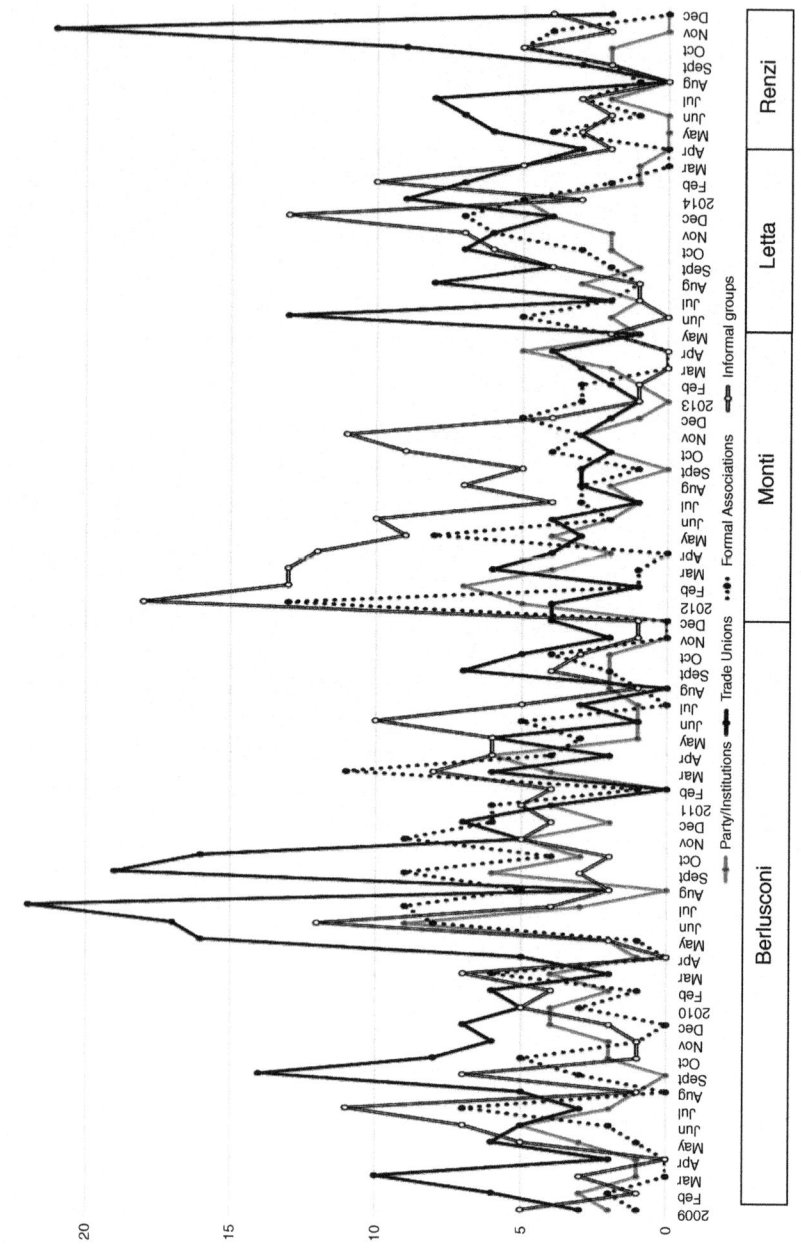

Fig. 7.5   Types of organizations protesting per month and government (absolute numbers) (Italy)

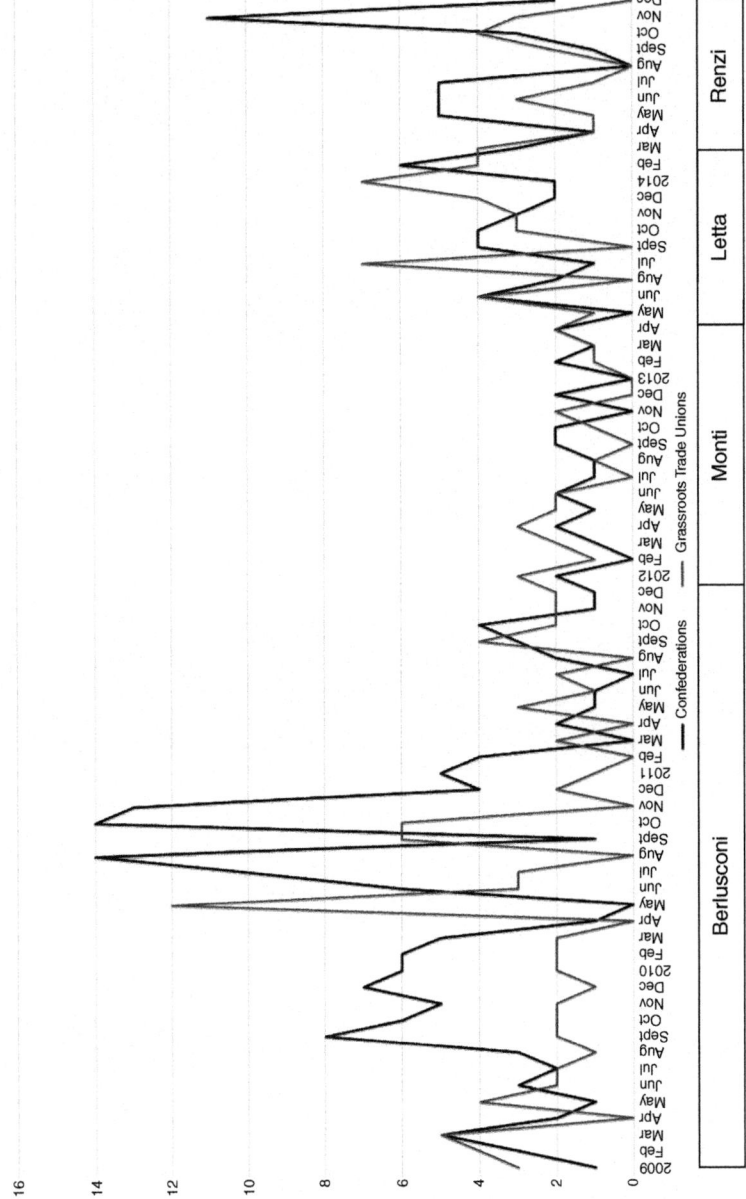

Fig. 7.6 Type of trade unions by month and government (absolute numbers) (Italy)

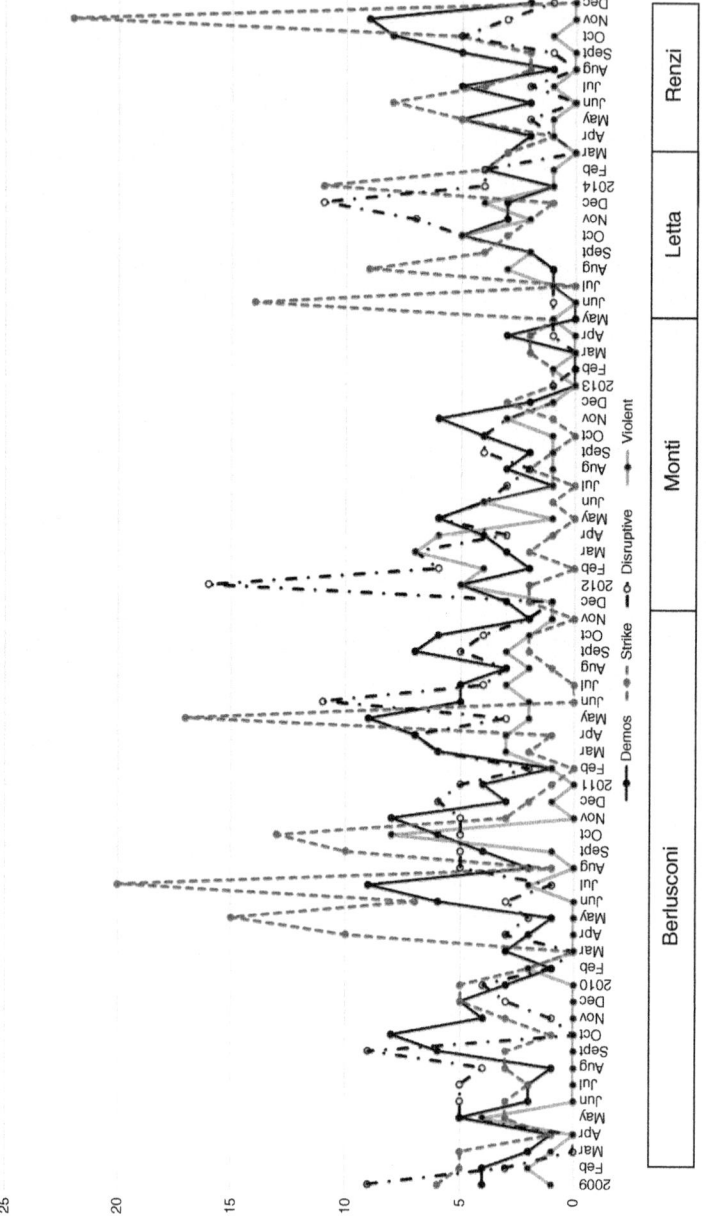

Fig. 7.7   Selected forms of action by month and government (absolute numbers) (Italy)

sometimes tense, with social movements. The long 1968 was characterized by the mobilization of both the student movement and the labour organizations; but even more recently, the Italian branch of the GJM (Global Justice Movement) was famous for its plurality and the renewed trust between old and new social movements of various kinds (della Porta 2009a, b). The threat of the economic crisis could have brought about a large coalition between the affected social groups and their organizations, but our data show that such an alliance failed. Although an anti-austerity claim was present in more than 80 per cent of the protests in which the two actors mobilized together, protests with co-mobilization of both types of actors amounted to only 7 per cent of the total protest events, further declining under the Monti and Letta governments (5 per cent), but rising slightly under the Renzi government (7 per cent). Violent actions were carried out in 20 per cent of those protests (versus 16 per cent of only social movement protests, 9 per cent in the protests in which both actors were absent, and 3 per cent of the protests staged only by trade unions). Many interviews with activists of both social movements and trade unions point to this tension and the failed attempt to create a strong alliance between different social actors (see the section on Anti-Austerity Repertoire).

Finally, there is a (minor and declining) role for political parties. After having been relatively active under the Berlusconi government, when all centre-leftist and leftist parties were in the opposition, their presence in the protest arena declined under the following governments, especially under Renzi (Fig. 7.6).

The relations among (leftist) parties, trade unions and social movements have always been controversially debated among social movement activists, but at the same time the alliance among movements, parties and unions had triggered some remarkable mobilizations in the past. It seems that something changed, and for the worse, in recent years. According to one respondent,

In Italy, there is like a pink thread from the Italian Communist Party (PCI) onward, that has never been really severed, because the Communist Refoundation Party had given impetus to the movements between 2001 and 2004, but when there is the 'call by the wild' [meaning the electoral and party alliance requirements] this link is broken ... It is like in Italy always existed this hood that jeopardized the conflictive realization linked to social movements within the parliament. Now there is Grillo, but he locked his party through barricades; he has nothing to do with social movements. (Interviewee IT1)

Party activists, especially the young party branches, have been active in the student movement, 'even though the party-movement relations became complicated' (Interviewee IT3). The leftist parties participated in the final phase of the water campaign, where party-movement relations have been at the centre of the campaign strategy: 'one of our goals has always been trying as much as possible to change the parties' agenda; the public debate during the electoral campaigns; forcing parties to publicly engage in favour of the campaign during the electoral phase' (Interviewee IT2). Another key witness argues that 'the workers' movement had its own national organization at the level of the political party, at level of the trade unions, and from this organization it built forms of internationalist solidarity … This clearly does not work any longer' (Interviewee IT4). Along a similar line, a key witness and precarious movement activist stressed that the party-led movement was 'an option at the end of the late nineteenth century'; while today 'there is an excess of "politicismo" [political orientation, meaning electoral and institutional orientation] of the bureaucratic parties and trade unions structures; this led them to orient any interactions with social movements in this view "politicista" … In its turn, this creates a lot of diffidence among social movements' (Interviewee IT5).

7.4   Anti-Austerity Repertoire

The Italian protest scene during the Great Recession seems to be characterized by a prevalently demonstrative (either a demonstration or a strike) and disruptive repertoire of action (Fig. 7.7).[10] Coherently with the Italian anti-austerity mobilization logic, led mainly by trade unions and socially based on the employed, the most visible demonstrative form has been the strike. This old form of action has been reinvented by grassroots trade unions, who called for what they named a 'social strike'. If the success of a traditional strike is linked to the number of workers who stop working, here,

> … who cares how many workers effectively did not go working? The production is in the city: we block the city for 24 hours. If you look at the strike [on 14 November 2014], the number of strikers is low, but the participation in the squares of 60 cities is very positive. The social strike was effectively coordinated and nothing wrong happened [meaning violent episodes or crashes with the police]. And this made a big impression … A kind of myth was created, like we moved an army, with a full control of the squares, with a very high participation.

As our interviewee observed, this form of action is resonant with transformation in the class structure:

> ... we think about new forms of mobilization which include the new 'partite Iva' [formally professionals selling their services, all the more used as dependent workers without contracts], the precarious workers, the students, but also the little shop owner... How do we ask people who cannot strike to strike? You can't strike, come to the square! We put in it a lot of narration, but the idea is simple. We gave the impression to some social sectors feeling as a sort of pariah—I'm not considered by them as they consider an employed because I can't strike—that their mobilization can make a difference. They cannot strike but they can join the mobilization once out of their work and create many more problems than by simply blocking for some hours a school or a factory. We gave them an option ... and now we are talking about a European social strike. (Interviewee IT1)

From a call for a meeting held in Rome in February 2015, the strike meeting, reads as follows:

> Not only the numbers, which have been also powerful, but also the spatial extension (more than 45 cities involved) and the time covered (24 hours); above all, the involvement of a broad social coalition, made of temporary workers, students, unemployed, grass-roots unions, committees in defence of commons and many more. A coalition that, overcoming the traditional form of the strike, was able to innovate practices, exhibiting the extension of exploitation outside the work place, from education to reproduction, from life forms to social relations. Nothing more than the beginning, no doubt, but a beginning that has left its mark.[11]

One of our key witnesses also presented this form of action as innovative, 'because it politicizes some forms of protest which spread in the years of the crisis and at the same time it has the ambition, potentially speaking, of building a new "common space"' (Interviewee IT4).

The metalworkers' unions affiliated with the CGIL, the FIOM, also participated in the social strike, and a FIOM activist presented it as an important step towards the construction of a new 'social coalition', bringing all forms of workers—precarious, autonomous and dependent—together with students and unemployed:

> ... if there is a goal our opponents aimed at it has until now been fragmentation and division ... this initiative is a way to overcome such fragmentation,

it is a way to speak of a new collective identity, of what we call a 'social coalition' ... The social strike involved forms of work of the future labour ... those who work in the logistic sector, the cognitive workers, the workers in the service sector, in the cooperatives, in the intellectual reproduction; that is, all those milieus which are de-structured from the point of view of the contracts. This is why we need a social strike: because you normally can call a strike in a metallurgic factory, but for those workers this is not possible. The social strike has to do with how you build a sociality in a broader space, in the country; it has to do with the welfare, which has been privatized in the last years; it has to do with the precarious workers of the school and the university, with a world that the traditional trade unions was unable to include, it has to do with a new form of trade unionism. (Interviewee IT6)

This activist also argues that 'the strike is the first step toward a process of identification, which I found very interesting because it re-builds a collective identity: without the production of identity we would not collectively recognize each other ... '.

Besides the classic demonstrations, demonstrative forms include symbolic actions to attract attention to the austerity measures and their consequences. One example is the academic researchers 'climbing on the roof' against the so-called government bill (DDL) Gelmini, which was considered as:

... innovative, though in a little pauperistic view, and this in fact was used also in the struggles against the crisis and the austerity: 'you want us under the bridges, we will climb the roofs' was the slogan. I remember a graffito in the Polytechnic in Milan, during the Pantera (Panther) movement [Students Movement, 1990–1991], with a panther's footprints climbing till the roof, 'from here we get to the sky'. (Interviewee IT5)

Another example of innovation comes from:

... the occupation of the Italian monuments, the Coliseum in Rome, the Pisa tower, the Valle Theatre in Rome as these actions were meant to stress that it was not only the university, but all the cultural work to be under attack. The occupation of the theatre, the intuition of the students with the 'book bloc', though the media represented them as aggressive, they were very ironic. This idea comes directly from Genoa [2001],[12] through the idea of protection, with the Plexiglas shields, with the white hands, the coloured hands, but here the idea is that you metaphorically protect yourself with the same instruments used for your educational formation ..., [with this form of action] you re-introduced the public dimension of the culture, by showing some titles like 'omnia sunt communia' [All is common] ... etc. The occupation of public monuments, the book bloc, the climbing of the roofs, all this was then reworked by the trade unions, in the campaign 'embrace the culture', with a sit-in 'embrace the Coliseum', but only after. (Interviewee IT5)[13]

It is worth noting that violent and disruptive forms increased following the fall of the Berlusconi government, with the beginning of strong austerity policies, in the years between 2011 and 2013 (Fig. 7.7). Thus, violence and disruptive forms of action increased when established trade unions and formal social movement organizations decreased, under peculiar political opportunities, their presence in the protest arena. One example of that radicalization in that period can be traced through the student movement. Although the *Onda* was initially moderate in terms of forms of action,

> ... occupations spread instead in several Italian cities in the 2010 student mobilization ... and in 2011 there is a sort of radicalization, with the use of the *manif sauvage*, from the French movements, that is non-authorized demonstrations, during which the march moves very fast through the city, and blocks some key city streets. The idea of the 'block' was already present in 2008, and was linked to the view that if the role of the student in the knowledge economy is an integrated role into the economic and productive process, while the worker can strike, what does the student do? The student must block the flow of goods, the productive flow. This is strongly linked with the slogan often chanted during the student demonstrations, 'If they block our future, we block the city'. (Interviewee IT3)

The repertoire of action is one of the key dimensions in which social movement organizations, trade unions and other organizations divide in Italy. At the same time, the radicalization of some protest events reveals the tensions between the different sectors of the anti-austerity protest. According to our data, in fact, violent forms characterize especially those protest events in which both traditional actors, such as trade unions, and social movements (especially informal) are present (in 17 per cent of such episodes, violent forms have been reported in newspaper articles, against only 8 per cent of protests in which both trade unions and social movements are absent, 3 per cent of protests staged only by trade unions, and 14 per cent of protests staged only by social movement organizationss). Activists confirmed that violent forms spread with tensions between different sectors of the protest field. For instance, one of the many attempts to create a broad coalition against austerity policies a few weeks (15 October 2011) before Berlusconi would resign as prime minister (12 November 2011) failed, as 'Many of us had the idea that the demonstration would stop in San Giovanni square (Rome), where we wanted to set our tents, after the American and the Spanish model... But a group of people wearing black at a certain point of the march start setting fire to anything they met, cutting the march and making the demonstration no longer manageable' (Interviewee IT3). Behind the scenes, in the preparatory meeting, there was 'a very much conflictual dynamic, in which tensions emerged on basically anything, the grassroots unions against the FIOM, and against each other, the FIOM against the CGIL, the Left, Ecology and Liberty Party against the Communist Refoundation Party, etc.... Internal rivalry between different sectors, with some who want to radicalize their action and others who want to keep a control on the protest' (Interviewee IT3) (see also della Porta and Zamponi 2013).

7.5   FRAMING THE CRISIS AND SEEKING DEMOCRACY

Most of the mobilizations in the last years in Italy have been linked to the economic crisis and the austerity policies. The crisis has been obviously at the centre of the trade unions' framing, and crosses all the national and local disputes, strikes and mobilizations against the several policies cutting the public expenses and reducing the welfare state. According to an activist of the FIOM-CGIL (metalworkers' trade union),

> ... the impact of the crisis was strong, with a campaign of layoffs, and disputes to avoid the loss of work, etc. For sure, the most important conflict between the FIOM and the firms develops in 2010. In Pomigliano, the FIAT imposes a specific contract ... outside of the collective contract ... the intention of the firm was to propose an exchange to the metalworkers and to the trade unions, which is more or less, 'in a phase of crisis, we guarantee you the job ... and in exchange you give all the acquired rights up'. (Interviewee IT6)

The leaflet of a general strike under the Berlusconi government reads: 'The thirty-four months of the Berlusconi government have impoverished the country; increased unemployment and the pressure of taxes; cut welfare; punished the pensioners; attacked schools, universities, research and our cultural heritage; increased inequalities.'[14]

Anti-austerity frames became even more widespread under the Monti government. In 2012, part of the CGIL and the FIOM called, with other grassroots trade unions and social movements, for a national mobilization against the government led by Mario Monti, and

> ... its economic policy, which produces precariousness, layoffs, unemployment, poverty ...; against the European austerity policies, and for the 'common goods'. At the same time ask for 'a decent work', the welfare state, the income, for all native and migrant men and women, ... for the common goods, the school, the public research, the health and the environment, for another economic policy paid by the banks, the cuts in the military expenses ... and for the cancellation of all treaties which have centralized the decisional power in the hands of an oligarchy... for a democracy in the country and in the work places, based on the participation, the conflict and the right to decide on the European treaties too.[15]

A month later, on 14 November, the CGIL called for an additional four hours of general strike during the 'European Day of Action and Solidarity. For Job and Solidarity in Europe. No to Austerity' called for by the European Trade Union Confederation.[16] In November 2013, against the same government, the three Italian trade unions confederations proclaimed another general strike, asking to stop the horizontal cuts in the public expenses foreseen in the new stability law for 2014.[17]

Anti-austerity frames were also used in protests (such as the ones in November 2014) against the policies of the government led by Matteo Renzi, leader of the PD; grassroots trade unions, student movements, movements for the commons, social centres and others organized the 'social strike' (see the section on Anti-Austerity Repertoire). The declaration proclaiming the day of action in several Italian cities reads: 'We know how much more difficult it is to strike today, for those who have the right to strike, but see it as conditioned by too many limitations. It is difficult because they have to give up a part of their salary when the crisis deepens and money is lacking. It is even more difficult for the precarious workers, because they risk their job ... and for the unemployed and the intermittent workers.' Against these difficulties, the network invites students, dependent workers, young unemployed, precarious workers and citizens in general to participate in the social strike in their cities—during working hours, if they can strike, before or after, if they cannot—against the new government policies on the labour market (the Jobs Act), which 'will make the job ... a blackmail'.[18] It also asks for free education, a guaranteed income and a new plan of public investment in welfare, education and the common goods.[19]

In these movement activities, the idea that the crisis and the austerity policies are reducing the democratic spaces is central. As an interviewee noted,

> ... the European Commission, the troika etc. influenced by the corporative interests of the companies, the financial powers, the economic powers ... the possibility to decide is progressively expropriated ... This is why citizens vote less and less in our country... Democracy means that you can decide. If you can no longer decide, because Europe decides on the economic policies and the firms decide on your workplace, people start to think that democracy is irrelevant because it changes nothing in their life. (Interviewee IT6)

Austerity and (deteriorating) democratic quality are linked to the idea of crisis. As already noted, the 2008 student movement was the first to raise the issue of the crisis with slogans such as 'we won't pay for the crisis', when the economic crisis was not yet so evident in Italy. According to an activist,

> Italy was already in difficult economic conditions well before the crisis, this is why the crisis became immediately politicized by the students, somehow as a metaphor of a generational situation of precariousness, of lack of perspectives, etc. It became even more central in 2010–2011, to the extent that the path of the students crossed the path of the metalworkers, of the movement for the commons, because you build an idea in which the precariousness is the unifying condition, and the latter is understood and interpreted as linked to the austerity policies, also with a view of searching for solutions against the crisis, that is to invest on culture and knowledge, on rights, on the commons ... (Interviewee IT3)

As for the diagnostic frame, a 2011 document from the student network 'Link' indicates in the government choices the causes of what is considered as the 'destruction of the right to study', as the choices made 'were not forced by the crisis, but political choices, which go in the direction of privatizing and making the university less and less accessible'.[20] Another document recently published by the national network of student grassroots unions (Atenei in Rivolta) reads: '"Surely, not working less, but working all", the goal of the reforms and the laws on the university and the labour market is to create a mass of impoverished, indebted and above all traumatized workers, willing to work for free.'[21] The connection between the crisis of the austerity policies, the precariousness of the labour market, and the student conditions became central in the student movement's framing. This is why, according to one respondent, the student movement:

> ... is the actor which builds coalitions with others, especially in the years 2010–2011, with the mobilizations linked to the work, with a big national dispute carried out by the FIOM, in the FIAT case ... a labour issue linked to the issue of the democracy in the workplaces, then connected with local disputes, with the workers on the cranes, In this phase also the work was framed under the label of a 'common good', then on the water issue which brought about a referendum. The slogan in the 2011 phase was 'Work, knowledge, common good' as the three pillars which connect the movements. (Interviewee IT3)

The issue of democracy is also central among the student activists, as according to them, the reforms of the university against which they mobilize 'cut the student representative power, give a lot of power to the rectors and put the private within the university governance' (Interviewee IT3). A leaflet calling for the 2011 world day of student mobilization reads:

> We students, without future, stolen by that 1 % of the population who decided to speculate even more on the crisis, who decided to save the banks and destroy the welfare, to guarantee the continuity of the capitalist system, by closing schools and universities, eliminating the rights and cancelling democracy... We want real democracy in a country expressing the misery of the power. We demand ... a real democracy: asking for the respect of the results of the referendum of 12 and 13 June [the referendum on the water management and the nuclear power], asking for a democratic vote on the new statutes of our universities, because we do not want to be the hostage of anybody and we want to decide.[22]

Democracy is also at the heart of the emerging discourse on the common good. As

> ... the crisis produces a drying out of the very formal and classic representative democracy, the fact that even the representative arenas from the town councils to the parliament are the more and more marginalized, and the sovereignty power moves toward the executives; and new set of laws are deepening all this, with always more majoritarian systems ... that is the representativeness is more and more eroded, most of the powers shift toward

non-elected organs, which actually determine the policies and the lives of all, and in this sense also the 'troika', the central bank, the IMF and the European Commission, which should be an executive, but it co-legislates with a very weak European Parliament. (Interviewee IT2)

An argument that calls into question the then national government, led by the leader of the PD and supported by a coalition with moderate parties is: 'within this plan, the democracy itself is put into discussion, with a new neo-authoritarian thrust, which removes representation to the legislative institutions (in particular with new electoral system "Italicum"), and increases the powers of the Government and of the Prime Minister, and with the attack to the public and social function of the local governments'.[23]

If the crisis accelerates, with the erosion of formal democratic representation, according to the 'common goods' discourse, its effects are also heavy on the forms of participative democracy:

> ... to all this that should have been integrating the representative democracy, forms of participative and deliberative democracy, from the participative budgets to the possibility for the citizens to be involved in the decision making of the fundamental public services, the democratization of water and transports management, in general the democratization of public spaces, including the school where we send our children... Against the provisions foreseen in our Constitution, and that in a certain phase of the history of our country were made available ..., there is now this disregard of the direct democracy elements that, though weak, are part of our legal system and this, in my view, indicates the ultimate cleavage. (Interviewee IT2)

The issue of democracy is also addressed by the No Tav network (no high speed train), which produced one of the most visible mobilizations well before the period of crisis (della Porta and Piazza 2008). Also here, 'the reading not so much of the crisis per se, but of the austerity as subtraction of democracy, of the diktats coming from ECB and IMF, which the people must accept, resonates a lot with the No Tav discourse, that always was a democracy frame, the democratic idea that "we want to decide on our land"' (Interviewee IT3). To be sure, some No Tav documents explicitly refer to the economic crisis:

> To resist one minute more than them [the pro High Speed train coalition] in the Valle is possible only if at the same time we bring the struggle on a more national and general political level, as we are sure that when the crisis

produces its effects in Italy, our movement has anticipated and acted upon the crucial question of the conflict, the question of the sovereign debt as a mortgage on the future of all our lives. The debt is 'public' only when we must pay the financial loss, while the profit is always and rigorously private. The No Tav reasons are potentially the same of those who will have to stand against the tears and blood plans.[24]

The democracy frame refers not only to 'we decide on our land', but also to 'who decides about the public financial resources': 'the decision on the public expenditure is not only the business of the bankers, EU commissions, corporate lobbies or of the corrupted, but it also concerns us as a struggle and social conflict field against the regime of austerity and precariousness'. In fact, instead of unnecessary and harmful big public works, such as the high-speed railway system, 'together with movements, associations, committees and social centres, we are collectively claiming that the only big work our society needs is: house, income and dignity for all'.[25]

Summarizing, the frame of the crisis prevailed in all sectors of mobilizations. The cause of the problem is not attributed to the crisis per se but rather to the policies of austerity imposed by European and domestic institutions, without the citizens' consent, which deepen rather than solve the crisis. The cuts in public expenses, the welfare state and basic services; the measures cutting pensions and reducing the role of the 'public' in many respects; the reforms of the educational system: all of these impoverish the population, while the privatization of state properties does not allow for the use of public resources to protect citizens, especially on basic needs such as work, housing, health and education, and relaunching the economy.

Trade unions and social movements alike consider the national governments, whatever their colour, as the principal ones responsible, together with the 'owners', for having invested too much in the deregulation of the labour market, diminishing workers' rights, expanding precarious work and increasing unemployment. All those 'wrong' decisions, they contend, are taken by centralizing decision making, reducing political representation and containing the political participation of the citizens. The prognostic frames point at the creation of a different model of society. The economy is to be re-embedded in the society through a political sphere in which citizens' participation becomes central. Strengthening, deepening, expanding democracy is at the core of many sectors of the anti-austerity protests.

7.6   EXPLAINING MOBILIZATION IN THE CRISIS

Notwithstanding intense mobilization, its political outcomes are still limited. Apart from limited concessions—such as delaying some law projects on educational policy, the (non-implemented) referendum results against the privatization of water, the spreading of the 'common good' frame in the 2013 electoral campaign by the centre-left coalition, limited defensive achievements in some local and national labour disputes, or the temporary inclusion of migrant families for the assignment of public housing (Interviewees IT1, IT2, IT3, IT4, IT5, IT6 and IT7)—all of our respondents shared the opinion that a 'cause' that could have been won was instead being lost.

Among the shared hope is the construction of a cross-sector mobilization similar to the one in Greece or Spain. As an interviewee observed, 'if till recently this for various reasons has not been possible, the mobilization for the general strike, but especially the success of the social strike at the end of 2014 is a good signal. This autumn I have seen the squares as full as never since 2011' (Interviewee IT3). In Greece and Spain, innovative elements are singled out as 'a break has been produced, several innovations have been produced ... and this made a new path possible, with a certain efficacy from the political and social point of view' (Interviewee IT4). Praised is, indeed, 'the bottom-up dynamics they are producing' (Interviewee IT6). However, the need for developing 'a big unitary anti-austerity mobilization' remained unfulfilled (Interviewee IT2).

Also shared is the perception of the necessity to go beyond the national level, building a long-lasting mobilization at the European level targeting both Brussels and the Troika (Interviewee IT3). This is considered all the more important as 'also the Greek experience, with the problem of the Greek government with the troika and the European Commission, shows that addressing the national level is not sufficient...' (Interviewee IT4). Attempts are therefore made to 'expand the idea of the social strike at the European level' (Interviewee IT1); or 'to bring our constitution in Europe: you can't think that you rewrite democracy in Italy, that you oppose authoritarian dynamics in Italy... The feeling you get is that you decide on nothing... Because the decisional power is more and more centralized, the democratic institutions are more and more emptied, the parliament is emptied, ... powers are shifting toward places which are not democratically legitimized' (Interviewee IT6).

With minor or major emphasis, our respondents agree on the failure in unifying the different sectors of mobilization in Italy and in Europeanizing the anti-austerity protest. The crisis is considered as jeopardizing both aims, as it 'has brought about a weakening of the social fabric of solidarity among people, and this makes the organization more difficult, even if at the same time it is a trade union duty' (Interviewee IT8). The crisis has indeed strengthened the divisions, as

> movements had their own specific history, preceding the crisis, with thematic boundaries that they have been building with their campaigns with a clear definition. When the crisis arrived they felt even more the necessity of defining their boundary and within it accentuating their struggle, the mobilization on those objective, somehow by closing themselves... Those who had reasoned on the water issue and the common goods thought their theme was the central one: those who were struggling for their territory the same and so on, like the reaction to the crisis was a reaction of more closure. (Interviewee IT3)

The crisis is in fact perceived as 'a depressive element ... it scared people, it made the fragility of a mass response more evident' (Interviewee IT1), as 'the more crisis, the more fear, closure, diffidence ... the crisis produce enormous difficulties for the house occupation. It is difficult to be listened to, to intercept the people, to convince them to struggle, because when you lose your house, your job, you do not want to mobilize... There is, then, more hassle in building participative processes, paths of resilience, of empowerment ...' (Interviewee IT7).

The crisis is also seen as jeopardizing the possibility to develop transnational mobilization—as 'also at the European level, the movements were closed in their crisis, isolated in their country crisis, and this weakened a lot the movements at the European level' (Interviewee IT3). The perception is that

> ... the development of the European politics has been profoundly marked by the failure of the European constitutional treaty with the referendum in France and in Holland in 2005, and there was a tendency toward the renationalization of the political discourse ... and then it was more difficult to carry on these paths... Thus, we entered the crisis of 2008, but more visible in 2010–2011, fundamentally disarmed; we lacked strong instruments of organization at the right level... That is why the struggles against the austerity, against the crisis, have been characterized by the process of nationalization, even if we look at them, the European Union significant, within those struggles, is evidently the enemy. (Interviewee IT4)

The divisions of the Italian anti-austerity movements, according to our respondents, are however also influenced by domestic factors, first and foremost by a political context in which austerity measures were first promoted by the centre-right, then by a take-care government with the support of the major centre-left party (PD), and finally by coalition-based governments led by PD leaders.

These political opportunities acted upon the traditional dependence of part of the civic society, including the unions, from party alliances. According to one of our interviewees,

> … in Spain and in Greece you had centre-left governments facing the crisis and implementing austerity policies and then they created informal movements. There, a cleavage was created between the electoral constituency and the social democratic parties. You did not have this in Italy. The enemy was Berlusconi, then Monti. Yes, the PD supported the Monti government, but it was Monti, not the PD, who governed. Then the big coalition with Letta etc. and now Renzi, who has the possibility to say 'I've nothing to do with the austerity', and then receive an electoral consent that the Socialists in Spain and Greece dream. (Interviewee IT3)

In fact, 'In the school too, until you had Gelmini [former minister of the education in the Berlusconi government], the mobilization was high, when the Berlusconi government collapsed, the political sector of the movements, the CGIL and the PD stopped supporting the movements and in 2011–2013 you had a decline of the mobilization' (Interviewee IT1). The traditional link between the most important Italian trade union—the CGIL—and the former Communist Party transformed first in the social-democratic PDS and, after the fusion with a party with a Christian democratic tradition, in the moderate PD, is considered as crucial:

> … in comparison with Podemos in Spain, but the thing is different for SYRIZA in Greece, in Italy there is a tradition of trade unions which are much politicized, which are always in between the protest and the institution, the political party. Something that you have less in Spain, and this brings organizations with a traditional leftist orientation within the movements. This makes the Italian articulation of social movements, different from Podemos, which is more individualist, less linked to an organization. There is less organizational competition in putting the hat on the mobilizations. In Greece, it is still different, trade unions are very politicized. Probably there the crisis was so strong that it disrupted all fences, because in Greece they needed to adapt their organization to save the people from hunger. (Interviewee IT3)

These explanations confirm those that have emerged in other research (Zamponi 2012; Andretta and della Porta 2015) and underline how the traditional link between the former Communist Party, civil society and social movements operates as a mediation between the political opportunity structure and protest mobilization:

> for sure, the political framework had an effect (on the fragmentation of the anti-austerity mobilization), because Italy is the only country in Europe in which the obsession of the 'single party', the single communist party, continued to work even when the party changed 5/6 names, 7/8 faces, and, PCI and CGIL in the collective imaginary of this country, are the Trade Union and the Party. But, while the Party does not exist any longer, the Trade Union exists. (Interviewee IT1)

Finally, according to many, the presence of the Five Star Movement and its recent electoral success occupied the space for the building of a type of collective identity able to transcend the movement's borders and to constitute the backbone of a new political action:

> In Italy the Five Star Movement is certainly a form of collective action born in the years of the crisis... But the Five Star Movement is very heterogeneous, in Veneto it collected the vote of the Northern League, in Sicily those of Berlusconi, it is very peculiar. In Spain too, Podemos say we are neither left-wing nor right-wing, but they are clearly leftist; the Five Star Movement is instead a different subject that occupied the space. (Interviewee IT4)

Another interviewee concurred that:

> In Italy there is the Five Star Movement, born before Podemos and SYRIZA, which in this phase of the crisis is gathering the possibility for hope and that at a certain point absorbs some themes of the movements and puts them at the centre, but then it betrays some promises of change ..., it takes the scene with the name of a movement, but actually it is not a movement, but a political electoral project... This occupation of the space of critique to politics ... complicates the building of a project similar to that of SYRIZA or Podemos ... (Interviewee IT2)

In fact, at least in a region with a strong participative tradition, such as Tuscany, many activists who joined the local organizations of the Five Star Movement have a leftist background and come from social movement organizations (Andretta 2015).

7.7   ANTI-AUSTERITY MOBILIZATION IN ITALY: SOME CONCLUDING REMARKS

The empirical findings of this chapter reveal the importance of the political opportunity structure, which operated as a filter between 'threats' (Van Dyke and McCammon 2010) or 'grievances' (Snow 2013) and protest mobilization in the Italian social movement tradition, and keeps working in the current anti-austerity mobilization. The key variable seems to be the behaviour and the position of potential allies within the political system (Tarrow 1989; Kriesi 1993). It is not by chance that the initial success of the Italian branch of the GJM against neoliberalism came into being when a solid centre-right government led by Silvio Berlusconi was ruling the country and all the potential allies were in a strong opposition position (Andretta et al. 2002; della Porta et al. 2006). In that situation, notwithstanding the critical attitude towards the GJM of the major leftist party, the important structures of civil society, mostly linked to leftist parties, were relatively free from party controls and their social bases could socially appropriate their organizations to participate in the protest field. Agency could also create new identities and a relatively new logic of actions and collective coordination.

Party allies, considered crucial in important pieces of social movement literature (della Porta and Diani 2006), are particularly relevant when social movements are embedded in a civil society historically built through party links. Comparing Italy and Spain, for instance, Riley and Fernandez found a strong but less autonomous civil society in Italy: this seems particularly true for the relations between trade unions and political parties (2014, 454–459). Indeed, the traditional reliance on left-wing parties, which had turned to the centre, might have contributed to weakening contentious capacities in Italy, especially after the PD started to support or participate in governments that were perceived as implementing the neoliberal agenda. Perception of opportunities is a key mechanism through which the political opportunity structure (POS) conditions social movements and protest actors (McAdam 1986) and it is thus worth noting that the interviewed activists and privileged observers have on different occasions elaborated on the POS, the social movement tradition, and the role of parties and unions in Italian civil society.

The anti-austerity mobilization in Italy was dominated by lawful strikes and rallies, with unions and traditional organizations as main collective actors (della Porta, Mosca and Parks, 2015; della Porta and Andretta 2013), and failures in the attempts to create broad coalitions, due to the tensions between actors, organizations and practices, and with little space for new actors and practices to emerge. While, of course, the more rapid and dramatic impact of the financial crisis in Spain and Greece versus Italy can in part account for the more dramatic expression of discontent in the former than in the latter, protest repertoires appeared as influenced by different political contingencies working upon different types of civil society and traditions. In Italy, the traditional political tensions among different social movement sectors emerged again in the declining phase of the GJM (Andretta and Piazza, 2010), when the 'potential allies' won the 2006 elections and remained visible in the years to follow. The most intense anti-austerity mobilization, with some connections among different sectors, was produced under the last Berlusconi government, when the main centre-left party (the PD), with its traditional links with the biggest trade union (CGIL), supported the protest. However, as the centre-right government was replaced by a grand-coalition in support of the self-defined 'technical' government led by Mario Monti, the implementation of anti-austerity measures found weak opposition from unions and associations that had traditionally developed near the centre-left parties. To which extent, under the Renzi government, which is pursuing very aggressive anti-union policies, the leftist part of the CGIL will be willing to cut loose from the traditional 'umbilical cord' is still to be seen.

7.8   List of Interviewees

IT1, member of Cobas, 2 February 2012, Rome

IT2, member of the Italian Water Campaign, 10 February 2015, Florence

IT3, former student movement activist, key witness, 28 January 2015, Florence

IT4, key witness and pro-immigrant activist, 24 February 2015, Bologna

IT5, member of precariousness movement, key witness, 26 February 2015, Rome

IT6, member of FIOM, 6 March 2015, Rome

IT7, member of House Movement—ACTION, 5 March 2015, Rome

IT8, member of NIDIL-CGIL, 6 May 2015, Florence

IT9, member of No Tav Movement, 6 June 2015, Susa-Turin

IT10, member of Social Centre, 5 June 2015, Turin

APPENDIX: SELECTED ORGANIZATIONS FOR ONLINE
DOCUMENT ANALYSIS

Trade Unions
Cobas Nazionale
Cub [confederazione unitaria di base]
CGIL
UIL
NIDIL-CGIL
Felsa CISL
FIOM-CGIL
USB
Cobas scuola

==

Precarious Movements
Freelance: Acta: associazione freelance
Euromayday
San Precario
Federazione Lavoratori della conoscenza
Rete 29 aprile
Coordinamento precari università

==

Movements of the Unemployed
Movimento Disoccupati (Napoli)
Disoccupati Organizzati (Napoli)
Rimanflow fabbrica recuperata

==

Environmental and Territorial Movements and Campaigns
No Tav
No Tav (terzo Valico)
No Muos
Difendiamo il Parco Trenno dalla Via d'acqua
No Expo
Non Lavoro Gratis per Expo
Genuino clandestino [comunità in lotta per l'autodeterminazione alimentare]
Comitato milanese audit del debito pubblico [bilancio del comune di Milano]
Forum dell'acqua
Legambiente

Greenpeace Italia
Zero Waste

==

Student Movements
Link—Cordinamento universitario
Air Atenei in rivolta [Coordinamento collettivi Sapienza]
Coordinamento nazionale scuola
Global project
Forum Studenti
<u>Social Strike 14 November 2014</u>

==

Women's Organizations
Associazione Filomena
Comitato pari o dispare
Di Nuovo
Se non ora quando
Usciamo dal silenzio

==

Online Groups
Anonymous Italia
Avaaz Italia
Moveon Italia

==

Groups Against the Crisis
Assemblea di San Giovanni
No debito
Draghi Ribelli
Indignati

==

Groups Against Cuts on Culture
Movimento Centauri
Teatro valle occupato
Zero Punto Tre

==

Social Centres
Askatasuna (Torino)
Cantiere (Milano)
Zero 81 (Napoli)

===
Information and Democracy
Articolo 21
Libertà e giustizia
Popolo Viola
Valigia blu
===
Political Parties
Sel sinistra ecologia e libertà
Movimento 5 stelle
Partito Comunista dei Lavoratori
Sinistra Critica organizzazione per la sinistra anticapitalista

NOTES

1. The source of the data is the AMECO database, reported in Armingeon and Baccaro (2012).
2. The Popolo della Libertà was founded in 2009, merging Silvio Berlusconi's former Forza Italia with the heir of the post-fascist MSI party, Alleanza Nazionale (AN, National Alliance) led by the same leader, Gianfranco Fini, who transformed the MSI into the AN.
3. The PD was founded in 2007 as a result of merging the Democratici di Sinistra (DS)—the heir of the former Italian Communist Party, which in 1991 took the name of Partito della Sinistra (PDS, Party of the Left) and in 1998 that of DS—and La Margherita, a party born in 2002, in which converged the Partito Popolare+ Italiano (PPI, Italian Popular Party, founded in 1994), the leftist heir of the former Christian Democratic Party (DC).
4. SEL was founded in 2009, merging several leftist and ecological groups, most of which were part of the Partito della Rifondazione Comunista (PRC, Communist Refoundation Party), born in 1991, when the left of the former Italian Communist Party (PCI) decided to create a new party after the transformation of the PCI into the Partito della Sinistra (PDS, Party of the Left).
5. Source:Istat,http://scenarieconomici.it/i-dati-del-pil-tra-2001-e-2014-di-tutte-le-regioni-italiane/.

6. Debating Europe Poll, see http://www.scribd.com/doc/172138343/Gallup-Debating-Europe-Poll-Austerity-Policies for the main results.

7. The newspaper articles were selected from the online version of the daily *La Repubblica* using the keyword 'protest*'. From all articles with 'protest*' in the text or the title, only those referring to protest events carried out by more than five people were selected. The data on 2011 and 2012 were gathered by Lorenzo Mosca and Louisa Parks, while the data on the remaining years were collected by Marta Bonetti.

   La Repubblica is a left-liberal newspaper. To control for potential bias linked to the editorial political profile, parallel research was conducted in selected months (January–May and September–October) for two years (2009 and 2010) in the competing national newspaper, *Corriere della Sera*, with a conservative orientation. The data show some differences in how the two newspapers covered the protest events in that period: in 2009, *Repubblica* reported 93 events, while the *Corriere* reported 89—although in 2010 the latter reported 128 events and the former only 108. If we look at the types of organizations covered by the newspaper accounts, both newspapers reported on institutional or party organizations in 37 per cent of events; but while the *Corriere* reported on trade unions in 52.5 per cent of the protest events, *Repubblica* covered them in only 38 per cent; the latter seems to pay a bit more attention to associations and formal movement organizations (55 per cent versus 46 per cent), but the former focuses a bit more on informal actors such as social centres, squatters, and similar groups (19 per cent versus 14 per cent). Finally, regarding the forms of action covered, *Repubblica* reported on conventional actions (petitions, leaflets, public assembly, lawful demonstrations and symbolic actions) in about 60 per cent of the covered events, versus 51 per cent by the *Corriere*; non-conventional forms (strikes, sit-ins, public building squatting, *acampadas* and similar) in 63 per cent versus 72 per cent; and violent actions against things or people in 9 per cent versus 10 per cent.

8. For a similar classification of anti-austerity issues, see Ortiz et al. (2013) and Accornero and Pinto (2014).

9. Other actors are intellectuals, artists, journalists (present in 5.4 per cent of cases), women (2 per cent) and citizens in general (15 per

cent); while in 6 per cent of cases the social profile has not been identified.

10. Taking the lead from other research (della Porta and Mosca 2015; della Porta 2004; Tarrow 1989), we recoded the forms of action reported in newspaper articles as follows: conventional (leaflets, press conferences, public letters, petitions, scientific reports, legal actions); demonstrative (demonstrations, legal strikes, sit-ins, public meetings, symbolic actions); disruptive (non-violent illegal actions such as squatting, occupation of public and private buildings, non-authorized demonstrations and strikes, roadblocks and so on); and violent (any violent action against things and people). Of all the protest events during the selected period, as many as 87 per cent were characterized by at least one demonstrative form of action, 23 per cent by a disruptive form, 12 per cent by a conventional form, and 11 per cent by a violent form.

11. See the document at http://www.dinamopress.it/multilanguages/strike-meeting-act-ii-13/14/15-february-in-rome.

12. On this see: http://criticallegalthinking.com/2012/09/03/from-white-overalls-tute-bianche-to-the-book-bloc/.

13. 9 April 2011 (http://www.cgil.it/news/Default.aspx?ID=16013).

14. See the call for General Strike, 20 May 2011, http://www.cgil.it/Archivio/EVENTI/Sciopero%20Generale%20%206%20maggio%202011/volantino%20A4%20ultimo%204colori%20QRcode.pdf.

15. See the call for Mobilization—No Monti Day, 27 October 2012, https://sites.google.com/site/nomontiday27ott2012/manifestazione-nazionale-roma-27-ottobre.

16. http://www.cgil.it/news/Default.aspx?ID=20034.

17. http://www.cisl.it/Sito.nsf/in-primo-piano/2013/11/05/articolazione-sciopero-nazionale-cgil-cisl-uil-legge-stabilita?opendocument.

18. Social Strike: declaration 3, 14 November 2014, http://archivio.scioperosociale.it/portfolio/declaration03/

19. Social Strike: declarations, 14 November 2014, http://archivio.scioperosociale.it/declaration/.

20. Document: Il diritto allo studio è un lusso!, September 2011, http://linkcoordinamentouniversitario.it/documenti/.

21. Document: Studiare meno, studiare gratis, February 2014; http://ateneinrivolta.org/approfondimenti/universit%C3%A0/studiare-meno-lavorare-gratis.

22. Call for the World day of Student Mobilization, 17 November 2011,http://www.retedellaconoscenza.it/17nov-perche-scendiamo-in-piazza/.
23. Leaflet of the National Forums of the Movement for Water, 24 April 2014, http://www.acquabenecomune.org/notizie/naziona li/2647versolamanifestazionenazionaledel17maggio.
24. Document of the No Tav network, 'No Tav and the question of the debt', published on 8 July 2011, http://www.notav.info/ post/notavelaquestionedeldebitolapiazzastatutodeibenicomuni/.
25. Leaflet published on the No Tav website, on 11 February 2015, http://www.notav.info/post/152bolognarisorseedenaropubblico chidecide/.

REFERENCES

Accornero, G., and P.R. Pinto. 2014. "Mild Mannered"? Protest and Mobilisation in Portugal under Austerity, 2010–2013. *Western European Politics* 38(3): 1–25.

Alonso, S. 2014. "You Can Vote but you Cannot Choose": Democracy and the Sovereign Debt Crisis in the Eurozone. Instituto Mixto Universidad Carlos III de Madrid—Fundación Juan March de Ciencias Sociales, *Working Paper 282*, 1–29.

Andretta, M., and D. della Porta. 2015. Contentious Precarious Generation in Anti-Austerity Movements in Spain and Italy. *Revista OBETS* 10(1): 37–66.

Andretta, M., and G. Piazza eds. 2010. Le sinistre nel movimento globale: Ascesa e declino dell'attivismo transnazionale? *Partecipazione & Conflitto* 1: 5–20.

Andretta, M. 2015. Il Movimento 5 Stelle in Toscana: Un movimento post-sub-culturale? In *Dal web al territorio. Gli attivisti del Movimento 5 Stelle*, ed. R. Biorcio, 111–123. Milan: Franco Angeli.

Andretta, M., D. della Porta, L. Mosca, and H. Reiter. 2002. *Global, noglobal, new global. Le proteste contro il G8 a Genova*. Roma-Bari: Laterza.

Armingeon, K., and L. Baccaro. 2012. Political Economy of the Sovereign Debt Crisis: The Limits of Internal Devaluation. *Industrial Law Journal* 41(3): 254–275.

Bordignon, F., and L. Ceccarini. 2013. Five Stars and a Cricket. Beppe Grillo Shakes Italian Politics. *South European Society and Politics* 18(4): 427–449.

Ciocca, P. 2010. La specificità italiana nella crisi in atto. *Moneta e Credito*, 63(249): 51–58.

Corsi M., C. D'Ippoliti, F. Lucidi, and G. Zacchia. 2007. Giovani, donne e migranti: I "giacimenti" del mercato del lavoro visti in un'ottica regionale. In

Generazioni flessibili, nuove e vecchie forme di esclusione sociale, ed. P. Villa, 75–99. Rome: Carocci.

D'Ippoliti, C., and A. Roncaglia. 2011. L'Italia: Una crisi nella crisi. *Moneta e Credito* 64(255): 189–227.

della Porta, D. ed. 2004. *Comitati di cittadini e democrazia urbana.* Soveria Mannelli: Rubbettino.

——— ed. 2009a. *Democracy in Social Movements.* Houndsmill: Palgrave.

——— ed. 2009b. *Another Europe.* London: Routledge.

della Porta, D., and G. Piazza. 2008. *Voices of the Valley, Voices of the Straits.* Oxford: Berghahn.

della Porta, D., and L. Mosca. 2015. Conflitti e proteste locali fra comitati, campagne e movimenti. In *L'Italia e le sue regioni (1945–2011)*, eds M. Salvati and L. Sciolla, Vol. 4, 203–319. Rome: Treccani.

della Porta, D., and L. Zamponi. 2013. Protest and Policing on October 15th, Global Day of Action: The Italian Case. *Policing and Society* 23(1): 65–80.

della Porta, D., and M. Andretta. 2013. Protesting for Justice and Democracy: Italian Indignados? *Contemporary Italian Politics* 5(1): 23–37.

della Porta, D., and M. Diani. 2006. *Social Movements: An Introduction.* Oxford: Blackwell.

della Porta, D., L. Mosca, and L. Parks. 2015. 2011. A Year of Protest on Social Justice in Italy. In *Subterranean Politics in Europe*, eds M. Kaldor and S. Selchow. London: Palgrave.

della Porta, D., M. Andretta, L. Mosca, and H. Reiter. 2006. *Globalization from Below. Transnational Activists and Protest Networks.* Minneapolis: University of Minnesota Press.

Ferrera, M. 2006. *Le politiche sociali: L'Italia in prospettiva comparata.* Bologna: Il Mulino.

Franzosi, P., F. Marone, and E. Salvati. 2015. Populism and Euroscepticism in the Italian Five Star Movement. *The International Spectator: Italian Journal of International Affairs* 50(2): 109–124.

Galbraith J. K., and E. Garcilazo. 2004. Disoccupazione, disuguaglianza e politica dell'Europa: 1984–2000. *Moneta e Credito* 57(225): 3–29.

Kriesi, H. 1993. *Political Mobilization and Social Change: The Dutch Case in Comparative Perspective.* Avebury: Aldershot.

Lucidi, F., and A. Kleinknecht. 2010. Little Innovation, Many Jobs: An Econometric Analysis of the Italian Labour Productivity Crisis. *Cambridge Journal of Economics* 34(3): 525–546.

McAdam, D. 1986. Recruitment to High-Risk Activism: The Case of Freedom Summer. *American of Sociology* 92(1): 64–90.

———. 1988. Micromobilization Contexts and Recruitment to Activism. In *From Structure to Action*, eds. B. Klandermans, H. Kriesi, and S. Tarrow, 125–154. Greenwich, CT: JAI Press.

Nastasi G., and G. Palmisano. 2015. The Impact of the Crisis on Fundamental Rights Across Member States of the EU. Country Report on Italy. *Report commissioned by the LIBE committee*, European Parliament. Accessed 28 July 2015 http://www.europarl.europa.eu/thinktank/it/document. html?reference=IPOL_STU%282015%2951 0018

Natali, D. 2007. *Vincitori e perdenti. Come cambiano le pensioni in Italia e in Europa.* Bologna: Il Mulino.

Ortiz, I., S. Burke, M. Berrada, and H. Cortes. 2013. World Protests 2006–2013. New York: Friedrich Ebert Foundation. Accessed 30 May 2014 http://cadtm. org/IMG/pdf/World_Pro tests_2006-2013-Final-2.pdf

Riley, D., and J. Fernandez. 2014. Beyond Strong and Weak: Rethinking Postdictatorship Civil Societies. *American Journal of Sociology* 2, 432–503.

Snow, D. 2013. Grievances, Individual and Mobilizing. In *Blackwell Encyclopedia on Social and Political Movements*, eds. D. Snow, D. della Porta, B. Klandermans, and D. McAdam, 540–542. Oxford: Blackwell.

Standing, G. 2011. *The Precariat: The New Dangerous Class.* London: Bloomsbury Publishing.

Sylos Labini, P. 2009. Le Prospettive Dell'economia Globale. *Moneta e Credito*, 62(245–248): 61–89.

Tarrow, S. 1989. *Democracy and Disorder: Protest and Politics in Italy, 1965–1975.* Oxford: Clarendon Press.

Van Dyke, N., and H.J. McCammon, eds. 2010. *Strategic Alliances: Coalition Building and Social Movements.* Minneapolis: Minnesota University Press.

Zamponi, L. 2012. Why don't Italians Occupy? *Social Movement Studies* 11(3–4), 1–11.

CHAPTER 8

Cyprus' Explosion: Financial Crisis and Anti-austerity Mobilization

Markos Vogiatzoglou

8.1 INTRODUCTION

Cyprus became a full member of the European Union (EU) in 2004. Its leadership at the time had the explicit goal of securing the country's participation in the Eurozone as soon as possible, with the hope of thus resolving the longstanding political issues deriving from the island's de facto division into the northern and southern sectors, following the Turkish Army's 1974 invasion and the military occupation of the country's northern part. Indeed, Cyprus adopted the euro in January 2008, just a few months before the collapse of Lehman Brothers signalled the start of a chain of events that would later culminate in the so-called 'Eurozone crisis'.

During the years that preceded the 2008 crisis, thanks to its booming tourist industry and steadily increasing financial sector, Cyprus had achieved relatively high rates of increase in GDP. As was the case with other EU countries, though, Cyprus' development had fragile foundations. Its banking sector—accused by many of providing money-laundering and tax-haven services—was unable to sustain the combined systemic shocks of the post-2008 recession, its exposure to the Greek public debt, and the tremendous 2011 explosion at a military base, which destroyed the country's main electricity plant and, according to estimates, caused damages amounting to almost 10 per cent of the Cypriot GDP.

D. della Porta et al., *Late Neoliberalism and its Discontents in the Economic Crisis*, DOI 10.1007/978-3-319-35080-6_8

In the explosion's aftermath, the government launched negotiations with the EU in the direction of securing a bailout agreement that would allow the country's banks to remain afloat. The austerity measures that would accompany the prospective deal provoked the first wave of public outrage and protest: in November and December 2012, citizens' groups, unions and the newly formed 'Alliance Against the Memorandum' staged a series of protests. In March 2013, the negotiations' failure and the imposition of capital controls and bank deposit levies caused a second, equally short-lived round of protest.

In sum, although the financial meltdown did have an important impact on the Cypriot economy, and notwithstanding the local social movement's efforts to construct coalitions with other societal groups in order to counter the austerity measures, organized resistance to the crisis' consequences was scarce and limited, from a certain point on, to individual or uncoordinated actions. Explanations for the above phenomenon include the relative weakness of civil society, the time frame of the protest development, and the strong presence of pre-existing, yet marginal, leftist organizations, which hampered the emergence of new protest actors with which a majoritarian part of the society could identify.

In what follows, we examine the socio-economic and political conditions that characterized the Cypriot case, then focus on the organizational formats and main actors of the protests, as well as their framing. The chapter concludes with an analysis and discussion of what we consider as the weakest link in the chain of anti-austerity protests that took place in Europe in the aftermath of the 2008 financial crisis.

8.2   THE SOCIO-ECONOMIC AND POLITICAL CONDITIONS

It is not possible to understand the socio-political background of any development occurring in Cyprus without reference to the island's de facto separation in the northern and southern sectors, after the 1974 invasion of the Turkish Army that led to the occupation of some 37 per cent of the island's territory. The Turkish invasion was the conclusion of a turbulent period that followed Cyprus' 1960 independence from the British Empire. The country was then inhabited by a majority (77 per cent) of Greek-Cypriots and a minority (19 per cent) of Turkish-Cypriots. Soon after the establishment of the Republic, violent inter-communal episodes took place, leading to hundreds of deaths, the destruction of dozens of Turkish-Cypriot villages, and the displacement of their inhabitants (Ker-Lindsay 2011). In 1974, the Greek military dictatorship organized a coup against the legitimate leader of the island, Archbishop Makarios, in order to replace him with a new leadership that would proclaim the island's union with Greece. Turkey's Armed Forces invaded the island to prevent such an occurrence. Thousands were killed during the invasion and the ensuing fights, and tens of thousands of citizens from both communities were relocated to their respective sectors. Although the United Nations (UN) condemned the invasion, the situation has remained in a stalemate ever since, minor concessions from both communities aside. Technically speaking, the whole of the island was accepted as an EU member; yet, the application of EU legislative provisions has been suspended for the northern sector, until a final decision on the island's division is achieved (Levin 2011). It is important to note that, since 1974, the division and the diplomatic and political efforts to resolve the issue have always been present as the leitmotif of Cyprus' social and political life.

With respect to its political system, Cyprus is a presidential republic: the President is elected by universal suffrage for a five-year term. Executive power is exercised by the government, with legislative power vested in the House of Representatives, whilst the judiciary is independent from both the executive and the legislature (Ker-Lindsay 2011; Orphanides 2014). In 2003, centrist DIKO (Democratic Party) president Tassos Anastasiadis was elected President of the Republic. Anastasiadis secured Cyprus' entry into the EU and the Eurozone, yet his mandate is mostly remembered for the referendum on the UN-proposed solution for the reunification of the island, a proposal that the Greek-Cypriot community rejected by a landslide. In February 2008, shortly after the adoption of the euro, AKEL's Dimitris Christofias won the national elections with 53 per cent and was sworn in as the country's first left-wing President. AKEL (Progressive Party of Working People) identifies itself as a communist party—yet its positions and policy choices whilst in power pertain to a more moderate euro-communist tradition. Christofias' government was broadly considered responsible for a series of mishandlings of the events that led to the banking sector's collapse in 2012–2013. As a consequence, AKEL lost the elections of February 2013 to the centre-right DISY (Democratic Rally) party, and its leader, Nikos Anastasiadis, was sworn in just a few days before the country's bank closure and the signing of the Economic Adjustment Programme that led to the bail-in imposed by the Troika of creditors—European Commission (EC), European Central Bank (ECB) and International Monetary Fund (IMF).

With less than half of the electors participating, the three aforementioned parties still gathered some 75 per cent of the vote at the 2014 European elections,[1] although with quite a significant loss for AKEL— which dropped to 27 per cent from 35 per cent at previous European parliament elections—while the other two parties remained stable. The centrist parties EDEK (Movement for Social Democracy) and Citizen's Alliance earned 7.6 and 6.8 per cent, respectively. The country's political scenery is complemented by the newly formed anti-Memorandum Message of Hope party (3.8 per cent) and the extreme right ELAM (National Popular Front) (2.8 per cent), which is an ally of the Greek neo-Nazi party Golden Dawn.

With respect to the Cypriot economy, the country had enjoyed a relatively stable annual GDP increase in the years that preceded the 2008 financial crisis. The driving forces of the smooth economic development were dual: on the one hand the—traditionally strong—tourist industry of the island; on the other, its rapidly expanding financial sector. As analysts noted, 'friendly laws and low taxes for financial companies had made Cyprus an attractive destination to conduct international business in Europe' (Trading Economics Indicators 2015). As Fig. 8.1 shows, Cyprus' debt-to-GDP ratio was lower than the EU average until 2012.

Yet, as the summer of 2011 events showed, the economy's health proved to be much more fragile than one might consider at first glance. In May 2011, the country lost access to the international financial markets—and thus, the ability to refinance its public debt. According to some, this was due to the reckless fiscal policies of the left-wing government in a period of international economic turbulence (Orphanides 2014), whilst others have primarily attributed Cyprus' exclusion to its exposure to the Greek public debt (Kouloudi 2014).

To make things worse, in July 2011, a tremendous ammunition explosion that occurred at the Evangelos Florakis Naval Base destroyed the nearby power station, which supplied 50 per cent of the country's electricity (Bank of Cyprus Economic Research Division 2012). The economic impact of the incident was significant: some 4.5 per cent of the country's GDP evaporated immediately, whilst, according to some, the overall damage amounted to 10 per cent of Cyprus' GDP.

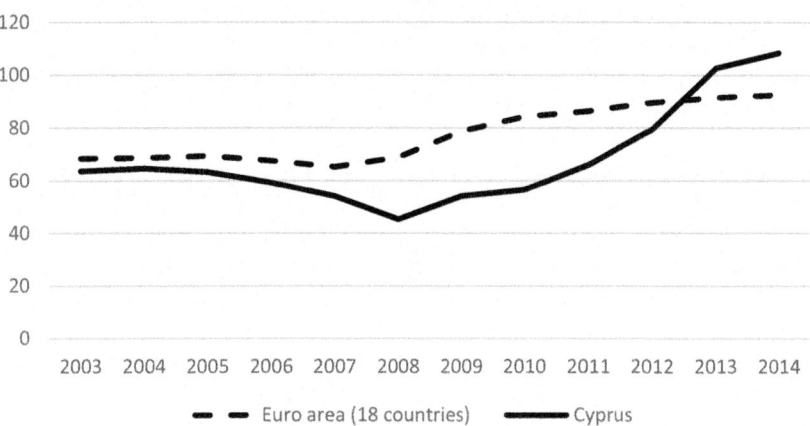

Fig. 8.1 General government debt as a percentage of GDP, 2003–2014; Eurozone and Cyprus *Source*: Eurostat

Unable to access the international markets in order to gather the much-needed funds required to redesign its energy production system, in 2011 Cyprus resorted to an emergency loan of 2.5 billion euros from Russia, which was later expanded to 5 billion euros (European Commission 2015).

In February 2012, the Greek public debt haircut gave the final blow to the country's weakest economic pillar: its banking sector. The rapid expansion of financial services, as well as the 'friendly tax environment' noted above, had allowed for a significant inflow of international depositors to the Cypriot banks. 'Cyprus had maintained a cozy relationship with Russian financiers, who made judicious use of the state in Cayman island-like tax evasion and money laundering ventures', Hess notes (2015, 14). He eloquently summarizes the sequence of events that led to the fall of Cyprus' largest private bank, Laiki Bank, and forced Christofias' government to request a bailout agreement from the Troika:

> As part of its EU accession and adoption of the Euro, Cyprus was forced to meet financial convergence criteria that included that rapid liberalization of its fiscal policy and financial industries. Perhaps due in part to this sudden expansion of the financial sector, within three years of adopting the Euro

the top Cypriot banks soon found themselves in possession of assets over 8 times the GDP of the small island nation. [...] In addition to these factors, Cyprus's historical and economic ties to Greece led them [the banks] to take on major shares of Greek bonds. When the financial crisis tanked Greece's economy, borrowing costs in Cyprus skyrocketed; when Greek foreign debt was partially forgiven, the Cypriot economy crumbled'. (Hess 2015, 14)

Negotiations with the EU, ECB and IMF on the terms and conditions of a bailout were initiated in November 2012. Given that the Cypriot population was well aware of the harsh austerity measures that accompanied the Troika interventions in other southern European countries, it is not surprising that the negotiations were met with a first wave of popular anti-austerity protest. The discussions failed to arrive at a fruitful conclusion until February 2013, when elections were held and Nikos Anastasiadis replaced his left-wing predecessor. On 16 March, the Troika submitted its final proposal, which was voted down by an overwhelming majority of the Cypriot Parliament on 18 March (Wearden 2013). Less than 24 hours later, a bank closure was proclaimed, and capital controls were imposed in order to prevent a bank run that would totally shatter the country's banking system (Treanor et al. 2013). Finally, on 25 March 2013, President Anastasiadis and the Parliament agreed to a renewed Troika proposal—the so-called Cyprus Economic Adjustment Programme, which included, among others, the following terms:

- Laiki Bank was split into two parts, a 'bad bank' and 'good bank', before being closed.
- Deposits in Laiki Bank of less than 100,000 euros (effectively the 'good bank') would be insured by EU law and were transferred to the country's biggest bank, Bank of Cyprus.
- Deposits in Laiki Bank of more than 100,000 euros, which were not insured by EU law, were transferred into the 'bad bank'.
- Deposits in this 'bad bank' and deposits of more than 100,000 euros in Bank of Cyprus were frozen and used to pay Laiki's debts and recapitalize Bank of Cyprus. These uninsured depositors faced a 47.5 per cent deposit levy.
- The levy produced some 4.2 billion euros. In addition, some 10 billion euros in loans were granted to Cyprus in order to cover for its refinancing needs for the period 2013–2016.
- State property privatizations and austere budgetary policies were also included in the Economic Adjustment Programme, in exchange for the aforementioned loan.

Summing up, the Troika intervention in Cyprus included both a bail-out element (similar to the ones implemented in the cases of Greece, Spain, Portugal and Ireland) and a—unprecedented for the Eurozone's economic policies—bail-in, theoretically designed in a way as to mostly harm big-shot Russian depositors (Orphanides 2013).

These developments sparked the second wave of protest in the Cypriot society (March 2013), the main target of which was the bail-in and the consequences it would have on the country's economy and the citizens' savings alike.

8.3   PROTEST EVENTS AND PROTEST CAMPAIGNS

8.3.1   Collective Action Repertoires, Organizational Forms and Resources

The anti-austerity protest in Cyprus occurred in two brief yet intense waves. It is important to note that in the years and decades preceding the crisis, Cyprus had experienced few large protest events. As Quaranta demonstrated, Cyprus ranked last among the 20 western European countries he examined, in terms of citizens' political participation (Quaranta 2013). This was partly due to the prevalence of the country's division/reunification issue on the social and political agenda. Indeed, the last major protest wave the country had experienced was in 2004, when the UN reunification plan was put to popular vote under a simultaneous referendum that took place in both communities—the Turkish-Cypriot and the Greek-Cypriot alike. However, our interviewees, as well as pre-crisis research conducted on the field, also provided an alternative or additional explanation for the lack of significant collective action instances in pre-crisis Cyprus. Party proximity was in fact an important (positive) indicator for citizens' mobilization in the past decades. The weakening of political party affiliations that had ensued in the 1990s and 2000s had significantly diminished Cypriots' direct participation in collective action. 'The concept of party crisis is a plausible explanation for current Cypriot political behaviour, which might aptly be termed "couch activism"', notes Katsourides (2013, 87). This is particularly relevant in the case of the most important left-wing party AKEL, which was in power during the crucial 2008–2013 years.

The first protest against the Troika intervention was organized on 8 November 2012 by ERAS (Committee for a Radical Left Rally, see the section on Protest Actors, Aims and Framing for more information)

(Kathimerini 2012a). Protests resumed a couple of days later outside the Ministry of State Finance in a demonstration called by the short-lived 'Alliance Against the Memorandum'. Construction workers went on strike on 21 and 22 November. According to reports, the protest on 18 November was 'one of the biggest the country has seen to date' (Davis 2013). On 26 November, thousands of high-school and university students protested outside the House of Representatives (the Parliament of Cyprus) (to vima 2013). The student protest was organized through Facebook, a tool that was widely used by both non-organized and organized anti-austerity activists throughout the two brief protest waves (Triga and Papa 2015). That evening, riots erupted during a bank employees' protest (Euronews 2013). Once again, and similar to other national cases of anti-austerity protests, the physical location of the protests was around the Parliament and the Ministry of Finance, that is, where the decisions—perceived as negative or threatening to the population—were being taken. On the 29th of the same month, seasonal and hourly contract-holding schoolteachers staged a protest at the Parliament, and then at the Ministry of Finance, against one of the Memorandum draft's provisions, which called for the cutting of some 1000 temporary contracts in the public education sector. The protest was turbulent: the teachers invaded both buildings, causing a ruckus and the interruption of the parliamentary session (Kathimerini 2012b). The first wave of anti-austerity protest reached its peak from 11 to 13 December 2012, when members of the Large Families' Association, state bond-holders and trade unions (mostly from the education sector), as well as leftist and anarchist organizations, marched outside government buildings (Sigmalive 2012b). As an AKEL member (who did not participate in the protest due to the fact that his party was in power) noted: 'In my opinion, the protests of the 12th of December were the only real ones of the period. In the sense that you had wide participation, many hundreds of people, [members of] many associations, unions and so on. Not only the usual leftists' (Interviewee CY2). The protesters tried to storm several buildings, caused minor property damage, and threw eggs at the Parliament's external walls (Sigmalive 2012a).

The second wave of anti-austerity protest developed in the period between 16 and 26 March 2013, upon the release of the Troika bailout plan that included the levy on bank deposits mentioned above. The demonstrations were daily and much larger than those of the previous winter.

After the bailout/bail-in plan was finalized and approved by the Cypriot House of Representatives, social tensions subsided. Sporadic protests, though, some of them quite large by Cypriot standards, continued to take place in the years that followed the Memorandum's adoption. It is interesting to note that these demonstrations were mostly called by trade unions facing privatization and threats of job cuts (Euronews 2013; To Pontiki 2014). A major cross-sectoral demonstration took place in October 2013, when public hospital workers, pensioners and municipality employees jointly protested in front of the House of Representatives (APE-MPE 2013). The protests occasionally featured scuffles with police and minor damage to public buildings, but public order officers seldom, if ever, faced a serious challenge by the demonstrators.

8.3.2 Protest Actors, Aims and Framing

Traditional, pre-existing actors constituted the core of both stages of protest. In November 2012, trade unions and small leftist organizations were leading the demonstrations.

With respect to the trade unions, the most visible organizers were productive sector and professional trade union sections (or 'guilds'— συντεχνίες, as they are usually called in Cyprus) that are members of the left-wing federation PEO (Pan-Cypriot Workers' Federation) and also contributed to populating PEO affiliate's grassroots platform 'Movement against the privatizations and austerity policies', as well as the socialist DEOK (Democratic Workers' Federation of Cyprus). The high-school teachers' union OELMEK was a leading entity of the teachers' mobilization, yet unions from all three educational levels participated in the public school employees' demonstrations.

With respect to left-wing parties, one needs to note first of all the important absence from the protest of organized elements of the AKEL party, at least until the February 2013 elections. Apart from the obvious contradiction of protesting against one's own government, the crumbling popularity of President Christofias in the aftermath of the 2011 explosion (Orphanides 2014) had already demobilized and demoralized his party supporters. As an AKEL supporter stated: 'the political leadership never recovered from this tragedy [the explosion]. We kind of lost our pace, but it is absolutely not true that all the mishandlings should be attributed to Christofias: it was the failure of the whole of the political leadership that brought the country to its knees' (Interviewee CY3).

The other two left-wing parties present at the time were the small, extra-parliamentary leftist ERAS and the Trotskyist NEDA (New Internationalist Left). The former was founded in 2011, and dissolved in 2014. A part of it participated in the European elections under the name DRASY (Bi-communal Radical Left Cooperation), in collaboration with Turkish-Cypriot candidates. It only gathered some 2200 votes (0.86 per cent of the electorate), failing to elect any of its candidates as an MEP (Agiomamitis 2014). The latter did not participate in the European elections.

Several civil society organizations held a prominent role in the anti-austerity protest. The pensioners, as well as the large families' associations from all over Cyprus, demonstrated numerous times against cuts in their pensions and benefits.

Finally, an actor that had a noteworthy, yet short-lived, presence in the protest was the 'Alliance Against the Memorandum'. As stated in their founding text, dated 5 October 2012:

> The 'Alliance Against the Memorandum' was established in the People's Assembly in Nicosia and Limassol and aims to unite in common actions against the upcoming memorial. We understand that the measures proposed will irreparably affect our lives and lead many to misery. The experience of many other countries confirms this effortlessly. We invite everyone to motivate with us or to self-organize in their own area—city—village. The social solidarity and resistance will be important in the difficult times ahead. [...] The crisis we are going through is a systemic crisis and cannot be solved simply by the disappearance of some social groups. (Alliance Against the Memorandum 2012)

It is interesting that the 'Alliance' makes specific reference to the 'experience of many other countries'. The fact that the Troika-led austerity policies landed in Cyprus in late 2012, two to four years after the other austerity-ridden European countries, made it easier for activists to identify and frame the bailout programme as a threat to social cohesion and the population's well-being.

In a qualitative content analysis of Facebook posts and online comments during the second protest stage (March–April 2013), Triga and Papa confirm that the broad time frame of the protests facilitated the threat recognition by protesters and their potential allies, bringing forward a broad set of recurring themes and frames that characterized the Cyprus protests: Raising the awareness of common grievances, identifying opponents, calling on the people to 'get off the couch' and participate in direct actions were the main categories that they identified (Triga and Papa 2015). Along these lines, in what follows we shall examine the main protest aims, as well as the accompanying frames, perceived threats, opportunities and constraints the Cypriot anti-austerity protesters faced during the turbulent months of 2012–2013.

First, with respect to the shared grievances, the danger and threat the bailout and the deposits' haircut posed to the Cypriot economy and society was pointed out. A Greek citizen we interviewed, who was working in Cyprus between 2011 and 2014, recalls being told numerous times by protesters or pro-mobilization Cypriots that 'we shouldn't allow Troika to do [in Cyprus] what they did to your country [Greece]' (Interviewee CY1).

According to Triga and Papa, the crisis and the haircut were often depicted as 'part of a conspiracy against Cyprus'—this was also a frequent understanding of the situation in Greece. What differed, though, when compared with most other European countries was the depiction of the crisis as a manifestation of *colonial* capitalism. This resonated well with potential participants, who were reminded of the country's anti-colonial struggle against the British Empire (1946–1960).

When it comes to the definition of the opponents, the enemies identified were both external and internal, as often occurred in other national contexts. The external enemies included the Troika—as 'the ultimate symbol of austerity and enslavement' (Interviewee CY3), the EU, the ECB, and 'the bankers'. In less abstract terms, individuals were also targeted, with a special preference for prominent pro-austerity European politicians. On several occasions, the anti-austerity demonstrators carried photos and masks, and impromptu banners featuring pejorative characterizations of German Chancellor Angela Merkel, Finance Minister Wolfgang Schauble and so on.

The country's presidents during the decisive months (Christofias at the beginning, Anastasiadis after February 2013) were the main internal adversaries. Cyprus' presidential system explains, to some extent, why the heads of the state were targeted, rather than the government, the MPs or even the political system as a whole—as was the case of Spain and Greece.

To give just an illustration, protest outside the Cypriot Parliament on 30 April 2013—the day when the Economic Adjustment Programme was approved by a parliamentary majority—showed a banner of the small centrist party 'Citizens' Alliance'. The banner reads: 'The ex [President] brought the Troika. The current one, conceded everything to it.' It is interesting to note that the protesters holding the banner are also holding the AKEL (the 'ex') flag, alongside the Greek and Cypriot flags and several banners merely comprising the word 'No' ('OXI')—a laconic message that would later gain international prominence during the campaign for the Greek referendum of July 2015. As Triga and Papa note, 'Such actions are qualified positively through the use of metaphors that express them as the regaining of the power by the people. The rhetorical form in which the action of resistance is presented is often by the use of the word "No"' (Triga and Papa 2015, 207).

The dual production of non-partisan discourse on the one hand ('All Cypriots united') and politically connoted references on the other was comparable to the discursive mechanisms employed in other countries as a way to mobilize the broader population, without alienating the experienced activists that are traditionally suspicious of de-politicized protests.

8.4   Concluding Notes

Summing up, the two anti-austerity protest waves that emerged in 2012–2013 in Cyprus were the Cypriot society's response to what it perceived as direct threats to its well-being and social cohesion: the potential intervention of Troika at first, and then the concrete bailout/bail-in plan proposed in March 2013, which would require a significant deposits' levy to be applied in order to recapitalize the country's banking sector. The protests, though, were significantly weaker than in all the other European countries where the Troika intervened in the aftermath of the 2008 financial crisis. In particular, they were significantly less attended and shorter lasting than the Icelandic ones of 2008–2009, the only perhaps directly comparable country case in terms of size and population. The main actors that contributed to the mobilization were trade unions, student unions, non-governmental political parties, the 'Alliance Against the Memorandum' and impromptu online collectives (Facebook groups, web pages, and so on), which set the tone for the discursive production of the anti-austerity movement. The weak presence of newly emerging, non-politically affiliated actors serves as a partial explanation of the movement's inability to expand in time and be embraced by larger parts of the society. This is also associated with the fact that the governments that resorted to Troika assistance came from both sides of the political spectrum, the left wing and the centre-right.

What is more, the anti-austerity mobilization in other European countries had as a mid-term consequence either the emergence of new political actors (Podemos in Spain) or the meteoric rise of pre-existing ones (SYRIZA in Greece), which undertook the responsibility of bringing anti-austerity ideas and political proposals to the central political scene. This was not the case with Cyprus. The only noteworthy party that emerged in the aftermath of the 2013 bank closure was the centrist, anti-memorandum party 'Citizens' Alliance'—which was founded on 28 April 2013 but failed to impress in the 2014 European elections (it was unable to elect an MEP representative, as it only got 6.7 per cent of the vote).

Yet, although it would be erroneous to ignore the movement's constituency characteristics, it would also be over-simplifying to attribute to it full responsibility for the limited mobilization's outcome. A comparison with other European countries' anti-austerity movements shows that, in cases such as Greece, the presence of 'traditional' actors did not hamper the mobilization in the long-term; rather on the contrary, it offered a sturdy base to build upon and a temporal perspective, once the Indignados-style protest wave subsided.

In terms of action repertoire, the forms the protest took were traditional and very similar to the broader European anti-austerity protest. Social media campaigning and protests in front of the physical location where the decision-making body is to be found—the Parliament, in the case of Cyprus—were a leitmotif of the European anti-austerity mobilization. An interesting difference when it comes to claim making, though, was that the Cypriot movement mostly focused on demanding the Head of State's resignation, rather than raising proposals in the direction of a deeper reform of the country's political and economic system.

The time frame of the protest should also be examined: the Cypriots' anti-austerity mobilization was the last to emerge in Europe. The first protests were organized towards the end of 2012, four years after the Icelandic financial meltdown and one and a half years after the Arab Spring and the Indignados-style protests in Spain and Greece. This aspect had a dual consequence for the way in which the movement developed. On the one hand, the dire consequences of the austerity mechanisms that accompanied the Troika-drafted bailout packages had already been well documented in countries such as Ireland, Portugal, Spain and Greece; therefore, the perceived threat was clearly identified and became less of a public debate than in the aforementioned cases. Yet, the inability of popular anti-austerity protest in the other countries to produce immediate and concrete outcomes did demoralize the population, as our interviewees confirmed. This is particularly relevant in the case of Cyprus, where, for geopolitical reasons, the potential of a Eurozone/EU exit was off the table and in fact never examined.

Finally, when trying to understand why the Cyprus memorandum did not spark as intense a popular resistance as in other southern European countries, one should also examine the content of the Economic Adjustment Programme itself. Although the bank closure and the deposits' haircut were undoubtedly extreme, unprecedented measures, they presented two characteristics that are of importance to our analysis. First, the 47 per cent levy was imposed on deposits exceeding 100,000 euros and mostly targeted Russian and other foreign depositors. The weakest strata of the population were not *directly* harmed by it (although, of course, the dismantling of Cyprus' banking sector as a 'safe haven' for foreign money did have grave, albeit indirect, consequences on the overall economy). Second, the fact that the banks were recapitalized through the bail-in, and not through state contribution as in Ireland and Greece, implied that the loan needs of the Cypriot State were significantly lower than in the former cases. As shown in Fig. 8.1, despite the recession of the crisis years, Cyprus' debt-to-GDP ratio never exceeded 110 per cent—remaining lower than in Portugal, Italy and Greece, just to cite some examples. Therefore, the austerity measures imposed on the country in the aftermath of the adoption of the Economic Adjustment Programme were significantly milder than in cases where horizontal cuts were imposed across State and welfare expenses. Indeed, in Cyprus the cuts were targeted towards specific groups (public schoolteachers, medical personnel, privatizations), which did mobilize in the years that followed the 2013 bailout/bail-in; yet, there was no incentive to form the types of wide cross-sectoral anti-austerity alliances that constituted the bulk of the mobilizations in southern Europe. The relatively low debt-to-GDP ratio allowed Cyprus to regain access to international financial markets as early as 2014.

The combination of mild austerity and re-establishment of alternatives to the Economic Adjustment Programme refinancing routes allowed for limited GDP growth in 2015, for the first time after 2011. It is forecast that these mildly positive perspectives for the Cypriot economy will be retained for the next two years (European Commission 2015). What the above signifies is that, even in the case of late neoliberalism in southern

Europe, where the patterns of austerity interventions are shockingly similar, scholarly research needs to take into account nation-case variations in the application of the neoliberal diktat.

8.5   List of Interviewees

CY1, observer, working in Cyprus from 2011–2014, 4 June 2015, Athens
CY2, AKEL member, 3 December 2015, Nicosia
CY3, AKEL member, 2 March 2016, Athens
CY4, non-organized participant at the demonstrations, 9 December 2015, Nicosia

Note

1. Euro elections serve as a good indicator for the Cypriot political parties' relative strength, as the national elections are more focused on the candidate Presidents than the political parties standing behind them; for example, in the 2013 elections, DIKO supported the candidature of Anastasiadis, yet in the first round, the percentage Anastasiadis received was less than what his party received in 2014, despite that DIKO stood no longer in alliance with DISY.

References

Agiomamitis, N. 2014. Drasy-Eylem Shall Continue. *ERAScy.blogspot.com.* http://erascy.blogspot.gr/2014/05/eylem_29.html

Alliance Against the Memorandum. 2012. Who we are. *symmaxiaem.wordpress. com.* https://symmaxiaem.wordpress.com/about/

APE-MPE. 2013. Protest Against Austerity in Cyprus—29/10/2013. *pronews.gr.* http://www.pronews.gr/portal/item/%CE%BA%CF%8D%CF%80%CF%81% CE%BF%CF%82-%CE%B4%CE%B9%CE%B1%CE%B4%CE%B7%CE%BB%CF %8E%CF%83%CE%B5%CE%B9%CF%82-%CE%BA%CE%B1%CF%84% CE%AC-%CF%84%CF%89%CE%BD-%CE%BC%CE%AD%CF%84%CF%81%C F%89%CE%BD-%CE%BB%CE%B9%CF%84%CF%8C%CF%84%CE%B7%CF%8 4%CE%B1%CF%82

Bank of Cyprus Economic Research Division. 2012. *Cyprus Economy,* Nicosia. http://www.bankofcyprus.com/Documents/Publications/Country reports/ I100341.pdf

Davis, C. 2013. Cyprus Bailout Protests: Cypriots March Against Bank Deal. *Huffington Post.* http://www.huffingtonpost.com/2013/03/18/cyprus-bailout-protests_n_2902406.html

Euronews. 2013. Cyprus: Blood Boiling Over the Banks. *euronews.com*. http://gr.euronews.com/2013/03/27/cyprus-blood-boiling-over-the-banks/

European Commission. 2015. *Country Report Cyprus 2015*, Brussels. http://ec.europa.eu/europe2020/pdf/csr2015/cr2015_cyprus_en.pdf

Hess, K.C. 2015. *Disparity in the Responses to the European Financial Crisis: Cyprus and the State of Bail-In Policy*. Portland: Portland State University.

Kathimerini. 2012a. On Thursday the First Protest Against the Memorandum. *Kathimerini Cyprus*. http://www.kathimerini.com.cy/index.php?pageaction=kat&modid=1&artid=111637

———. 2012b. Significant Incidents at the Parliament and Ministry of Economics, Provoked by Seasonal and Hourly-Contract Teachers. *Kathimerini Cyprus*. http://www.kathimerini.com.cy/index.php?pageaction=kat&modid=1&artid=114278&show=Y

Katsourides, Y. 2013. "Couch Activism" and the Individualisation of Political Demands: Political Behaviour in Contemporary Cypriot Society. *Journal of Contemporary European Studies* 21(1): 87–103. doi:10.1080/14782804.2013.766478.

Ker-Lindsay, J. 2011. *The Cyprus Problem: What Everyone Needs to Know*. Oxford: Oxford University Press.

Kouloudi, E. 2014. Understanding of the Financial Crisis in Cyprus, its Effects and the Post Crisis Strategy. Thessaloniki: University of Macedonia. https://dspace.lib.uom.gr/bitstream/2159/16940/6/KouloudiEiriniMsc2014.pdf

Levin, P.T. 2011. *Turkey and the European Union*. London: Palgrave Macmillan.

Orphanides, A. 2013. What Happened in Cyprus: An Interview with Athanasios Orphanides. *The Economist*. Accessed 3 December 2015 http://www.economist.com/blogs/freeexchange/2013/03/interview-athanasios-orphanides

———. 2014. *What Happened in Cyprus? The Economic Consequences of the Last Communist Government in Europe*, London. Accessed 9 June 2015 http://www.lse.ac.uk/fmg/workingPapers/specialPapers/PDF/SP232-Final.pdf

Quaranta, M. 2013. Measuring Political Protest in Western Europe Assessing Cross—National Equivalence. *European Political Science Review* 5(3): 457–482.

Sigmalive. 2012a. Clashes and Riots Outside the Parliament. *Sigmalive.com2*. Accessed 11 January 2016. http://www.sigmalive.com/news/local/20781/symplokes-sti-vouli-sti-diamartyria-ton-polyteknonvinteo

———. 2012b. The Education Associations are also Reacting. *Sigmalive.com*. http://www.sigmalive.com/news/local/20874/antidroun-kai-oi-ekpaideftikes-organoseis

To Pontiki. 2014. Riots in Cyprus: Protesters Entered the Parliament's Courtyard. *Topontiki.gr*. http://www.topontiki.gr/article/68324/epeisodia-stin-kypro-diadilotes-mpikan-sto-proaylio-tis-voylis-video

to vima. 2013. Cyprus: Students Protest Outside the Parliament. *tovima.gr*. http://www.tovima.gr/world/article/?aid=504407

Trading Economics Indicators. 2015. Cyprus GDP Growth Rate 2001–2016. Accessed 1 February 2009. *www.tradingeconomics.com*. http://www.trading-economics.com/cyprus/gdp-growth

Treanor, J. et al. 2013. Cyprus Bailout: Fury as Banks Closed to Avert Run. *The Guardian*. Accessed 2 February 2015 http://www.theguardian.com/business/2013/mar/18/cyprus-closes-banks-bailout-package

Triga, V., and V. Papa. 2015. The Poor Have Been Raped": An Analysis of Politicised Collective Identity in Facebook Groups Against the Financial Crisis in Cyprus. *Cyprus Review* (Jan.).

Wearden, G., 2013. Cyprus Parliament Overwhelmingly Rejects Bailout Savings Tax. *The Guardian*. Accessed 9 February 2016 http://www.theguardian.com/world/2013/mar/19/cyprus-parliament-rejects-savings-levy

CHAPTER 9

Late Neoliberalism and Its Discontents: A Comparative Conclusion

Donatella della Porta

Late neoliberalism, defined as neoliberalism in the Great Recession, had similar characteristics all over Europe, with policies of privatization, liberalization and deregulation-cum-austerity reducing the state's capacity to fulfil its promises to the citizens. Throughout the continent, in different forms, neoliberalism, with its emphasis on the free market and departure from social protection, produced increasing inequalities as well as decreasing support for institutions. Late neoliberalism added austerity measures as a way to address the financial crisis that deregulation policies had created. While recession had effects everywhere, late neoliberalism did not impose cross-national convergence: rather, inequalities increased between macro regions, but also between countries and even within Europe. In fact, at the European Union (EU) level, 'progress in convergence of both bond yields and unemployment rates was dismantled by the financial crisis' (McGrath 2015, 100).

This volume has suggested that those different contextual conditions were reflected in some characteristics of the movements that mobilized over discontent with neoliberalism during its crisis. In this conclusion, we will first compare the social movements that developed in the European periphery we have studied in reaction to austerity policy. We will then link those movements to the different domestic characteristics of late neoliberalism as well as of the related crisis of political responsibility. Finally, we

© The Author(s) 2017
D. della Porta et al., *Late Neoliberalism and its Discontents in the Economic Crisis*, DOI 10.1007/978-3-319-35080-6_9

shall discuss some caveats of our research as well as some directions for future expansion of the comparison.

9.1   COMPARING SOCIAL MOVEMENTS IN TIMES OF CRISIS: A TYPOLOGY

Literature on social movements has focused on movements in times of affluence, particularly those developing in advanced democracies, with expanding welfare provisions and well-established political parties and representative institutions. The movements of the crisis (della Porta and Mattoni 2014) have instead grown under conditions of deep recession, with retrenching welfare states and de-legitimated representative institutions. In the European periphery, the socio-economic and political crises have been fuelled by the EU's structural features as well as its contingent choices. As the research collected in this volume has shown, contentious politics in times of austerity has reflected these contextual characteristics, trying to change them but also being forced to adapt to them.

In fact, to a certain extent, the movements we studied have some assonance with those that have been described as typical of crisis periods: Polanyi's reactive countermovements, but also Wallerstein's and Arrighi's proactive anti-systemic movements. These movements have in fact a strong emphasis on the defence of the losers, calling for a return to previous conditions. With a strong ethical appeal, they denounce the betrayal of existing social pacts by immoral and greedy elites. Appealing to a diverse social base, they also mobilize different types of organizations that have traditionally defended the rights of workers and citizens—from unions to human rights groups. However, they also innovate on these traditional forms, with new repertoires of contention and organizational formats as well as visions of the future.

Comparing our cases, we can notice that, while Polanyi's type of countermovements mobilized everywhere, movements of anti-systemic character have emerged especially where the socio-economic crisis had more disruptive effects on citizens' everyday lives. As Borland and Sutton (2007) had noted in their study of the Argentinian crisis in the beginning of the 2000s, the disruption of subsistence routines as well as the threats to established expectations increase propensities towards collective action frames and identities. When the quotidian rhythm is disrupted, for example through loss of jobs, health, housing and the like, 'action is inhibited, routine is stymied, and uncertainties emerge' (Snow et al. 1998, 5). Casting doubt on taken-for-granted assumptions, these situations make individuals more risk-seeking and 'powerfully motivated to engage in collective action to reconstitute the quotidian and recoup what they have lost' (Snow et al. 1998, 17). In fact, it was especially in Iceland, Greece and Spain, where disruption of the quotidian rhythm was most dramatic, that the agentic power of the contentious citizens has fuelled discontent with political authorities, entangled in a strong crisis of responsibility, testified by the fall of trust and legitimacy indicators as well as the (unexpected) emergence of new parties. However, in Portugal, Ireland, Italy and Cyprus, protests, even when strong, remained more bounded to traditional contentious traditions and actors, putting forward claims of defence of previous conditions.

In *Spain*, the protest on 15 May 2011 started a long and strong wave of contention that innovated within both social movement and traditional political arenas. Although including some more traditional forms of contention (among them, prominently, strikes and marches), the protest repertoire was largely transformed by the emergence of new forms, such as the *acampadas* (camps), but also the re-emergence of old forms of contention, similar to charivari, which singled out alleged perpetrators for public shaming rituals. Although mainly peaceful, the protests underwent heavy repression, having to adapt to the closing down of political channels of access to institutions. The organizational forms within the social movement arena were also influenced by the wave of protest, with the strengthening of a horizontal, inclusive, assembly-based model that had already spread during the global justice movement (della Porta 2007). The youth played a particularly important role in the mobilizations.

The contentious framing included a defence of citizenship rights, but also proactive visions of progressive transformations of the welfare system towards conceptions and practices of the commons. Strongly oriented to denounce the immorality of the degenerated system, protesters also imagined ways to transcend existing state and market institutions. Experimenting with different strategies and playing within different arenas, the Spanish cycle of anti-austerity protests empowered the citizens, who participated en masse, also having transformative effects on the party system (della Porta et al. 2017). While unions organized several strikes, their interactions with the social movement organizations of the 'horizontal' sector remained tense. The movement's ideas and practices, nurtured within local assemblies and self-managed collectives, also influenced labour conflicts through the so-called 'waves' (*mareas*) in the public sector. Values of equality, inclusiveness and dialogue were practised within deliberative and participatory conceptions of democracy.

Similarly, as the square camps moved to *Greece*, anti-austerity protests also acquired very innovative characteristics, mobilizing as much as one-third of the population in multi-class and multi-actor coalitions (Rüdig and Karyotis 2014). The well-established horizontal tradition that characterized the Greek movement was reflected in the organizational structure as well as the repertoire of action of the protest cycle. As was especially the case in Spain, the protests mobilized many previously uncommitted citizens who had been directly hit by the crisis, and claims in defence of social rights were accompanied by proposals for reinventing democracy. Unions of various forms, sizes and persuasions mobilized the workers in numerous strikes, while the citizens took the square and camped, protesting but also discussing potential economic, social and political alternatives (Diani and Kousis 2014). Met at times with brutal repression and developing within an already radicalized milieu, the protests occasionally escalated into violence. Outrage at political scandals fed mistrust in the political class, as well as calls against the immorality of the institutional system, accused of betraying the citizens and discharging their rights (Sergi and Vogiatzoglou 2013). Massive participation in anti-austerity protests also empowered the citizens towards the development of various self-help and direct actions, including the occupation and self-management of factories or the organization of grassroots activities against the suffering and deprivation produced by the crisis. Local assemblies and social solidarity spread all over the country. While alternative forms of self-organization were experimented with, the electoral arena was also affected by the protests, with the strengthening of the radical left, culminating in SYRIZA's conquering of the government in 2015.

In *Iceland*, as well, the protests erupted unexpectedly, involving a large part of a population whose experience with contentious politics was extremely limited. Against the government, which wanted to blame the global crisis, protesters spread a moral frame stigmatizing the political corruption of an octopus-like elite, made up of businesspeople and politicians, which had acted out of greed against the tradition of solidarity of Icelanders. While the traditional role of the state was reclaimed, protests also empowered new visions within the very horizontal organizational format of a citizens' movement. The mobilizations that started—with a rock concert—by the agency of a tiny and unpolitical group, spread quickly and massively. As Bernburg (2015, 13) summarized, public protest meetings in downtown Reykjavik became a regular occurrence, attracting a growing number of individuals and working as

> ...a platform for challenging the way in which the authorities framed the crisis as a global, as opposed to a local, problem. In the course of a few weeks, thousands of individuals began to attend the meetings, including nationally known intellectuals, critics, and activists, who argued that Iceland's political leadership had led the nation into crisis due to corruption and blind faith in market forces. Collective demands emerged: the ruling government was called on to resign, along with the Chairman of the Board of Governors of the Central Bank, and the Director of the Financial Supervisory Authority.

With contentious activities growing, and political leaders perceived as insensitive to citizens' suffering, disruptive protests were called in order to push the government to resign. On 20 January 2009, thousands of people gathered in front of the parliament in Reykjavik, remaining in the central square for three days:

> Most were committed to peaceful action, but some frontline protesters engaged in vandalism and confrontation with riot police who lined up with shields to protect the parliament building. The protests went on for three successive days and created an atmosphere of civil unrest and disorder throughout the downtown area, and the noise could be heard kilometres away. In the evenings, bonfires were lit, and the demonstrations turned into riots; police used gas and batons to disperse the crowd. Referring to their use of kitchen utensils, the protesters claimed that a 'pots-and-pans revolution' (búsáhaldabylting) was in process. (Bernburg 2015)

While remaining mainly peaceful, the protest forms included several innovations, from the pots and pans demonstrations to the bottom up process of constitution writing. In a virtuous circle, the massive response increased the sense of efficacy by participants, fuelling further participation. Organized horizontally, the protest activities were capable of empowering the Icelandic people, producing innovative ideas.

In *Portugal*, protests also increased steadily during austerity times, but with particular growth in more traditional forms such as strikes (including five general strikes), marches (almost 600 protests were registered in

266 D. DELLA PORTA

Lisbon in 2012 alone), and petitions, but with less success for *acampadas*. Contentious politics remained, moreover, peaceful, and very much linked to the national institutions—with direct targeting of the parliament and, at times, the presidency, to which specific claims were addressed, sometimes successfully (Accornero and Pinto 2014). With large participation of traditional actors, including trade unions, political parties, and even police and military personnel organizations, protesters advocated the defence of labour and citizens' rights. While new actors were also present, mobilizing especially the young precarious generation, they tended to adapt their organizational forms to open channels of access to institutions. Symbols, such as slogans and music, were used to root the protest within the glorious past of the carnation revolution of 1974 (Baumgarten 2013). While some innovative conceptions of democracy emerged, with appeals to citizens' participation, contentious politics remained rooted in more conventional visions, with requests for 'more' and 'better quality' democracy. Coordinatory committees for anti-austerity protests included new and old organizations, with the left in Parliament increasing its support throughout the protests.

Similarl to the Portuguese case, in *Italy* there was also a growth in protests in defence of challenged citizens' rights, but overall contentious politics was more reactive than proactive. In fact, the arena of anti-austerity protest was populated mainly by more traditional collective actors, remaining generally fragmented (della Porta et al. 2015; della Porta and Reiter 2012; della Porta and Andretta 2013). While labour conflict was sustained, it was not systematically linked to other types of mobilization that emerged on public education or the right to the city. Main unions called for strikes, but they were not only divided among themselves but also without connections to the social movement organizations that had emerged in the global justice movement as well as in successive waves of protest. Innovative forms, such as social strikes, were invented, but without sustained empowering capacity. No strong social or political coalitions formed to challenge neoliberal reforms. In a situation traditionally characterized by a large but not autonomous civil society, rather accustomed to search for support in the centre-left parties and their collateral organizations, social movements had weak capacity to mobilize against governments that were supported by the centre-left party and its successor. This was reflected in the repertoire of protest, which remained in part anchored in the past, with attempts to build camps in the city squares encountering very little success.

While protest remained mainly peaceful, tensions within the social movement sector itself produced occasional radicalization. From the point of view of framing, as well, the reconquering of lost rights dominated, with only limited attempts to single out proposals for the building of participatory forms of democracy and a practice of commons. While achieving an important victory in the referendum in defence of water as a public good, and notwithstanding the electoral punishment of the main two parties in the 2013 general elections, no new vision of justice and democracy was forged during the protests. Parliamentary opposition to austerity policies was in fact carried out by the Five Star Movement, which had a tense relationship with social movements on the left.

In *Ireland*, protest was certainly not absent, but here as well it took more traditional forms in defence of established rights. While there were, especially at the beginning of the crisis (2008 and 2009), strikes and mass demonstrations organized especially by the unions, rooted in particular in the public sector, protests then subsided when the unions accepted austerity policies, in the hope of some future rewards. In particular, in March 2010, the *Public Service Agreement 2010–2014* 'copper-fastens previous unilateral pay reductions while containing a tentative commitment to avoid additional pay cutting measures, unless faced with a further economic crisis' (McDonough and Dundon 2010, 558). Some protest camps were organized in 2011, the idea spreading from Southern Europe, with innovative character but very limited capacity for mobilization. Discontent with the government was instead channelled into the electoral arena. The most innovative protests have developed since 2014, with the emergence of social movement organizations after the peak of the crisis—for example, the Right2Water campaign's experimentation with new forms and frames.

In *Cyprus*, negotiations with the Troika, initiated by the left-wing governments in 2012 and continuing after the change in government by the right-wing party in 2013, brought about opposition both in the streets and in parliament. Two intense but short waves of protest developed in the most important moments of negotiation with the European Commission (EC), European Central Bank (ECB) and International Monetary Fund (IMF) in the autumn of 2012 and the spring of 2013. The protesters took up frames of defence of national sovereignty, sometimes revisiting the anti-neocolonialism discourse developed during the struggle for independence from the United Kingdom. As in Ireland, contentious politics was mainly moved by more traditional actors, such as the public sector trade unions that were at the core of the Alliance Against the Memorandum. They also took the more traditional forms of strikes and demonstrations, often in front of parliament, although with some use of social media campaigning as well. As the bail-in hit especially foreign (Russian) investors and the sum gathered from the bail-in (rather than state funds) were used for recapitalizing the banking sector, the potential for building up a broad social coalition was limited. Weak traditions of protest but high degrees of control of civil society by the main party of the left also explain the weak capacity for autonomous mobilization of the society.

As we will see in what follows, the characteristics in terms of repertoires of action, organizational forms and framing of the protests relate to the characteristics of the crisis itself. Contrary to expectations present in much of the sociological literature (e.g. Kerbo 1982), however, more transformative movements emerged when and where the crisis was most acute.

9.2   Socio-Economic Crises in the EU Periphery

Although the crisis was one and the same, it had different timing and characteristics in different countries, influenced as it was by previous structural conditions as well as contingent developments. Variables that are usually mentioned when assessing the economic conditions that affected the evolution of the world crisis are related to the size of the public debt, but also its composition; the amount of the public deficit; the relationship of private debt versus savings; the financing of debt through domestic versus foreign financial institutions; the payment balance; the competitiveness of the economy. The timing and speed of the manifestation of the great recession is also relevant. In general, socio-economic indicators converge in pointing at the increasing misery in all the countries analysed in the European periphery.

Research has stigmatized the extreme level of deprivation in recent times. In her book on *Expulsions*, Saskia Sassen has singled out an emergent systemic trend that allowed for extreme concentration of wealth and rapidly increasing inequalities, with the development of 'predatory formations' as 'a mix of elites and systemic capacities with finance a key enabler, that push towards acute concentration' (2014, 13). She points indeed at the exceptionally high profit-making capacity of some service industries, also through new technologies that facilitate hypermobility. The degrading of the welfare state project thus brings about 'a shrunken space with relatively fewer firms, fewer workers, and fewer consumer households, all indicators of a system gearing towards expelling what does not fit in its evolving logic' (Sassen 2014, 217).

As Thomas Piketty (2014) has recalled, today's unequal distribution of wealth is similar to that of the end of the late nineteenth century, as the capital rate return is greater than the economic growth. This inequality in turns produces social and political instability, with often dramatic existential effects of inequalities in terms of disruption of everyday life (Therborn 2013). Inequalities also developed within the Eurozone, as

> during these 15 years of its existence, the Eurozone has been characterized by high structural heterogeneities between countries, high inflation differentials, the absence of optimum currency area criteria, and the absence of functional equivalents (such as common budget, common taxes, or automatic cyclical stabilizers such as a common unemployment insurance or a cyclical shock insurance). (Dawson et al. 2015a, 19)

While our countries fit this picture quite well, we did notice significant variation in the forms and degrees of dispossession. To cite only a few examples, Eurostat data on the unemployment rate (that is, the number of people unemployed as a percentage of the labour force)[1] show the highest values and most rapid increases for Greece and Spain, followed by Cyprus (see Fig. 9.1). A similar trend can be noted in long-term unemployment (Fig. 9.2), referring to the number of people who are out of work and have been actively seeking employment for at least a year, as well as on youth unemployment (Fig. 9.3). On the latter, Italy and Cyprus show very high values, which approach those of Spain and Greece.

Eurostat data also point at an increase in material deprivation, especially in its most severe forms.[2] Here as well, Greece has the most dramatic features, followed by Italy, Cyprus and Spain (see Fig. 9.4). In all cases, the youth is particularly hit by these various forms of material deprivation (Fig. 9.5), and also highly at risk of poverty (Fig. 9.6).[3]

Variations in the degree of disruption in everyday life can be explained by contextual conditions in some countries, which buffered the effects of the financial and social crises—as was the case, for instance, in Italy, given the high saving tendency; in Portugal, given a more protective welfare system; in Cyprus, given the composition of the bank deposits; or in Ireland, given the high import of capital. Vice versa, the disruption to daily life was higher, given high private indebtedness and/or weak social protection, in

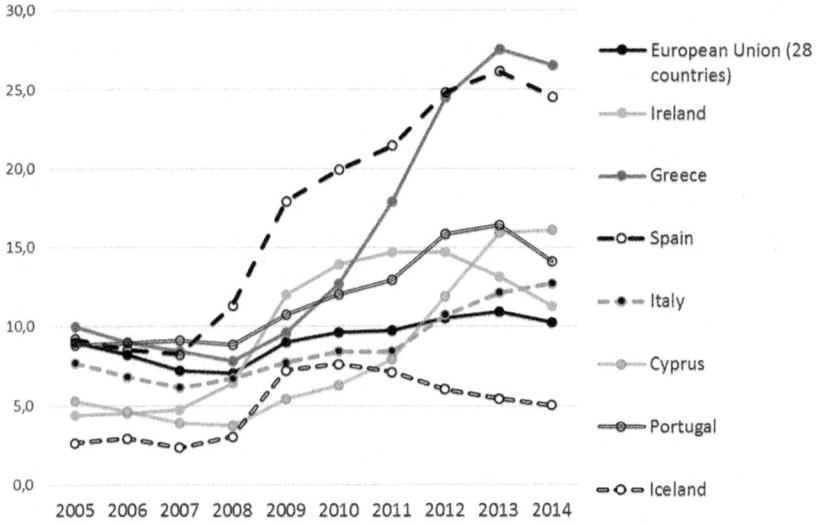

Fig. 9.1 Unemployment rate as percentage of active population in selected European countries. *Source*: Eurostat

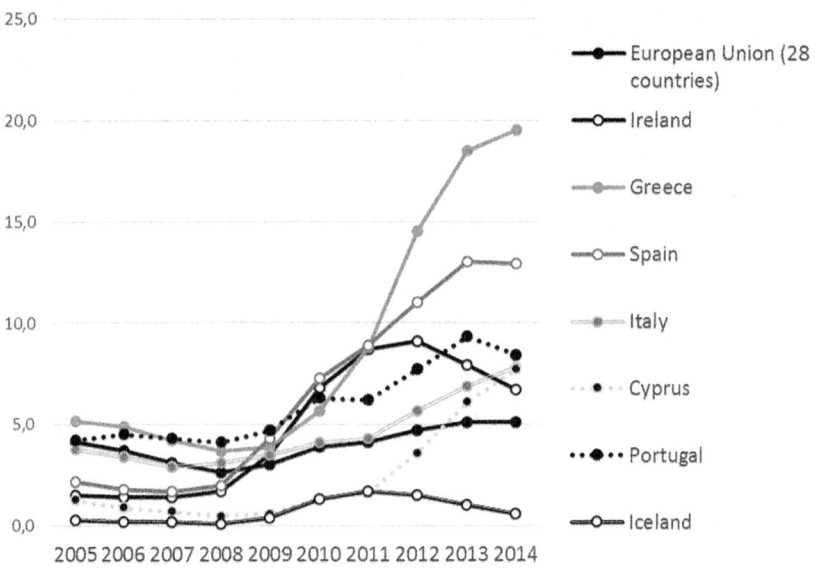

Fig. 9.2 Long-term unemployment rate as percentage of active population in selected European countries. *Source*: Eurostat

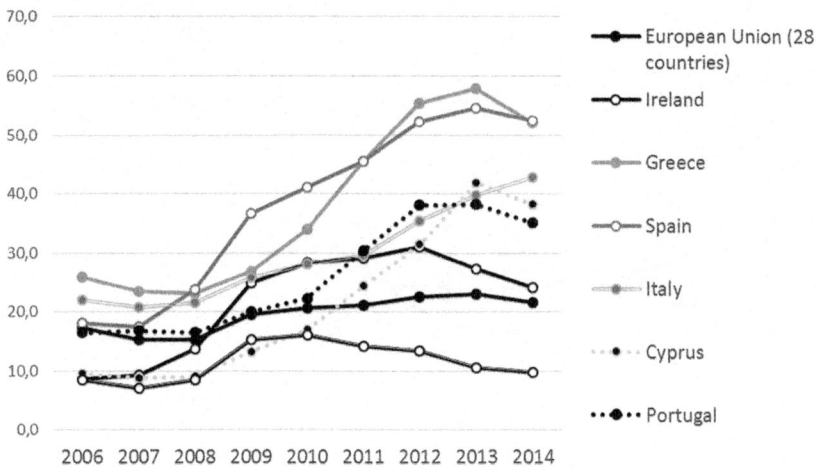

Fig. 9.3 Youth unemployment rate as percentage of youth active population in selected European countries. *Source*: Eurostat

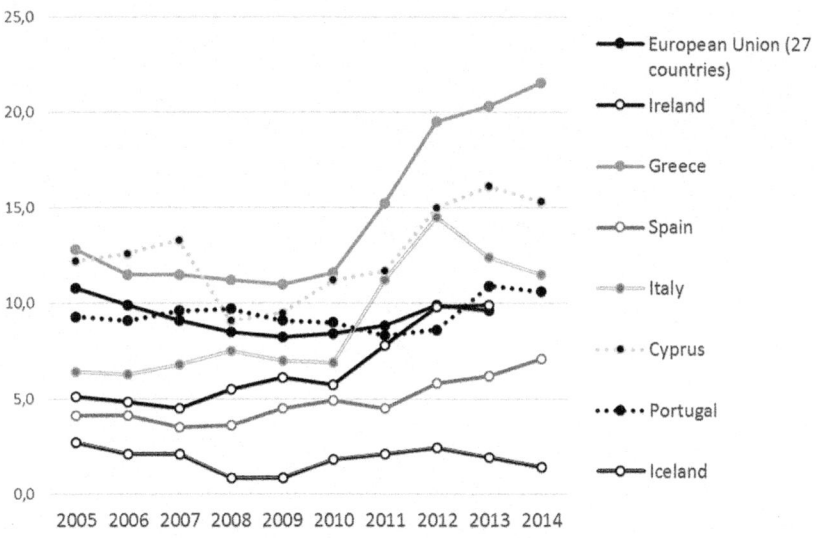

Fig. 9.4 Severe material deprivation index in selected European countries. *Source*: Eurostat

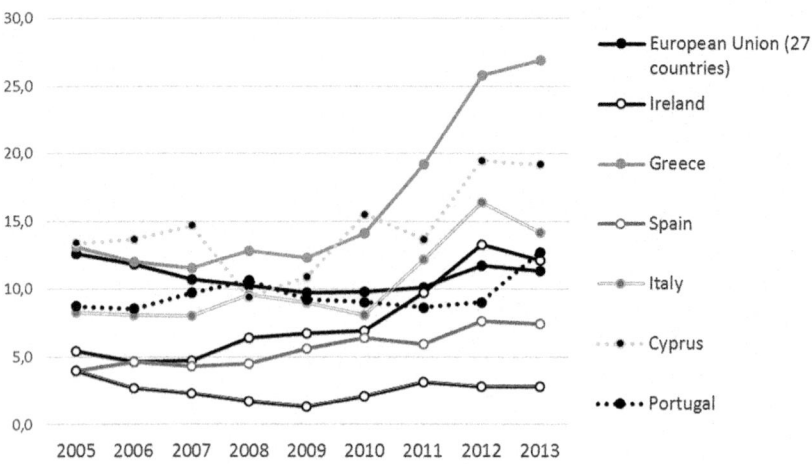

Fig. 9.5 Severe material deprivation of young people (15–29) in selected European countries. *Source*: Eurostat

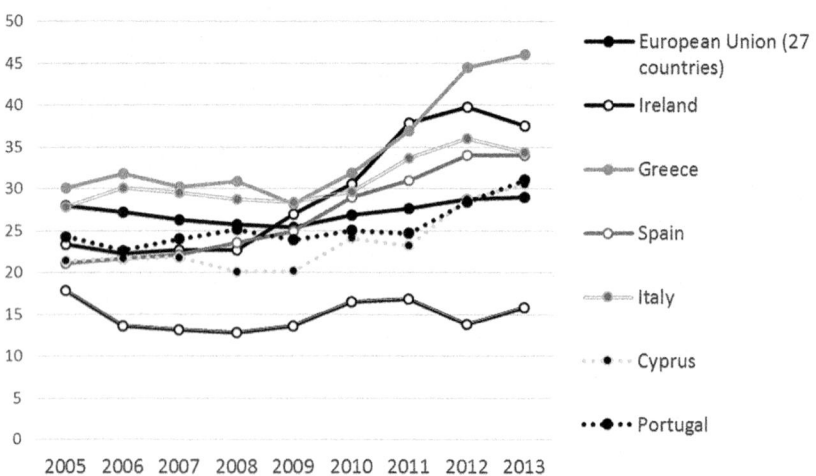

Fig. 9.6 Young people (15–29) at risk of poverty: percentages in selected European countries. *Source*: Eurostat

Iceland, Greece and Spain, where indeed more radically innovative movements developed.

In *Iceland*, citizens reacted swiftly due to the speed and breadth of the crisis. As has been observed,

> The quick onset of the economic crises in Iceland in 2008 was perhaps its defining feature. While it would be an exaggeration to say that things fell apart overnight, it wouldn't be all that far from the truth. In the span of a few days Iceland's three largest banks were placed into receivership and every day appeared to bring a new batch of bad news. Icelanders felt the consequences of the collapse of the banking system immediately. People who had invested in the banks' stocks saw their savings wiped out. While perhaps not significant in itself there was no way to get money in or out of the country for a few days, which bred feelings of isolation and helplessness among many. Most importantly, the banking crisis was accompanied by a significant devaluation of the Icelandic krona. While a fall in the value of a currency has substantial effects on consumption in countries that rely heavily on imports, there were additional complications in the Icelandic case. Interest rates had been kept very high in Iceland and, as a consequence, taking out mortgages and other loans in foreign currency—at substantially lower rates—had become quite common. The devaluation of the Icelandic krona meant that many people faced mortgage payments twice what they had been at the origination of the mortgage. (Indridason 2014)

The disruption of Icelanders' everyday lives was indeed dramatic, as 'the crisis did more than create widespread anticipation of personal economic loss. It produced a collectively experienced disruption in taken-for-granted reality; it disrupted taken-for-granted assumptions and ideas about Icelandic society, thus resulting in a shared experience of a problematic present' (Bernburg 2015, 41). At the same time, however, Iceland did recover quite quickly through heterodox policies, as decisions not to repay bank debt proved effective. Given the incapacity of the small Icelandic state to act as a lender of last resort, it focused on protecting domestic investors, leaving the banks insolvent in their international operations and deflating the krona (Bernburg 2015). So, while the recession was full blown in the rest of the EU periphery,

> Under the recovery programme, Iceland's recession has been shallower than expected, and no worse than in less hard-hit countries. At the same time, the krona has stabilized at a competitive level, inflation has come down from 18

to under 5 per cent, and CDS spreads have dropped from around 1,000 to about 300 basis points. Current account deficits have unwound, and international reserves have been built up, while private sector bankruptcies have led to a marked decline in external debt, to around 300 per cent of GDP... while the IMF is demanding that Ireland cut minimum wages and reduce unemployment benefits, its mission to Iceland praised the 'focus on preserving Iceland's valued Nordic social welfare mode'. (Krugman 2013)

In *Greece*, as in the other cases in Europe's periphery, the crisis arrived as a shock after a period of foreign investments (especially in banks, communication and infrastructures) and apparent growth. The depth of the transformation—and the blatant challenges to democratic accountability and national sovereignty in the political reactions to it—contributed to a broad and deep social movement, with ultimately strong political effects. The socio-economic situation was dramatic at the onset of the crisis and even worsened. Persisting structural problems reverberated in the crisis—among them, 'problems of clientelism and corruption, problems of policy making and governance, and problems of competitiveness (a weak industrial base, strong product market rigidities and a mounting current account deficit)' (Monastiriotis et al. 2013, 4).

In part due to these weaknesses, the crisis was reflected in an increase in the budget deficit, which climbed to 15.8 per cent in 2009, with borrowing rates up to 10 per cent. As mentioned in the chapter on the Greek case, under these conditions, in 2010, the EC and IMF accorded an emergency loan, which—here as in Ireland—implied 'a strict and pervasive conditionality for the implementation of a broad range of reforms and fiscal consolidation actions' (Monastiriotis et al. 2013, 4). As lending institutions set unrealistic benchmarks, this allowed 'the markets to declare an imminent default (and a "Grexit") every time any of these projections failed to materialize' (Monastiriotis et al. 2013, 7). The effect was, between 2010 and 2013, a fiscal tightening of about 20 per cent of GDP, which had immediate and dramatic reverberations on the everyday lives of most Greek citizens: an increase in unemployment, from 9 per cent in 2009 to 26 per cent in 2012; cuts in salaries (by 25 per cent) and personnel in the public sector; increases in the VAT rates; increases in pension age; and reduction of pension amounts. Liberalization of professions, privatization and a flexibilization of the labour market included 'reduction in notice periods, rise in the lawful redundancy rate, softening of unfair dismissal rules and a drastic cut in severance pay entitlements' (Monastiriotis et al. 2013, 6).

The weak welfare state, with its lack of general safety nets and low social spending, aggravated the disruptive effects of the crisis on the daily lives of a large majority of the population.

Similarly to Greece, in *Spain* the crisis was deep and dramatically affected citizens in their everyday lives. As in Ireland, it was initially not linked to sovereign debt: rather, the public debt increased as Spain had to respond to increasing unemployment, linked to the collapse of the housing market and related fall in revenue. The response to the financial crisis then led to a deep social crisis. After the first years of the recession, Spain had in fact the highest level of unemployment and one of the highest public deficits in the entire Eurozone (Conde-Ruiz and Marín 2013). Public accounts shifted from a 2 per cent surplus in 2007 to a deficit of 11 per cent in 2009, while the public debt jumped from 36 per cent in 2007 to 54 per cent in 2009 (Conde-Ruiz and Marín 2013).

As in Greece, the policy responses to the crisis in Spain dramatically affected the day-to-day lives of citizens through reductions in public investment (which dropped by 60 per cent since 2009) and in public employees' wages, along with increases in the VAT and in personal and corporate income taxes (Conde-Ruiz and Marín 2013). While temporary contracts had spread since the deregulation of 1984, with strong dualizing effects on the labour market (Picot and Tassinari 2014), the management of the crisis also imposed a stripping of workers' rights in the once protected main labour market. After the EU Eurogroup meeting in May 2010, EU institutions increased pressures for austerity policies, particularly insisting on the flexibilization of the labour market, which was passed unilaterally, after negotiations with unions failed. The new regulations facilitated dismissals, reducing compensations in cases of unjust dismissal while the unemployed were compelled to commit themselves to a specific plan for counselling and training set up by the public employment services. Agreements with social partners were looked for only occasionally, and disposed of in case of disagreements, with a decline in union rights and decentralization of collective bargaining. The effect was

> ...strong labour market deregulation by itself, not matched by a corresponding recalibration of protections. The decentralization of collective bargaining was equally drastic and may represent the starting point of a systemic change in Spanish industrial relations. It shifts the balance of power towards employers, sanctioning the priority of flexibility and adaptability to firms' productivity needs, and is likely to bring about considerable wage modera-

tion and further decline in the power of Spanish unions. (Picot and Tassinari 2014, 15)

Related to the specific dynamics of the crisis, the bank crisis, with its linkages to credits in the construction sectors (the so-called construction bubble), was one of the most disruptive aspects of the Great Recession. Bank customers who could not repay their mortgage debts were evicted from their homes at a rate of two per day (Romanos 2014).

The socio-economic conditions were hard in the other peripheral countries as well. However, as mentioned, they were, somehow, buffered by factors such as foreign capital investment in Ireland, an inclusive welfare state in Portugal, the composition of bank deposits in Cyprus, or conservative economic behaviour in Italy.

In *Ireland*, where protests were limited during the peak of the crisis and instead grew from it, the crisis was fuelled, as in Iceland, by the weakness of the financial system. The most dramatic effects emerged as public debt boomed (from 40 per cent of GDP to about 120 per cent in 2013) following the 2008 government's decision to save heavily indebted banks (Hardiman and Regan 2013). This bailing out was indeed a different move from Iceland's, imposing an austerity policy strongly based on cuts in public spending that certainly affected the citizens, especially those working in the public sector. In total, between 2008 and 2015, the Irish economy is estimated to have experienced total cuts of as much as 20 per cent of GDP (Hardiman and Regan 2013).

Relevant in assessing the dynamics of the crisis, and of social movements' reactions thereof, is the broad agreement among political actors and unions to continue to attract capital investment through low taxation, as well as the economic dualism, with an export-oriented sector that remained less affected by the recession. Austerity policies were in fact based on a compromise to maintain a low tax regime, especially for the business sector, keeping a 12.5 per cent corporate tax rate as well as low social insurance contributions for employers, with fiscal adjustment based instead upon cuts in pay and services in the public sector. While low taxation rates had been a structural weakness already in the buoyant years, it certainly contributed to a deficit of 7.3 per cent of GDP in 2008 and 14 per cent the year after, while foreign-based investors repatriated the profits (Hardiman and Regan 2013).

Addressing the crisis, in 2011, the Fine Gael-Labour government continued, in fact, with policies oriented to attracting foreign capital, new tax breaks for the financial sector, but pay cuts in the public sector (by about 15 per cent) as well as in the minimum wage and in social welfare. While unemployment increased from 6.4 per cent in 2008 to about 15 per cent in 2012 (Hardiman and Regan 2013), early retirements were used to reduce employment in the (already small) public sector, especially in health and education (Hardiman and Regan 2013). The trade unions were involved in this deal through the Croke Park Agreement, which included 'a government commitment not to impose further pay cuts until 2014 in return for industrial peace and productivity increases, reform of the bonus payment system, a recruitment embargo in the health and education sectors, and significantly reduced pay and conditions for new entrants to the public sector' (Hardiman and Regan 2013, 12).

Also in *Portugal*, as in Spain, the crisis developed from financial problems linked to speculative reactions to the information spread about the sovereign debt crisis in Greece. In addition, as in Spain and in most of the European periphery, its dynamics were in part fuelled by the external debt and the negative balance of payments crisis. Low competitiveness, already a structural problem of the Portuguese economy, brought about its most dramatic effects when Portugal joined the euro, and the trade deficit and related net external debt could no longer be controlled through devaluation. Thus, 'the main reason Portugal presently faces an external debt crisis is not that its export sector lost competitiveness, but instead that the adoption of the euro removed the automatic stabilizers that helped maintain the levels of net external debt and balance of income deficits in check' (Cabral 2013, 27).

The effects of the recession were aggravated as Portugal had to sign a memorandum with the ECB and EC, which considered the crisis as derived from 'fiscal laxity' and related failure to comply with the Stability and Growth Pact (Cabral 2013). Aiming at reducing the payment balance, the Memorandum of Understanding (MoU) thus imposed very specific measures, triggering a social crisis as well as a democratic one. With its 222 main action items spread across 34 pages, the MoU imposed a new bank recapitalization programme, leaving decisional power in private hands. It also increased the VAT as well as the fees to access public services such as hospitals, the court system and public highways. With a freeze on hiring and promotions in the public sector, cuts affected all services, education being the hardest hit. The sacrifices demanded by lending institutions proved ineffective, as the general government debt rose from 93.5 per cent in 2010 to 120.5 per cent of GDP in 2012 (Cabral 2013).

As the chapter on Portugal indicates, however, while the crisis also had dramatic impoverishing effects here, the most dramatic changes in the everyday lives of citizens were somehow buffered by a welfare state whose bases were built in the years immediately after the carnation revolution (Fishman 2011). The Social Emergency Plan, building on traditional partnerships between the state and civil society organizations, provided for some social protection.

In *Italy*, as well, the crisis was related more to low productivity than to public debt. It arrived later than in the rest of the European periphery, and the response was also somehow delayed. Over the past decade, Italy's real GDP growth per capita has been among the weakest in the OECD (Organization for Economic Cooperation and Development), reflecting very low underlying productivity growth (Goretti and Landi 2013). Here as well, 'when fears of contagion rose, structurally low growth even before the Great Recession (with real GDP growth rate at 1.3 per cent per year on average between 1995 and 2008) and policy stalemate (with the Berlusconi government incapable of making tough decisions due to internal cabinet rifts and a divided majority) did nothing but contribute to the flee from Italy's sovereign debt' (Sacchi 2015, 81). From April to July 2011, Italian credit default swaps tripled, only shortly after the European Council had endorsed a plan oriented to achieve a balanced budget in 2014 (Sacchi 2015). However, the effects of a very high public debt were buffered by high private savings, as 'net households' wealth was at 8.6 trillion euro in 2011, about 5.4 times the GDP, and considerable primary budget surpluses have been run since 1991 with the sole exception of 2009 (−0.7 per cent despite a GDP plunge of 5.5 per cent) and 2010 (an immaterial −0.1 per cent)' (Sacchi 2015, 81).

Similarly to Spain, even without having signed an MoU, Italy was still subject to heavy conditionalities, as 'while acting to ease the pressure on the Italian bonds by making purchases on the secondary market, the ECB imposed certain conditions that, despite not being formalized in MoUs, were nonetheless stringent and pervasive, as the ECB was setting the policy agenda, alternatives and instruments to be adopted in exchange for its support' (Sacchi 2015, 83). After Berlusconi resigned, the grand coalition government led (as in Greece) by a so-called technocrat, Mario Monti, implemented all the points included in a letter from the ECB leaders to the Italian government, with particular emphasis on labour market flexibility and pension system restructuring. In addition, with support from EC institutions, the Monti government 'did nothing to conceal blatant distaste for the trade unions, perceived and portrayed as forces for the preservation of the status quo and partly responsible for the country's dramatic situation. This also meant the introduction of reforms that would deeply affect categories of workers ("insiders") largely untouched by previous reforms' (Sacchi 2015, 85). Reforms included the implementation of a minimum retirement age of 67 by 2019, as well as the abolition of seniority pensions, with strict monitoring by the European institutions. Reforms of the collective bargaining system were imposed 'to allow firm-level agreements to tailor wages and working conditions to firms' specific needs', and for 'reviewing the rules regulating hiring and dismissal of employees, to be adopted in conjunction with the establishment of an unemployment insurance system and a set of active labour market policies capable of easing the reallocation of resources towards the more competitive firms and sectors' (Picot and Tassinari 2014, 17). In this period, demands by the ECB were strategically used by Italian policymakers to implement decisions that had been opposed by the unions.

The socio-economic structure in *Cyprus* was similar to the Irish one in terms of reliance on low taxes and favourable laws in order to attract foreign financial capital. As in Iceland, the breakdown of an oversized financial system (the bank system being in possession of assets of eight times the value of Cyprus' GDP) reverberated on the entire economy, with the country losing access to international financial markets in 2012. The bailout agreement with the troika brought about austerity policies that penalized the public sector and the public services. However, given a low public deficit, as well as a mix of bailout and bail-in measures, the crisis hit the population less harshly than in other cases.

The socio-economic dynamics of the crisis, particularly its disruptive effects on the everyday lives of the European citizens, also had an impact at the political level.

9.3   Political (Lack of) Legitimacy in the Great Recession

In all of our countries, the growing amount of suffering was translated, although not linearly, into political de-legitimation of existing institutions and parties in power. In fact, neoliberal policies of privatization and deregulation, especially when combined with austerity, drastically reduced the capacity of governments to address citizens' demands. As mentioned, protesters often claimed that what was at stake was citizenship rights and, with them, democracy. Everywhere, increasing constraints by international organizations of dubious accountability have reduced (and been perceived as reducing) the quality of democracy. Post-democracies appeared as increasingly corrupt. However, these general trends towards a crisis of responsibility have either been enhanced or reduced by the characteristics of the economic crisis, as well as by structural and conjunctural dynamics in the political system.

This was all the more the case in the EU and, even more, in the Eurozone. As Christian Joerges (2015, 81) noted, 'In post-war Europe, the responsibility for ensuring welfare, balancing social inequalities, and creating infrastructure for economic development has become a common feature of the nation state with constitutive importance for its social legitimacy.' EU-imposed conditionalities that acted against this type of intervention have brought about a de-legitimation of national and European institutions alike. The democratic deficit has increased, as 'new forms of EU governance have often been adopted without significant reflection on their accountability implications' (Dawson, Enderlein, and Joerges 2015a, 17). In sum:

> Nationally, strong constitutional courts like the German Bundesverfassungsgericht have defended the prerogatives of the German Parliament by insisting upon strict conditionality for loan assistance to southern European debtors. In the very act of doing so, however, they may have limited the ability of other constitutional courts to defend rights to equality, social assistance and employment as guaranteed under national constitutions. Supranationally meanwhile, the coordinative method is often elaborated through soft law or vague, indeterminate economic benchmarks that are unamenable to judicial review. Just as parliamentary scrutiny of EU governance has become more difficult, avenues for legal control of EU economic governance have also become increasingly scarce. (Dawson et al. 2015a, 21)

Indeed, the crisis challenged previous modes of legitimation of European institutions, as 'through the supervision and control of macroeconomic imbalances, Europe's praxis disregards the principle of enumerated powers and competences and cannot respect the democratic legitimacy of national institutions, in particular the budgetary powers of the parliaments' (Joerges 2015, 87). So, 'the institutional and decision making framework emerging from the crisis has created a number of gaps in this accountability structure. The coordinative method tends to render obsolete traditional mechanisms of judicial review and parliamentary control without substituting new models in their place' (Dawson 2015, 43). Essentially, the crisis triggered an extension of the so-called coordinative methods from social to fiscal issues with financial coercion, not uniform by state, increasing EU power: 'The coordinative method involves a significant reconfiguration of the balance of power between the EU and its member states. Not only is EU intervention more regular, but it is also deeper, extending beyond traditional areas of EU competence and including detailed, rather than general, policy prescriptions' even 'in areas going far beyond official EU competence (e.g. in pensions, tax, health, and other areas of policy' (Dawson 2015, 54–5). So, 'the notion that states should be subject to equal obligations has been gradually abandoned' (Dawson 2015, 56).

Electoral accountability declined, with parliamentary institutions at all levels being considered as 'the great "losers" in this time of emergency' (Joerges 2015, 90). While new treaties—such as the Fiscal Compact and the European Stability Mechanism (ESM)—do not even mention the European parliament, as recommendations are made by the commission and the council (Ecofin) alone, the 'sidelining of the European Parliament has often been matched during the crisis by a declining role in budgetary policy for national parliaments'. Among others, the new rules even limit the time available for national parliaments to control budgetary decisions by setting a deadline of 30 November for the commission to assess the drafts of national budgets, with 31 December as the deadline for budget adoption at the domestic level (Dawson 2015, 59). The EU institution that acquired more power during the great recession was the ECB, which is 'one of the world's most independent central banks' (Dawson 2015, 60). Legal accountability through the constitutional courts has also been hampered, given vague parameters (for example, 'serious macro-economic imbalances' or 'budgetary objective') as well as very opaque decisions by the Commission. A deferential approach by the European court has been noted, with 'The court's failure to consider whether lending conditions under the ESM might threaten social rights protected under the EU Charter—a question it has repeatedly refused to answer, in spite of several references from national courts' (Dawson 2015, 62). Furthermore,

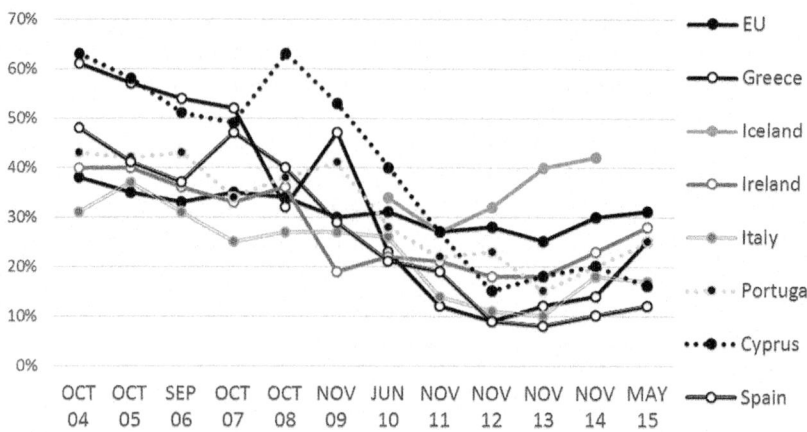

Fig. 9.7   Trust in national parliament (% of tend to trust). *Source*: Eurobarometer

> At a legal level, the reliance under EU economic governance on discretionary fiscal standards and the increasing use of international law agreements among member states has made it more difficult for citizens to exercise their rights of individual judicial review. At a political level, the rise of executive institutions in the fiscal field, such as the Eurogroup or the European Central Bank (ECB), has correlated with the tendency to marginalize parliamentary institutions. (Dawson et al. 2015b, 118–19)

Eurobarometer polls capture an indicator of the crisis—if not directly of legitimacy, at least of consent. In particular, they show a marked decline of trust in political institutions that, in our peripheries, is much sharper than the EU average. Greece and Spain have the lowest levels of trust in national parliaments, which, from relatively high levels, dropped enormously during the crisis. While recovery is very limited in southern Europe and Ireland, only in Iceland have recent years seen a substantial increase in trust in parliament. Very similar is the trend for trust in parties, declining everywhere, but especially in Greece and Spain, which had started with relatively high levels but dropped to its lowest level (5 per cent) during the crisis (see Figs. 9.7, 9.8, and 9.9).

The decline is even more dramatic with regard to EU institutions. The 'sleeping giant' of discontent with European politics (Franklin and van der Eijk 2004, 47) has indeed been fully awakened by the crisis. The European periphery, which had started with higher-than-average levels of trust in the EU parliament and the EC, saw a massive reduction in confidence,

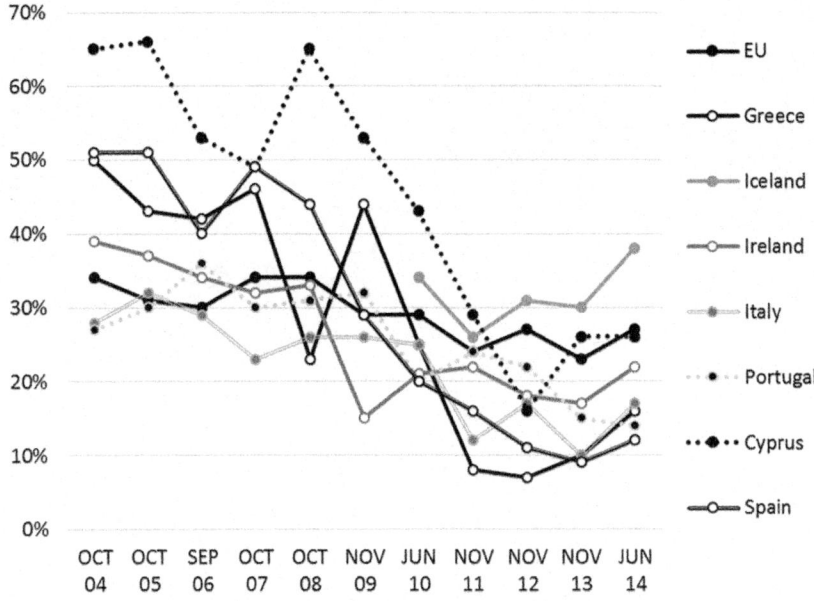

Fig. 9.8   Trust in national government (% of tend to trust). *Source*: Eurobarometer

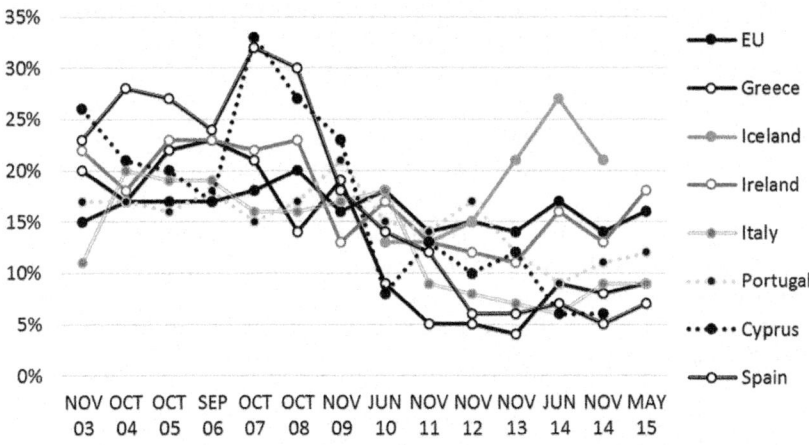

Fig. 9.9   Trust in political parties (% of tend to trust). *Source*: Eurobarometer

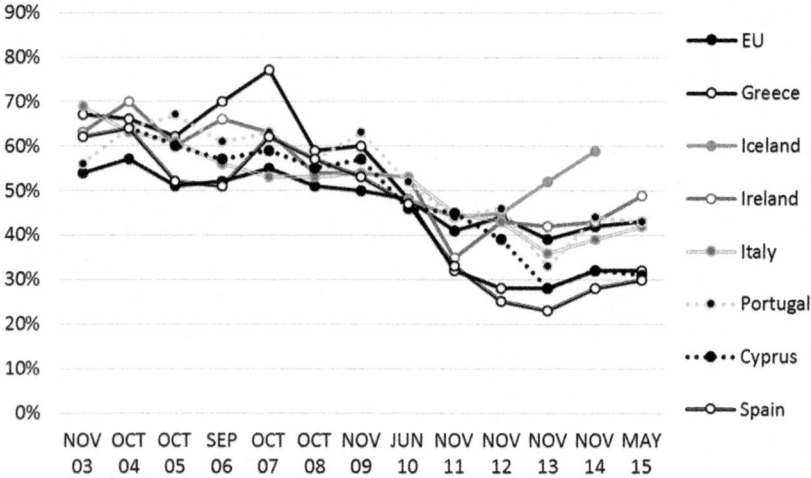

Fig. 9.10   Trust in EU parliament (% of tend to trust). *Source*: Eurobarometer

with Spaniards and Greeks leading the trend and Italians following very closely behind. Both institutions saw dramatic falls in citizens' trust (cut by at least half) between 2003 and 2013, with limited recovery thereafter (see Figs. 9.10 and 9.11). Similarly, citizens' trust in the European Central Bank was in sharp decline during the crisis, particularly in Spain and Greece (see Fig. 9.12).

In general, in fact, a strong association between unemployment and mistrust in EU and national institutions was noted in the EU countries that had been hardest hit by recession (McGrath 2015). Our case studies indicate, however, that this crisis of legitimacy took different characteristics given different attribution of opportunities.

In *Iceland*, the crisis and the response to it interacted with a deep change in the political system that was reflected in a drop of the confidence in representative institutions—with trust in parliament falling from 40 per cent before the crisis to 13 per cent afterwards, and high distrust for the political parties as indicated, among other events, by the victory of the newly founded Best Party in the local election in Reykjavik (Indridason 2014). During the financial crash,

> …the unfolding crisis undermined the legitimacy of the authorities, especially in the period from early October through November 2008. After

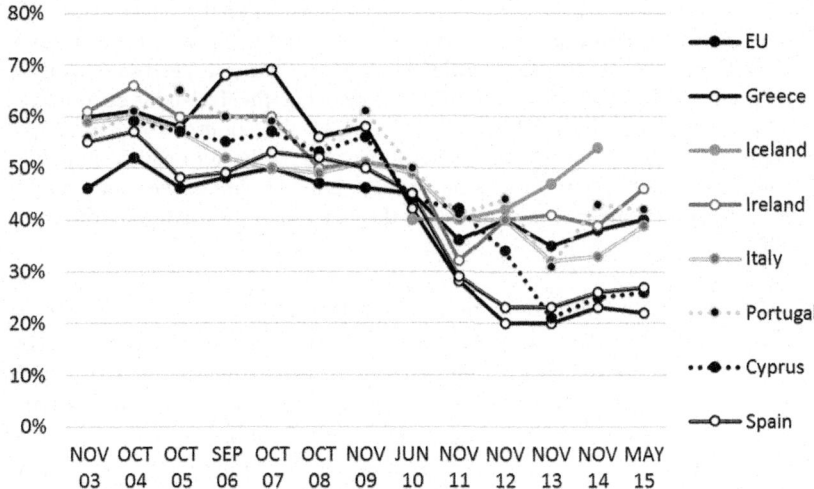

Fig. 9.11 Trust in European Commission (% of tend to trust). *Source*: Eurobarometer

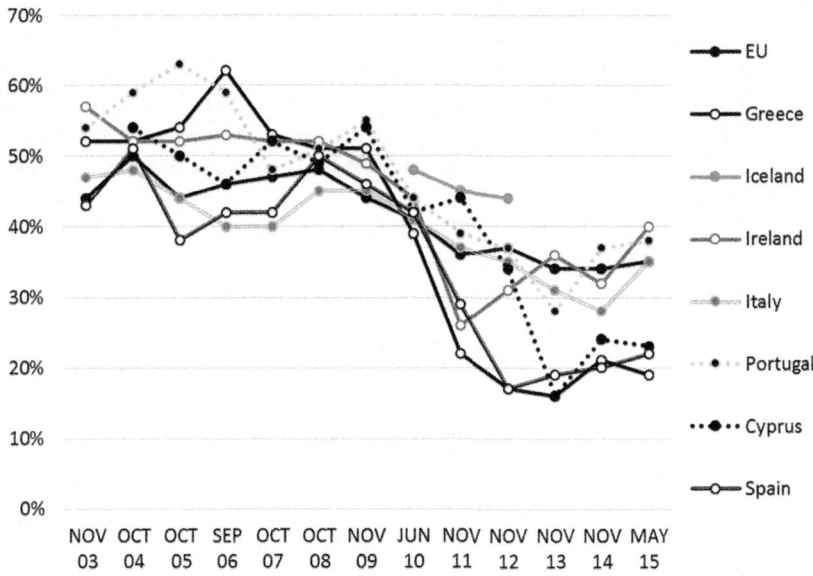

Fig. 9.12 Trust in European Central Bank (% of tend to trust). *Source*: Eurobarometer

liberating capital from state restraints and privatizing the banks, neither the present nor the previous government, nor the supervisory agencies (the Central Bank and the Financial Supervisory Authority) had sufficiently restrained the financial sector from outgrowing the Icelandic economy, threatening state insolvency and jeopardizing the country's welfare system. Ambitiously unleashing market forces, the authorities had seemingly done nothing to prevent the public from potential harm; they had stood by watching the banks accumulate risk at the expense of the public. (Bernburg 2015, 45)

Mistrust fuelled indeed an electoral earthquake at the national level, as the Independence Party, in power at the moment of the crisis, lost 13 per cent of the vote, while its ally in government, the Progressive Party, gained 3 per cent. In particular, the left parties increased their presence, with 2 per cent more going to the Social Democratic Alliance, while the Left Movement and the Citizen's Movement each gained over 7 per cent of the vote and up to five seats in parliament. The Social Democratic Alliance and the Left Movement went to government, first within a minority coalition and, since May 2009, acquiring a legislative majority (Indridason 2014). The so-called 'pots and pans' revolution was indeed able to find alliances within the institutions, imposing a referendum on the payment of the banks' debt to foreign owners. This initiative was then won by the movement supporters, as well as giving an impetus to a constitutional process, which involved a participatory process. While the constitutional proposal built by the citizens has not been implemented, the alternative Pirate party, which has its roots in the pots and pans revolution, has been leading the polls.

In *Greece*, the spiralling crisis had political roots as well, having even more dramatic effects in terms of transformation of the party system. Political de-legitimation of the old party system was fuelled by the 'inconsistency of policy at the international level, which created a setting of never-ending policy shocks: seemingly every month or so, the question of a Greek default resurfaced and a new minicrisis triggered a new round of emergency eurogroup meetings and contradictory policy statements by officials' (Monastiriotis et al. 2013, 7). As the chapter on Greece explains in detail, already in 2012 there had been a dramatic fall in the popularity of PASOK and New Democracy at the national elections, with neither reaching a majority notwithstanding the 50-seat bonus for the first party. After that, the decline of the centre-left strengthened the radical left at the party level as PASOK, which had led the government that negotiated the first bailout deal in 2010, saw its votes dropping from 44 per cent in 2009 to 13 per cent in May 2012. At the same time, SYRIZA saw its electoral support booming to 16 per cent in May and 27 per cent in June of 2012. The effects of the crisis included, in 2011, the resignation of PASOK Prime Minister George Papandreou and the formation of a new government led by former ECB Vice President Loukas Papademos. Later on, the new elections ended with a grand coalition in government, which brought about, in 2012, the collapse of the two main parties which together received less than one-third of the electorate—down from approximately 80 per cent at the beginning of the crisis (Teperoglou and Tsatsanis 2014). Besides economic voting, which traditionally punishes incumbent parties in times of crisis, the electoral results also reflected a more general disaffection with the existing party system, particularly by the young generation, as trust in parliament dropped from 60 per cent in 2004 to 10 per cent in 2011. The same was true for party identification (Teperoglou and Tsatsanis 2014).[4] The political crisis of responsibility was indeed most widespread in Greece, leading SYRIZA to the national government.

In *Spain*, as well, the dramatic socio-economic crisis translated into an equally dramatic crisis of political legitimacy for an institutional system that relied upon the power of the executive, moderated only at the territorial level by the increasing power of the regional *autonomias* as well as by the alternance between the two main parties, which controlled a very high percentage of the electorate. Here as well, democratic accountability at the domestic level, already shaken by a series of scandals related to political corruption, fell dramatically as the Spanish governments conformed to the recommendations by ECB and EC. In this situation, 'The power of unions to oppose or substantively influence the reforms, either through social pacts or general strikes, was very limited, as negotiations failed on numerous occasions and both the PSOE and PP governments went ahead unilaterally' (Picot and Tassinari 2014, 17). As in Greece, at the electoral level, the political legitimacy crisis was reflected in very high levels of electoral volatility. Both main parties on the right and on the left dropped steadily, and new parties (such as Podemos and Ciudadanos) emerged rapidly (Romanos and Sádaba 2015; della Porta et al. 2017). In fact, while economic voting penalized first the PSOE, in power at the moment of the emergence of the crisis, and then the PP, which had taken over governmental positions, dissatisfaction with the management of the crisis—filtered through the assessment of political responsibilities

(Torcal 2014)—was accompanied by a decline of political trust in existing institutions and a pressure for renovation. The traditional closure towards social movements was reflected in high levels of repression of the protest—which backfired, further increasing discontent (Fishman 2011).

Incumbent parties were also punished in *Ireland*, although no new challenger emerged in the electoral arena. Certainly, 2011 saw 'one of the most dramatic elections in European post-war history in terms of net electoral volatility. In some respects the election overturned the traditional party system' (Marsh and Mikhaylov 2012, 161; see also Mair 2011). The main party in government, Fianna Fáil, fell from the first to the third position; while the other centrist party, Fine Gael, became the first party for the first time, forming a governmental coalition with the Labour Party, which had almost doubled its support in the elections. In general, the parties on the left gained a very high 31 per cent of the vote (Marsh and Mikhaylov 2012).

A relevant difference in comparison to Iceland is Ireland's loss of national sovereignty, as it signed an agreement with the EC, IMF and ECB for a loan programme in December 2010. This has hugely constrained domestic budgetary discretion, as 'all budget decisions must be cleared with the troika, fiscal performance is subject to quarterly reviews and troika personnel are embedded in the core government departments' (Hardiman and Regan 2013, 30). It was noted, however, that electoral results represented 'a conservative revolution, one in which the main players remained the same, and the switch in the major government party was merely one where one centre-right party replaced another' (Marsh and Mikhaylov 2014, 161). The important role of personal ties seems indeed to have mitigated the intensity of the political changes, as did traditional ideological proximity among the main parties (Marsh and Mikhaylov 2014). The traditional localism-cum-clientelism of Irish politics, the weakness of the left, and the feeble power of the parliament (Mair 2014) all contributed to prevent those most dramatic expressions of the legitimacy crisis that we saw in the Greek or Spanish case.

The political effects of the crisis were also visible in *Portugal*, but here in a less dramatic fashion than in Greece or Spain. As in Greece, the centre-left Socialist Party, in power when the Memorandum of Agreement was signed, earned its worst electoral results immediately thereafter. What is more, even if it campaigned for less austerity, the electorate did not recognize its diversity in social and economic policies. As in Ireland, EC plus IMF interventions suspended not only democratic accountability in terms of decision making, but also the democratic dialectics between the government and the opposition as the austerity memorandum had to be signed by all main parties: the government's Socialist Party (PS) as well as the centre-right opposition Social Democratic Party (PSD) and the Social and Democratic Centre-Popular Party (CDS-PP, on the right) (Magalhães 2014). In fact,

> Many of the measures contained in the very detailed memorandum of agreement pointed to a rolling-back of state functions and spending and to a generically market-oriented liberalization. In other words, the basic tenets of the policy endorsed by the PSD, which the Socialists harshly criticized during the campaign, were, after all, the same that all major parties, including the PS itself, had committed to implement with the EU and the IMF after the election took place. (Magalhães 2014, 193)

Throughout the crisis, the constitutional court repeatedly intervened, however, by blocking some austerity provisions (including the abolition of bonuses, reforms of labour codes, and cuts in public service salaries) considered as unconstitutional. Immediately going into opposition was, moreover, a blessing for the PS, which could from there criticize austerity policies. Hit by scandals and members' disaffection, the PS underwent internal reform and moved to the left, while adopting open primaries, thus recovering some support in the electorate (Raimundo and Pinto 2014). However, it was especially the radical left (including the older communist party and the newer Block of the Left) that made substantial (even if delayed) electoral gains in the general elections of 2015, ending up supporting the new centre-left in the government.

In *Italy* as well, the social crisis interacted with a political crisis, as the alignment to EC requests penalized parties on the centre-left as well as the centre-right, even if not to the extent it had in Greece or Spain. After the Berlusconi government failed to pass some of the agreed upon austerity measures, 'in an unprecedented step with a country that had not signed any MoU, the heads of state and government of the eurozone entrusted the EC with the task of providing "a detailed assessment of all the measures and monitoring their implementation", inviting "the Italian authorities to provide in a timely way all the information necessary for such an assessment"' (cit. in Sacchi 2015, 84). A letter to the Italian Treasury Minister, Tremonti, on 4 November 2011, made 'no less than 39 detailed remarks on which it elicited a response within a week...On this backdrop, with Italy haunted by outright lack of credibility, the only lifeline could come from ECB purchases. However, at the beginning of November, members of the ECB governing council discussed (and disclosed) the possibility of stopping the purchase of Italian paper if the Italian government failed to implement the promised reforms' (Sacchi 2015, 84).

Berlusconi encountered political difficulties in approving austerity packages, as requested by the Council recommendation of 12 July 2011. However, after his resignation in November 2011, Monti's bipartisan government—as well as other large coalitions under PD Letta (in coalition with Forza Italia) and Renzi (in coalition with a splinter FI faction)—proceeded speedily to the implementation of EC requests. The comprehensive labour market reform adopted in June 2012 met with the opposition of the main union, the CGIL, which was problematic for the Democratic Party. The EU institutions instead supported the government's intransigent line.

Here as well, the crisis implied a loss of domestic power and electoral accountability. 'The labour market reform is monitored at every juncture, its contents thoroughly scrutinized, warnings are issued in a way that could easily make defenders of old-school democracy raise an eyebrow, and the parliamentary process is followed day by day' (Sacchi 2015, 89). While unions initially retained some ability to influence the process, finding some political support, the austerity measures strongly affected union power through a general reduction of labour rights at the workplace, as well as decentralized bargaining. In the process, EC institutions are said to have encouraged national governments to go ahead even without the approval of the unions, which they stigmatized as conservative.

After a year of grand coalition, supporting Mario Monti's government, the 2013 elections brought about a drastic loss for the main parties as, on the right, the People of Freedom (PoF) reached only 21.3 per cent (against 37.2 per cent in 2008) and, on the left, the Democratic Party (DP) achieved 25.5 per cent (against 33.1 per cent in 2008)—while the Five Star Movement (5SM), in its first experience with national elections, obtained 25.1 per cent of the votes. Indeed, the electoral results were notable for the 'greatest vote-swing in the history of the Italian Republic, with an index of aggregate volatility of 39.1 %' (Bellucci 2014, 244). A good percentage of the voters for the 5SM came indeed from former centre-left electors (Bordignon and Ceccarini 2013). In parallel, the indicator of trust in parties (measured on a 0–10 scale) fell from 3.2 in spring 2011 to 2.1 a year later (Bellucci 2014).

In *Cyprus*, in 2008, just after the adoption of the euro, the left-wing candidate from AKEL (the Progressive Party of Working People), Dimitris Christofias, won the presidential elections with 53 per cent of the vote. Under his government, Cyprus' banking sector collapsed. While the new election, in 2013, punished the left, giving the victory to the centre-right party DISY (Democratic Rally), no major transformation happened in the party system. The newly formed Message of Hope party, which had mobilized against the Memorandum, earned only 3.8 per cent of the vote.

Indeed, AKEL's mass-party structure helped to maintain its influence on the society. Crisis notwithstanding, AKEL is a rare example of a mass party, with mass membership and deeply rooted mass ancillary organizations. Based on democratic centralism, it is articulated in branches and cells, with no recognized factions and 'a hierarchy built as a pyramid, with those standing in the upper levels having the power to assist selected people in the lower levels to get promoted. … the pyramidal structure of power, with the integration of lower bodies into a central bureaucracy, leaves little or no room for autonomous, decisive action by lower bodies, thus limiting attempts for bottom-up change' (Charalambous and Christophorou 2013). Besides these mass ancillary organizations,

> AKEL's relations with society can only be fully seen when one examines the nature of the left–right cleavage and its impact on daily life. AKEL's almost unhindered development in the very early stages of its life, in 1941–42, fiercely opposed by an initially leaderless and non-organized conservative social body and the church, led to a deep, radical divide. The places where one sought to buy goods and services, the brands of coffee and other drinks and beverages one consumed, were dictated by the left–right cleavage and designated the camp one belonged to. AKEL promoted the creation of left-wing industries and businesses under the effective control of party officials and both camps mutually excluded their adversaries from employment. While the impact of the cleavage may have weakened today, hundreds of families continue to earn their living in left-wing-controlled businesses that supply the market with products for daily consumption and services. The circular bond established between the party, employment, production and consumption reinforces AKEL's already strong influence on large parts of society. The very strong cooperative movement and businesses in Cyprus (banks, supermarkets and product trading unions) have also constituted a sector in which AKEL has extended its activity and influence since the 1940s. (Charalambous and Christophorou 2013)

In sum, in the European periphery, as in Latin America, domestic political opportunities (especially the position of the centre-left parties) had a strong influence on the forms and intensity of anti-austerity protests.

9.4   COMPARING CRISES AND MOVEMENTS: SOME CONCLUSIONS

In sum, our research testifies to the ways in which a common crisis had different dynamics in the various countries of the EU periphery. Various other factors—including the characteristics of the welfare state, propensity towards saving, amount of public and private debt, and presence of foreign investment—also had an impact on the disruptive effects of late neoliberalism on the everyday lives of European citizens. Moreover, the political context in which protests developed also influenced their size and forms. As we noted, the most empowering effects of movements, which can be defined as anti-systemic, developed where disruption of daily life was higher. Vice versa, more defensive forms of protest, resonant with Polanyi's countermovements, spread in those cases in which the effects of the crisis had been heavy but somehow buffered by different social and political circumstances.

Three caveats are in order in these concluding remarks. First, reflecting on the effects of the socio-economic and political context at the domestic level should not lead towards structuralist interpretations that deny agency. Indeed, a main result of our research is that movements in times of crisis do not always comply with the expectations spread in social movement research: rather than small, violent, regressive and unsuccessful, they can be massive, peaceful, innovative and even successful. Protest has in fact transformative effects, creating the conditions for its own development (della Porta 2015). Second, the focus on cross-national comparison should not bring back methodological nationalism (Beck 2006). The dynamics of late neoliberalism at the domestic level can indeed be understood only within the world-system of capitalism, and the crisis of responsibility is strictly linked to the shifts in power towards international organizations and multinational corporations. Third, focusing on southern Europe and Iceland plus Ireland, we have singled out the dynamics of the crises in countries whose similar positions in the Great Recession have often been stressed (for example, by the spread of acronyms like PIIGS or GIIIPS). Our research does not, however, cover another part of the EU-periphery: the one in the east (but see della Porta 2017). This is certainly an important gap to fill in further research.

NOTES

1. An unemployed person is defined by Eurostat, according to the guidelines of the International Labour Organization, as: someone aged 15 to 74 (but aged 16 to 74 in Italy, Spain, the United Kingdom, Iceland, Norway); without work during the reference week; available to start work within the next two weeks (or has already found a job to start within the next three months); actively having sought employment at some time during the last four weeks. See Eurostat http://ec.europa.eu/eurostat/statistics-explained/index.php/Glossary:Unemployment_rate.
2. Material deprivation rates measure the inability to afford some items considered by most people to be desirable or even necessary to leading an adequate life, such as paying rent, mortgage or utility bills; keeping their home adequately warm; managing unexpected expenses; eating meat or proteins regularly; going on holiday; owning a television, a washing machine, a car and a telephone. Severe material deprivation rate is operationalized as the enforced inability to pay for at least four of the above-mentioned items. (http://ec.europa.eu/eurostat/statisticsexplained/index.php/Glossary:Severe_material_deprivation_rate).
3. The at-risk-of-poverty rate is the share of people with an equivalized disposable income (after social transfer) below the at-risk-of-poverty threshold, which is set at 60 per cent of the national median equivalized disposable income after social transfers (http://ec.europa.eu/eurostat/statistics-explained/index.php/Glossary:At-risk-of-poverty_rate).
4. Moreover, surveys at demonstrations showed that only 24 per cent believed in taking decisions through elected governments and representative institutions (24 per cent), while 58 per cent called for referendums and people's assemblies (Kollia 2012).

REFERENCES

Accornero, G., and P.R. Pinto. 2014. "Mild Mannered"? Protest and Mobilisation in Portugal Under Austerity, 2010–2013. *Western European Politics* 38(3): 1–25.

Baumgarten, B. 2013. Geração à Rasca and Beyond: Mobilizations in Portugal after 12 March 2011. *Current Sociology* 61(4): 457–473.

Beck, Ulrich. 2006. *Cosmopolitan Vision*. Cambridge: Polity Press.

Bellucci, Eftichia. 2014. The Political Consequences of Blame Attribution for the Economic Crisis in the 2013 Italian National Election. *Journal of Elections, Public Opinion and Parties* 24(2): 243–263. doi:10.1080/17457289.2014.88 7720.

Bernburg, J.G. 2015. *Economic Crisis and Mass Protest: The Pots and Pans Revolution in Iceland*. Farnham: Ashgate.

Bordignon, F., and L. Ceccarini. 2013. Five Stars and a Cricket. Beppe Grillo Shakes Italian Politics. *South European Society and Politics* 18(4): 427–449.

Borland, E., and B. Sutton. 2007. Quotidian Disruption and Women's Activism in Times of Crisis, Argentina 2002–2003. *Gender & Society* 21(5): 700–722.

Cabral, Ricardo. 2013. The Euro Crisis and Portugal's Dilemma. *Intereconomics* 48(1): 27–32.

Charalambous, G., and C. Christophorou. 2013. A Society Within Society: Linkage in the Case of the Cypriot Communist Party. *South European Society & Politics* 18(1): 101–119.

Conde-Ruiz, J.I., and C. Marín. 2013. The Fiscal Crisis in Spain. *Intereconomics* 48(1): 4–32.

Dawson, M. 2015. The Euro Crisis and its Transformation of EU Law and Politics. *Governance Report 2015*, eds. Hertie School of Governance, 41–68. Oxford: Oxford University Press.

Dawson, M., H. Enderlein, and C. Joerges. 2015a. Introduction. Exploratory Governance in the Euro Crisis. *Governance Report 2015*, eds. Hertie School of Governance, 13–24. Oxford: Oxford University Press.

———, 2015b. Outlook. Where do the EU and the EMU go from here? *Governance Report 2015*, eds. Hertie School of Governance, 117. Oxford: Oxford University Press.

della Porta, D. 2007. *The Global Justice Movement in Cross-national and Transnational Perspective*. Boulder, Co: Paradigm.

——— 2015. *Social Movements in Times of Austerity*. Cambridge: Polity.

della Porta, D., and A. Mattoni. 2014. *Spreading Democracy*. Essex: ECPR Press.

della Porta, D., and H. Reiter. 2012. Desperately Seeking Politics. *Mobilization: An International Quarterly* 17(3): 349–361.

della Porta, D., and M. Andretta. 2013. Protesting for Justice and Democracy. *Contemporary Italian Politics* 5(1): 23–37.

della Porta, D., J. Fernandez, H. Kouki, and L. Mosca. 2017. *Movement Parties in Times of Austerity*. Cambridge: Polity.

della Porta, D. (ed.). 2017. *Global Diffusion of Protest. Riding the Protest Wave in the Neoliberal Crisis*. Amsterdam: Amsterdam University Press.

della Porta, D., L. Mosca, and L. Parks. 2015. Subterranean Politics and Visible Protest in Italy. In *Subterranean Politics in Europe*, eds. M. Kaldor, and S. Selchow, 60–93. London: Palgrave.

Diani, M., and M. Kousis. 2014. The Duality of Claims and Events: The Greek Campaign Against Troika's Memoranda and Austerity, 2010–2012. *Mobilization: An International Quarterly* 19(4): 387–404.

Fishman, Robert M. 2011. Democratic Practice After the Revolution: The Case of Portugal and Beyond. *Politics and Society* 39(2): 233–267.

Franklin, M.N., and E. van der Eijk. 2004. *Voter Turnout and the Dynamics of Electoral Competition in Established Democracies since 1945*. Cambridge: Cambridge University Press.

Goretti, C., and L. Landi. 2013. Walking on the Edge: How Italy Rescued Italy in 2012. *Intereconomics* 48: 14–21.

Hardiman, N., and A. Regan. 2013. The Politics of Austerity in Ireland. *Intereconomics* 48: 9–14.

Indridason, I.H. 2014. The Collapse: Economic Considerations in Vote Choice in Iceland. *Journal of Elections, Public Opinion and Parties* 24(2): 134–159. doi: 10.1080/17457289.2014.889699.

Joerges, C. 2015. The Legitimacy Problématique of Economic Governance in the EU. *Governance Report 2015*, eds. Hertie School of Governance, 69–94. Oxford: Oxford University Press.

Kerbo, Harold R. 1982. Movements of "Crisis" and Movements of "Affluence": A Critique of Deprivation and Resource Mobilization Theory. *Journal of Conflict Resolution* 26: 645–663.

Krugman, P. 2013. "Lands of Ice and Ire", The Conscience of a Liberal. http://krugman.blogs. nytimes.com/2010/11/24/lands-of-ice-and-ire/

Magalhães, P.C. 2014. The Elections of the Great Recession in Portugal: Performance Voting Under a Blurred Responsibility for the Economy. *Journal of Elections, Public Opinion and Parties* 24(2): 180–202. doi:10.1080/174572 89.2013.874352.

Mair, P. 2011. The Election in Context. In *How Ireland Voted 2011: The Full Story of Ireland's Earthquake Election*. Basingstoke: Palgrave Macmillan.

——— 2014. Explaining the Absence of Class Politics in Ireland. In *On Parties, Party Systems and Democracy: Selected Writings of Peter Mair*, ed. I. van Biezen. Colchester, UK: ECPR Press.

Marsh, M., and S. Mikhaylov. 2012. Economic Voting in a Crisis: The Irish Election of 2011. *Electoral Studies* 30: 1–7.

McDonough, T., and T. Dundon. 2010. *Thatcherism Delayed? The Irish Crisis and the Paradox of Social Partnership*. Rochester, NY: Social Science Research Network.

McGrath, L. F. 2015. Governance Indicators. In Governance Report 2015, eds. Hertie School of Governance, 95–116. Oxford: Oxford University Press.

Monastiriotis, V., N. Hardiman, A. Regan, C. Goretti, L. Landi, J.I. Conde-Ruiz, C. Marín, and R. Cabral. 2013. Austerity Measures in Crisis Countries: Results and Impact on Mid-Term Development. *Intereconomics* 48(1): 4–32. doi:10.1007/s10272-013-0441-3.

Picot, G., and A. Tassinari. 2014. Liberalization, Dualization, or Recalibration? Labor Market Reforms Under Austerity, Italy and Spain 2010–2012. Nuffield College Working Paper Series in Politics.

Piketty, T. 2014. *Capital in the Twenty-First Century*. Cambridge: Harvard University Press.

Raimundo, F. and A. C. Pinto. 2014. When Parties Succeed: Party System (in) stability and the 2008 Financial Crisis in Portugal. Paper Prepared for the 2014 Annual Meeting of the American Political Science Association, Washington, DC, 28–31 August.

Romanos, E. 2014. Evictions, Petitions and *Escraches:* Contentious Housing in Austerity Spain. *Social Movement Studies* 13(2): 296–302.

Romanos, E., and I. Sádaba. 2015. La evolución de los marcos (tecno) discursivos del movimiento 15 M y sus consecuencias. *Empiria* 32: 15–36.

Rüdig, W., and G. Karyotis. 2014. Who Protests in Greece? Mass Opposition to Austerity. *British Journal of Political Science* 44: 487–513.

Sacchi, S. 2015. Conditionality by Other Means: EU Involvement in Italy's Structural Reforms in the Sovereign Debt Crisis. *Comparative European Politics* 13(1): 77–92.

Sassen, S. 2014. *Expulsions*. Cambridge, MA: Harvard University Press.

Sergi, V., and M. Vogiatzoglou. 2013. Think Globally, act Locally? Symbolic Memory and Global Repertoires in the Tunisian Uprising and the Greek Anti-austerity Mobilizations. In *Understanding European Movements: New Social Movements, Global Justice Struggles, Anti-Austerity Protest*, eds. C.F. Fominaya, and L. Cox. London: Routledge.

Snow, D., D.M. Cress, L. Downey, and A.W. Jones. 1998. Disrupting the "Quotidian": Reconceptualizing the Relationship Between Breakdown and the Emergence of Collective Action. *Mobilization* 3: 1–22.

Teperoglou, E., and E. Tsatsanis. 2014. Dealignment, De-legitimation and the Implosion of the Two-party System in Greece: The Earthquake Election of 6 May 2012. *Journal of Elections, Public Opinion and Parties* 24(2): 222–242. doi:10.1080/17457289.2014.892495.

Therborn, G. 2013. *The Killing Fields of Inequality*. Cambridge: Polity.

Torcal, M. 2014. The Incumbent Electoral Defeat in the 2011 Spanish National Elections: The Effect of the Economic Crisis in an Ideological Polarized Party System. *Journal of Elections, Public Opinion and Parties* 24(2): 203–221. doi:10.1080/17457289.2014.891598.

INDEX

Note: Page numbers with "n" denote notes.

© The Author(s) 2017   297
D. della Porta et al., *Late Neoliberalism and its Discontents
in the Economic Crisis*, DOI 10.1007/978-3-319-35080-6

Printed by Printforce, the Netherlands